Butte Voices:
Mining, Neighborhoods, People

Enjoy the book
Pat Kearney
8-1-00

written by
Pat Kearney

edited by
Zena Beth McGlashan

front and back photos by
Mike Kearney

layout by
Wes Harr and Jim Feickert

map illustration by
Jim Duran

published by
Skyhigh Communications

printed by
Artcraft Printers of Butte

ISBN C-9661688-3-6

FORWARD

Butte, Montana, has been called "the richest hill on earth." Its rich in minerals, but rich in so many other ways as well. The most profitable mining camp in the world has produced a lot more than just copper, silver and gold.

It is a place where immigrants from around the globe planted their roots to become Americans. A place that put Montana on the map and Butte in the world spot light. A place where living one day at a time was more than just a motto, it was a fact of life due to the potential grim reality of a mining accident. A place where a hard day's work was demanded and a fair day's wage was expected. A place where corporate interests met face-to-face with union concerns, where lock out met "can do", where neighborhoods met ethnic pride, where our lady met her mountain. This place called Butte, Montana, is bound to leave a lasting impression on you. It is one of the most unique, colorful, historic towns in this country.

The history of Butte has been tainted through the paper and pen of The Anaconda Company. The Company did provide jobs, opportunities, and hope, but they also started riots, producing bloodshed, death and destruction.

This book will focus on the Butte people. It tells their story about mining, ethnic pride, neighborhoods, games they played, accomplishments they achieved, the love they have for their city. It is *Butte Voices: Mining, Neighborhoods, People.*

This book examines a number of aspects on Butte history, however, it can not cover everything. Frankly no book can achieve that because of the vast volumes of history that has occurred here in this mining camp called Butte.

The book took three years to complete. There was a lot of research and a lot of help given to me to finish this manuscript. I must say thank you to those helping me with research: Ellen Crain of the Butte Silver Bow Archives, Jim Street a Butte High history teacher, Jerry Bugni of Butte, and especially to my brother Tim Kearney who was very diligent in making sure facts were accurate.

A special thank you must go to my proof readers who spent time and thought with the manuscript. Thank you to: Tina Anderson, Terry Courtright, Melanie Marotta-Cox, Carol Feickert, Bob Kearney, Cheri Meier, Raynita Meier, Tom Mulcahy, Cathy Nickisch, Mary Pahut, Paul Tash and Hudson Willse.

Thanks also to longtime friend Jim Duran for his map on the Butte neighborhoods.

A thanks must go to Jim Feickert and his staff at Artcraft Printers in Butte who provided helpful hints on the layout and completion of the book.

My final thanks must go to the person who gave me the most encouragement and direction to complete this book: my editor Zena Beth McGlashan. Zena, a Butte native, spent countless hours reading the manuscript. It is easy to see through her dedication to this book the love and passion she has for her hometown. My heart-felt thanks to her for wisdom, patience and understanding with me.

Butte Voices: Mining, Neighborhoods, People gave me an opportunity to visit some of the most special people in the world. I want to dedicate this book to the Butte people.

Pat Kearney
author

I was sitting in the day room in Ondal, India, during my World War II days. Someone turned on the phonograph and from the speaker came the voice of Deanna Durbin singing, "I Can See The of Lights of Home." As I listened my thoughts drifted ten thousand miles away to the top of Harding Way and my eyes became filled with tears, as I remembered the bright lights of Butte from that vantage point."

Howie Wing memoir, a Butte native and World War II veteran

Butte Voices: Mining, Neighborhoods, People

Table of Contents

CHAPTER 1

Mining

First Glance

It is dark as you head west on Interstate 90. Shortly after passing the small community ofWhitehall, you start to climb up the steep mountain pass called Homestake. The winding highway eventually takes you to the top of the Continental Divide over 6,400 feet above sea level. Your vehicle now starts down the west slope of the pass. You turn a corner and suddenly there it is, Butte, Montana. The glistening diamond of lights in the distance is of a community a mile high above sea level. You will soon discover its colorful history glows as brightly as the lights from afar.

As night turns to day, the glowing flow of lights are replaced by a town with some of the most unique characteristics of any city on the face of the earth. Every place you turn, the mining industry grabs your attention.

The northeastern corner of the community is a massive hole known as the Berkeley Pit. The Anaconda Company developed open pit mining here in 1955. Operations continued until April 23, 1982, when ARCO, the firm now running the Berkeley Pit, elected to suspend mining at the Pit. ARCO decided to shut off the pumps which kept water from flowing into the Berkeley Pit from the massive number of underground mining tunnels. The Pit slowing turned from a major hole into a gigantic lake.

The Berkeley Pit is just one sign of Butte's mining past. The only mining activity still left in town is just east of the Pit. Called the Continental Pit, it is operated by Montana Resources, a company which restarted the Butte mining operations in 1986. The new mine was in production three years after ARCO turned off the keys to their shovels and trucks for good on June 30, 1983.

Once you leave the pit area and start penetrating the town, Butte's mining past is still remembered by numerous gallows frames located around the community. These massive black steel structures symbolize abandoned underground mining operations in Butte. The gallows frames were used to lower miners and animals to the underground operations. The structures would also pull up copper ore dug out by the workers. It is only fitting that these symbols of the past should remain, because mining is what turned the small gold mining camp of Butte into "the richest hill on earth."

Gold Rush

It seemed like gold was everywhere when William Allison and G. O. Humphrey discovered some nuggets in an area called Baboon Gulch at the north end of Summit Valley in May, 1864. The discovery came less than two years after similar findings had been uncovered in Bannack and Virginia City in Southwestern Montana. A few months after Allison and Humphrey found their nuggets, gold was located on a creek a couple of miles west of Baboon Gulch at a place called Silver Bow by Peter McMahon, one of four men in a party who located the gold treasure.

Both discoveries lured hundreds of miners from the bustling gold mining camps of Bannack and Virginia City into the area. Within a year over 1,000 miners called Silver Bow Village their home. In Baboon Gulch, just east of Silver Bow Village, the discovery by Allison and Humphrey led to a mining camp called Butte named after the large butte overlooking the valley. The town of Butte had 50 residents in 1866. By the next year, the community had grown to 500 people. In the early years, placer mining was the easiest way to extract the gold. Miners spent long hours panning the waters and streams. During the three years after the gold discovery, over $1.5 million worth of gold was washed out of Silver Bow Creek.

Once the gold in the Summit Valley started to be worked out and disappear, so did most of the miners. Silver Bow Village ended up as a ghost town. By 1874, the mining camp of Butte almost shared the same fate with only 200 residents left in the small outpost. A majority of the people still living in the mining camp were Chinese. They reworked the old claims left behind. The town was down to a pair of bars and no stores.

The only saving grace for Butte were major quartz deposits that remained on the hill just below the large butte overlooking the town. A Deer Lodge banker, William Clark, visited the mining camp in 1872. Like many people who visited the region before him, Clark was overwhelmed by the large black quartz reefs on the hill. The miners told Clark that the black quartz rock held some combination of precious metals; however, the question was how to smelt down the rock to get at the valuable nuggets.

Clark saw the potential of mining on the hill and so he purchased four mining properties: the Original, Colusa, Mountain Chief and Gambetta Mines. After he completed the sale, Clark took some mineral samples from his properties and hauled them back to New York City. During the winter, Clark took some mining classes at Columbia University. The Deer Lodge banker wanted to learn as much as he could about mining and smelting. Clark had his mineral deposits assayed and found out the black quartz rocks contained enormous potential. Clark returned to Butte the next spring and started to plan the development of his mining properties. He put his brother, Joseph Clark, in charge of making sure his mining properties were operated correctly.

Silver Time

William Clark was not the only man who uncovered the rich value of the Butte hill. William Farlin located some silver nuggets near what came to be known as the Travona Mine. Farlin took his deposits to Owyhee, Idaho, to have them assayed. He was told the silver was of high value. After he found out the assay results, Farlin returned to Butte. On January 1, 1875, he legally jumped the Travona Lode claim because federal law stated at least $10 worth of work per 100 feet had to be done on a claim during a year or someone else could file a claim on that mining property. Butte would soon be in the silver mining business.

Lacking financial backing, William Farlin was forced to take out a $30,000 loan from William Clark's Deer Lodge bank to try to develop his silver vein. Farlin built the Dexter Mill to help process the silver ore. His lack of cash flow soon caught up with Farlin. He was unable to make his loan payments and saw William Clark foreclose on Farlin's property.

The silver mining business was much different than panning for gold. It took a great deal of capital to realize a profit in silver mining. The capital expense of building an underground mine was one factor the silver industry had to overcome. A second factor was the development of an adequate smelter to process the ore. William Clark and another banker, William Jefferson Davis, had the financial resources. Both men put vast sums of money into their mining operations and both were greatly rewarded for their efforts.

Davis had acquired the Lexington Mine for $20 and a white horse. The Lexington proved to be one of the most profitable silver operations on the Butte hill. When Davis finally sold the property in 1887 to the Butte and Boston Mining Company, he received $1 million.

William Clark also realized a nice profit for his foreclosure on Farlin's operation. First, though, he had to solve the dilemma of smelting. The Dexter Mill built by William Farlin, like similar experiments before it, was not adequate enough to smelt the silver from black quartz rock. So Clark, through the help of his friend Nathaniel Hill, built the Colorado and Montana Smelter in 1879 just south of the Travona Mine. It was Butte's first large-scale smelter operation. The smelting plant meant that Butte became a big-time player in the mining industry.

The silver boom turned Butte from a small mining camp of 200 in

1874 into a community of 3,000 people by 1879 which was the year local officials incorporated Butte as a city. By 1885, there were 22,000 residents in the town.

The mining industry was growing in Butte just as quickly as the city's population. By 1884, there were over 4,000 mining claims in the county and over 300 operating mines. The town had nine quartz mills and four smelters in operation. William Clark was the leading mine owner controlling the interests in 46 different properties on the hill. Butte was the second leading silver producer in the world from the mid 1880s until the 1893 Depression. Its productivity led to the nickname "Silver City" in the 1880s.

A critical milestone establishing the camp as a national mining region came on December 21, 1881, when the Utah and Northern Railroad successfully completed a link between Ogden, Utah, and Butte. Two years later, the Northern Pacific Railroad moved into Butte providing an east/west route to the camp. Prior to the railroad's appearance in Butte, ore was smelted in crude open-air roasting bins in the town or was shipped over 400 miles to Corrine, Utah, to hook up with rail service. The ore bodies were then taken to a small smelter in Baltimore plus the only large copper smelting complex in the world at Swansea, Wales.

Copper

The rail service did provide the town with a boost, but the biggest impact turning the small mining camp into the richest hill on earth was still to take place. When the silver rush hit in the 1870s, a young Irish mining foreman, Marcus Daly, was sent to Butte by the Walker brothers, Joseph, Samuel, Matthew and David of Salt Lake City, Utah. Daly had served as a successful foreman for the Walkers' mining properties in Utah. Daly was ordered to assess what mining potential Butte had for the possible purchase of property by the Walkers. Daly arrived in Butte on August 25, 1876.

What Marcus Daly found in Butte was to be a pot of silver at the end of the rainbow, literally. The Rainbow Belt was a half-mile wide and a two-mile long strip of silver veins located in the northern section of the valley. Through his advice, the Walkers purchased the Alice Mine property for $25,000 from Rollo Butcher. The Walkers put Marcus Daly in charge of developing their Butte mining properties.

In a short time, Daly turned the Alice Mine into the richest, most profitable operation in the Butte district. Through a series of water pumps, Daly overcame a myth that ore could not be mined below the water table. Within a year after taking over the Alice Mine, Daly's workers were already mining some 25 feet below the water line. The achievement led others to dig deeper in search of ore.

In addition to going below the water table, Daly discovered large deposits of copper ore in the underground mines. He believed copper ore could have as much financial value as silver.

Daly was not the first to explore the possibility of mining copper. In 1868, William Parks, a miner with a hunch, thought copper could be a vital metal. Parks calculated that the landscape in the region dictated that a copper vein was close to the surface. He started digging the Parrot Mine by himself in 1868. For eight years Parks was called crazy and various other names by the residents of the community. Yet, he had the last laugh finally uncovering a large vein of pure copper a couple hundred feet below the surface. Parks made a nice profit from his mine and then sold it for $10,000, a fraction of its value.

Parks' mine was a short distance from where Marcus Daly located large copper ore bodies 300 to 500 feet below the surface. Daly, like William Parks, believed copper would be an even more valuable metal than silver if an economical smelting process could be developed. Daly told the Walker brothers about the potential to mine copper, but they were not interested. So Daly sold his interest in the Alice Mine for $100,000 and decided to branch out on his own by purchasing the Anaconda Mine from Mickey Hickey.

Hickey had fought for the Union Army during the Civil War. He remembered reading an editorial once from Horace Greeley of *The New York Tribune* which said, just before the battle of Richmond, "Grant's army will encircle Lee's forces and crush them like a giant anaconda snake." Hickey liked the name "Anaconda" and thus named his property after the giant snake in October, 1875. Hickey could not know just how important the name Anaconda would become in the mining industry.

The Anaconda Mine was the property where Daly had uncovered the most promising copper ore. There were copper veins 50 to 100 feet wide in the property with copper assaying as high as 55 percent. When the first copper ore from the mine was shipped to Swansea, Wales, for smelting, the workers there thought a new way to concentrate copper had been discovered because they had never seen the red metal that pure before.

Despite the pure ore from the Anaconda, Daly realized that to be successful in copper mining he needed money and investors. Daly talked to California businessman, George Hearst, a man he became friends with while working at the Comstock Lode in Nevada. Daly convinced Hearst and two business associates, James Haggin and Lloyd Tevis, that Butte had enormous mining potential in copper. Together the four men devel oped a partnership that became the most powerful mining firm in the world.

The partnership quickly purchased all the mining properties around the Anaconda like the Mountain Con, Neversweat, Bell-Diamond, Modoc, High Ore, Green Mountain and the Wake Up Jim. The new copper partnership would put a stranglehold on the Butte mining district.

Daly's bold move to mine copper came at just the right moment in history. Alexander Graham Bell had invented the telephone on March 10, 1876. Thomas Edison had developed the incandescent light on October 21, 1879. Both inventions required copper because it was a great conductor for electricity.

Edison extended his new lamp into the Pearl Street Generating Station in New York City. The plant went on line in 1882, the same year Marcus Daly took control of the Anaconda Mine. The Pearl Street Generation Station was the first step toward the electric lighting of New York City then the rest of the world. The Anaconda Mine was the first step toward making copper a means to wealth and fame.

The outside factors like the light bulb and electricity would prove to be helpful for Daly's copper partnership. However, men from the Michigan copper mines tried to counter-act Daly's movement into the copper industry. The Michigan mining companies, owned by Boston bankers, dominated the copper market in 1882. They set the price. When the Michigan partnership found out about Butte's potential, they lowered the price for the red metal from 18 cents a pound to 15 cents in 1883. Instead of driving Daly's copper machine out of business with the move, the drop in price would back-fire on the Boston bankers. Daly's Anaconda Mine only increased production.

The Boston bankers decided to increase the pressure on Daly by lowering the price to 10 cents a pound in 1886. The move put every Butte mine out of business expect for those operated by Marcus Daly. He continued producing copper ore. His mines were not making any profit on copper, but they were still operating because the by-product of silver was making money.

Daly's ability to remain open despite the drop in copper prices proved to be a vital turning point in the development of Butte. It broke the Michigan monopoly on the copper market.

When the Michigan-Montana price war ended, Daly faced a similar challenge from a group of European bankers who formed a cartel to try to control the price of copper. They purchased copper from the Anaconda mines for 13 cents a pound and sold it for 18 cents. The cartel tried to up their selling price to 20 cents, but the greed of the Europeans backfired on them because it caused chaos on the copper market. The price fell to 5 cents a pound. The cartel collapsed in June 1888, and the attempts to corner the copper market by outside forces beyond Butte were over, at least for awhile.

After the European cartel dissolved, a meeting was held by copper producers to shore up their industry. They elected to sell copper at 12 cents a pound and slowly allow over 4 million pounds of produced ore to filter on the market. It saved the industry and added muscle to Daly's Anaconda Copper Mining Company.

The ability to fight off outside market forces made Daly's partnership the most powerful copper company in the world. The group had a huge advantage in Butte because of all the property they had purchased around the Anaconda Mine. This led to enormous profits for Daly's syndicate.

Production numbers in the Butte mines prior to 1880 and during the decade indicate just how much money was being pumped out of the Butte mining operations by Marcus Daly and others. It also reflects how copper turned the Butte mining camp from just another producer into the "richest hill on earth."

Butte Mining District

1864-1868 placer gold mining	$ 8,450,000
1864-1878 quartz product with silver mining	11,500,000
1878	800,000
1880	1,000,000
1881	1,247,600
1882	2,000,000
1883	4,160,000
1884	6,720,000
1885	11,479,000
1886	13,246,000
1887	16,143,000
1888	19,500,000
1889	22,055,689
1890	25,327,149

In the eleven years from 1880 to 1890, the Butte mines produced $122,799,387 in ore. It is staggering to look at early copper production in 1883 when Daly and his associates began full time efforts to mine the red metal and compare it to numbers just seven years later in 1890.

Copper was good for electricity, but electricity was also good for

Butte and its underground mining operation. When electricity was introduced with the first lights glowing at the Alice Pit on November 18, 1880, it ignited Butte's electrical age in mining. Electricity allowed hoist systems to be dug deeper into the mountain which in turn produced more copper.

Prior to the use of electricity, everything below the surface in Butte was accomplished by manual and animal labor. Miners dug holes with sledge hammers, jacks, picks and shovels. They mucked by hand the loosen ore rock into cars which were pulled by horses and mules along a track to the hoist area.

The horses and mules were primary fixtures in Butte's underground mines. Its estimated that 1,000 mules worked at one time underground and that prior to 1910 over 10,000 animals had labored in Butte's mines. Once they were taken below the surface, the animals only came back to sunlight if a long strike took place or they became too old to work. The animals like the miners worked an eight-hour shift. When their work duties for the day were done, the horses and mules were taken to a livery stable underground.

Each mine employed a veterinarian and blacksmith to tend to the needs of the animals.

The introduction of electrical, battery and gas cars plus drills started to make life easier for both man and beast in the 1910s. Yet, despite the coming age of electricity to Butte's underground mines, horses and mules were still being used until 1934 when the final work animals were pulled out of the St. Lawrence and Emma Mines.

A year after starting their copper operation in the Anaconda Mine, the California group under Daly's advice, built a smelter near Warm Springs Creek, 26 miles northwest of Butte, at a cost of $4 million. Once the Old Works Smelter was put into operation on September 3, 1885, copper was now truly king on the Butte hill. The amount of ore being pulled out of the Butte mines had tripled from 1883 to 1885 when the smelter began operations.

The Old Works and later the Washoe Smelter built in 1902 resulted in the emergence of the community of Anaconda at the site. Train loads of ore were shipped to the new smelter by the Montana Union Railway. Marcus Daly believed the Montana Union Railway was charging excessive haulage fees in 1892 to transport his product so he shut down his Butte mines for five months to protest.

Daly and James J. Hill, the president of the Great Northern Railroad, incorporated the Butte, Anaconda & Pacific Railroad on September 30, 1892. Daly's idea was to build his own rail system to Anaconda for hauling copper ore. He also wanted to extend the line to Hamilton and Kalispell to gain valuable timber supplies needed for his Butte operations. He had plans to extend the line to San Francisco and thus the name the Butte, Anaconda and Pacific Railroad.

The new rail system constructed by Hill's Great Northern began operations on December 1, 1893. A month later, on January 1, 1894, the Butte, Anaconda & Pacific Railroad officially took over the line from the Great Northern and Marcus Daly had his own railroad to haul copper ore to Anaconda.

The rail lines to Hamilton and Kalispell were never completed, but the 26-mile route from the Butte mines to the Anaconda Smelter was put to heavy use by Daly's mining operations. It was dubbed, "the Biggest Little Railroad in the World." The first raw ore hauled on the new line was December 3, 1893. A year later, the BA & P started providing daily passenger train service between the two towns. The passenger train ride continued until April 17, 1955.

The BA&P Railroad was eventually electrified from its original steam-generated system in 1913. The electricity allowed bigger volumes of ore to be shipped at much faster speeds to the Anaconda Smelter. The BA&P had over 1,400 hopper cars with most being in service on a 24-hour bases. The 18-ton hopper cars could haul up to 50 tons of copper per car.

The combination of copper, rail service, plus effective smelting operations in Anaconda and eight smaller smelting operations in Butte pushed the community into the forefront of mining. Butte was now the copper king of the world.

A number of mining firms, besides The Anaconda Company, made huge profits from the underground operations. One of the most successful was the Montana Copper Company formed by two New York brothers, Adolph and Leonard Lewisohn. The chief mining foreman for the company was Charles Meader, who came to Butte in 1879 and purchased a number of properties on the east end of the mining district for the Lewisohn brothers. Meader also constructed a smelter for the brothers in a section of town that would later bear his name, Meaderville.

The Montana Copper Company later joined forces with Boston businessmen, Albert S. Bigelow and Joseph Clark, to form the Boston and Montana Mining Company. The mining firm was well-financed and became one of the most profitable mining operations in the Butte district. A key component to the firm's success was their huge smelting operation in Great Falls, Montana, which was completed in 1893.

The battle for copper money led to clashes between the major power brokers of the Butte mining properties. The Lewisohns were able to avoid the confrontations. The chief opponents in the "War of the Copper Kings" in the early years were copper barons, Marcus Daly and William Clark. The exact point which triggered their feud is not clear. What is very evident is both men would do whatever was necessary to get their way in mining, politics and prestige.

The first public battle between the two copper barons who were both Democrats took place in 1888. Clark was seeking to become a delegate to the Congress from the Montana Territory. Daly backed little known Helena lawyer, Thomas Carter. Few people gave the Republican much of a chance against the wealthy William Clark.

Marcus Daly and some of his partners in the lumber industry were under investigation for illegally cutting down timber through their firm called the Montana Improvement Company. They believed Carter had a better chance of stopping the federal investigation against their company since it became clear that Republican Benjamin Harrison was going to beat incumbent Democrat Grover Cleveland in the 1888 Presidential election.

Marcus Daly influenced his mine workers into voting for Carter. Daly also got his lumber partners to pressure their workers into also casting ballots for the Helena attorney. Carter won the election by 5,126 votes. It was William Clark's first defeat in his ambition to become a political leader. Clark had lost round one in his political battles with Marcus Daly.

A few years later, during the 1893 Montana Legislative session, Daly's efforts kept Clark from winning the nomination as a Senator from Montana. During that time, the state legislature voted for its Senators. William Clark's effort in 1893 fell 3 votes shy of election.

Following the deadlocked legislative session, Montana Governor John Rickards appointed a political puppet of Daly's, Butte mayor Lee Mantle, to fill the Senate seat. The Senate refused to seat Mantle because he was a political appointee. Thus, Montana went over a year with only one of their two Senate seats occupied.

Clark gained some sweet revenge in 1894 when his choice for the state capital, Helena, beat out Daly's favorite, Anaconda, by less than 2,000 votes. Helena received 27,028 votes, while Anaconda's total was 25,118. The two copper kings combined spent over $1.5 million on promoting their choice for the seat of state government.

The 1899 Montana Legislature stands as the ultimate battle between the copper warriors. Clark made it known early in the legislative session that he would do whatever it took to win the nomination as the state's Senator.

Clark reportedly spent over $400,000 bribing lawmakers to vote for him in the Senate race. As Clark boldly stated, "I never bought a man who wasn't for sale." After weeks of ballots, Clark got his way and won the nomination; however, when he went to Washington, the Senate refused to seat him because of the alleged bribery charges. An investigation resulted and on April 10, 1900, the Senate Committee on Privileges and Elections declared Clark's election through the Montana Legislature as null and void. For the second time in less than a decade, Montana would have only one of its two Senate seats filled for over a year.

The controversy surrounding the 1899 Montana Legislative session and Clark's alleged bribery charges started the process for the 17th Amendment to the Constitution. The amendment was ratified in 1913 allowing the general public's popular vote to decide United States Senators rather than election through state legislatures.

Clark's troubles with being barred from the Senate came during a time of great transition which changed the city of Butte forever. The mining property owned by Marcus Daly and his California syndicate was purchased by the Amalgamated Copper Company. The new mining firm was headed by Standard Oil executives, Henry Rogers and William Rockefeller.

Prior to the transfer, capital investments to make improvements in their operations forced Marcus Daly and his syndicate to incorporate their mining company on January 19, 1891. A few weeks after the incorporation, the majority shareholder, George Hearst, died leaving his holdings to his wife, Phoebe, and their son, William Randolph. The Hearst family sold their shares of the corporation, roughly 25 per cent of the company, to a group of European investors led by the Rothchild family. The Rothchild family eventually sold their shares in the mining company.

The move forced the company to reorganize and reincorporate into The Anaconda Copper Mining Company on June 18, 1895. The reorganization left Marcus Daly and the lone remaining California investor still alive, James Haggin, in firm control of the company with over 50 percent ownership of shares.

Following the reincorporating in 1895, The Anaconda Copper Mining Company made over $12 million in profits over a 3-year period. It was simply too good a business venture for other Wall Street investors not to try to buy out Daly and Haggin.

Two Boston men, Thomas Lawson, a speculator, and Albert Burrage, a capitalist, convinced Henry Rogers and William Rockefeller, two key executives in the Standard Oil trust, that a take over of the lucrative Butte mining operations was possible. Rockefeller was the younger brother of John D. Rockefeller, the founder of Standard Oil, who refused to participate in the copper buyout.

The Eastern syndicate first tried to buy shares of the Boston and Montana Mining Company owned by the Lewisohn family. The maneuver ended in litigation. Then, the Standard Oil executives turned their attention to The Anaconda Copper Mining Company. Both Daly and Haggin realized that they might face litigation too with the financially powerful Standard Oil Company. The two, both now in their later years in life, agreed to sell their shares of Anaconda to the Standard Oil executives on April 27, 1899. Haggin made $15 million in the transaction, while Daly netted $17 million which he reinvested in the new company. In the settlement for selling his shares, Daly was allowed to remain as president of Anaconda. The firm was now under the umbrella of the newly created holding company, the Amalgamated Copper Company, which remained in place until 1915.

At the time of the sale The Anaconda Copper Mining Company was netting $5.4 million a year in mining. They owned the Anaconda Smelter, the Butte, Anaconda and Pacific Railway plus three large department stores.

The take over by the Standard Oil Company of the Butte mining operations became a key political issue for Daly's bitter enemy, William Clark. He joined forces with a rising copper king in the town, F. Augustus Heinze, to form the Fusion Party, a combination of Democrats and Populists, for the 1900 elections.

Heinze was born on December 5, 1869, in Brooklyn, New York, a son of German immigrants. After earning a mining engineering degree from Columbia University, Heinze came to Butte in 1889. He joined the engineering staff of the Boston and Montana Consolidated Copper and Silver Mining Company and worked in the underground mines. Heinze quickly became acquainted with the workings.

After working two years in Butte, he went to Germany and studied for a couple of years before returning back to the mining camp. Shortly after his arrival in the city, he received $50,000 from the estate of his late grandmother. Heinze used the money to create the Montana Ore Purchasing Company in Meaderville. His knowledge of Butte's underground operations led in 1895 to the purchase of the Rarus Mine for $300,000 on the east end of the mining camp. Heinze developed the Rarus Mine and soon became a major force in the war of the copper kings.

During the 1900 election campaign, Clark and Heinze portrayed Standard Oil as a big Eastern conglomerate that cared little about the Montana workers. They also told workers that Marcus Daly had sold them out for his own personal gain.

Clark and Heinze announced in the form of letters on Miners' Union Day, June 13, 1900, that their mines would institute an eight-hour work day without a reduction in pay. The miners had long been seeking such a work schedule and the announcement was well-received within the community. The Anaconda Copper Mining Company did not grant an eight-hour work day until 1906.

The message of big Eastern money combined with the eight-hour work day got through to the Butte voters. The Fusion Party did very well during the 1900 elections in Silver Bow County.

Also the influence of Clark's money bought enough supporters so the copper king won a majority of the seats in the Montana Legislature. This led to Clark's easy approval from the 1901 Montana Legislature as the state's Senator.

But, the key reason for the Fusion Party's success was the health of Marcus Daly. The copper king grew ill the year before in 1899. He traveled to various parts of the world seeking help for diabetes. When he returned to the United States, Daly was ordered to a bed in the Hotel Netherland in New York City rather than be allowed to travel back to Montana to battle the Clark-Heinze Fusion Party in the 1900 election. Six days after the general election on November 12, 1900, Marcus Daly died.

The combination of Clark and Heinze working together for a political purpose ended shortly after the 1900 election. When he was finally seated in the Senate, Clark made peace with the executives of The Anaconda Copper Mining Company. Heinze called Clark "the Traitor of Montana" for the move. Heinze would do battle on his own for the next five years with the giant Anaconda Copper Mining Company.

The year after the election, the Standard Oil executives were able to take over control of the Boston and Montana Mining Company from Leonard Lewisohn. The buyout left Clark's and Heinz's companies as the remaining two large independent mining firms left on the Butte hill. By this time, Clark was devoting much of his attention to matters in Washington rather than his Butte mining operations. This left Heinze as the lone gladiator against The Anaconda Copper Mining Company.

Heinze's secret to success on the Butte hill was displayed not in his engineering skills, but in his manipulation of the local courtrooms. Heinze controlled two local judges, William Clancy and Edward Harney. This was extremely important in the maneuvers Heinze made to gain control of the Butte hill over the Standard Oil trust.

Heinze bought property next to holdings of The Anaconda Copper Mining Company. Under the apex law Heinze followed a vein down into property controlled by Anaconda. The Standard Oil executives tried to stop Heinze's moves in litigation; however, both Judges Clancy and Harney always ruled in Heinze's favor. So, the copper baron could do just about anything he wanted to on the Butte hill and get away with it.

One of Heinze's boldest moves was to break down underground bulkheads of connecting Anaconda Copper Mining Company mines and have his workers remove valuable ore from Amalgamated's own property. This led to open warfare underground by miners from Heinze's camp and Anaconda's work force. The two sides fought with fists, shovels, pickets and most of all dynamite. The main battleground was a mile and a half strip of underground land connecting Heinze's Minnie Healy Mine and the Pennsylvania Mine, a property operated by Anaconda. This led to the deaths of Sam Olson and Fred Divel, two Anaconda workers employed in the Pennsylvania.

The Standard Oil executives had enough of Heinze's courtroom control after Judge Clancy ruled against Anaconda's two-year legal fight with minority stockholders who were controlled by Heinze. When Clancy ruled in Heinze's favor, the giant Anaconda Company struck back by suspending all their mining operations in Montana for two months from October through December, 1903. This forced over 6,500 workers in Butte and over 20,000 people across Montana out of work.

Standard Oil executives said the mines would not be reopened until the Montana Legislature passed a Fair Trials law which allowed district judges to be dismissed from a case because of bias, allowing a new district judge to hear a case. After a six-week standoff, Governor Joseph Toole agreed to call a special session which quickly passed the Fair Trials legislation on November 11, 1903.

The maneuver broke Heinze's mining career in Butte. Heinze had used the courtroom successfully for nine years to get his way in Butte's underground mines. Now, his only defense was gone and Heinze had little choice but to sell his holdings to The Anaconda Copper Mining Company. It took over a year but he finally worked out an agreement with Arthur Carson who was acting as an agent for Thomas Cole and John D Ryan. Cole and Ryan had been high school classmates in Houghton, Michigan. Ryan, who was made president of The Anaconda Copper Mining Company in Butte in 1905, used the assistance of his old classmate to get F. Augustus Heinze to sign over his United Copper Mining property holdings to The Company on February 13, 1906. Heinze received $10.5 million for his properties. He later lost most of that trying his luck on Wall Street. Heinze died a broken man in 1914 in Sarasota Springs, New York.

The buyout of Heinze saved The Anaconda Copper Mining Company large amounts of revenue. The legal battles with Heinze were costing The Company over $1 million a year. The settlement freed up $70 million worth of valuable mining properties that had been tied up by the 110 legal cases still pending. The mining properties had to suspend their operations until a legal ruling had been made on their various suits. All that was wiped out with the Heinze buyout.

The buyout of Heinze left the Standard Oil executives in almost total control of the Butte hill except for William Clark's mines and some other smaller operations. Anaconda acquired some of Clark's holdings in 1910 and the rest of his mining properties following the settlement of his estate in 1928, three years after Clark's death. The remaining smaller operations eventually came under the control of The Anaconda Copper Mining Company which would later be shortened to The Anaconda Company in May 1955.

The Union

The shift of power from local owners to Wall Street corporate executives had a major impact on the workers at the Butte mines. In the past, differences over working conditions, wages and other issues could be easily resolved with local owners like Daly, Clark, Heinze and Lewisohn who understood the mining business. Now with executives from Wall Street like Rogers and Rockefeller running the operations, the only issue that really mattered was getting the rock out to make the bottom line. This led to major confrontations between workers and mine owners over the next 20 years.

Yet, long before The Anaconda Company curled a stranglehold around the Butte hill, the underground miners realized their best course for protection was banding together as one. The Butte Miners' Union was formed on June 13, 1878, as the Butte Working Men's Union. The union was formed after some mine owners told workers they were going to cut their wages. The workers revolted when they heard the news, quickly formed a union and stopped the wage cut.

It was the first union of its kind in the state and the first large-scale miners' union in the country. Its purpose was threefold: develop better working conditions underground, develop a sick and death benefit for union members' families and develop a better wage scale.

The Butte Working Men's Union joined forces with the Western Federation of Miners in 1893. The Butte group was the first to join the WFM and thus was given the union number of one. The Butte Miners Union built a union hall in 1888 on North Main Street. The completion of the hall came a year before Butte's first major mine disaster. On November 23, 1889, a fire broke out in the Anaconda Mine. The blaze took place between shifts so only a handful of men were underground when the inferno broke out. There were six men killed and two others badly hurt in the fire.

The story of mine disasters and fires were a major component of life in Butte. Four years after the Anaconda Mine fire on April 21, 1893, an inferno broke out in the Silver Bow Mine. Nine workers lost their lives. A blaze at the High Ore Mine on January 14, 1911, resulted in two deaths. A blast of 600 pounds of dynamite at the Granite Mountain shaft on October 19, 1915, claimed 16 workers. A couple of months later, on February 14, 1916, a blaze ignited at the 1200-foot air shaft inside the Pennsylvania Mine resulting in 21 workers losing their lives. The Butte mines were the most unsafe hard-rock operations in the world. Accidental deaths occurred on a monthly basis with over 2,100 workers losing their lives underground during the duration of mining in Butte.

The fear of accidents and death is something Butte mining families had to endure every day.

"I use to worry all the time about my husband," remembered Maurine Higman Dennehy. "There was one time he was suppose to go with three other men from the Badger to the Leonard Mine underground to check out the tunnel. He got sick beforehand and never went with them. Well, all three miners got into some bad air and died. Thankfully, my husband was not with them or he would've been dead too."

Larry Maki said, "I remember a guy working with me in the Belmont Mine got his leg cut up really bad when it got caught in the tracks. The experience was so bad I had a tough time eating for a week after the accident."

Beatrice Lockett Scalabrin recalled, "As a child I use to watch my dad go off to work every day. One day he never came home. He was killed in an accident at the West Colusa Mine. It was hard on my mom raising four kids. She had to work a lot just to make ends meet. As I got older bitterness developed inside me because my dad was such a good man and to die such a tragic way inside one of those mines was simply awful."

Jenny Serich said, "I lost my father in the mines when I was 16-years-old. It was a real shock and it took a long time to get over."

Evelyn Eva explained, "I was frightened for my husband, Tom, every time he went to work. What scared me the most was him traveling down that cage because it could really get going. In fact, one time the cable broke and the cage went crashing down below. My husband and the others were hurt and taken to the hospital. Thankfully, no one was killed."

Jack Harris, a former miner said, "Some people thought The Anaconda Company was great because they provided jobs. Yet, I'll bet those same people never went underground working for Anaconda. It was tough work in horrible conditions."

Bob Koprivica recalled, "The working conditions those miners had to endure you wouldn't put your dog through they were so bad. I remember as a kid watching those miners come out of the hole in Dublin Gulch. Why their clothes were all yellow and they were spitting all over the place trying to get the dust out of their mouth. It was absolutely terrible how they were treated by The Anaconda Company."

Rich Holman looks back at that time and remembered, "Every time that whistle blew at the various mines my entire family held their breath. My dad worked on the cages which was a dangerous job. We were always concerned when that whistle went off that it could be our father. It was only after the ambulance had come to the site and hauled out the injured miner did we breath easier when we discovered it was not our dad on the stretcher."

Harris added, "People talk all the time about all the deaths in the Butte mines. Few realize that all the accidents in the mines kept the hospitals as busy as the undertakers. There were wards full of miners in the hospital all the time with broken legs, ankles, backs, arms and other things from working underground. It was a very unsafe profession especially in Butte."

Bev McClafferty, a former nurse at St. James Hospital remembered, "The hospital wards were always filled with miners. They had something once a week in the emergency room of the hospital called "miners hours." It was during this time that miners could come in and receive medical attention from local doctors for cuts, bruises and other injuries suffered on the job. When it came time for miners hours, trust me, we were always busy."

The Anaconda Company and the various other mining firms offered no health or life insurance on its workers.

"When my father was killed in the mines we got nothing from Anaconda," said Jenny Serich. "We were thankful he had a small life insurance policy because that was the only way we could afford to bury him."

The miners were forced to protect themselves in case of sickness or death, a critical matter that united all miners. Miners compensated for a lack of insurance by placing a portion of their weekly check in a union fund to help pay workers and their families for any sickness or death that resulted from a mine accident.

If workers were not being either hurt or killed in the mines, they were certain to be dying a slow death through breathing the dirty air underground. Only a few mines on the hill had any type of ventilation system which alleviated the dry, dirty air that workers were forced to inhale while mucking out the ore. The dirty air eventually led to silicosis or in Butte lingo "miners' con." It impacted any worker who went underground and would lead to an early grave site for many hard working miners. The average life span of a Butte miner was 45 years. There was also the factor of the copper sulfur which miners came in constant contact with during their shift. The copper sulfur produced burns on clothing and the flesh.

Despite the unsafe conditions, the life of a miner was a special one in Butte. They performed a unique, complicated craft and were professional in every sense of the word.

"I worked with some of the best miners in the world," said Mike McGrath, a former miner motorman. "There were people like Bill Gilbert and Steve Ryan. They were contract miners and boy were they good at what they did for a living.

"When we started a shift I took them back to their drift. The first thing they did was make sure everything around them was safe. They knocked down large rocks and other things that could be a hazard during their shift. The number one concern for them was always safety. They made sure everything was okay before digging or drilling began for the day.

"Once they got going, I used a mucking machine to load the ore cars. The bucket came right over my head with very little clearance with the ceiling above me. The other two guys directed me on operating the mucking machine with head signals because it was the only way we could communicate. It was dark and noisy down in the hole."

Andy Kankelborg, a former miner recalled, "I loved the fellowship that was there between the miners. You always had this special feeling of being a team underground that you found no where above the surface. Everyone depended on their partner to stay alive. You were always looking out for the other guy. It did not matter what ethnic group you were or the color of your skin. When you were underground working in Butte, Montana, everyone was equal.

"It was a status symbol that when you were a miner you worked like hell underground. There were never any bosses around. You never really needed a boss, though, because as a contract miner it was up to you to muck out the ore if you wanted a decent paycheck."

Mike McGrath added, "I loved the life of a miner. It was such a unique way to make a living. The pay was good. The fellowship between workers was second to nothing. More than anything, though, I was just proud to be a miner. Believe me the only reason The Anaconda Company got to be the world's largest mining outfit was through the tremendous hard-working miners."

The pride developed underground by miners did not help them once they were back on the surface especially during the winter. The underground mine temperatures were sometimes well over 100 degrees which produced a lot of sweat from miners. When they were brought back to the surface, the miners would be dripping with perspiration. They had to walk home wet from perspiration in temperatures often below zero during the winter. This situation was alleviated when a building called the dry was set up in a mine yard. It allowed miners to change from wet work clothes into dry clothing for the walk home.

The union fought for a better pay scale. They received $ 3.50 a day in 1878, a good wage at the time. However, that same standard carried through for the better part of 40 years with only slightly higher standards during upswings in the price of copper in the 1910s.

One of the few times copper prices and wages were high was between 1913-1917. The wage scale was $4.75 a day. The Butte mines employed over 15,000 men in 1915. There were 83 shafts in operation with 56 mines producing ore. When the United States entered World War I in 1917, copper was selling at a robust 26 cents a pound.

The problems confronting the mine workers of Butte were obvious, unsafe working conditions, no benefits, low wages and Wall Street's non-mining personnel running the operations. Yet, the hidden agenda and greatest obstacle for the union to overcome was fighting among members themselves.

A major segment of the fighting by members was caused by The Anaconda Company, the United States Army and members of the Bureau of Investigation which later became the Federal Bureau of Investigation. All three groups had agents infiltrate and disrupt union activities. The agents caused turmoil within the union ranks and gave both Anaconda and federal officials advance knowledge on what steps union officials were going to take next. A government investigation years after the infiltration agreed with the suspicion of union leaders that both The Anaconda Company and the federal government had secret agents working inside the ranks of the local unions.

There were two general courses of action workers in the early 20th century could take to overcome the Wall Street corporations like The Anaconda Company. One was to achieve power for the working man through peaceful negotiations. The second was the creation of a single industrial workers' union which took whatever means necessary to achieve their goals. The ideological differences produced fighting between union members that was as vicious as their battles to gain better wages and benefits from the mining companies.

The conservative branch of the union, made up primarily of Irish and Cornish miners, wanted to do whatever was necessary to keep peace with The Anaconda Company and remain on the job. They took no direct action during contract talks in 1906 and 1911 with Company officials to achieve safer working conditions underground. No action meant mine accidents and deaths were allowed to continue at an alarming rate.

The conservative branch of the union also worked out in their 1906 and 1911 contract a wage agreement that tied their pay directly to the price of copper. If the price of copper rose between 15 to 18 cents a pound the miners received $3.75 a day. If the copper price went above 18 cents a pound the miners wages went up to $4.00 a day.

Shortly after the deal was finished, the price of copper hit a 25-year high of 25 cents a pound in 1907. This meant a short term pay increase for miners; however, the price fell under 15 cents a pound in 1908 and workers were back to a wage scale of $3.50 a day. It was the same scale they worked for over three decades earlier in 1878.

The progressive members of the union, made up mainly of Finnish miners, called the conservatives "stooges" for Anaconda. The progressive members were in favor of taking whatever radical means necessary to achieve better conditions for miners. The progressive supporters were looked at as possible agents for The Anaconda Company by the conservatives. They felt the progressives were trying to disrupt union activities keeping the unions weak and Anaconda strong.

The progressives' philosophy of direct action against the giant corporation was preached by the Industrial Workers of the World, known as the Wobblies. They believed only direct action by workers through a general strike or sabotage brought about the destruction of capitalist companies like Anaconda and thus lead to a cooperative commonwealth controlled by the working class.

The progressive union members wanted to go out on strike in 1912; however, the conservative branch of the union fought and were successful. They kept the mines open through an election of conservative union officers that progressive members claimed was rigged.

Through the help of the conservative union members, The Anaconda Company developed a rustling card system for miners to work underground which was started on December 1, 1912. A miner had to receive a rustling card from Company officials before going underground. A background check of radical union members led to flushing out trouble-makers from Company property.

This resulted in progressive members refusing to show their rustling cards to union officials at the gates of the Speculator Mine before starting a shift. The union officials had taken the action to try to assure The Company that all the workers were in good standing, each with a rustling card. The progressive members left the Speculator and marched over to the Black Rock Mine where workers there joined in the protest. Later that night, the group formed their own union called the Butte Mine Workers' Union on June 12, 1914, at the Finlander Hall. In less than two weeks, this new organization was able to sign up 1,430 new members.

The pot of tension boiled over the next day on June 13, 1914, Miners' Union Day. During the annual Miners' Union Day parade, progressive union members developed a blockade on Park Street stopping conservatives from completing their annual march through uptown Butte. The action started a riot in the business district as the two sides turned their anger on each other.

Progressive members were looking for the local head of the Western Federation of Miners, Bert Riley, and his officers. Riley and his men managed to escape the riot scene and, through the help of local police officials, were removed from the area.

Once progressive members realized they could not get Riley and his men, they bolted toward the Miners' Union Hall on Main Street. They pushed aside conservative union men who were trying to protect the building. They went inside and ransacked the Hall, breaking all the windows and tossing furniture, paper and other items outside on Main Street. The acting mayor of the town, Alderman Frank Curran, pleaded with the men to stop the riot. They tossed Curran out a second-story window. The injured Curran was taken to the nearby Murray Hospital.

Authorities tried to stop the riots by closing all the taverns in town, which was done by two o'clock in the afternoon. Later that night, the members from the new union held a meeting. Following their deliberations, they went back up to the Miners' Union Hall and hauled away the union safe.

The men took the safe south of town near the Tivoli Brewery. They blew up the safe before 1,000 spectators, including both Police Chief Jerry Murphy and Silver Bow County Sheriff Tim Driscoll. Both men felt it was helpless trying to stop the mob. The damage had been done. The mighty union town had been split in half.

Ten days after the riots on June 23, 1914, more trouble developed at the Miners' Union Hall. Progressive union men took over the building while conservative members, led by the national Western Federation of Miners president, Charles Moyer, were trying to hold a meeting inside.

The trouble began when union member Pete Bruno tried to go inside the hall and up the stairway to attend the meeting. He was shot in the head by union members inside the building. The conservative members inside the hall had brought lots of rifles and other weapons into the building earlier in the day through the back entrance. They were ready for a fight and the shot that hit Bruno started open warfare.

The conservatives opened fire on the men outside the building. Ernest Noy, who was walking up the opposite side of the street during the gun battle, was shot and killed. Six people were hurt during the battle.

The men outside retaliated, firing shots back at the members inside. When that happened, the conservatives quickly left the hall through the back entrance where they slid to safety down a plank which had been put into place earlier in the day. The progressive members continued shooting inside the building for thirty minutes.

It was then decided to take more drastic action against the conservative members. The progressive members raced up Main Street to the Steward Mine. They held the chief engineer of the Steward at gun point while they took 10 boxes loaded with dynamite which they used to blow up the Miners' Union Hall. It took 15 blasts before the building had been almost completely destroyed.

The leaders of the Butte Mine Workers' Union Muckie McDonald, Joe Bradley, Joe Shannon and James Chapman were all arrested after the bombing. A lawyer tried to get Charles Moyer arrested for the death of Ernest Noy; however, the local authorities refused to press charges.

Prior to the destruction, McDonald and his officers had handed out over 5,000 handbills to the members of their new union. The handbill provided the following message, "Fellow workers, in the name of your new union, keep peace and go home." Another union leader, Dan Shovlin, pleaded with the workers to go home in a speech before the first shots were fired.

Despite the efforts by McDonald, the president of the union, and Bradley, the vice president of the organization, both were tried in a court case held in Boulder, Montana. Both men were convicted and sent to prison. Shannon was released to take care of his wife and six kids. A number of union members maintained that releasing Joe Shannon without any legal trial was a sign he was an agent working for The Anaconda Company.

James Chapman was released without standing trial for no apparent reason. He went to Arizona and his activities there led many to believe that he was an agent working for The Anaconda Company. Because of alleged agents some historians maintain The Anaconda Company did have an actual part in the destruction of the Butte Miners' Union building.

That belief can be supported by testimony during the corner's inquest of Ernest Noy's death. It revealed that a number of the gunmen both inside the hall and on the outside were not familiar with local union leaders. Edwin Duncan, the son of mayor Louis Duncan, was inside the hall attending the meeting when the shooting began. He testified that the gunman who fired the first shot was a new face to the union meeting. A local detective for 15 years in Butte, George Ambrose, also stated that the men doing all the shooting both inside and outside the building were all unfamiliar to him. He calculated that all the men were from outside the area.

Charles Moyer, the head of the Western Federation of Mines, claimed all the new faces in town were members of the International Workers of the World, or Wobblies. He said 140 Wobblies had arrived in town just a few days before the shooting.

Union members from the new Butte Mine Workers' Union said the new faces in town were all agents working for The Anaconda Company and against the formation of a strong union.

A federal investigation and report done by the United States Justice Department after the destruction reveals that Moyer's claim of IWW involvement in the Miners Union destruction is simply not true. The report stated that the IWW had very little influence on Butte union activities in 1914. The report also indicates that The Anaconda Company had agents planted within the Western Federation of Miners. The investigation revealed the agents were the real culprits behind the dynamite blasts that destroyed the union hall.

All this did little to solve the issue of who killed Ernest Noy. The corner's inquest in Ernest Noy's death resulted in the conclusion that the man had been killed from a shot fired from the second floor of the union hall; however, no one was ever arrested for the murder.

The Miners' Union Hall destruction led to the impeachment of Sheriff Driscoll and Socialist Party Mayor Duncan by the city council. The local council believed neither official took decisive action to stop the destruction. Driscoll had been totally unprepared for the night of violence. He was stationed at the site with only two other deputies. Why more officers were not at the hall especially after the destruction less than two weeks earlier was one of the main questions he was asked by city officials. Duncan had tried to take appropriate actions to try to stop the violence. When the shooting started he immediately ordered all the saloons in town be shut down. The bars were closed within 30 minutes of the order before the shooting had stopped and the blasts had started at the hall.

Duncan had been a favorite of the progressive union members. A segment of the progressive branch felt they could achieve working class control through politics and the Socialist Party, a political stance that the conservative union members strongly opposed. Despite the large population of Irish and Cornish miners in Butte, the Socialist Party started to gain strength when The Anaconda Company took over majority control of the Butte mines. It took a number of years, but the Socialist Party made up primarily of working class progressive union members achieved their ultimate prize when their candidate, Louis Duncan, was elected mayor of Butte in 1911. He won again in 1913, but infighting developed among Socialist Party members over political appointees to city jobs. Duncan lost plenty of party support with his appointee decisions and lost the full support of the party when the Miners' Union Hall was blown up.

A few days after the destruction a member of the new union, Erik Lantala, walked into Duncan's office on July 3, 1914, and demanded that the mayor deport newspaper writer, Frank Altonen, from Butte. Altonen worked for the *Tyromles* a newspaper in Hancock, Michigan, which supported the Western Federation of Miners. When Duncan refused, Lankala pulled out a knife and stabbed the mayor three times. Duncan grabbed a gun and shot Lankala. The Finnish miner later died from the gun shot wound to the stomach. Duncan was not charged with murder because he had acted in self-defense. The incident illustrated that Duncan's main political support had vanished in the progressive wing of the union.

After the destruction of the Miners' Union Hall, tensions remained high in Butte, climaxing on August 30, 1914, when the rustling card office at the Parrot Mine was blown up. Anaconda Company officials claimed they would pay $10,000 for information leading to the arrest and conviction of the culprits. Union members vehemently maintained that Company men had deliberately blown up the office so they could get federal troops to come into town.

Governor Samuel Stewart mobilized the National Guard and brought troops to Butte on September 1, 1914, to control the hostilities. Officials established martial law and set aside all civil court proceedings. A number of union members were thrown in jail with no charges being filed against them.

The muscle of the federal troops allowed Company officials to declare that members of the Butte Mine Workers' Union would be blacklisted and kept off their property.

Company official Con Kelley declared on October 11, 1914, that their mining properties were now an "open shop." This meant that miners no longer had to be affiliated with the local union to work for The Anaconda Company. It essentially was the end of unions in Butte which is exactly what Anaconda wanted with the potential for enormous profits because of the start of World War I. The Company could now deny collective bargaining for the union on behalf of workers, making the unions powerless against The Anaconda Company.

Times were good for The Anaconda Company. They had total control over their operations and, with an increasing demand for copper, The Company was making enormous profits. Copper was selling for 32 cents a pound, the highest figure for the red metal in over 30 years.

Total control by Anaconda and federal troops was maintained for almost three years until June 8, 1917. A fire on that June evening in the Granite Mountain and Speculator Mines killed 168 miners. The response to the disaster was a general strike by all workers on the hill. They also wrote to US District Attorney Burton Wheeler seeking his help in asking President Woodrow Wilson to send someone from the Department of Labor to come to Butte to investigate the mining operations.

The timing of the strike and the request to Wheeler could not have come at a worse time for miners trying to establish better working conditions. The United States had just entered the three-year-old World War I on April 6, 1917. Butte with its precious copper metal was desperately needed by the Allies in the war.

The miners demanded six things before they would go back to work underground:

1. fully safeguard the lives of miners
2. develop proper ventilation systems underground
3. have water systems installed to lay down the dust and reduce miners' consumption
4. no man could be left to work alone in dangerous places underground
5. abolish the rustling card system
6. establish a work scale of $6.00 a day

It is interesting to note that four of the six demands dealt with working conditions and not wages. Miners simply wanted to feel safe at the work place. The workers wanted a committee established made up of both workers and Company managers. The committee would inspect the mines once a month for safety. They also wanted all new workers to learn where the escape routes for each mine were located and they wanted the bulkheads to be guarded so the areas would be safe if another fire erupted.

The issue of wages had been burning for some time. In 1917, miners were making $4.75 based on copper selling for 27 cents a pound. They were suppose to receive a wage increase of 25 cents for every 2 cents the red metal was selling above 32 cents. Copper ore had been selling above 32 cents since February 1917, but the workers had not been given a raise. They believed The Company was cheating them of entitled wages. Yet, the workers could do little about it because the mines were operating as an open shop. The workers had no way of conducting collective bargaining with The Company.

The Department of Labor sent W. H. Rodgers to Butte to try to settle the strike. The President of the American Federation of Labor, Samuel Gompers, also came to town, but the miners refused to affiliate themselves with Gompers' organization.

Three weeks after the Granite Mountain disaster, there were over 15,000 workers out on a picket line. Other skilled craft unions joined the miners in their efforts to receive better working conditions. Anaconda Company officials refused to acknowledge the miners' demands. Instead, they helped create better working conditions and wages for the skilled crafts people who went out on strike with the miners. This weakened the impact of the miners' strike. Union members were being thrown in jail by federal troops for trying to distribute strike pamphlets.

Frank Little, a national leader for the Industrial Workers of the World, came to town a month after the accident to champion the cause for better working conditions. He also tried to better organize the new Metal Mine Workers' Union. Little believed the only way to change things in Butte was to have a massive strike of all workers against the mining companies. Earlier that year he had been deported from Brisbee, Arizona, for trying to organize labor. His background included being jailed in Spokane, Washington, in 1909 and Fresno, California, in 1910 for trying to organize workers.

Little arrived in Butte on July 18, 1917, with a broken ankle the result of a fight he had with a gunman at his previous stop in El Paso, Texas. He held well-attended rallies at the Finlander Hall next to the boarding house where he was staying. He also spoke at the Columbia

Gardens amusement park east of town. Little was promoting his cause to shut down all the mines in town. Little blasted the entrance of the United States into the World War as a way for capitalists to continue making a large profit at the expense of the working class. He told the crowds that capitalists, not any one nation, were the real enemy of the working people.

On the evening of July 31, Little was told by a local bartender that a vigilante group had been formed to stop him. Little thought little of the rumor as he went to his Room 32 in the boarding house. A few hours later at three o'clock in the morning of August 1, a black Cadillac pulled up to the front of the Steele Building and Mrs. Nora Bryne's boarding house at 316 North Wyoming Street. Six men wearing masks got out of the car. Five of the six went inside looking for Little. After crashing through the door at Room 30 and finding nothing, they were confronted by Mrs. Bryne. The men told her they were with the Sheriff's Office and they had come to take away Frank Little.

When she told them Little was in Room 32 the five men crashed inside, gagged Little with a towel, and dragged him from the room. Once outside and away from the boarding house, they tied Little with a rope to the back of the car. They dragged him down the road. The men took Little south of town where he was hanged to death from the Milwaukee Railroad trestle west of Montana Street.

The killers left a note on Little's underwear a card which read:

Others take note
First and Last Warning
3-7-77
L-D-C-S-S-W-T

The L had been circled indicating that Little had been taken care of while the other letters represented union leaders and Wobblies the vigilantes claimed would be next to get it like Little. D was William Dunne the head of the Electricians' Union; C for Tom Campbell president of the Metal Mine Workers' Union; S was William Sullivan an attorney for the union; another S for Dan Shovlin a union official; W was for John Williams a known Wobbly, and T was for John Timosh a Wobbly and friend of Frank Little. The 3-7-77 is a cryptic notation used by the vigilantes in their 1860s roundup and execution of the Plummer gang in Virginia City.

Who killed Little was never discovered despite an investigation by both local, state and federal officials. State Attorney General Sam Ford came to Butte the day after the hanging to conduct his own investigation. Many people who had seen the car were brought before Ford. The witnesses were so frightened that Ford never could get his investigation off the ground. United States District Attorney Wheeler a key proponent to stay out of World War I, conducted an investigation and like Sam Ford came up with nothing.

The Strike Bulletin, a local union newsletter, stated that the six men included William Oates, Herman Gillis, Pete Beaudry, a "rat" named Middleton and the chief gunman named Ryan. There were many theories, but never any answers, solutions or arrests in the murder case.

The various theories of Little's death have been discussed at length through the years by Butte citizens. The only thing for certain is that six masked men forced Frank Little out of his boarding house room in the early morning hours of August 1, 1917. He was found dead the next morning hanging from a railroad trestle south of town. It was Butte's first lynching since 1868 when three Chinese men were hung to death.

Little's death produced one of the largest funerals ever in the community on August 5, 1917. Over 10,000 people looked on during his procession which ended at the Mountain View Cemetery.

The union strike continued after Little's funeral. Yet, its strength weakened with each passing day as more and more workers went back to their jobs. By August 21, 1917, the Company reported that 75 percent of their employees were back at work. The walkout was finally called off on December 18, 1917.

Congressional Representative Jeannette Rankin came to Butte in 1917 to try to help workers. She conducted her own investigation over a four-day period. She finished her work by giving a speech at the Columbia Gardens ballfield before over 6,000 people on August 18, 1917. Rankin told the audience that the miners were just in their cause to seek higher wages and to abolish the rustling card. She called the rustling card system a form of blacklisting people. She wanted a federal investigation conducted of the Butte mining operations. Rankin returned to Washington DC and wrote letters to both the Secretary of Labor and the Secretary of Defense demanding that the rustling card system be abolished.

US District Attorney Burton Wheeler also asked that rustling cards be eliminated. He called the workers grievances just. Instead of eliminating the rustling card, The Anaconda Company with the federal troops as protection put a tighter hold on their operations. The troops remained at the mines until January 8, 1921.

One of the officers of the federal troops right after Little's death was Captain Omar Bradley, who went on to be an Allied general in the invasion of Europe during World War II. Bradley remained in charge of the troops in Butte until September 16, 1918, when he was assigned to other duties.

The division between the conservative and progressive union members only grew after the 1917 strike. The progressives with strong ties to the Wobblies tried to influence the conservatives over the next three years. Yet, their movement never took hold in Butte. A federal government report estimates that only 10 percent of the Butte work force was ever associated with the Wobblies. The limited impact by the IWW lasted only until 1920.

The hanging of Little during a time of war led to a special session of the Montana Legislature in 1918. Lawmakers created the Montana Sedition Act, limiting free speech especially concerning national interests during the time of war. The seeds of the Montana Sedition Act later led to a similar measure across the country.

In addition to keeping people quiet through the Montana Sedition Act, The Anaconda Company was also given more muscle. Company guards were allowed to carry weapons to protect Anaconda property on August 23, 1917. Local authorities received numerous reports of unarmed people being pistol-whipped by Company guards for no apparent reason.

The Company put their muscle to work with more than just guns and a rustling card. They developed their own internal information card file on radical union members. Company officials would put notes on a card to identify union troublemakers. An example of an information card is the one on Mike Manhart.

It reads as follows:

> Mike Manhart 7/3/22
> Is a dangerous IWW, very strong against ACM,
> says if he had a chance, he would blow them up,
> claims he knows the parties that killed Little
> and would do anything he could to get even

The Company took things into their own hands if a worker obtained a rustling card by providing false information. In 1918, James Ferriter, a known radical union member, was issued a rustling card under a different name. Two days after he started to work, Ferriter was found dead in the mines.

The Anaconda Company was not the only ones taking matters into their own hands. A federal investigation by the US Department of Justice stated that army troops broke the law on numerous occasions. During a February 1919 strike, troops bayoneted eleven men at a picket line who were unarmed. There were times when troops arrested people for no apparent reason.

During their stay in Butte, federal troops witnessed four more walkouts by workers in a three-year period. The threat of a walkout and violence were a reality in the mining camp. Both the union and The Anaconda Company tried to flex their power for control of the situation.

On July 6, 1919, The Anaconda Company's pay office was dynamited, leading to more unrest and resulting in miners receiving a dollar increase in their pay through a settlement agreement reached with The Company on July 16, 1919.

The federal troops saw the power of The Company get completely out of hand. During one strike, on April 21, 1920, Company guards fired into a crowd of unarmed civilians leading to the death of union member, Tom Manning. The gunmen claimed they were protecting Anaconda property at the Neversweat Mine. Company gunmen told a coroner's inquest that Sheriff John O'Rourke had ordered the crowd estimated at near 400 to leave the area three different times. O'Rourke told local newspapers that he believed the first shot came from the Simons' Boarding House at 246 Anaconda Road. However, that testimony was disputed by 17-year-old Central High School student, Madeline Lynch, who told the coroner's inquest that she was in the house at the time of the shooting with friends Dennis and Mary Lowney. Lynch testified that no shots came from the home. The statement was backed up by Mrs. John Lowney.

The coroner's inquest also revealed that union members did not have guns during their protest. It showed that union protesters were hit with clubs and the butt end of weapons carried by Company gunmen prior to the shootings. The coroner's inquest went on for 11 days, hearing over 100 witnesses. When it was finally over no one was ever arrested or convicted for the death of the 35-year-old Manning.

After the inquest, *The Strike Bulletin* ran this commentary concerning the judgment.

"Sheriff O'Rourke states his men did no shooting. The city police state they did no shooting. The question occurs, "Did the 15 miners shoot themselves?" By process of elimination we arrive at the answer. The answer forced by the testimony of the copper press is the miners were shot by the gunmen of The Anaconda Copper Mining Company."

Two key figures present as Company gunmen during the shootings were William Oates and Jack Ryan. Oates was accused of butting union members in the head with his rifle. Jack Ryan was accused of being the man in charge of the gunmen. They allegedly took their orders from Roy Alley, secretary for The Anaconda Company. He had been infuriated the day before the shooting by an unfavorable article about him in a union newspaper.

It's interesting to note that Oates and Ryan were listed three years earlier in *The Strike Bulletin* union newsletter as two of the six men who killed Frank Little. In that article, Ryan was called the chief gunman of the group. Through testimony in the inquiry, Alley is reported to have told his gunmen, "Go get them boys! Give them son-of-a-bitches hell!" Following the inquest, Alley was quickly eased out of his position at The Anaconda Company.

Fourteen other union members and one police officer were hurt in the incident. Five of the injured union men were seriously wounded. All the union members had been shot from behind. They recovered from their wounds except for Manning who died three days later. The police officer, Samuel Hautnen, was hit with a rock and received a cut in the head.

The labor troubles in the late 1910s and early 1920s hurt copper production. So did a surplus of copper on the world market once the War was finished. The price fell sharply, mines around the country suspended operations. In Butte, The Company first tried to lower wages a dollar a day to keep men working. The belt tightening did not help enough so Anaconda suspended their Butte operations on April 1, 1921. The suspension lasted nine months until January 16, 1922.

The nine-month mine closure had a drastic impact on the city. Butte had tripled its population every 10 years beginning in 1870. Its peak came in 1918 when the Polk City Directory listed 93,300 residents in the community. The next year the same Polk City Directory had only 67,000 people calling Butte home. The reason for the enormous one-year drop is the price of copper. In January 1919, it was selling for 20 cents a pound. A month later, the metal had dropped to 17 cents. People were leaving the town by the train load as jobs became harder to find with layoffs taking place at the various mining operations.

The copper industry made a slight comeback in 1922 when the price went up and the mines reopened. The bottom line for The Anaconda Company started to improve. In 1923, Anaconda purchased a majority of shares in the Chile Copper Company for $77 million from the Guggenheim family. The price of copper was good and so were times from both The Anaconda Company and union members working in Butte. Miners' wages went up and remained that way until the Wall Street's Stock Market crash in October 1929. The price of copper fell hitting an all-time low of 4.7 cents a pound in 1933. The Great Depression had a devastating impact on workers in Butte. They were helpless because the drop of copper prices meant the loss of jobs. The Company reduced their Butte mining operations to part-time on January 21, 1930. All the Company's zinc mining operations were cut off in June 1930, and remained dormant until May 1933 when the Orphan Girl was put back into business.

The reduction of mining operations in Butte forced many miners to work on a very limited scale. Hundreds of men standing at the gate of a mine looking for work on a daily basis was a common sight.. Company officials could only use a handful of men every day.

During the 1930s Butte lost 6 per cent of its entire population.

The price of copper finally started to rise. As the price went up, so did the number of miners working.. Better times in the copper industry also produced a labor force in Butte that wanted a bigger chunk of the pie. A way to achieve that was a walkout. Mine workers went out on strike on May 8, 1934. It was the first large-scale walkout by workers since the 1921 mining suspension.

Union leaders had been taught some valuable lessons from previous walkouts. The strikes of the 1910s were disrupted by Company and federal agents who infiltrated the rank and file of the union. The workers realized if they were going to achieve anything during a walkout they needed to take extra steps to make sure Company agents were no longer union officials. Union members became better organized and more violent in their attempts to win concessions from The Company. The union workers showed they were not going to help Anaconda in any way during the 1934 walkout. It marked the first time in a Butte mine strike that union members had not delegated some of their members to maintain property during a walkout.

A new tactic used by union members in the 1934 strike was to get other workers to support their walkout. During the 1934 strike, the clerks' union sided with the miners by refusing to bring food to the homes of 175 Anaconda Company workers who crossed the picket lines to maintain mining property. Another new twist in 1934 was the "serenade." A group of people gathered in front of homes of known "scabs" people who continued to work for The Company during the shut down. They shouted sometimes in vulgar language to scab families to stop supporting The Company by continuing to work. Some in the crowd wrote SCAB on the side of the house.

Union members also got young members of the community involved in the walkout. "I remember the 1934 strike," said Emma Strike Smith. "The union guys came around to our neighborhood and gathered all the kids up they could find. We were told to pick up as many rocks as we could locate. Next, we were escorted into a convertible car and off we went to scab homes. Once there, we threw rocks at the scab's homes while union members wrote the word SCAB on the side of the house."

A better organized union with new tactics beyond the gates of the mine paid off. The pressure put on Anaconda forced a settlement on September 13, 1934. It was touted by union members as a major break through against The Company. Workers received a 50 cent-an-hour increase in pay up to $4.75 a day. The major point won by the union went beyond money. The Anaconda Company agreed to establish a "closed shop" for their underground mining operations. It meant that a miner had to be a union member to work underground. This wiped out Anaconda's open shop policy which had been in force for 20 years.

A better agreement with The Anaconda Company plus better copper prices meant better times for union workers. By 1937, copper prices were up to 16 cents a pound and there were over 9,000 people working in the Butte mines.

Those numbers started to fall sharply again a few years later. This time the decline was directly tied to World War II. One reason was men heading off to serve their country. Another factor was people leaving town to work in safer jobs elsewhere in the United States. During World War II, about 3,000 miners worked in Butte. The Company estimated they had another 1,500 to 2,500 jobs available working underground, but they could not fill those positions. The reduction of miners forced The Anaconda Company to cut their number of active operations down to 10 mines. This is in sharp contrast to World War I, just 25 years earlier, when Anaconda had 56 mines pumping out copper ore.

Despite The Company's cut back in the number of operations, the danger in underground mines was not reduced. During the four years of World War II, 62 miners were killed working in the Butte mines.

"The miners were trying to get out manganese," said Kevin Shannon, a former Anaconda Company worker. "The Russians had cut off our supply of tungsten. So the United States tried to compensate for that by replacing it with manganese which was plentiful near the surface on the Butte hill. Yet, the ground near the surface was very unstable and it caused a lot of accidents and a lot of deaths. The Butte miners were in their own war and it was not easy winning the battle to mine manganese."

Manganese was used as a bomb alloy and was also a key component in the production of airplanes. Butte became the manganese capital of the world producing 285 million pounds of manganese during 1943 alone. The local mines supplied 97 percent of all the United States' manganese production used in the Allies' war effort.

Jack Harris recalled, "The World War was a tough time to be working as a miner in Butte, Montana. We were making $7.75 a day for an eight-hour shift which is less than a dollar an hour. The Company did not give a damn about the worker because they were being subsidized by the federal government.

"Everything was done to favor Anaconda. As a contract miner you were paid once a week by the amount of cubic feet of ore you moved or mucked out during the week. The Company was always the one measuring with their tape and sometimes they robbed a miner blind by calculating only portions of the distance actually achieved by the miner. You did it their way if you wanted a job."

When World War II was over the battle for control of the Butte hill only intensified between The Anaconda Company and the unions. The first major confrontation took place in 1946. Union workers went out on strike April 9, 1946. This time the serenades and writing the word SCAB on the side of a home grew into activities which were much more violent. A few days after the walkout began, youths began ransacking Anaconda Company employees' homes. The houses belonged to Company workers who crossed picket lines to maintain mine property. During two nights of terror, mobs of youngsters ripped more than 10 Butte homes completely apart. They destroyed everything. The youngsters smashed doors, broke windows, destroyed mirrors, tossed refrigerators outside, cut up pianos with axes and chopped up furniture to bits.

During the destruction people gathered around the targeted homes and watched. It was estimated that over 3,000 people witnessed the demolition at one home. Police officials maintained the mobs were too large for them to stop the looting. Yet, some city officials believed that authorities did little to halt the destruction. Alderman Tom Morgan said he saw one police car just drive around the block at one home while it was being destroyed rather than try to stop the violence.

The two days of riots resulted in two youngsters being shot. All the activity put Butte on the front page of newspapers around the country. Newspaper reporters from across the land came to town to give accounts of the destruction.

Anaconda Company employees were taken to local hotels for safety reasons, but chambermaids refused to change the beds of Company employees. It just further added tension to a delicate situation.

"I remember my father taking our entire family up to the destroyed homes," Lee Masters said. "Boy, it was really, really bad. No one approved of what happened to those people."

Maurine Hignam Dennehy remembered, "I recall during the 1946 strike union members going down to Meaderville. There was one man down there working for The Company. They killed all his chickens, rabbits and everything else. It was terrible!"

Eleanor Hanni remembers, "My husband, Charles, was a member of the Company's management team. He called me from inside the mine property and told me to take the kids and get out of town before anything happened to us. I took the kids and went to Salt Lake City to live with my mother until things settled down in Butte. It was a real scary thing and gave Butte a terrible black mark."

Martin Hannifin, a former Anaconda Company manager said, "I've been around the world and never saw anything like a strike in Butte. Some management people had their wives and kids leave town until the walkout was over so they would be safe. When I was down in Chile, even if the workers were on strike they would let you through peacefully to the mine which was not the case in Butte. The managers and bosses had to stay on the mine grounds behind fences to protect themselves from the strikers. Why, they even hauled passenger train cars onto the site so management people had a place to eat and sleep."

The Anaconda Company tried to blame unions for all the violence during the 1946 strike. They called the looters an "undisciplined mob" in their Company-owned newspapers. Yet, the looters were anything but undisciplined. The mobs did not touch one home which housed a regular worker out on strike. All the targeted homes were Anaconda Company management personnel working inside the mining operations.

Feelings about the scabs were understandably high in the town.

"If I had a chance I'd hang a scab," said Harris. " I had no use for them."

Cathy Brozovich James recalled, "My father was a strong union man. One time during a strike a neighbor, who was a Company boss, crossed the picket line and went to work. My father went down to the man's house and got into an argument with him. Afterwards, my father never talked to the man again. I mean to my father crossing the picket line was worse than committing murder. It was lower than low for a human being to do!"

Anaconda Company officials asked for assistance from state officials through the help of the National Guard troops. The move to call for troops had been used successfully in the past by Company officials. This time state officials refused to send troops. The Anaconda Company was on its own to try to restore peace with union members.

The Company tried a different tactic to gain support. They ran numerous stories in their Company-owned newspapers about the families impacted by the rioting. The Company also formed a task force to try to find out the names of looters. A cash reward was offered to any person providing information that led to the arrest and conviction of the vandals. Local police officials did question over 30 suspects, but did not make any arrests.

Peace in the community was finally restored between the union and The Anaconda Company on April 18 when a new working agreement was signed. The 1946 strike was one of the shortest on record, but it produced a major impact on the town.

The 1946 violence led to a much more restrained relationship between the union and The Anaconda Company.

"I believe everyone learned plenty of valuable lessons from the 1946 strike," said Jim Carden, a former Anaconda Company manager. "The first lesson was The Anaconda Company never again tried to use scab labor to try to maintain their mines during a walkout. Future contracts had written clauses which required the union to provide personnel to maintain the mines and the water pumping systems during a time of strike. If the union did not honor that clause in the contract The Anaconda Company was willing to go to court to force the union to uphold their part of the agreement. The union always cooperated and really caused no problems with the maintenance issue.

"I think a second lesson was each side had to better learn how to respect the other side. When it came to future contract talks, it was more a business proposition rather than an issue of hatred or trying to get even. The strikes after 1946 seemed to involve more complex issues and were more difficult in a lot of ways to solve, but there was more respect for each side which helped ease the tensions."

The Mines

The vast majority of residents were involved in underground mining. It really did not matter which mine a man worked in, they all had the same trait: every mine was very dangerous. The Butte mines had the highest accident rate of any hard-rock mining operation in the country.

Most of the operations were linked by tunnels. There were over 2,590 miles of tunnels and over 41 miles of vertical shafts. The tunnels underground looked the same; however, each mine below the gigantic steel gallows frames had its own unique characteristics just like a human being.

The names of the mine operations were as colorful as the unique features that lay underneath them. From the time underground mining began in the 1860s these are some of the mines which were in operation at one time or another: Acquisition, Adirondac, Alice, Allie Brown, Anaconda, Ancient, Angelo Saxon, Anselmo, August Flower, Bachelor, Badger, Balaklava, Banker, Bell, Belle of Butte, Belmont, Berkeley,

Betsy Dahl, Black Rock, Black Warrior, Blam, Bluebird, Blue Jay, Blue Wing, Bologna, Bonanza, Buffalo, Bullwhacker, Bullion, Bully Boy, Bummer, Burlington, Burnett, Butte, Can Can, Carte Blanche, Centennial, Champion, Clear Grit, Cleopatra, Clipper, Colorado, Confidence, Cora, Crotch, Czarina, Davis-Daly, Destroying Angel, Diamond, East Colusa, Eighth of May, Elm Orlu, Emma, Estella, Exchequer, Exile of Erin, Fashion, Fifth of July, Fourth John D, Fredonia, Free For All, Flag, Fraction, Gagnon, Gambetta, Gem, Glengarry, Goddess, Gold Hill, Gold King, Gold Smith, Gopher, Granite Mountain, Great Republic, Green Copper, Green Mountain, Grey Eagle, Grey Rock, Ground Squirrel, Hattie Harvey, Hibernia, High Ore, High Top, Hope, Ida Montana, India Queen, Iodine, Jelly Man, Josephine, Kelley, Lackawanna, La Plata, Late Acquisition, Leonard, Lexington, Liquidator, Little Cinnamon Bear, Little Darling, Little Ida, Little Minah, Lizzie, Look Out, Lost Anaconda, Louis Barber, Macawber, Magna Charta, Main Range, Mamie, Margaret Ann, Mark Anthony, Mastadon, Mayflower, Michael Davitt, Midnight, Minne Healy, Minnie Jane, Missing Link, Missoula, Modoc, Mollie, Moonlight, Moose, Morning Star, Mount Moriah, Moulton, Mountain Chief, Mountain Con, Mountain View, Narrow Gauge, National, Neptune, Nettie, Neversweat, Night Hawk, Nipper, None Such, North Star, Ophir, Old Glory, Olive Branch, Oro Butte, Original, Orphan Boy, Orphan Girl, Otisco, Pacific, Parnell, Parrott, Pawn Broker, Pay Master, Pennsylvania, Pilot, Pittsmont, Plutocrat, Poorman, Poulan, Poser, Quarter Moon, Ramsdell, Rarus, Ready Cash, Rising Star, Robert Emmett, Robert McMinn, Rob Roy, Rose, Rubber Neck, Scottish Chief, Self Riser, Shark, Shonbar, Silver Bow, Sinbad, Smokehouse, Snoozer, Snow Ball, Snowflake, Speculator, Spread Delight, Star of the East, Star West-Salisbury, Silversmith, St. Lawrence, Stevens, Steward, Sulvadore, Sunnyside, Tiger Lil, Ton a Minute, Toulumme, Tramway, Transit, Trevona, Tycoon, Unrepresented, Valademere, Valley Queen, Venus, Vesuvius, Virginius, Volunteer, Wake Up Jim, Washoe, West Colusa, West Gagnon, Wild Bill, Wild Pat, World, Yankee Boy, Yellow Jacket, and Young & Roundebush.

The most prominent mine during early times in Butte was the Anaconda which at the turn of the 20th century was producing almost 10 percent of the world's supply of copper. Close to the Anaconda were the Neversweat and St. Lawrence. All three mines were operations under the control of Marcus Daly and The Anaconda Company.

The Neversweat Mine featured seven stacks. The phrase "Seven Stacks of Neversweat" were the only English words some immigrants knew when they got off the boat in New York City. It gave port authorities an idea that these new folks in the United States wanted to go to

Butte, Montana.

Another key early mine was the Black Rock which was the world's leader of zinc production during World War I. It was the first mine on the Butte hill to have an electric hoist system installed on its gallows frame in 1910. The mine operated by the Butte and Superior Mining Company had a concentrator built next to the mine shaft in 1907. The entire operation of the Black Rock lasted about two decades until it became a victim of the Great Depression. The mine was torn down and the equipment was moved to other sections of the Butte hill with the gallows frame ending up at the Anselmo Mine.

The Anaconda, Neversweat and St. Lawrence shared the same fate as the Black Rock. All were eventually closed and capped with their head frames torn down. Yet, not all the mines suffered the same fate. Well over 100 years after mining operations began in Butte a number of steel gallows frames remain on the hill.

The oldest mining operation on the Hill was the Original. The property stood just a few blocks north of the business district between Main and Montana Streets. Mine diggings at the site can be traced back to before the white man even came into the valley. William Clark purchased the property in 1872 during his first visit to the mining camp. A main feature of any Clark mine was the brick hoist engine house. This was in sharp contrast to a Daly operation which used a tin steel hoist room. The Original Mine reached a depth of over 3500 feet before being closed in 1940.

On the other side of Main Street just north of the Original stood the Steward, a property once owned by William Clark. The Steward, like its neighbor the Original, supported a brick hoist room. The cage lowering miners below the surface was operated by a steam engine. The Steward gallows frame was completed shortly after the Diamond Mine head frame in 1898. The steel structure cost $9,000 to construct. Clark sold the Steward and Original mines to The Anaconda Company for $5.5 million in 1910 after receiving some false information from one of his engineers that the Steward's main ore body was "petering out."

The Steward was considered a hot mine with temperatures underground getting well above 100 degrees. The shaft extended down to 4600 feet before the mine was shut down for good in October 1974, after 80 years in operation. It was one of the final mines to close in Butte and the buildings in the mine yard contained many of the records of The Anaconda Company's underground operations.

"The miners called the Steward 'Chinese laundry' especially when you got deep down into the shaft," recalled former miner Tony Stosich.

"If you got down to say the 3600-foot level it was unbearably hot and made it tough to work."

Company officials tried to compensate for the heat when they installed a ventilation system for $1.2 million in 1961. It took 18 months to complete the project. Once done, the system pumped 550,000 cubic feet of air per minute into the Steward to help cool things down.

Further up Main Street, beyond the Original and the Steward stood the best copper producing operation on the Hill, the Mountain Con. The Mountain Con is located about halfway up the hill just below a section of town called Centerville. The miners who worked the Mountain Con were mainly Irish and Cornish immigrants who lived close to the property.

"The Mountain Con was like working in hell before they put the ventilation system in it," said Jack Harris. "The further down into the hole you went the hotter it got. Once the ventilation system was going, it cooled things down quite a bit and also provided much cleaner air to work in."

The shaft was sunk in 1890 and the operations continued until 1975. The shaft was sealed with concrete in January 1978. The Mountain Con produced the deepest shaft in Butte some 6,135 feet below the surface or only 842 feet from sea level. Workers achieved a milestone on July 12, 1961, when the shaft reached a mile deep below the surface, 5,280 feet. During the Greater Butte Project, the deep shafts of the Mountain Con produced rich deposits of copper which were hauled to the surface through the Kelley Mine shaft.

The longest standing gallows frame on the hill is the Diamond. The mine, located just northeast of the Mountain Con, was put into operation in 1882. The gallows frame was put into place in 1898. It continued producing copper until 1928 when the mine was shut down. The Diamond stands at the top crest of the Berkeley Pit overlooking the city.

Up Main Street, beyond the Original, Steward and Mountain Con, is the Lexington located at the top of the hill of Main Street just inside the city limits of Walkerville. The Lexington began operating as a silver mine in 1876 shortly after William Farlin's silver discovery and became one of the most profitable silver mining operations on the hill.

The Lexington reached a depth of 3,260 feet and remained in operation until 1957. Due to its location on the top of the hill, the gallows frame of the Lexington served as a guard tower for Company security personnel during strikes.

East over the hill from the Lexington, stood the Badger, Granite Mountain and Speculator Mines. All three were primarily copper producing operations. The Granite Mountain and Speculator Mines were controlled by the North Butte Mining Company. The firm was incorporated in 1905 in Minnesota. During its largest growth period in the city in 1917 and 1918, the North Butte Mining Company employed 3,000 workers.

The Granite Mountain and Speculator Mines were inter-connected which served as both a plus and a minus. It was a plus for mining allowing greater productivity for pulling out copper. At one time the twin mines employed over 1,600 miners and was the second largest copper producing operations on the Butte hill. However, the closeness of the two mines was a tremendous minus when fire broke out on the night of June 8, 1917, killing 168 workers. The irony of the disaster is that the operation had one of the most sophisticated safety systems on the Butte hill. The mine had the best ventilation operation in the district which actually helped fuel the fire.

The North Butte Mining Company survived the fire and stayed in operation until 1923. After that, their mines were operated off and on until they were sold to The Anaconda Company on January 21, 1953.

The Badger stood the test of time the longest of the three mines, staying in operation until December 1966. The first shaft for the Badger was sunk in 1905. A steel head frame replaced a wooden structure in 1927. During its final years of operations in the 1960s, the Badger became Butte's main zinc producer.

"I think one thing people tend to overlook is the amount of zinc and manganese the Butte hill produced," said Martin Hannifin. "At one time the Butte hill was mining up to 75 percent of the world supply of manganese and zinc. Mines like the Badger, Anselmo and Lexington were major zinc producing operations while the Emma Mine near Central Butte was a big supplier of manganese."

Back down the hill, southwest of the business district, stood the Travona Mine. It was here that William Farlin discovered silver in 1875 and led to a silver rush in Butte. Farlin called the mine Asteroid because it would out shine all other mine claims.

When Clark took over the operation after Farlin could not repay a loan for the nearby Dexter Mill, the property was renamed the Travona after a province in the Balkans. The Travona did not have a deep shaft, only 1,500 feet deep, but the property stayed in operation until 1954. It was one of Butte's best silver producing operations with its gallows frame coming from the Pennsylvania Mine.

Another large mine with a gallows frame still in place is the Anselmo. The mine is located about a mile north of the Travona just off Excelsior Street. The Anselmo mainly produced copper and zinc with some silver and manganese. It began operations in 1887. The boom period for the mine took place after the property was bought by the Anselmo Mining Company in 1921. During the next 20 years, the mine produced 300-million pounds of copper and 100-million pounds of zinc.

The profitable mine added a steel gallows frame obtained from the highly productive Black Rock Mine in 1936. The Anselmo was eventually purchased by The Anaconda Company in 1949. The property continued to operate until 1959 when a general strike across the hill led to a shut down of all mining operations. Once the strike was over, Company officials chose not to put the Anselmo back into production.

Today, the Anselmo provides more than just a head frame. It is the most complete mine plant left on the Butte hill. There is a complete hoist house in tact along with drys, the large rooms used by miners to change clothes following their shifts. The Anselmo was turned into a historic mine park by the Butte-Silver Bow government so tours can be conducted on the property.

Another mine operation that became a park is the Orphan Girl which began in 1875. The Orphan Girl is located west of the Montana Tech campus. The gallows frame for the Orphan Girl came from the Colorado Mine on Park Street in 1925. The Orphan Girl was located near two other mining operations, the Orphan Boy and Angelo Saxon, producing modest amounts of silver, zinc and lead. The Orphan Girl remained in operation until 1956 with the shaft reaching a depth of 3,200 feet. The mine was noted for its good ventilation which kept temperatures underground comfortable between 55 to 60 degrees above zero.

"I remember going down the Orphan Girl shaft in mid-July," said former miner Lyle Metz. "You got 500 feet down and their were icicles hanging off the wood. It was a much different mine to work in than others on the Butte hill."

The turnover rate of the work force was exceptionally low at the Orphan Girl due mainly to the cool working conditions underground. During its operation, the Orphan Girl produced over 7 million ounces of silver. After it ceased operations, the Orphan Girl was converted into a mine park called the World Museum of Mining.

Like the Anselmo and the Orphan Girl, the Belmont underwent a new use long after mining had ceased on the property. Located east of the central business district next to Mercury Street, the copper producing mine operated from 1900 until 1956.

The mine was closed in November 1956 as part of The Anaconda Company's Northwest Project. Company officials made the mine ready for future exploration with its vast ore reserves still underground. The suspension was dictated by the low price of copper which was 41 cents a pound in 1956. The copper market hit a recession starting in April 1956. The price of copper continued to tumble down for a number of years. The temporary suspension of the Belmont Mine became permanent due to the world market for copper.

The Northwest Project which was to be centered at the Ryan Shaft north of the Big Butte area was called off by Company officials. The Ryan was not really near a major ore body, but was going to be used as a hoisting and transportation area for other underground operations like the Belmont. Its location northwest of the city was perfect because it was away from the residential section of Butte. The shaft had been named after former Anaconda Company president, John D. Ryan.

The Belmont Mine was noted for being one of the hot mines on the hill with extremely high temperatures.

"Boy, let me tell you the Belmont was a hot mine to work in," remembered Larry Maki. "You could go down to the 2600-foot level or lower and only be there a few minutes before you already started to work up a sweat. It was miserable conditions to work in."

In 1996, a federal grant led to the conversion of the Belmont hoist room into a new senior citizens center for the community.

The last underground mine to cease operations on the hill was the Kelley Mine. The gallows frame is the largest on the Butte hill standing 178 feet tall and is the only one that faces east to west rather than north to south. It was located in the northeast corner of the mining district near the site of the Anaconda Mine. The Kelley Mine was the direct result of the Greater Butte Project.

Berkeley Pit

It became apparent to Anaconda Company officials prior to World War II that high grade copper veins, the most profitable form of mining, would be hard to locate in the future on the Butte hill. A lack of manpower and material during World War II prevented officials from starting a new plan to mine lower grade copper ore. When the War ended in August 1945 officials from The Anaconda Company began their idea to mine lower grade copper ore through a new mining adventure called the Greater Butte Project.

The announcement of the Greater Butte Project came on September 10, 1947. The chairman of the board for The Anaconda Company, Cornelius Kelley, told a capacity dinner audience, "The Greater Butte Project has been so named because to my mind it ushers in the greatest period of the long and exciting history of the richest hill on earth.

"For the first time through the Greater Butte Project with the carefully estimated tonnages known to be available for the production of low grade ore there is now the assurance of a longer period of activity than it has been possible to state positively at any proceeding time. With its high grade northwestern veins and extensive reserves of both copper and zinc and its reserves of manganese it is now possible to visualize many years of more varied and flexible mining operations than in the past.

"The Greater Butte Project not only means great industrial activity for Butte and a period of community longevity that will far extend beyond the mortal expectancy of anyone present in this room, but it should also be the dawn of an era of a greater, finer city."

The Greater Butte Project was the dawn of a new era for the city. No one attending the dinner on September 10, 1947, could realize just how much it would impact their town. Beyond the decision to mine copper, there is no other event in the history of Butte that changed the community more than the Greater Butte Project. It triggered the real beginning of the end of underground mining in Butte and the start of open pit mining in the region.

The Anaconda Company committed $20 million to the project with half of the money to be spent in the first year of the operation. Company officials estimated the Greater Butte Project would result in billions of tons of ore being taken out of the Butte hill in the future and a sharp increase in the city's population. The jump in population was certainly evident. A population base of 48,422 in 1950 increased to 59,600 by 1957.

The cornerstone of this new project was the Kelley Mine, named after Cornelius Kelley, located just south of the Mountain Con head frame. The shaft for the Kelley was started on April 17, 1948, with operations beginning the next year.

The Kelley Mine was a much different operation than previous Butte mining properties. It was more technologically advanced with a cage that could hold up to 50 miners at a time. That number compares to previous cages in older mines that could hoist down 6 miners at a crack. Bigger cages also meant more rock could be hauled to the surface at one time.

Besides bigger cages, the Kelley Mine also used a different type of mining method called block caving. Block caving was designed to mine ore too low grade for vein operations. Block caving allowed workers to dig out larger sections of low grade rock at one time, meaning higher productivity with fewer men which translated into higher profits for Anaconda. Block caving was essential for the project because it was the only way officials felt they could economically mine the low grade copper.

"Block caving was a proven method of mining that had been tried at various other locations around the world," said Martin Hannifin, the head mining engineer of the Greater Butte Project for The Anaconda Company. "I believe the first form of block caving took place in Michigan. I know they were block cave mining in Miami, Arizona, in the early 1900s. The method was also used in Chile, and Ely, Nevada. So it was nothing new in the mining industry, but it was something new to Butte.

"Block caving, in simple terms, is releasing the mine support beams and structures through blasting or other means and allowing the sides of the cave to collapse in the middle. You then muck out the ore body and start all over again. You go to a point blast, retreat and then go forward again. It was much different than vein mining which is what the Butte miners were familiar with working underground."

Rich Navarro, a former miner recalled, "Block caving at the Kelley was very dangerous. The Kelley had these big overhanging large rocks or duggans as we called them that meant instant death if they fell on top of you. Everyone had to be extra careful when we were block caving."

When Company officials began block caving, they estimated that there was 130 million tons of low grade of 1.2 percent ore to a depth of 3,500 feet. They also calculated there was even more low grade ore deeper under the surface, but Anaconda engineers were not sure how much more in ore rock was hidden under the 3,500-foot level.

Company officials estimated that they could mine 15,000 tons of low grade ore from the Kelley on a daily basis when the mine went into production on May 13, 1952. The bold prediction would be hard for Company workers to measure up to with only 5,500 tons of ore being pulled out of the mine daily during the first year of operation in 1952. It took until 1956 before workers could haul out the predicted 15,000 tons of ore a day out of the Kelley.

"Boy, we had a lot of problems in the early days with block caving in Butte," explained Hannifin. "First of all, we had heavy ground and had to blast all the time. We also had to deal with sticky ore which was hard to handle. We could only block cave in short lengths of say 100 to 300 feet at a time. The closer we were to the surface the shorter our length would be for block caving. In some other block caving operations I was at, we could do sections of a 1000 feet at a time. It was impossible to get that type of length underground in Butte because of the hard ground and sticky ore. It was a real challenge."

Jim Carden remembered, "The Greater Butte Project was a total flop with block caving. The grade of ore inside the Kelley was too low and they never developed a hoisting capacity that made block caving economically successful."

As the original shaft was slowly increasing its production, a second Kelley shaft was started in September 1952. When it was operational in March 1955, the second shaft served as a central hoisting system for taking out copper from deep reaches of the Steward, Belmont, Leonard and Mountain Con mines.

The original Kelley shaft was sunk over 2800 feet below the surface. It was dug down another 2000 feet beginning in 1961 to a depth of 4816 feet. Once at this depth, workers could take out over 7,000 tons of ore a day from the deepest levels of the mining hill. This arrangement lasted until 1975 when the Mountain Con was shut down for good.

In 1953, a few years after the Great Butte Project had been launched, members of The Anaconda Company's geology department started doing more churn drills to define the boundaries of their block caving operations at the Kelley Mine.

"Wallace O'Brien had put together the first series of maps for the Greater Butte Project and the Kelley Mine shaft," recalled Hannifin. "He did a great job working with old maps and other things to get an idea about what type of reserves we were working with at the Kelley. The geology department wanted to see how far we could stretch out the edge of the block caving method on the Butte hill because we were getting about 1.2 per cent ore through block caving and that was pretty good for low grade ore.

"The Company hired Lyon Drilling Company to do a series of churn drill holes that went down 300 to 500 feet which allowed our people an opportunity to determine where the boundaries were for these ore bodies. The more tests they conducted the more our geologist team came to the conclusion that it was much more practical to open pit mine the area rather than block cave. The low grade ore in many cases was less than .1 percent so it made sense to open pit mine."

The geology team continued their drilling for over a year to make sure their tests were conclusive. They were trying to develop several long crosscuts to better determine the mineralization value of the property. In a two-year period, they had drilled over 31 miles of holes to gain a better idea of the copper ore content. They also studied past data on the mining development in the area and the maps produced by Wallace O'Brien to analyze the potential of a future operation.

Finally a decision was made by Anaconda Company officials to try mining in the region through an open pit method. Open pit mining had been successful in other parts of the country, but in Butte the underground operations had remained king. Company officials had a proven track record with open pit mines in Chile and a new operation started in 1953 at Yerington, Nevada. Company officials estimated that there were 100 million tons of available low grade copper ore through open pit mining in Butte.

"You must realize that open pit mining meant much higher productivity," said Hannifin. "Open pit mining meant you could get out 200 tons per day a man; block caving was only 20 tons a day per man and vein mining was 3 tons a day per man. Open pit mining was a cheaper form of mining, resulting in higher productivity, plus we could select and separate the various grades of ore bodies dug up through open pit mining.

"Even after the decision was made to open pit mine, The Anaconda Company delayed the digging because a number of factors had to be looked at. First, the Washoe Smelter in Anaconda was producing maybe 20,000 tons a day. We needed the volume amount to be much higher because we would be dealing with a much lower grades of ore. Secondly, we had to look into the future at building a concentrator in Butte to reduce haulage cost to the Anaconda Smelter. We simply needed to be more cost efficient with our milling process. Thirdly, we had to figure out where to put all the tailings from an open pit mine because we would be dealing in much greater volumes of waste dirt than in any other mining venture ever previously undertaken in Butte."

The Anaconda Company hired F & S Construction Company to begin their open pit mining operation. The firm, owned by Les Sheridan and James Finlen, had the heavy equipment needed to begin the operations. It is interesting to note that James Finlen had very close ties to The Anaconda Company. He served as their main chief legal counsel from 1952 to 1958.

"I believe F & S was used in the beginning to break union contracts," said Kevin Shannon. "All the people who went to work for them had to start from scratch with no pension or benefits. It was a way for The Anaconda Company to maneuver around the unions."

Hannifin countered, "That is simply not true. F & S was a construction company that offered lots of flexibility for their workers. The Anaconda Company had become bogged down by union jurisdiction which really hurt the efficiency of the mining operations. Why sometimes it took three men to go out and do a job that one man could easily perform, but union jurisdiction really dictated how things had to be done in a certain way. F & S workers were not under that union jurisdiction so they could get a lot more done with fewer men.

"You must remember we were working with a marginal operation at the Berkeley Pit. We had to move large volumes of dirt and ore in order to make a profit. We needed to be cost efficient in order to make the Berkeley Pit a viable operation."

In March 1955, F & S workers started digging at the West Colusa Mine near Meaderville. They called their operation the Skyrme Pit after the Skyrme ore vein which ran all through the West Colusa Mine property. The Skyrme operation was considered an experimental pit to make sure the geological studies were correct. Workers were taking out about 3,000 tons of rock a day from the Skyrme Pit. Shortly after their operations began, F & S crews started working with their large 150-B shovels and their 34-ton Euclid trucks digging up and hauling dirt away from the nearby Berkeley Mine.

By October 1955, the shovels at the Berkeley Mine had dug 250 feet down through over 4.4 million tons of worthless reddish brown dirt before finally striking copper ore. It was the beginning of the Berkeley Pit.

"We knew right away that the Berkeley Pit was going to be big," recalled Shannon. "The Company had started the Skyrme Pit in the same area and had the Great Northern Railroad hauling away the dirt. When the Berkeley Pit was started, we were taking away much higher volumes of ore than the Skyrme operations ever did. It was easy to see that The Anaconda Company had every intention of making the Berkeley Pit a major part of their operations."

The beginning of the open pit mining era in Butte came during the best year to date for The Anaconda Company. Records indicate that the price of copper in 1955 was 44 cents a pound and Anaconda had a gross income of $636 million, the highest in Company history, representing an increase of $17.1 million in gross income in one year. The Company had a net income of over $65 million in 1955 which was almost $30 million more than Anaconda made the previous year.

The Berkeley Pit came just in time to help maintain a strong financial statement for The Anaconda Company. During the next four years, the price for copper dropped sharply, hitting a low of 23 cents a pound in 1959. Larger volumes of ore being processed were needed to balance out the sharp price decline. The Berkeley Pit was just the answer for The Anaconda Company.

In a few short years, open pit mining became a big business for Anaconda. The Company spent over $80 million on the Greater Butte Project from 1949 through 1961 developing their open pit mine while searching for low grade copper. During that time frame, the estimated income from that investment topped $3.5 billion.

By the early 1960s, the Berkeley Pit was the largest truck operated hard-rock mining pit in the United States. In less than seven years, over 500 million tons of ore had been extracted from the pit. The Anaconda Company estimated they had shipped 40 million tons of copper ore to their Washoe Smelter in Anaconda. The hole had grown to over one-mile wide and created 25 miles of roads inside the pit.

Since Marcus Daly and his California investors started The Anaconda Copper Mining Company back in the 1880s their operations produced some staggering figures for mine production in the Butte District. Company officials released these figures at the end of 1961.

The Anaconda Company Metals Mines Production 1880-1961

copper	15,459,962,614	pounds
zinc	4,584,104,699	pounds
manganese	3,667,017,242	pounds
lead	804,024,009	pounds
silver	627,753,711	ounces
gold	2,406,039	ounces

One way to help boost those numbers even higher was The Anaconda Company's decision to build a $40 million concentrator plant at the Berkeley Pit in the early 1960s. The construction work was started on March 15, 1962. The 82-acre complex was done by the Parsons Company. The 15-building facility named after an Anaconda Company president, Clyde Weed, was completed late in 1963.

Prior to the Clyde Weed Concentrator, when The Anaconda Company was mining strictly underground, their work force could get 80 to 100 pounds per ton of copper ore. The switch to lower grade ore from the Berkeley Pit reduced that amount down to 12 pounds per ton of copper. The modern concentrator in 1963 was essential to continue future operations at the Berkeley Pit.

The grinding process of the ore at the new plant was done by 12 large autogenous pebble mills covered with steel balls each over 12 feet long in diameter and 22 feet long in the primary crusher. The rock was sent to bins where it was mixed with high grade ore from the underground operations and then sent through a secondary crusher. The new plant allowed The Anaconda Company to process low grade copper ore more efficiently. They were processing 42,000 tons of copper ore a day.

The new concentrator meant the Berkeley Pit could expand beyond the eight electric shovels with six-yard baskets operating around the clock in 1962. After the concentrator was built, larger 15-yard basket shovels were utilized along with 65-ton Euclid and Mack trucks instead of the 36-ton trucks used prior to the concentrator. The larger trucks hauled greater mounds of dirt to the new concentrator built on the west end of the operations. Workers were scooping out over 215,000 tons of rock a day from the Berkeley Pit.

The development of the 65-ton truck was not without its problems.

"The biggest obstacle to overcome was the development of rubber large and strong enough to withstand the pressure of a 65-ton truck," said Joe Roberts, the owner of Roberts' Rocky Mountain Equipment, the firm that supplied much of the heavy equipment used at the Berkeley Pit. "They had a heck of a time making sure the rubber was strong enough for the trucks.

"Besides the rubber, a 65-ton truck needed to be two-axle instead of one which was not easy. A Portland firm came out with the first two-axle truck, but they had trouble with the tires. Then the WABCO Corporation from Illinois finally was able to construct a 65-ton two-axle truck which had the right combination of tires that could withstand the work load demanded inside the Berkeley Pit."

As time went on the equipment got even bigger inside the Berkeley Pit. By 1978, the operation was using a 22-yard shovel basket which loaded trucks with a 200-ton capacity. The 22-yard basket could load a 200-ton truck in just four scoops. The Anaconda Company had 133 trucks with a capacity of 100 tons or more operating in the Berkeley Pit. The 200-ton trucks were the largest vehicles to operate inside the Berkeley Pit. They were 24 feet wide, 43 feet long and stood 20 feet high. The truck tires alone stood 10 feet high and 7 feet wide.

During its first 20 years of operation, over 700-million tons of dirt had been moved in the Pit. Company workers were digging out 291,000 tons of dirt a day by 1976 with 46,000 tons of it being actual ore with an average ore grade of .69 percent. The Berkeley Pit had grown to be 6,500 feet long and 5,600 feet wide.

Besides the large hole, the Berkeley Pit had become a massive economic part of the Butte community. Figures released by The Anaconda Company concerning their 1962 expenditures showed that the mining firm spent over $143 million dollars.

1962 Anaconda Company Expenditures	
Payroll	$51,000,000
Supplies and equipment	50,597,000
Employee benefits	13,125,000

Freight	11,408,700
Electricity and gas	10,660,800
Montana state taxes	5,522,000
Social Security	1,400,000
Total	$143,714,587

To soften up the rock for hauling, explosive teams drilled 40-foot holes and filled them with a fertilizer grade of ammonium nitrate. The workers added one-gallon of diesel fuel for each 80-pound bag of powder nitrate. Dynamite crews were not new to the Butte hill. They had been used for years in the underground operations.

Yet, the advent of open pit mining produced an entirely new type of work force beyond just miners, laborers, explosive experts, ironworkers and some crafts people for The Anaconda Company. The Berkeley Pit needed mechanics, teamsters, parts professionals and so many more different types of crafts people. It was a new type of work and produced new sets of problems for Anaconda to confront in the future.

The first major problems between The Anaconda Company and union members after the Pit became a reality was in 1959. The two sides had struggled through a 53-day strike five years earlier before reaching an agreement on October 14, 1954. It was the year prior to the start of the Berkeley Pit.

Five years after the 1954 settlement, the stakes were much more complex with a new open pit mining operation and new concerns for both sides to worry about during negotiations. The two sides could not reach a new contract agreement over wages, benefits and something the union wanted: seniority based on service for their members. It led to the first of many long strikes by mine workers against Anaconda during the Berkeley Pit era.

The strike started on August 19, 1959, over the protests of women and children who sat outside the bargaining meeting room pleading with the two sides to reach an agreement. They did not and thus began one of Butte's longest walkouts. There were 2,100 men in Butte who went out on strike against The Anaconda Company. Across Montana the number totaled over 5,000 people carrying picket signs.

Unlike the strike of 1946, the walkout of 1959 was peaceful. When it began union members were prepared to go the distance to get their wishes granted in a new contract. The distance proved to be a marathon that many Butte residents felt would never end.

The smeltermen of Anaconda were able to reach an agreement with the mining firm on December 23, 1959, but the two sides in Butte could not reach a settlement. Joseph Finnegan a federal mediator, came to town and finally got the two sides to sit down and talk to each other again. The settlement was ironed out on February 11, 1960. The agreement came after three members from Finnegan's Federal Mediation Commission, George Hillenrand, Dan Edwards and Bob McClenand, put the two sides through a 19-hour marathon negotiation session at the Thornton Building. The strike lasted 177 days.

When it was over the union had won the seniority based on service clause they desperately wanted. It was the first time that had ever been included in a contract between The Anaconda Company and the local unions. The wages and benefits package agreed to was about the same as when the strike had started some seven months earlier.

"The union gained the seniority clause in the contract, but they lost the ability to go hustle a job at any mine," said Jim Carden. "Prior to the 1959 strike, a worker could go to any mine yard in town and hope to get hired by the mine foremen. He used to hire additional help if needed every day at noon. This took a lot of time away from running the mine operations so The Anaconda Company wanted to eliminate the process.

"When The Company gave the union the seniority clause, in turn the union gave up the right to be hired any day by any mine foremen. All the hiring for The Anaconda Company was now done through a central hiring office which I served as the manager of along with Gene Hogan."

Maurine Higman-Dennehy remembered, "The 1959 strike was just horrible. A lot of people had to leave town because there was no work. It really hurt the community."

Jack Harris said, "In 1959, you used what you had left and just tried to survive. It was a long strike and tough on everyone."

Another long walkout that once again crippled the operations at the Berkeley Pit began on July 15, 1967.

Rich Holman, a former Anaconda Company worker recalled, "That strike was a real bad deal. The workers at the Pit were talking about the strike a year before it even happened. They knew that the International Union wanted to strike, but the local guys never wanted anything to do with it. They felt a long strike would cripple Butte like it did in 1959 and that's exactly what took place."

The fears of local workers came true. In addition to the Anaconda Company, the International United Steelworkers of America Union, which the local Butte Miners' Union joined in 1962, set up picket signs against seven other non-ferrous mining operations throughout the United States. There were more than 60,000 employees out of work due to the strike.

The walkout cut off 90 per cent of the total copper production in the country and produced an economic impact of over a billion dollars.

President Lyndon Johnson and his staff were forced to intervene. On March 1, 1968, he called for industry leaders and union heads to meet at the White House for settlement talks. The discussions between the two sides started on March 6, 1968. A tentative agreement was not reached until March 24. The unions voted to accept the new contract package on March 30 some 260 days after the walkout began. It was the longest strike against one industry in the nation's history. It was also the first time a strike by workers in Butte had been settled outside of a direct negotiation between The Anaconda Company and local union representatives.

The long strike proved costly for Butte copper workers. The number of people employed after the walkout fell sharply in Butte compared to the other Anaconda Company's Montana operations.

Anaconda Company Employee Numbers

	1966	1967	1968	1969	1970
Butte operation	4,715	4,427	2,714	2,810	3,207
Anaconda operations	1,480	2,001	1,848	1,851	1,809
Great Falls operations	1,611	1,761	1,602	1,626	1,680

Fewer workers saved Anaconda over $4 million in payroll in 1968 in Butte. In fact, a payroll of $29 million for Butte workers in 1966 had been reduced to $16 million by 1968. During that same two-year period, The Anaconda Company had cut their overall expenses in the Butte operations by $33 million.

The reduction in workers and fewer paychecks did not stop another walkout by mine workers on July 1, 1971. It lasted 84 days and was finally settled on September 22, 1971. This time the strike ended without the intervention of the White House.

Last Days

Labor trouble at home was not the only problem facing The Anaconda Company. The mining firm had grown from its Marcus Daly roots in Butte to become one of the largest copper operations in the world.

One of the most important regions for The Anaconda Company was in South America. In 1923, The Anaconda Company spent over $77 million to purchase some very promising geological copper land in the Andes Mountains along the border between Chile and Bolivia. The property turned out to be the largest known copper deposit in the world. The Company developed the Chuquicamata Mine and similar operations like it around the region. The Chuquicamata Mine and the other Chile holdings by The Anaconda Company became even more precious to the mining firm than their operations in Butte.

In July 1971, less than two years after winning a close election, the new leftist president in Chile, Salvador Allende, took over control of The Anaconda Company copper mines in his country. Overnight Anaconda lost 75 per cent of its net annual income and more than 60 percent of their copper production. The Anaconda Company was suddenly in deep financial trouble which was reflected in a net loss of $375.3 million for 1971.

Company officials were forced to take some bold steps to offset their dramatic losses. They elected to sell some of their less valuable Montana properties such as their zinc operations in Great Falls and Anaconda. The move cost 600 workers their jobs. The headquarters of The Anaconda Company in New York City saw their work force trimmed from 480 to 180 people. By the end of 1972, The Anaconda Company had reduced 5,200 people from their payroll of 30,000 workers.

Besides the cutbacks, The Anaconda Company sold their vast timber holdings in Montana to Champion International for a price tag of $117 million. The timber sale plus shutting down some operations resulted in a $9.4 million profit for Anaconda during the first quarter of 1972, according to Company president John Place.

Hannifin recalled, "The Company really went into a panic when the Chile properties were taken over. We had reorganization after reorganization with some of the moves just not making any sense at all. One thing that hurt was most of the board of directors for The Anaconda Company at the time had no mining background. John Place, The Company president, was a vice-president for Chase Manhattan Bank. He had very limited knowledge of mining. When the Chile mines were taken over, The Anaconda Company took a nose dive and never recovered."

Cardin said, "Can you just image what it would be like to have 75 percent of all your income taken away just like that! All the money was gone and there was no way The Anaconda Company could recover losing their Chile properties."

The cutbacks continued in 1973 as The Anaconda Company shut down the Columbia Gardens, the amusement park east of Butte built by copper king, William Clark, at the turn of the century. The Company was spending some $200,000 a year to operate the facility. The park was being removed to pave the way for an open pit mining operation. The Continental East Pit was built at the site and lasted less than two years.

Company officials elected to suspend its operations in February 1975. Company officials discovered that various underground water springs in the Columbia Gardens area made it almost impossible to run heavy equipment over the surface, plus the ore grade in the region was very marginal.

Company officials also talked about starting the Continental South Pit in 1974 near the Hillcrest Dump south of the Columbia Gardens area. The proposed pit did not get beyond the talking stage.

The Anaconda Company's Butte operations president, Frank Monninger, tried to formulate a future mining plan through the guidance of a Swedish firm, Atlas Copco. A three-year study by the Swedish firm called for mining in two areas at the Kelley Mine site and also along the East Berkeley Pit. The plan was turned down in 1975 by Anaconda Company officials because they felt it was too expensive and involved too much capital investment.

Besides the mining plan, Company officials faced an economy that was not overly kind to copper production. The auto and construction industries had hit a slump. It resulted in a big drop in the copper price. The red metal was down to 63 cents a pound, 20 cents less than the previous year. It forced The Anaconda Company to make some drastic cutbacks in their Montana operations.

The Anaconda Company announced on February 19, 1975, that all their underground mining activity would stop on the Butte hill. The payroll at the Butte operations would be cutback by 30 percent resulting in the loss of 1,500 jobs. The hardest hit was the Butte Miners' Union. In 1974, the group had 1,030 paying members. Less than two years later, the number was down to 125 people.

Butte was not the only area hit by Company cutbacks. In Anaconda, 275 employees lost their jobs as The Company closed their Foundry and Concentrator operations. When the chopping ax was finished, 25 percent of the Montana employees working for The Anaconda Company were without jobs.

Company official, Robert Weed, cited four reasons why the cutbacks were needed in Montana. The first was the increase costs of materials and supplies. One major factor was the price of diesel fuel that doubled in less than two years to help run the large Berkeley Pit trucks. A second reason was the sharp drop of copper prices. A sagging economy plus one-million tons of a copper surplus on the world market hurt the price. The drop in copper prices was not anticipated by Company officials when they reached a new three-year working agreement with local unions in 1974. The drop in copper prices plus the rising cost of labor, which received an 18 percent increase overall in their wages and benefits during the three-year working arrangement, contributed to hurting the Company's chances of making a profit in 1975.

During 1975, Company stock lost $1.80 a share. The previous year Anaconda stock earned $4.83 a share. The Anaconda Company claimed they lost $39 million dollars in 1975. The production levels at the Berkeley Pit fell to 75,000 tons of copper a day down from 99,000 tons the previous year.

Weed said a final factor was environmental control costs which continued to go up each year. In 1975, Anaconda Company officials estimated they spent $43 million on environmental controls.

The dramatic drop in copper prices even with the cutbacks forced Company officials to realize the good times of the past were gone. Company shareholders started to shop around their firm in hopes of getting a buyout.

The Crane Company, known for manufacturing bathroom products, tried to buy up to 5 million shares of The Anaconda Company in 1975. Company officials and state government leaders saw the buyout as a hostile takeover that would result in the closure of Anaconda's mining operations in Montana. The Crane Company eventually purchased over 4 million shares at $20 a share, giving Crane an 18 percent share of Anaconda's holdings. Crane officials estimated they needed 23 percent of the Anaconda stock to take control of the mining company. Crane tried four different times to make a bid for the mining firm, but each time Anaconda Company officials managed to survive the hostile takeover.

Anaconda Company officials tried to react to Crane's bid by talking with officials from Tenneco in early 1976 about the oil firm taking over their mining operations. Talks between the two parties came to a halt in March 1976, as Tenneco backed out of any merger deal.

A new player emerged in the buyout of The Anaconda Company: Atlantic Richfield. On March 17, 1976, Atlantic Richfield, the eighth largest oil company in the country, offered to purchase Anaconda Company stock at $27 a share. Two days later, on March 19, 1976, Atlantic Richfield bought 409,000 shares of The Anaconda Company. By April 1976, Atlantic Richfield acquired over 6 million shares, representing 27 per cent of the Company's stock, at a price of $162 million. They also reached an agreement with the Crane Company to acquire their 4 million shares of Anaconda's holdings, pushing Atlantic Richfield's share of Anaconda's holdings up to 45 percent.

The purchase led The Anaconda Company shareholders to agree to merge with Atlantic Richfield on November 1, 1976. The merger occurred over the objections of the Federal Trade Commission which went to court to try to halt the business deal. The federal agency claimed that the merger broke anti-trust laws.

Investment experts at the time believed The Anaconda Company was a good acquisition by Atlantic Richfield due to the large carry-forward tax losses from expropriation of The Anaconda Company's Chilean operations in 1971.

What appeared on paper to be a good investment in 1976 would be something a number of Atlantic Richfield officials called years later "the biggest mistake in the history of their company." The acquisition of The Anaconda Company was filled with litigation and headaches almost from the time of its purchase.

The end of the Anaconda Company officially took place on January 12, 1977, when the once giant mining firm was disincorporated at the state capital in Helena and formally became a wholly owned subsidiary of Atlantic Richfield.

ARCO officials took steps to pump investment money into upgrading the Montana mining properties. They also reopened the underground mining at the Kelley Mine on September 11, 1979. Company officials had worked for three years and spent $5 million dollars trying to determine the mine ore body at the bottom of the Berkeley Pit. After analyzing the results, Company officials went ahead with their new underground mining operations. It put 60 miners to work and put ARCO in the underground mining business for the first time.

The new mine development was implementing the plans from the Atlas Copco study which had been turned down three years earlier by The Anaconda Company for being too expensive. The new operations soon had problems. In a short period of time, ARCO officials realized the high cost of production and low price for copper would not result in a profit.

The massive Berkeley Pit was becoming too big for effective copper production. As the pit expanded so did the distance a truck had to haul ore to the concentrator. Frank Monninger, the manager of the Butte mining operations for The Anaconda Company, told a Butte Rotary Club in 1973 that the number one problem his firm faced was increasing haulage costs. He forecast to the Butte service club a solution was needed or the handwriting was on the wall for the Berkeley Pit operations. In 1973, the average distance to haul ore was three miles. Five years later, the distance had increased to 3.3 miles. In addition to a longer distance, the grade of ore being pulled out of the Berkeley Pit in 1978 was less than .6 percent which was down from .7 percent just five years earlier.

The amount of copper being taken out of the Berkeley Pit had slipped from 18.5-million pounds per month in 1973 to 13-million pounds per month in 1978. Clearly the days of operations at the Berkeley Pit were growing fewer and fewer with each passing dig of the shovel.

The production of less ore tonnage out of the Berkeley Pit required few workers at the job site. The payroll total for the Berkeley Pit operations in November 1973, stood at 3,600 workers. Five years later, the payroll was under 1,900 employees.

On September 29, 1980, Atlantic Richfield took the first in a series of steps to shut down their Montana mining operations. ARCO officials announced that the Washoe Smelter operations in Anaconda and the Refinery Plant in Great Falls would be shut down immediately. The result was a loss of over 1,500 jobs in Montana.

Company officials believed the plants were too old and not efficient. A $15 million study done over an 18-month period by ARCO indicated it would take $300 million to $400 million to retrofit the Washoe Smelter to comply with new air regulations and make the plant effective. For ARCO, the cost was simply too high. The Company would now ship its concentrates to Japan and a smelter in McGill, Nevada.

Despite the closure, ARCO officials believed they could operate the Berkeley Pit in Butte for another 25 to 30 years.

Even with that claim, less than a year later, on June 15, 1981, ARCO laid off another 400 employees at their Butte operations. Atlantic Richfield was abandoning a $30 million project for block caving in the Kelley Mine that had only been started in 1979. During that short two year period, ARCO had spent $10 million on the project. Company officials blamed low copper prices, which at the time were around 75 cents a pound, along with a slump in the housing and car industries as reasons for trimming back. Company officials said that the production of copper was costing more than a dollar a pound and their Butte operations was losing $2.5 million a month. Company officials estimated the layoffs would trim their budget by $15.6 million annually.

Less than six months later, in January 1982, another 200 more workers were laid off by Atlantic Richfield. A tell-tale sign that the operations were near an end came on April 23, 1982. ARCO officials announced that another 270 workers would be laid off and they were discontinuing their only underground mining operations still in production at the Kelley Mine.

The Berkeley Pit, the center of mining activities since 1955 was also being abandoned. The elaborate pumping machines installed at the Kelley Mine to keep water out of the Berkeley Pit and the underground mining operations was turned off. For the first time in history all the underground mining operations in Butte would be allowed to flood.

Less than a year earlier on June 15, 1981, Bill Thompson, the general manager of the Butte operations for Atlantic Richfield, had said his firm had no intention of turning their elaborate pumping system off and flooding the mines. Yet, that is exactly what Atlantic Richfield did on April 23, 1982.

Pumping water out of the underground mines had been a ritual since the turn of the century. At one time, every mine in Butte had some type of pumping system to keep out water from various underground springs. When The Anaconda Company became the chief mine owner of all underground Butte operations, a central pumping system for all the mines was developed at the High Ore Mine near Walkerville. The High Ore pumps were shut down in 1968.

The chore to keep water out of the underground operations was transferred to the Kelley Mine. Workers at the Kelley Mine completed and put into service four large, new modern pumps along with two sump pumps. The pumps were located at the 3900-foot level of the mine. The switch was turned on for the first time on February 6, 1978. The new pumps kept water from reaching the 4000-foot level in the Kelley, Mountain Con, Steward, Original and Anselmo mines.

Some 50 months or just over four years after this elaborate pumping system was put to work, it was shut off for good. A major investment with a virtually brand new pumping system was washed away along with a vibrant past of underground mining operations in Butte.

Company officials estimated at the April 1982 announcement that it would take 20 years for the Berkeley Pit to fill with water. They also calculated that the layoffs reduced their net operating loss for the year from $50 million down to $26 million.

The shut down of the Berkeley Pit meant that ARCO would devote all their efforts at the East Berkeley Pit, started in the mid 1970s with the closure of the Columbia Gardens. The area immediately around the old amusement park did not prove fruitful in terms of ore; however, just west and over the hill of the Columbia Gardens, engineers uncovered a well-formed pocket of copper.

The East Berkeley Pit did not have as rich a body of copper ore as the Berkeley, producing .37 percent copper as opposed to .50 percent in the Berkeley, but the ore body was much closer to the surface. It was easier to extract and required less truck mileage to the Weed Concentrator than the truck distance inside the Berkeley Pit. The April 23, 1982, announcement indicated that only eight trucks would remain rolling with copper ore instead of the 20 used inside the Berkeley Pit.

This major decision by Atlantic Richfield in April 1982 did cut their losses, but with copper prices still low at less than a dollar a pound it became apparent that ARCO's mining days in Montana were near an end.

The final blow came less than a year later, on January 6, 1983. Atlantic Richfield officials announced they would suspend mining operations in Butte on June 30, 1983. The final 700 workers left on the payrolls by ARCO would soon no longer have a paycheck. The result was the loss of a $32 million annual payroll and $9 million in services in the Butte area.

Frank Gardner, the president of the Montana operations for Atlantic Richfield, called the work stoppage "a suspension not a closure or a shut down" of the mining activity. By announcing it was a suspension the laid-off workers would not be entitled to severance pay like their co-workers in Anaconda and Great Falls received when their plants were closed in 1980. Furthermore, the city of Butte could not receive the readjustment money both Anaconda and Great Falls got after their two facilities were shut down for good.

The announced closure day June 30, 1983, came on the final day of a three-year contract between the unions and Atlantic Richfield; however, Gardner maintained the suspension date and the end of a union contract were not related.

Gardner cited economic reasons why ARCO had decided to suspend mining operations in Butte. He stated that it cost his company about $1.20 a pound to produce copper while the world market rate for the red metal stood at only 69 cents a pound. Gardner said his firm had lost $65 million in 1981 at their Butte operations and another $32 million in 1982.

"We can not continue to operate in the face of the market conditions and prices far below the price of production," said Gardner.

The president of the Butte operations pointed to four key changes in the current situation for mining to resume again in Butte: a rise of copper prices, adjustments in the corporate metal mines taxes being paid by Atlantic Richfield, completion of union jurisdiction flexibility talks, and a major influx of $250 million in capital improvements to the Clyde Weed Concentrator.

Gardner stated that the corporate metal mines tax was simply too high for his company to make any type of profit at all. He said state officials needed to make adjustments to benefit ARCO so they could be more competitive on the world market.

The issue of flexibility with the unions had been a continuous battle for Atlantic Richfield. Union talks over flexibility went on for eight months in 1982 with no settlement of the issue. Talks continued in April

1983, but two more months of negotiations on union flexibility and severance pay for laid-off workers produced nothing.

The figure of a $250 million upgrade of the concentrator had been arrived at after ARCO had done a year-long feasibility study. The study, which cost over $1 million to complete, told officials it would take a quarter-of-a-billion dollar figure to produce the tonnage necessary to make the Butte mine profitable.

It was a remarkable turn of events for Atlantic Richfield. They had purchased The Anaconda Company back in 1977. During their short period of time in control, they had mentioned on various occasions that "they did not buy The Anaconda Company to just watch the demise of mining in Montana." Yet, in just six short years that is exactly what took place. The oil firm had dismantled the mighty copper industry in Montana shutting down plants in Butte, Anaconda and Great Falls. The net loss was over 3,000 jobs in Montana.

The reaction to the decision at the time to suspend the mining operations was met with bitterness from local union members.

"Here is a company that took over and made major promises to three communities on what they were going to do to be competitive," said Barney Rask, the director of the local Steelworkers Union in Butte. "I feel they had no intentions of doing anything. They're an oil company. They're more interested in the land that went with the takeover and the write-offs. I feel they had no intentions of doing anything in the three communities."

Ed Berry, a 19-year veteran at The Anaconda Company added, "It had to happen sooner or later. All I know is it was better when The Anaconda Company had it. It's gone down hill since ARCO took over."

Don Peoples, Butte-Silver Bow Chief Executive said, "Its like being told that a patient has a terminal illness. You first feel frustration, anger and then sit back and determine what to do."

Peoples decided immediately to figure out what the loss of mining would have on the city of Butte. He ordered Butte-Silver Bow Budget Director Gary Rowe to determine what the impact in tax dollars lost to the community would result from the closure of the Butte mines.

Rowe submitted his report to Peoples on January 25, 1983, less than three weeks after the announcement by Atlantic Richfield that they were suspending their Butte mining operations.

INVENTORY OF ANACONDA COMPANY TAXABLE VALUATION

Property Classification	1982 Taxable Valuation	1982-83 Taxable Valuation	1985-86 Estimated Taxable Valuation
GROSS PROCEEDS	$ 1,027,433.40	$2,485,265.00$	0.00
REAL PROPERTY			
Commercial	$ 827,804.76	$ 1,825,161.00	$ 1,440,000.00
Other	$ 102,312.95	$ 251,377.00	$ 198,000.00
TOTAL	$ 930,117.71	$ 2,076,538.00	$ 1,638,000.00
PERSONAL PROPERTY			
Furniture	$ 21,939.24	$ 53,069.00	$ 38,900.00
Pollution Devices	$ 2,013.30	$ 4,870.00	$ 0.00
Machinery	$ 3,403,664.68	$ 8,179,354.00	$ 3,975,000.00
Trucks	$ 654,967.12	$ 1,584,304.00	$ 792,152.00
Right of Entry	$ 1,072.96	$ 2,593.00	$ 2,593.00
TOTAL	$ 6,041,208.41	$14,385,993.00	$ 4,808,645.00

When Don Peoples saw the figures he knew Butte was in deep trouble. Yet, he could not know that the Atlantic Richfield announcement was just the beginning. In March 1983, Stauffer Chemical officials announced that they were shutting down one of their two burners at their Ramsay plant. It cost 75 people their jobs. Two weeks later, on March 28, 1983, Safeway officials announced that they were closing their Safeway Warehouse Distribution Center in May. The closure of the center, which opened for business in the 1950s, cost 135 people their jobs and add even more people to the unemployment lines. Another blow came in November 1983, when Northwest Airlines announced they were leaving Butte for good in a couple of months, costing 6 more people their jobs.

In one short year of 1983, over 1,000 people were put on the unemployment lines in Butte. It was a grim time for the community. Some of the 700 Anaconda Company workers had enough time accumulated to retire and receive a pension. The majority of the work force did not have that same benefit. The average age of a laid-off worker was 47-years-old. The average number of years worked for the Company was 24 years. These laid-off workers were faced with two very difficult choices, find mining work elsewhere, or try to go through a retraining program and hope to find a new job locally.

The laid-off miners could file for unemployment benefits. Each miner was entitled to $166 a week for 26 weeks. When that period of time was over the former mine workers faced no paycheck, no company, and, for some, no hope.

Even with all the job losses and the high unemployment Butte faced an even bigger blow through the loss of taxes with a silent mine sitting just east of town.

By the time the shovels were turned off, on June 30, 1983, Peoples and Rowe estimated that the taxable valuation would decrease between three to six percent during the next fiscal year. The numbers meant about $700,000 less for the school district and some $300,000 less for the local government in 1984.

The local school district reacted immediately. After a study by Montana State University, the local school board decided to shut down three elementary schools at the end of the 1983 school year. The closures did soften the blow of the mining closure at least in the short term. School officials were hopeful that some how the mine could resume operations within a couple of years when the impact of a lost metal mines tax kicked in and severely cripple the school district's budget. When the impact came a few years later, it forced the school board to shut down two more elementary schools in 1986 and consolidate two junior high schools into one plus convert the vacant junior high center into an elementary school.

Many longtime Anaconda Company workers were forced to leave town for good. Butte's population stood at 42,000 prior to the nationalization of the Chile copper mines by Salvador Allende's leftist government in 1971. During the decade of the 1970s as changes and layoffs were taking place, the city's population dropped to 38,092 by 1980. The suspension of the mining operation further eroded the city numbers down to 34,000 by 1990.

Montana Resources

Butte was faced with devastating losses in employment, property taxes and population. Local government officials under the leadership of Peoples frantically searched for some company to take over the ARCO's idle mining properties. The Butte-Silver Bow Chief Executive tried to remain optimistic despite all the gloom around him.

"Oh, we're going to survive", said Peoples in a 1983 television interview. " I am not pessimistic at all. I think Butte has a great future." Peoples set up 17 different volunteer committees to try to come up with economic development plans for the community, including the resumption of mining.

One person who was interested in the mining property was Dennis Washington. The Missoula businessman wanted to salvage the scrap metal from the Clyde Weed Concentrator. He had little interest in getting into the mining business. Washington came to Butte to try to work out a deal with the president of the Butte operations for ARCO, Frank Gardner, for the scrap metal at the concentrator. Instead of buying scrap metal, Gardner convinced Washington that mining could prove to be an even better investment for Washington. Gardner pointed out to Washington that if everything could be put into place, the mine could be turned into a low cost operation and make a profit.

Gardner calculated that diesel fuel, a large chunk of the mining operations' budget, was less than half of what it sold for three years prior when the mine was being run by Atlantic Richfield. He also explained to Washington that less than a half a ton of waste material had to be moved to get a ton of ore from the East Berkeley Pit. This figure was in contrast to removing three tons of waste to get one ton of ore in the Berkeley Pit.

The estimate by Gardner on how much ore could be hauled out of the East Berkeley Pit in a year was 75 million pounds of copper, 10 million pounds of molybdenum, and 31,000 pounds of silver. He calculated that, based on the current price of copper, molybdenum and silver a mine could bring in an annual revenue of $80 million.

"Frank Gardner spent a tremendous amount of time trying to determine what it would take to get the mine going again," said Ray Tilman his assistant. "He had a lot of pride in the mine because he was a Butte native. So he went around the country attending seminars on how to better understand the management-labor relationship and what could be done to change things. He was constantly evaluating every aspect of the mine to see how we could become a low cost producer.

"Dennis Washington was the only person to take a serious look at the feasibility of mining again in Butte. All the other mining firms in the country, Kennecott, Phelps Dodge, ASARCO and Rio Tinto had looked at the idle Butte situation and backed away. The overwhelming concern of the group was the issue of Superfund and the perception of labor troubles which had a long history in Butte."

Despite the potential obstacles, Dennis Washington could see the enormous possibilities for the operation. He was a good businessman who made a living by taking a gamble. In 1964, he borrowed $30,000 to start a construction business building roads for the United States Forest Service. He turned that loan into a $100 million a year operation. Washington's construction company had grown enormously starting in the mid 1970s. In 1976, his firm had $26 million in contracts. Six years later, in 1982, that number had skyrocketed to $121 million. His firm had become one of the top 15 heavy construction companies in the entire country.

The prospects of Washington taking a gamble on Butte mining came at a time when copper was selling for a spot price of just under 60 cents a pound. It was almost 20 cents less than what the red metal was worth when Atlantic Richfield decided to suspend operations in June 1983. The principal reason for the fall in copper was the continuous production of the ore in third world countries like Chile, Zambia and Zaire.

After some negotiations, Washington signed an agreement to buy 40,000 acres of land from ARCO on September 19, 1985. The deal was announced in Butte on September 23, 1985, that Washington had reached a tentative agreement with Atlantic Richfield to purchase their Butte mining operations.

"The Washington Corporation is looking very forward to the challenge to making Butte a successful, viable mining operation," said Dennis Washington in an announcement held at the War Bonnet Inn.

Atlantic Richfield also issued a statement at the press conference through a release from James Marvin, the former president of the Anaconda Minerals Company.

"We're very pleased with this agreement. We think it is good for the city of Butte and good for the State of Montana. Since our future doesn't include copper due to Atlantic Richfield Company's recent restructuring, we have worked very hard to find a quality Montana person or Montana organization to take these properties. We know Dennis Washington is the person who can grasp the opportunities these assets represent and we wish him success."

The final deal between the two sides was signed on December 17, 1985, in Denver, Colorado. The purchase price by Washington was never disclosed; however, *Pay Dirt* a monthly mining magazine based in Brisbee, Arizona, reported that Dennis Washington paid less than $10 million for the 40,000 acres of Butte mining property owned by ARCO. The magazine also stated that Washington paid probably around $7 million to $8 million for the operation. The magazine said its source for those figures was "well placed and has always been accurate in the past."

Even with the mine's potential there were a number of hurdles to overcome before Washington could start moving the shovels once again. One of the most complex was trying to gain approval from the Environmental Protection Agency to allow the mine to operate despite their declaration that the entire Butte mining district must be placed under Superfund. The EPA backed down from their declaration and made it possible.

The remaining hurdles involved financing. Washington wanted to insure that every possible step be made so the mine could remain a low cost operation despite the volatile price of copper. A financial package was not easy to put together. There were many barriers involved in financing the operation, including property taxes, power supply, operating capital, smelting and labor.

One of the first steps taken came from the Butte-Silver Bow government. They agreed to create a new three-year business tax incentive plan that reduced property taxes at the mine from $5.2 million a year down to $1.1 million annually.

"We had to be creative in order to get the trucks rolling again," said Peoples. "The local government had to take a chance that reducing the taxes for the new mining company over a short period of time would in the long run be a major benefit to the community."

The Montana Power Company agreed to supply electricity to the operation for 15 percent under their standard industrial enterprise rate of 2.6 cents per kilowatt hour.

A $12 million financial package involving the Montana State Board of Investments and banks was arranged to help get the mine back into operation. A majority portion of that start up capital $7.6 million, came from the state's coal severance tax fund. The five-year loan was the largest ever made by the State Board of Investments. Montana Resources also got a $3 million loan from Midwest Federal Savings in Minneapolis and $1 million from Norwest Bank of Butte.

A smelting contract to process the mine's copper ore was worked out with various firms in the Far East led by the Nippon Mining Company in Japan. Other stopping points in the Far East for smelting included Taiwan and Korea. The molybdenum concentrates were slated to be hauled to Europe and England for smelting.

Labor was also a big financial concern that had to be addressed by Washington. When Atlantic Richfield ran the mine operation, there were 13 different unions. The company had to deal with wages and jurisdiction.

Peoples explained, "The labor issue was a critical one in the eyes of the new mining company. I think the one key person who realized this more than anyone was Barney Rask, one of the union leaders. Rask was on our mining task force and he knew things had to change if Butte was ever going to have a chance to reopen the mines."

Dennis Washington wanted to run the mine differently than Atlantic Richfield with a "union free" operation. He wanted to develop a plan where workers were compensated for their less than union wages with profit sharing based on the company's performance. The elimination of union jurisdiction would, in the eyes of Washington's management team, make the mining operation more efficient with few workers being employed.

"Labor was behind Montana Resources in trying to develop a viable operation," said Joe Maynard, the former president of the Butte Miners' Union in a 1986 television interview. "Once Montana Resources got the flexibility they wanted, they came back and slapped us in the face and said they were going to be non-union.

"The jobs created in the new mine should've been ours. We were the ones most qualified. Our union was the one that made mining king in Butte. Instead, they hire an out-of-town company, Roundup Powder, to do their blasting. Those were duties our people did. What Montana Resources did was not right."

Ray Tilman, Montana Resources manager countered, "We never tried to slap anyone in the face. We needed to become a low cost producer. It was that simple. The operations had to have total flexibility over work duties.

"When the mine was run under ARCO the main office would get 100 grievances a week from workers. I would say 98 percent of those grievances were over union jurisdiction. The unions were fighting between themselves over work duties and ARCO was suppose to settle the difference. The fight over jurisdiction hurt productivity. We could not afford that if we wanted to be profitable.

"It seemed like under the old Anaconda Company and ARCO systems everything had been put into a bowl of spaghetti and been mixed up so much that it was a tangled mess. We needed to throw all the spaghetti onto the table and start from scratch. It was the only way Montana Resources could succeed."

Despite the complaints from union leaders, Montana Resources went ahead as a non-union operation.

All the various pieces to the puzzle for Montana Resources were put into place in a few short months. On July 16, 1986, the shovels and trucks began moving again as Washington and his newly named company, Montana Resources Inc, were in operations in the newly named Continental Pit, the operation started by The Anaconda Company in the mid 1970s.

As he watched the first trucks roll, Don Peoples said, "The mine reopening is a major development in Butte's economic recovery. It means the creation of 300 new jobs, a $9 million annual payroll which pumps an estimated $50 million into the community plus in three years an annual tax payroll of an additional $3 million to $4 million. I am very pleased to see the shovels rolling once again in Butte."

Local officials were pleased with the mine reopening, but the same could not be said for members of the Butte Miners' Union. They had suffered a total destruction of their union membership. They owed over $7,000 in back taxes for their building on Granite Street within one year of the 1983 mining suspension. It forced local union officials to close their building in June 1984.

The union was desperately trying to become a player in the new Montana Resources' operation. Butte Miners' Union members set up informational pickets at the mine site with the hope that Montana Resources would hire some of their members. Picket signs said Montana Resources was not being fair to former Anaconda Company workers. Union members claimed Montana Resources was hiring non-Anaconda Company employees. At the time of their claim Montana Resources had hired 167 former Anaconda Company workers out of a staff of 191 which translated into 85 per cent of the work force. Those numbers did not help the union's cause as they tried to get MRI workers and citizens in the community to support them. The efforts of the union were not successful. The pickets eventually came down and Montana Resources went on as a non-union operation.

"We hired as many former Anaconda Company workers as possible," recalled Tilman. "It only made sense to hire them because they had the experience. The people of Butte could see that in the numbers we released and got behind us in our effort to make the mine successful."

The make up of Montana Resources was vastly different from The Anaconda Company and Atlantic Richfield. The work force was only 300 workers compared to 700 employees when ARCO announced their shut down in 1983.

The development of a low cost operation by Montana Resources paid off. When the shovels first started digging in 1986, copper was selling for 60 cents a pound, about five cents less than what it sold for when Washington started to consider buying the mine. However, the price for molybdenum which was at $2 a pound when Washington started to look at the mine was now up to $3.15. Copper eventually rebounded and climbed to over a dollar a pound.

Tilman explained, "The thing that really has kept the mine open has been molybdenum not copper. Copper has been up and down, but moly has been much steadier price-wise which has proven to be a real stabilizer for the operations."

Montana Resources officials estimated they could take in about

$916,000 in net profit during their first-year of operation. The mine did even better than that with a net profit of $1.4 million some $500,000 more than anticipated. Within a couple of years of starting the operation, Montana Resources had an anticipated income of $140 million with a profit sharing pot of some $50 million. Some of the profit sharing money went to workers while some of the cash went back to Atlantic Richfield. When ARCO agreed to sell their Butte mines to Washington, they put in the sales agreement that they would receive a royalty payment from Washington if his new mining firm made a profit.

"Through profit sharing the employees realized that they had a lot more at stake than when many of them worked for The Anaconda Company," said Tilman. "We explained to them the cost of running every aspect of the operation. They realized if we needed spare parts for something it impacted the bottom line of the company and thus impacted their potential profit sharing. A number of workers came up with various ways to cut costs and save money.

"Beyond profit sharing, I know a lot of the workers take pride in proving to the world that this mine could be a low cost profitable producer. A number of top mining officials felt it could never be done here the way Montana Resources is doing it, but you know what we're the lowest grade mining operation in the world and we're making it work."

The Montana Resources mining operations in Butte was hauling out 44,000 tons of rock a day which translates into 16-million tons a year. It reduced down to one pound of moly and six pounds of copper per ton. In comparison, the Kennecott operations in Utah creates 16 pounds of copper per ton mined; the Chile operations, once controlled by Anaconda, gets 25 pounds of copper per ton mined, and the rich mines in Indonesia extracts 30 pounds of copper per ton.

Despite the low ore grade, Montana Resources was making money. Dennis Washington wanted to capitalize right away with his bonanza mining venture. A year after turning the shovels back on in Butte, Washington sold his interest in the underground mining properties in the district to a group of European and Australian investors. They bought the properties on April 24, 1987, for an undisclosed amount of money.

The new company was called Montana Mining Properties. Australian Laith Reynolds was put in charge of the operations. The company was hoping to use a technique called slot mining to help recover gold, silver, lead and zinc from Butte's underground mines.

The first project of the new mining firm was clearing out the Lexington-Alice tunnel near the Syndicate Pit which served as the staging area for the operations. The work began on May 20, 1987, and was cleared a few weeks later on June 11, allowing workers to travel underground from the Missoula to the Lexington Mine and also to the Syndicate and Alice Pits.

A few months later, on October 1, 1987, the new mining adventure was put on the London Stock Exchange and in one day the new firm called New Butte Mining Company was capitalized at $100 million.

New Butte Mining started actual mining near the Chief Joseph vein north of the Lexington Tunnel on June 2, 1987. The company estimated they could get 1,500 tons of ore out of the mine a day and employ between 50 to 80 people at their operations by 1989. The predictions by mine officials never even came close to being true. The mining venture was plagued by complaints from local residents over dust created by their operation and also trucking the ore on city streets. State and federal regulations put a final halt to the underground operations.

The operations shut down less than four months after they began, but the story of New Butte Mining would drag on for a number of years. Finally on May 19, 1998, Clive Smith and two of his associates, John Clarke and Malcom Clews, were found guilty of fraud by a British court. The three were charged with deceiving investors with exaggerating values on the precious metals and ore base in the Butte mine properties. The three men managed to raise over $100 million for the project and mining experts in Butte estimate around $15 million was actually used to invest in mining development. The three men deceived investors by shuffling the capitalized money into a web of offshore trust funds. Investigators had to travel to four different countries around the world just to track down where Smith, Clarke and Clews hid the investment money All three men were given jail time.

In addition to his sale to New Butte Mining, Dennis Washington worked out a deal so ASARCO could purchase 49 percent share of Montana Resources in 1989 for $125 million.

The introduction of ASARCO into the mining firm provided some changes in where to smelt the ore concentrates because ASARCO had put $260 million into upgrading their various smelting operations around the country. The improvements allowed Montana Resources to ship its ore concentrates to ASARCO's renovated plant in El Paso, Texas. Some of the concentrates also went to Hayden, Arizona.

Tilman said, "One of the things we look at all the time is where can we get the best price for smelting. We've been to Japan, China, Korea, Taiwan, Nevada, Arizona, Texas and Canada looking for the best deal. We have to do that because in order to remain competitive our smelting costs have to be as low as possible all the time."

The company continued to make a healthy profit until 1993 when copper prices fell and, for the first time since Montana Resources took over, workers did not receive profit sharing checks during the year. A couple of years later, in 1995, copper prices were back up again and MRI enjoyed its biggest profit margin year during its first decade of operation with $100 million in net profits. Under the system as a non-union operation workers shared 10 percent of the company's net profits through profit sharing, with payments occurring five times a year.

Washington eventually tried to capitalize even more on the booming copper industry. In 1997, he worked out a deal with Morrison Knudsen, of which Washington owned 37 percent share, to purchase his remaining 50.1 percent share of Montana Resources. Based on how the agreement was structured the deal could have netted Washington well over $200 million; however, the copper price tumbled shortly after the deal was announced. Morrison Knudsen stock also fell and Washington's agreement with the construction company was called off.

Washington benefited from the development of Montana Resources, but so did Butte and the State of Montana. During their first 12 years of operations, Montana Resources paid out an estimated $364 million in goods and services with 44 per cent of that total exchanging hands in Silver Bow County. The net payroll for workers was $153 million. MRI paid $43 million in local taxes and $46 million in state taxes during its first 12 years in operation.

Montana Resources decided to upgrade their operations in 1998. MRI workers installed three new crushers at the Weed Concentrator. The $4 million investment allowed Montana Resources to maintain their daily ore-milling pace of 48,000 tons of rock. It also allowed workers to crush much harder rock from the Continental Pit. This, the largest investment made by Montana Resources since they first started digging back in 1986, signaled that MRI was planning ahead to remain a competitive mine in the future.

"If we were going to remain profitable the new crushers were critical," explained Tilman. "We are currently mining .3 percent grade of ore. In ten years, the grade will be down to 2.5 percent. which means we must put more volume through the concentrator just to stay even with where our profit margins rest today.

"We're also encountering much harder rock which makes the whole process that much more difficult.

"As I look into the future this mine could operate for another 30 years if everything goes right. There is always a concern about the price of copper. The issue of deregulation of the utility industry will also keep us concerned because our number one cost is power for the plant. The unforeseen issue on taxes and Superfund in the future will also be factors in how long we can stay in business."

The goal Don Peoples tried to achieve in 1983 shortly after Atlantic Richfield suspended the Butte mining operations, which was to reopen mining and put more money back on the tax rolls, had worked to perfection. The shovels at Montana Resources have been going on a consistent basis for 12 years, the longest period of time in this century that the Butte mines have remained open without any long-term interruption.

Superfund

Even with the shovels back in operation plus an attempt to reopen the underground mines the city of Butte still faced another major obstacle called Superfund. The new federal law was developed in 1976 and passed in 1980 by Congress. The idea was to force companies and individuals that had caused major environmental impacts on the land during their operations to clean up the property even if the mess was legal to create at the time of production. If the offending party no longer existed, then the company that bought its assets inherited the liability for cleaning up the mess and maintaining the area.

Butte's mining mess was mainly created by The Anaconda Company. But, because its assets were purchased in 1976 by oil giant Atlantic Richfield, ARCO became the main responsible party for cleaning up a century of mining on the richest hill on earth.

The Environmental Protection Agency named the Silver Bow Creek drainage in 1983 as a Superfund area. Silver Bow Creek leaves the Butte mining district heading northwest extending 26 miles to the Warm Spring Ponds. The water flows into the Clark Fork River and heads on downstream to Milltown, near Missoula, which was also declared a Superfund site.

The entire Butte mining district was named as a Superfund area in 1987. The combination of the Butte mining district and the Silver Bow Creek area flowing down the Clark Fork drainage became the largest Superfund site in the entire country covering over 115 miles.

"I knew the Superfund site was large, but I was just overwhelmed with how massive the cleanup area was," said Sandy Stash, vice president of ARCO's Environmental Services Department for the Clark Fork Basin. "I laugh now at coming to town for the first time to interview for the job and driving by the Colorado Tailings. I thought that must be part of it and sure enough it was, but I found out later it was just a tiny part of the overall picture."

The Clark Fork River serves as a crucial watershed for Montana because its drainage flows into the Pacific Ocean. In fact, more water leaves the state through the Clark Fork River than departs from Montana in the Missouri or Yellowstone Rivers.

"Officials really were reluctant to name the entire Butte hill as a Superfund area," said Sara Weinstock, the EPA remedial project manager. "The same declaration had been done earlier in Leadville, Colorado, and that created a lot of problems because local homeowners there became responsible parties who were forced to pay for cleanup. We wanted to avoid that type of situation in Butte."

A key development which led to the Butte hill being declared a Superfund site came in 1986 when testing revealed high levels of lead and mercury in soil samples. The Sherman baseball field in Walkerville showed such high levels of lead and mercury that state officials fenced-off the area to keep the public away from the contamination. The high levels had health officials concerned because lead getting into the bloodstream of children less than six-years-old can cause potential mental and physical problems.

Weinstock added, "A unique problem with the lead contamination in Butte was the fact that many older homes had heavy coats of exterior lead paints. We cleaned up lead from soil in a local yard and come back to find more lead in the soil because it filtered off of the lead-based paints.

"So that forced us to create an entirely new program called the Residential Lead Abatement Program. It has been funded by the EPA and Atlantic Richfield with Butte-Silver Bow Health Department handling the program. Under the concept, instead of just cleaning up the lead from the soil in a local yard, we will completely rebuild a house to eliminate the lead paint when its warranted. So far a number of Butte homes have received major facelifts because of the program."

Stash said, "The Lead Abatement Program has been successful because we needed to come up with a unique way of solving more than just a reclamation soil problem. A majority of the money has gone to cleaning up lead paint rather than soil. Its important from our point of view not to waste money, but put it in the right places to make sure the cleanup is done correctly the first time. Its exactly what has taken place with the Lead Abatement Program."

The program has worked so well that other communities like Leadville, Colorado, Smelterville, Idaho, and East Helena, Montana, have started similar remedial processes in their towns.

After years of study, the first extensive cleanup began in 1986. Atlantic Richfield spent $800,000 during the year to reclaim some of their mining properties on the hill at the Anselmo Mine. The waste piles were covered with lime and then later converted into a green landscape. During the next few years, ARCO turned a number of mine dumps into grassy hills.

During its first ten years of reclamation efforts, ARCO workers had reclaimed more than 400 acres. The Anselmo Mine area was the first of many dumps that received reclamation work. So far over 100 mine sites have been cleaned up by Atlantic Richfield and EPA.

"I think one of the key reasons why so much has gotten done has been ARCO's willingness to do the work," said Weinstock. "In many cases, ARCO and the EPA have begun cleaning up sites while the study plans for the area were still being developed. The EPA came up with a unique way of allowing the work to go forward without getting bogged down in lots of red tape."

Stash added, "Cooperation has been the most important step we can take to make this thing work. At most Superfund sites $20 million is spent studying the clean up methods before ever moving any dirt. Here both EPA and ARCO have been willing to roll up their sleeves and get working on clean up rather than being bogged down in red tape. It has worked well in most cases.

"It seems like our most successful clean up projects are the ones where everyone is on the same page. The best example of that was the Old Works Golf Course in Anaconda. The city fathers right down to almost every Anaconda citizen wanted to see the Old Works Smelter site turned into a golf course. I will never forget watching people come out to the site to look in sheer amazement at grass growing for the first time in the area. It was the first time Anaconda people had seen anything green at that location in over 100 years."

The Old Works Golf Course designed by golf legend, Jack Nicklaus, cost Atlantic Richfield $40 million. It was opened to the general public for the first time in 1997.

A key concern in Butte has been water runoff from mine sites into local sewers and also Silver Bow Creek. Of the five drainage areas on the Butte hill, the largest is Missoula Gulch. The main source for mine runoff in the Missoula Gulch comes from mining areas in the community of Walkerville located just north of the site. During the summer of 1997, Atlantic Richfield did a massive cleanup effort in the Missoula Gulch area. The project cost $4 million to finish.

"The Missoula Gulch project was one where we received a lot of support especially from the neighborhood people at the clean up site," said Stash. "The neighborhood people were so anxious to get the project done they brought cookies and other things out to the workers to munch on during their breaks."

Weinstock explained, "Its crucial that we try to work as closely as we can with ARCO and others to get the work done. Its so important that the water drainage areas be fixed. As we try to reclaim Silver Bow Creek, we need to eliminate a main source for the contamination which is the mine water runoff from the five drainage areas."

Water runoff eventually filters down to Silver Bow Creek. It was at this location that officials had another massive area to cleanup, the Colorado Tailings. The site was created by copper king , William Clark, in 1879, as a smelting location for the silver being pulled out of the ground from the nearby Travona Mine.

Atlantic Richfield started hauling the tailings away by rail cars to a location near the Anaconda Smelter. Progress of the clean up was extremely slow until a better solution was developed for the site.

"We worked out a deal with Butte-Silver Bow to move the tailings to a site near their old dump site and the Clark Mill," said Stash. "The tailings were moved by truck less than a mile to the dump location. In a relatively short period of time we had moved the necessary tailings from the area. Now we can try to restore the Colorado Tailings back to something more inviting to look at. In addition, our next step is to cap the spot where the tailings were put and eventually build a new sports complex with baseball fields and other things at the location.

"When done the Colorado Tailings will be gone, Butte will have a new sports complex and Atlantic Richfield will have taken three full years off of their timetable for cleaning up that area. Its a win for everyone when we can come up with solutions like the Colorado Tailings."

Another major area of concern is the water rising in the Berkeley Pit. Water first appeared at the bottom of the Berkeley Pit at the 4263-foot level about a year after the pumps to keep water out of the mines were turned off by ARCO officials on April 23, 1982. Since then, the massive Berkeley Pit hole has been turned into a large "Berkeley Lake." In a 15-year period, the water has risen to a depth of over 800 feet.

Federal, state and mining officials were not sure exactly how long it would take for the water to reach a critical stage of 5410 feet above sea level. It would be at this point that the contaminated Pit water intersected the alluvial groundwater aquifer that supplies water to some local well users in the valley.

Thirty monitoring wells were set up by state officials at sites like the Anselmo, Granite Mountain, Kelley, Belmont and Steward Mine Shafts. Through this effort officials were able to keep a close eye on the rising water.

"The real critical well is at the Anselmo Mine site," said Weinstock. "The Anselmo is the trigger point because it's at least 100 feet higher than the Berkeley Pit. Right now the water in the Anselmo is flowing down into the Berkeley. When the well hits 5410 feet in the Anselmo, then it's time to take action to get a water treatment plant built at the Pit site to keep water from reaching the critical stage."

Test results from the Anselmo Mine reveal the water level at 5175 feet in December 1996. A year later in December 1997, the level was at 5189 feet a rise of 14 feet during the course of 12 months. The numbers indicate it will be some time before the water treatment plant will be needed at the Berkeley Pit site.

The water treatment plant will be a massive construction when officials are forced to build it. The project will likely top $50 million. It will be used to both pump out and treat the water which will keep the water below the crucial 5410 feet level.

Yet, even before the critical level has been reached, efforts have been taken to reduce the inflow of water into the Berkeley Pit. The first project to reduce the water flow took place in 1996. Montana Resources set up a pump station at Horseshoe Bend inside their mining properties. Some of the water flowing into the Pit was diverted into a pond where it was treated and used again at the Clyde Weed Concentrator. The actions by Montana Resources cut the flow of Pit water in half during its first nine months of operation.

The Horseshoe Bend pumping station was one of the first visible signs of cleanup efforts at the Berkeley Pit. It will take years of effort to reclaim the Berkeley Pit and other sections of the Butte mining district.

Weinstock said, "The EPA realizes its going to take a long time to clean up the mining problems of Butte. During our first 15 years of work here, we have done more remediation work on the Butte hill that was accomplished in the previous 100 years.

"The clean up efforts have created lots of jobs and pumped thousands of dollars into the local economy. The EPA helped pay for the Granite Mountain Memorial, was instrumental in the construction of the new Chamber of Commerce office on George Street, created the development of a greenway along Silver Bow Creek, and helped Butte-Silver Bow acquire GIS equipment that has helped bring the local government into the 21st century in technology. There has been a lot done here already and certainly a lot more to do in the future."

Stash estimated that "so far Atlantic Richfield has spent over $360 million on clean up efforts for the Clark Fork River. The figure will only increase as we tackle projects like the Water Treatment Plant, Alice Mine

Dump and other things that need to be cleaned up in the future."

The process for Superfund cleanup takes lots of litigation between state and federal officials along with companies like Atlantic Richfield plus Montana Resources to determine responsible parties. The process can take years of courtroom battles before the matter is resolved.

A major stumbling block in the clean up efforts was a 1983 lawsuit filed by the State of Montana against Atlantic Richfield. State officials were seeking $765 million for the clean up of the Clark Fork River. State officials and Atlantic Richfield lawyers agreed on a $215 million settlement for the clean up of the Clark Fork River on June 19, 1998. The Silver Bow Creek area received $80 million from the settlement.

The whole issue of Superfund will be with Butte residents for a long time into the future. It creates a messy end to a glorious time of mining for "the richest hill on earth."

REFERENCES USED IN CHAPTER ONE

A BRIEF HISTORY OF BUTTE, MONTANA by Harry Freeman published in 1900
TRUTH ABOUT BUTTE written by George Tompkins published 1917
US Department of Justice report on use of military force to quell domestic disturbances in Butte
The Strike Bulletin newspaper
BUTTE MINING DISTRICT International Geological Congress XVI published 1932
Inventory of County Archives of Montana by Work Projects Administration published 1939
BUTTE WAS LIKE THAT written by Joe Duffy published 1941
COPPER CAMP by William Burke published 1943
September 10, 1947 speech by Con Kelley
The Frank Little Episode and the Butte Labor Troubles of 1917 by Donald Garrity published 1957
OUR FAIR CITY by Joseph Kinsey Howard published 1947
ANACONDA by Isaac Marcosson published 1957
ANACONDA COMPANY TRAILSMAN magazine published on May 1, 1962.
MONTANA PAY DIRT by Muriel Sibell Wolfe published in 1963
SKETCHES OF OLD BUTTE by Jacob Ostberg published in 1972
SKETCHES OF WALKERVILLE by Beverly Brothers published in 1973

Arrowhead magazine by Atlantic Richfield published September, 1978
THE BATTLE FOR BUTTE by Mike Malone published in 1981
K Ross Toole's audio tapes produced in 1981
June 15, 1981 interview Bill Thompson
THE ORPHAN GIRL MINE by Nanny Chaleen, Al Hooper, Robert Rugh published 1981
January 6, 1983 speech by Frank Gardner
January 6, 1983 interview Don Peoples
January 6, 1983 *Montana Standard* interview Barney Rask
January 6, 1983 *Montana Standard* interview Ed Berry
June 30, 1983 interview Don Peoples
September 23, 1985 speech by Dennis Washington
September 23, 1985 press release from James Marvin
Butte Mines by Dennis Glich and Butte Historical Society published 1985
THE SPECULATOR magazine by Butte Historical Society Winter 1985
1986 interview Joe Maynard
July 16, 1986 interview Don Peoples
FORBES magazine September 8, 1986 article by James Cook
THE GIBRALTAR by Jerry Calvert published in 1988
BUSINESS WEEKLY magazine July 18, 1988 article by Sandra Atchison
THE SMITHSONIAN magazine November 1992 article by Dan Baum and Margaret Knox
THE PROGRESSIVE magazine November 22, 1994 article by Tom Hillard
BUTTE'S PRIDE - THE COLUMBIA GARDENS by Pat Kearney published in 1994
The Anaconda Company's Greater Butte Project & Kelley Mine by Martin Hannifin published in 1996
Notes from Alex Koprivica
The Butte Miner newspaper
The Montana Standard newspaper
Butte Archives
1996 interview Bob Koprivica
1996 interview Lyle Metz
1996 interview Emma Strike Smith
1997 interview Maurine Higman Dennehy
1997 interview Jack Harris

1997 interview Martin Hannifin
1997 interview Cathy Brozovich James
1997 interview Larry Maki
1997 interview Joe Roberts
1997 interview Beatrice Lockett Scalabrin
1997 interview Kevin Shannon
1998 interview Jim Carden
1998 interview Evelyn Eva
1998 interview Eleanor Hanni
1998 interview Rich Holman
1998 interview Andy Kankelborg
1998 interview Lee Masters
1998 interview Bev McClafferty
1998 interview Mike McGrath
1998 interview Rich Navarro
1998 interview Jenny Serich
1998 interview Sandy Stash
1998 interview Tony Stosich
1998 interview Ray Tilman
1998 interview Sara Weinstock

Working in Butte mines
photo courtesy World Museum of Mining

William Clark

Marcus Daly

photos courtesy A Brief History of Butte, Montana by Harry Freeman

Anaconda Mine in 1900
photo courtesy A Brief History of Butte, Montana by Harry Freeman

Hungry Hill with Seven Stacks of Neversweat Mine
photo courtesy A Brief History of Butte, Montana by Harry Freeman

Miners at Steward Mine
photo courtesy World Museum of Mining

F. Augustus Heinze
photo courtesy A Brief History of Butte, Montana by Harry Freeman

Miners drilling
photo courtesy A Brief History of Butte, Montana by Harry Freeman

Miners underground - photo courtesy World Museum of Mining

Miners Union Hall destruction
photo courtesy Butte Silver Bow Archives

Grante Moutain Mine
photo courtesy World
Museum of Mining

Frank Little
photo courtesy World
Museum of Mining

Frank Little funeral pallbearers with casket
photo courtesy Butte-Silver Bow Archives

Federal troops marching out of County Courthouse
photo courtesy World Museum of Mining

Miners underground
photo courtesy Jerry Bugni, World Museum of Mining

Miners ready for a blast in the Steward Mine
photo courtesy World Museum of Mining

Steward, Kelley and Original Mines - photo courtesy Pat Kearney

Kelley Mine electric train - photo courtesy World Museum of Mining

Anaconda Smelter - photo courtesy World Museum of Mining

Skyrme Pit early stages in 1955 led to the Berkeley Pit
photo courtesy Jerry Bugni, World Museum of Mining

Skyrme Pit looking down at Meaderville in 1955
photo courtesy Jerry Bugni, World Museum of Mining

Berkeley Pit - photo courtesy World Museum of Mining

1981 aerial shot Berkeley Pit and Butte, Montana
photo courtesy World Museum of Mining

Berkeley Pit blast - photo courtesy World Museum of Mining

Truck on the move at Montana Resources
photo courtesy Montana Resources

Continental Pit
photo courtesy Montana Resources

Montana Resources
photo courtesy Montana Resources

Original Mine
photo courtesy Pat Kearney

Berkeley Lake
photo courtesy Raynita Meier

Butte, Montana and Berkeley Lake from East Ridge Range
photo courtesy Raynita Meier

CHAPTER TWO
Business District

The Foundation

When the first prospectors started searching for gold in the Summit Valley, they worked along Silver Bow Creek and paid little attention to the giant hill overlooking the waterway. That attitude changed as the gold played out and the prospectors' interest shifted to the hill as they searched for ore veins. A business district for Butte developed around the permanent underground mines on the hill. The early business area was filled with small wooden shacks.

The landscape started to change with the discovery of silver by William Farlin in 1875. Within a year of his findings, the original town site was plotted on August 10, 1876. It contained 42 acres extending west to Jackson Street, north to Copper Street, east to Arizona Street and south to Gold Street.

Soon after drawing the town map, more permanent commercial buildings started to appear. One of the first such structures was the First National Bank. Andrew Jackson Davis, a mine owner and successful mercantile operator, along with Samuel Hauser, built the bank in 1877. The Hauswirth Hotel on Main Street was also built during this time.

In 1879, a major fire destroyed numerous buildings on Main Street. The blaze made local officials realize brick buildings rather than wooden structures would be safer. Shortly after the fire, the first brick building was constructed at the corner of Granite and Montana Streets by Henry Jacobs, the city's first mayor.

The Jacobs' home triggered the brick and stone era in Butte. During the next 20 years, enormous building growth took place. A majority of the structures were made of brick and stone with some having very elaborate, unique designs added to the facades.

The local government made its presence known with one of the first prominent brick buildings on Park Street. The first city hall built in 1884 served as the home for the local government through the 1880s. The original city hall was converted into a fire hall until a more permanent fire station was constructed on Quartz Street in 1900. The building then was used by numerous businesses and eventually became what it is today: Ming's, a Chinese restaurant. A larger city hall, costing $37,000 was built on Broadway Street after voter approval on August 5, 1890.

County officials were also busy. Silver Bow County had been created out of Deer Lodge County in 1881. Two years later, county voters passed a $100,000 bond issue to construct a courthouse which was built on the corner of Granite and Montana Streets in 1884. The building was torn down in 1910 and replaced by a new courthouse at the same location for a cost of $482,000. The new courthouse was dedicated on July 4, 1912. The structure was located next to a jail complex that was finished and put into use in 1909.

The construction boom was not just confined to government bodies. Church leaders were also busy. Roman Catholics purchased property at Mercury and Washington Streets on February 5, 1878. On August 1, 1879, a simple wooden-framed mission church was dedicated and called St. Patrick's Church. It was Butte's first church. The town's population was growing quickly so the folks at St. Patrick's soon wanted a bigger church. They built a more permanent brick structure just east of the wooden church in May 1882. The church cost $18,000 and featured a 108-foot steeple which still exists over 100 years after it was completed in September 1884.

During the same year the first St. Patrick's Church was under construction, ground work began for the Mountain View Methodist Church. The church was completed in July 1881 on the corner of Montana and Quartz Streets.

Other denominations followed the lead of the Catholics and Methodists.

The first Episcopal services held in Butte took place on October 20, 1875. The service was conducted by Rev. M. N. Gilbert from Deer Lodge. In June 1881, ground was broken for a permanent church on the corner of Broadway and Idaho Streets. St. John's Episcopal was finished in just a few months, with the first services being held on November 13, 1881. The church was rebuilt after a 1918 fire destroyed the original structure but, this time, it took three years to complete the new St. John's.

The First Presbyterian Church was completed in 1896 on the corner of Broadway and Idaho Streets. The church eventually closed and was sold to local businesswomen, Ann Cote Smith. After some remodeling, she turned the church into a summer theater called "the Garden Court Theater." The summer theater lasted two years, closing its doors for good after the 1965 tourist season.

Two decades later, in the spring of 1984, Smith sold the building to a local non-profit theater organization called, "Broadway 215." After the building was remodeled, the theater enjoyed a brief period of success before closing its doors.

Since then, the building has sat vacant.

The First Baptist Church was constructed on the corner of Broadway and Montana Streets in 1907.

Church life was a key component for Butte residents. By 1915, there were 42 churches in the community with many in the business district. The list of denominations included Adventist, Baptist, Catholic, Christian, Episcopal, Greek Orthodox, Jewish, Lutheran, Methodist, Mormon, Presbyterian, Reorganized, Scientist, Serbian Orthodox and Unitarian.

Medical centers were another key component of the district. Three different hospitals were located in the area with only the Murray Hospital surviving for any length of time.

The Murray Hospital was built in 1888 on the corner of Quartz and Alaska Streets and named for its director, Doctor Thomas Murray. The success of the hospital can be reflected in the numerous expansion projects. The two-story brick building was enlarged in 1890 with two additional floors. In 1907, two more floors were added making the hospital a six-story building. A few years later, in 1918, the Murray Hospital started a nursing home and a school for nursing. The facility served as a hospital until January 21, 1952, when the Butte Community Hospital, was opened for business. After it was closed, the Murray Hospital was torn down.

The name Murray and medicine continued in the area for years. Doctor Murray opened the Murray Clinic in 1910 on the corner of Granite and Main Streets. It served patients at that location until March 26, 1973, when the clinic was shut down and a new center opened at 401 South Alabama Street.

Through the development of commercial buildings, churches, and hospitals, Butte had the look of a major metropolitan city. The construction boom created buildings housing mercantile stores, insurance companies, grocery stores, butcher shops, clothing stores, dress shops, furniture stores, restaurants, cigar and tabacco stores, food stands, noodle parlors, hotels, boot repair shops, laundries, blacksmiths, theaters and bars.

The Growth

A sure sign of growth in the district was the emergence of Montana's first "skyscrapers." A number of structures built around 1900 featured more than one or two floors. The first large department store, Hennessy's, opened for business on November 21, 1898, at the corner of Granite and Main Streets. The Hennessy's store had five floors plus a mezzanine full of merchandise and carried everything from kid gloves to cast iron cooking pots. The mezzanine between the first and second floors featured a china department and a book store. At one time Hennessy's also sold groceries, booze and had a soda fountain.

Hennessy's was the brainchild of Daniel Hennessy who came to Butte in 1879 to work for Edward Bonner, one of the city's first successful mercantile store owners. Hennessy branched out on his own in 1886 eventually constructing his large department store. In addition to all the merchandise, the Hennessy Building served another important function in the community. The sixth or top floor was the headquarters of The Anaconda Company for many years.

There were other department stores in the district. One of the most popular was Symons' on the corner of Park and Dakota Streets. It was opened for business in 1897 by brothers, William and George Symons, along with their partner Joseph Oppenheimer. The store carried a wide variety of clothing, furs, hats, boots and other items.

Symons became the Burr's Department Store in 1946. Burr's featured Butte's first escalator. A main attraction of the department store was the second floor where women's clothing was located. Like Hennessy's, Symons and later the Burr Store featured high quality clothing and other items.

Another major department store that became a part of the business district was JC Penney's started in 1930 at the corner of Park and Dakota Streets. There was also the Strain Brothers at 32 East Granite that was replaced at the same location by the Sears Department Store in the 1950s.

All the department stores made the district a great place to shop for women. In 1925, there were 19 women's clothing stores in the district. Thirty years later, in 1955, there was only a slight drop to 14 women's clothing shops in business. The women could purchase any style of dress for any price in the district.

"One of the most expensive and popular dress lines was Lilli Ann manufactured in San Francisco," said Brian Mogren. "The Lilli Ann brand did so well in Butte that the company came to town twice a year to sponsor a fashion show at Hennessy's.

"A Lilli Ann dress cost almost three times as much as a regular brand name dress, but that did not stop the Butte women. They saved money to get the best they could afford. You must remember that Butte was a town where your fortunes could change over night with a mine disaster. So the Butte women 'lived for the day,' just like the miners. It is said that next to San Francisco, Butte's women were the best dressed in the west."

Other popular women's clothing stores included Boyington's Gown Shop on the corner of Main and Broadway Streets. It featured a unique higher end product. The same can be said for both Emil Maran's store at 16 North Montana Street and his brother, Ed Maran's store at 48 West Park Street. There were some stores that remained in operation through most of the 1940s and 1950s. They included: Cannon's at 39 West Park, Art Connee Shop at 22 South Main and Joe Rose Shoppe at 14 North

Main. Ladies stores that emerged in the 1960s included Gene's and the Diana Hughes Shop. They remained open until the 1970s when numerous fires destroyed large sections of the district.

A favorite stop for many ladies was Weinberg's established in 1907 at 58 West Park. The store had top-of-the-line women's dresses and featured an outside glass showcase.

Mogren explained, "The outside showcase was just prior to walking inside the store. I have been told many young girls walked around the display window gazing at the new expensive dresses dreaming about one day owning one. It is a place where almost every women had to stop while shopping in the business district."

The second floor of Weinberg's was the location for perhaps the district's best women's hat shop run by Elizabeth Haggerty. Every large department store in Butte had a hat department. Hats were an essential part of a women's outfit up until the 1960s. Hat stores included: Broadway Hat Shop, Park Hat Shop and the Hat Shop.

Another item in high demand especially through the 1950s were furs. Every major store had a fur department and also independent fur places like National Fur were in business on Park Street.

Jewelry Stores were also plentiful in Butte's business district. In 1925, there were 20 jewelry stores in the district. Thirty years later, in 1955, there were 14 stores selling jewelry in the area. One of the oldest and most successful operations was Towle-Winterhalter-Hannifin's at 109 North Main Street. It featured china, silverware, crystal and jewelry. Early day stores that lasted at least twenty years through 1945 included: Ley's and Neyman's Exchange. Other jewelry shops that were operated at least ten years from 1945 to 1955 included Jacob Alanko, Globe Jewelry, Gordan's Jewelry, Hord's, S & S Jewelry, Sheets-Powell, James Uncles, and Fred Young's.

There were other stores located in the district on Park Street. They included H. L. Green's Five and Dime Store, Montgomery Ward's, the Army-Navy Store and F.W. Woolworth's which was constructed in 1930 at a cost of $200,000 with the Butte store becoming the ninety-sixth chain operation built by the company in the United States.

When the men shopped they had lots of choices. The men's stores included Richards and Rochele's plus the Toggery both located on Main Street. There was also Joe Schwartz Store, Thomas' Apparel, Hub Clothing, Morris Schwartz, Grand Clothing, Louie Moses' Store, and Wein's Men's Store.

Furniture stores were also a major industry in the business district. Stores included: Finberg's, Rosenberg's, Christie's, Shiner's and

Rudolph's Standard Furniture. Finberg's was located at 44 East Park. Rosenberg's opened in 1934 at 120 North Main. The store was relocated to South Montana Street in 1976. Christie's sat at 20 West Broadway. Shiner's at 75 East Park Street was opened in 1898 and remained in business until 1980. The only furniture store still in operation in the business district is Rudolph's Standard Furniture at 65 East Park. Its Montana's oldest furniture store. Rudolph's Standard Furniture was opened in 1919 by Kalman Rudolph, a Russian Jewish immigrant. The first store was located at 215 East Park. Rudolph moved the store to its present location in 1939.

Sporting good shops featured Treasure State Sporting Goods and Butte Sports Shop both on Park Street plus Phil Judd's on the corner of Wyoming and Park.

The wide variety of merchandise made Butte a shopping mecca from the 1900s through the 1960s. Extra wide sidewalks were needed to handle the vast number of people in the area. Shoppers could hear numerous languages being spoken all the time by the various ethnic groups who had come to Butte for a new opportunity. It was a district that was full of life 24 hours a day. It gave Butte the feeling of a large American city.

Other large buildings also gave Butte that feeling of being a metropolitan city. One of the early day "skyscrapers" was the Hibour Building located on the corner of Broadway and Main Streets. Taller than Hennessy's, the Hibour Building was eight stories high. It was completed in 1901. Like Hennessy's, Hibour Building workers used a steel frame and curtain wall construction allowing the structure to be more than just a couple of stories high. When it was first opened the bottom floor of the Hibour Building served as a grocery store while the upper floor rooms were rented out.

Another building using a steel frame and curtain wall construction was the Metals Bank Building on the corner of Park and Main Streets. Copper king, F. Augustus Heinze, financed the construction for $325,000. The building was completed in 1906. The building served as a bank and offices for professional business people for many years. When the bank was moved, the bottom floor of the building was converted into the Metals Banque Restaurant.

The construction of large hotels also added to the feeling of a major city. The Thornton Hotel was completed at a cost of $75,000 in 1900 at the corner of Wyoming and Broadway Streets. President Theodore Roosevelt dined there during his visit to the city on May 27, 1903. The Thornton served as a hotel until 1947 when it was taken over by The Anaconda Company. The mining firm converted the building into a club which included a theater, barber shop and bowling alley. The Anaconda Company sold the Thornton Building to the Montana Power Company in the 1970s. The utility firm maintained the beautiful tiled fireplace and nicely polished wooden floors in the Thornton. Also left in place was the mirrored ballroom.

The McDermott Hotel, across the street from the Thornton, was purchased by mining pioneer, Miles Finlen, who changed the name to the Finlen. His son, James Finlen, tore down the original building in 1923 and constructed the new Finlen Hotel for $750,000. It was completed and open for business on February 9, 1924. The hotel was modeled after the Hotel Astor in New York City with identical twin towers. The west tower was completed to nine stories but, due to a lack of money, the east side tower was scaled down to only three floors. The Finlen was Butte's main hotel for many years. Under its copper-shingled roof, the hotel served as a place for dances, dinners and large social gatherings in the Treasure State Ballroom and Copper Bowl Room. A number of famous Americans stayed at the Finlen Hotel, including aviator Charles Lindbergh when he flew into Butte on September 5, 1927. Senator John F. Kennedy and his wife, Jackie, were guests on March 8, 1959. Kennedy was elected President the next year.

Besides large hotels, the district featured apartments and boarding houses. The construction of the Napton and Leonard Apartments in 1906 provided the first permanent apartment buildings. There were also a series of boarding houses built with the Girton House on Quartz Street being the first.

The boarding houses established in the business district and in various neighborhoods were an important element of early day Butte. The boarding houses were used by the vast number of single miners who came to town looking for a job.

The hotels, apartments and boarding houses led to the natural creation of many restaurants and cafes in the district. One of the favorite early spots prior to 1900 was Leu's, a Chinese restaurant in China Alley just a short walk below the district. It featured Butte's best noodles, chop suey and chow mien.

The flavor of delicious Chinese food continued after Leu's through the Pekin Noodle Parlor opened on South Main Street in 1909. The Wong family operated the restaurant for the remainder of the century.

A noteworthy eating place was the Success Cafe on Broadway Street. If a person labeled success with small, then the cafe was a perfect fit. The cafe was 3 feet wide and 13 feet long. It had four stools and always had a waiting line of customers.

Another popular spot was Carkulis' Cafe at 9 1/2 North Wyoming Street. A patron could get a hamburger for a nickel. It was especially popular for kids after they attended a Saturday afternoon movie in the 1930s and 1940s. Carkulis' was not the only spot serving cheap hamburgers. Gus's on the corner of Montana and Mercury Streets sold the greasy sandwiches for only a dime in the 1950s.

Other favorite eating establishments for both adults and kids included the American Candy Store on Park Street and the Beehive on the corner of Park and Montana Streets. There was also Bartlett Cafe, Butte Grill, Chequamegon, Creamery Cafe, Davey's Grill, Ed's Cafe, George's Coffee Shop, Green's Cafe, Harrington's, Iona's Cafe, Kenoffel's Spokane Cafe, Leland's Cafe, Lockwood Cafe, Moxom, S & L Ice Cream Store, State Cafe, Truzzolino's and Walkers' Cafe. The various restaurants operated some time between 1920 to 1965.

The old cafes eventually gave way to modern restaurants like the Acoma, Bronx, Columbian Gardens Espresso, Doreen's, Gold Rush Casino, Ming's, Northwest Noodles & Wrap, Trafford's and the Uptown Cafe.

One of the few old-style restaurants left in Butte is Gamer's Cafe. Walt Gamer opened Gamer's in 1904 at the corner of Park and Montana Street. A 1932 fire forced Gamer's sister-in-law, Sophia Gamer, to relocate to the Curtis Music Hall on Park Street. In 1944, Mrs. Gamer was bought out by Carl Rowan and George Schotte. Carl Rowan operated the place until Paul and Pam Cote purchased the restaurant in 1993.

"I think what makes Gamer's an institution in Butte is the total old-cafe style atmosphere it provides," Paul Cote said. "It takes a glimpse back into what a bustling uptown Butte was like 30 or 40 years ago. I know folks who once lived in Butte come into our restaurant during the summer and comment on how this is the way they always remembered the place.

"People enjoy dining in the old wrap-around booths. The kids get a big kick out of sitting at the soda fountain ordering a shake.

"If an architect came into this building today he would shake his head at the way Gamer's was designed with the upstairs dining area. Yet, it's what people like about the place.

"There is always a lot of activity here but its also a very relaxing place. I know for a fact that a lot of civic and business decisions for this community are made right here at Gamer's over a cup of coffee."

Bars

Plenty of places offered miners a chance to wet their whistles after a tough day underground. The city of Butte had 206 saloons in 1906. The number of drinking holes remained consistent up until Prohibition in 1919.

There were four types of drinking establishments: the clubs for the elite members of the community, the bars in the business district, the neighborhood bars or saloons, and the down-and-out saloons featuring "rock gut" liquor for transients.

A number of the clubs in the business district served imported beer from overseas or Eastern brews. The most famous club was the Silver Bow which was built in 1906 on Granite Street. During its hey-day, the Silver Bow was considered one of the top men's clubs in the state with over 500 paid members. It was rivaled only by the Montana Club in Helena. The price for a drink in the Silver Bow Club was higher than any other place in town because it was a gathering place for the wealthy. When the Silver Bow Club was discontinued, the building became home for the Butte Miners' Union in 1954. After the union shut down the hall because of back taxes in 1985, the building was converted into a professional office center.

The bars in the business district and around town catered to the miners with affordable beer and liquor prices. A favorite drink served by every establishment was a Shawn O'Farrell. It was actually a series of two drinks. The first was a shot of whiskey followed by a slug of beer as a chaser. The drink was especially popular with miners just getting off shift.

The main difference between bars in the business district and in the local neighborhoods was ownership. Most of the bars in the business district were owned and operated by local people, while many of the neighborhood bars were handled by local brewery companies.

Of the five local breweries, the Centennial, Olympia, Tivoli, Crystal and Butte, the only one located in the business district was the Butte Brewery. The Butte Brewery was established in 1885 by German immigrant, Henry Muntzer, at 200 North Wyoming Street just below Anaconda Road and Dublin Gulch. The location was perfect for capturing the thirsty miners' trade. Anaconda Road was the main artery leading to the Anaconda, High Ore, St. Lawrence and Neversweat mines. It was the first stop miners encountered coming off the hill following a tough shift.

"The miners never missed a chance to hit the Butte Brewery," according to Vince Downey. "They would load up the bottom half of their bucket with beer going to work and would visit the place for a 'quick one' after their shift before heading home."

The brewery made Butte Special Beer. In 1919, when Prohibition took affect, the brewery switched to making soft drinks. Once Prohibition ended in 1932, the Butte Brewery went back to manufacturing what made it famous, beer. It is the only brewery in town to survive the Prohibition era. The Butte Brewery Company stayed open for 80 years. It was shut down in 1965 to make way for the Capri Motel.

All the drinking establishments featured Butte beer and many other brands. Of course, the uptown bars featured more than just beer. There was wide-open gambling everywhere with someone always willing to take a miner's money in any type of game of chance. A man could try his luck at any time of day or night because the joints stayed open 24 hours. The bar owners simply threw away the keys.

Some bars like Clifford's, the Board of Trade, M & M, the Sportsmen, Walker's and the Classic featured ticker-tape information from major sporting events. The ticker tape in bars was sometimes a better source of information than the local newspaper. On numerous occasions reporters would call a local bar to obtain information on a sporting event. There were baseball pools for gamblers with people playing the pool by shaking dice and receiving eight teams based on the dice. The winner would be the person with the top run production total from their eight teams on a given day.

Besides gambling, uptown bars had plenty of free food. One way to attract patrons was featuring enormous spreads.. A person could eat anything available so long as they had a drink in their hands. The bars offered platters of bologna, anchovies, corn beef, frankfurters, ham and a half dozen other cold cuts.

Butte's uptown bars were big and elaborate like the Atlantic which extended its bar from Park Street to Galena Street, a full city block. It was called "the longest bar in the world."

Another unique bar was the Orpheum on West Broadway which was operated by Danny Mack and Jimmy Carey. The Orpheum Bar was a favorite night spot in the 1900s and 1910s for many theater stars who came to Butte. A number of the celebrities had their photos taken there. When Mack and Carey decided to sell their place they had over 1,000 photographs and autographs from the biggest celebrities in show business. Unfortunately, all the collectibles were sent to the Lamb Club in New York City. The Orpheum was torn down to construct the Leggat Hotel.

The names of the uptown bars were as colorful as the patrons who occupied them. The list includes: Alley Cat, Atlantic, Big Stope, Board of Trade, Bronx, Cabin, Cesspool, Classic, Clifford's, Club 13, COD, Collar, Council, Elbow, Frozen Inn, Good Old Summer Time, Gold Rush, Graveyard, Irish Times Pub, Keyboard, Main Street Lounge, Maloney's, Montana, Oasis, Ocean, Open All Night, Orpheum, Pat Day, Radio, Room 71, Shanty, Sportsmen, Silver Bow, Silver Dollar, Terminal, Water Hole and Zebra.

Most of the old-time bars disappeared from the uptown district. One remaining relic is the M & M Cigar Store. It was named after the original owners, Sam Martin and William Mosby, who opened the bar in 1890.

"I think one of the reasons why the M & M is so popular is that nothing really changes," Charlie Bugni, M & M bar owner, said. "We have people who come in here all the time and say that this is the way they always remembered the place." The M & M features a bar and lunch counter. It is common to see a bank president in a business suit seated next to a less-than-wealthy man in old baggy clothes eating a meal. There is no social discrimination in the M & M; everyone is treated equally.

A person can get a meal at the M & M every day of the year at any time of the day except for Christmas when the restaurant takes its annual 24-hour break.

Bugni said, "I think one thing that has made the M & M popular is the quality of the food we serve here. I know people don't leave here hungry after eating one of our meals." One of the more popular days for local people is Super Bowl Saturday. The M & M features T-bone steaks, fries and salad for $5.50. During the day, over 700 steaks are served, with people lining up behind someone eating at the counter just waiting to sit down on a stool.

The place is full of activity 24 hours a day. There always seems to be a card game in progress or someone playing the video gambling machines. In past years, a person could also get a drink any time of the day, but that has all changed through tougher state regulations.

"Running this place has really changed during the 25 years I've owned it," Bugni said. "In the old days you could go gambling or drinking in any of the uptown joints any time of the day you wanted. It was a wide-open place. Now, it seems like you have rules for everything. You can only serve liquor a certain time of day. You can only allow certain types of gambling devices in your place. You have to be extra careful not to serve minors. A lot of the fun of owning a joint is gone."

One thing that has made the M & M famous is St. Patrick's Day. It's the main watering hole for many people celebrating the Irish holiday.

Bugni said, "At one time St. Patrick's Day use to be a lot of fun.

Heck, I remember back when I first bought the place in 1972 there was only one other bartender and myself running the place on St. Paddy's Day. We were busy, but we could handle it. We served corn beef and cabbage for 75 cents a plate and sold a shot of Bushmills for 25 cents and the people loved it!

"I guess the shots for 25 cents got too popular because each year we have more and more people in the joint. Now, St. Paddy's Day is a big pain because it takes so much work to just survive the day. We have to do so much just to protect the place because it's always wall-to-wall people.

"The first thing we do is haul all the chairs, tables and gambling machines out of the place. Next, we extend the bar 30 feet. We have to go under the joint and brace the floor with 4-by-4's. We have to run at least 8 large 4-by-4's down the center of the floor just to keep it stable.

"We have to hire a full compliment of bartenders. We have five or six on duty all the time. We also hire security personnel at least two at a time to man the door to allow only so many people inside at one time.

"The thing that gets me the most about St. Paddy's Day is we once had a pretty good party here, but all the college kids have come into town and taken over. All my older patrons leave the joint for the day. I guess it will never be the same again. Its just like all the old Butte bars. It will never be the same again, but at least they still have the M & M to try to remember what it was like in the good old days."

Ladies of the Night

When a miner left the bar he still had lots of other forms of entertainment. Dance halls were popular with early day miners. There were a couple of prominent dance places in the district, the Renshaw Hall on the corner of Park and Dakota Streets and the Caplice Hall just down the road on the corner of Montana and Park Streets. Bowling at the Marquette Lanes located on Park Street above the PO Newsstand or the Winter Garden Lanes on Montana Street was an option.

Another form of "entertainment" was within easy walking distance of the uptown bars. It was Butte's red light district on the southern edge of the business area. It became one of the largest red light districts west of the Mississippi River prior to the 20th century. There were two solid blocks of brothels on Galena and Mercury Streets.

Prostitutes worked in one of three types of operations: the cribs or one-room shanties located next to an alley or street, private homes throughout the city run by a "landladies" and brothels or parlor houses with more elegant surroundings in a hotel-style building operated by "madams".

The "cribs" were small rooms with a bathroom, closet and window. They were located in the red light district along East Galena and Mercury Streets. The one-room structures were lined up next to each other in Venus Alley between East Galena and East Mercury Street and also in Sullivan's Alley between South Wyoming and South Arizona Streets. A "working girl" in a crib stood in the doorway trying to entice customers or sat next to a window hitting chopsticks against the glass trying to attract male customers. They paid a daily rent of $2.50 to a madam who owned their crib.

A patron wanting to look at the "working girls" in the cribs passed through a gate patrolled by police officers to get to Venus Alley which was bordered by a green fence. Through the years authorities made occasional raids and arrested prostitutes for "city vagrancy." Even during their raids, the police were being paid off by "madams" and "landlords" to keep the red light district in operation.

Former "madam" Ruby Garrett told *The Montana Standard* in an interview that "the old-time police wanted the line and sanctioned it. Any time a new prostitute came to town she would be fingerprinted and photographed at the police station and undergo a health screening before she was allowed to work. That was a way to stop someone if they came in with syphilis and gonorrhea."

The ladies in these crude crib structures soon competed with more elegant surroundings when the 1880s construction boom led to large brick buildings like the Dumas Hotel. It was built by French-Canadian brothers Joseph and Arthur Nadeau in 1890. The Dumas was especially designed as a brothel with three floors of rooms. The basement contained smaller crib rooms with the main floor housing larger rooms and parlors. The upstairs featured larger rooms and suites.

The Nadeau brothers were the "landlords" of the Dumas Hotel for a number of years until they sold it to Dick Walden. He and his wife, Lillian, ran the operation until 1950 when Elinor Knott took over the building. Elinor committed suicide in an upstairs room in 1955 after her boyfriend died of a heart attack. A women named Bonita ran the Dumas from 1955 until 1971 when Ruby Garrett became the "landlord" running the facility until its closure in 1982.

The Dumas was not the only brothel in the red light district. Another such facility was operated on East Galena Street by Blonde Edna. She catered to the rich people of the community.

"There was sure a lot of money exchanged in the red light district," said Bob Kissell, a former driver for the Meaderville Mercantile Store. "I especially remember every time I had a delivery to a brothel run by

 Blonde Edna on Wyoming Street. She always paid you in silver dollars no matter if the bill was for five bucks or fifty dollars. In those days silver dollars were not common. So you can just imagine the type of money that was being made in the red light district."

Dorothy Lombardi remembered that Blonde Edna "ran quite the place at 14 South Wyoming Street. She had high-class girls who were well-dressed and groomed. Blonde always had the girls over to my hairdresser shop getting made up for the clients. She always made sure her girls did not steal any money from the customers.

"One time Blonde had her white poodle stolen. She was furious. A couple of days later, the dead poodle was throw on the front porch of her house on Wyoming Street. Blonde was naturally heart broken. She had a funeral service for the dog and buried it under the big tree in front of her house. All the ladies of the house and myself attended the funeral. Blonde had us all fold our hands in prayer to send good wishes to her lost dog. She was quite a character."

Other parlor houses in the red light district included the Windsor on East Galena Street, the Royal and the Victoria both on East Mercury Street and the Copper Block on the corner of Galena and Wyoming Street. The large Copper Block building constructed by the Nadeau brothers in 1892 contained a brothel called the Empire Hotel. There was also the Stockman's Bar located in the block operated by "Dirty Mouth" Jean Sorenson. The Copper Block was eventually closed and torn down.

The prostitution was wide-open in Butte operating 24 hours a day with three shifts of women working all the time just like the miners digging underground. Hundreds of ladies were in the trade with some making decent money with tips of cash, jewelry, clothing and furs from clients.

The vice of prostitution did not go unnoticed by Butte citizens. As early as 1881, some residents began complaining about it; however, local officials never tried to end the operations in the red light district. The only time the activity was stopped in the Butte brothels and parlor houses came during World War I and World War II when a federal government order shut down all the brothels in the country. Officials requested the closure for fear that the soldiers would contract sexually transmitted diseases at the brothels before going to fight in battle. The second shutdown by federal officials in 1943 resulted in the final closure of all cribs in the country.

Once the World Wars were over, the parlor houses and brothels were back in business. It remained that way for a number of years. The number of brothels declined down to seven by 1953 and to a couple by the

1970s. Local officials finally shut down the business for good in 1982 after the last remaining brothel in operation, the Dumas, was robbed by a pair of men.

Ruby Garrett, the final "landlord" at the Dumas sold the building to Rudy Giecek in 1990. He renovated the building so it looked like a brothel during its busy time period in earlier years. Giecek operated the Dumas as an antique mall. In 1998, Giecek sold the building to the International Sex Workers Foundation for Art, Culture and Education. The group held a ceremony on August 27, 1998, at the former site of the Copper Block. They dedicated the Copper Block Park honoring the "working girls" who were employed in the district . The organization plans to turn the Dumas Brothel into an International Sex Worker Museum. It will be through the museum and the Copper Block Park that the Butte's notorious red light district will remain a memory for many years into the future.

Show Time

Butte has a reputation as a rough-and-tough mining camp with wide-open gambling, beer halls and prostitution. It is hard to imagine a town with so much vice having a cultural heritage as well. Yet, Butte boasted one of the top theater towns west of the Mississippi River.

The business district was a mecca for plays, concerts and vaudeville acts. Butte served as the primary stop between Seattle and Minneapolis for successful shows.

John McGuire was considered the father of entertainment in Butte. The native from County Cork, Ireland, came to Butte in 1875. He found no adequate facility for his one-man theatrical performance. After moving from place to place, McGuire built and ran the Grand Opera House on Broadway Street. The doors to McGuire's theater opened for the first time in 1882. He was a constant promoter of early day shows. The Grand Opera House was considered one of the best show palaces in the western region of the United States. *The West Shore,* a Portland newspaper, called the Grand Opera House "the best on the Pacific Coast outside of San Francisco."

The Grand Opera Theater was destroyed by fire on July 24, 1888. A few weeks after the blaze, numerous fund raising efforts helped provide the capital McGuire needed to build a second Grand Opera Theater. It opened for business on February 28, 1889, on West Broadway Street with Rose Osborne playing in "A Celebrated Case."

In 1902, McGuire sold his theater to J.P. Howe of Seattle and retired. John moved to San Francisco where he died on March 23, 1912. A few months later, the Grand Opera was destroyed by a fire on May 25, 1912.

A colorful character following McGuire's footsteps was "Uncle Dick" Sutton, who operated a series of theater houses. His main attraction, the Sutton, was built and held its first show "The Belle of New York" on September 29, 1901. A feature of the Sutton was a massive stage, allowing large theatrical groups to bring Broadway shows from New York to Butte. It was the city's largest theater seating 2,282 people. The theater was renamed the Broadway in 1915 and the Montana in the 1930s. This movie palace remained open until 1969 under the ownership of the Fox West Coast Theater Corporation which purchased the entertainment center in 1946. Once the final curtain came down, the theater was never used again and was torn down in 1989.

The efforts of John McGuire and Dick Sutton began an enormous boom in Butte's theater industry. Theaters located in the district included: the American, Ansonia, Bow, Broadway, Empire, Empress, Family, Fox, Grand Opera, Imperial, Liberty, Lyric, Lulu, Majestic, Orpheum, Park, Pavilion, Peoples, Princess and Rialto.

One of the biggest stars ever to play in Butte was Charlie Chaplin. He was a member of the Fred Karno London Pantomime Company. A popular favorite of Chaplin's was the show called "A Night in an English Music Hall."

Sam Spiegel, a veteran stage hand of over 60 years told *The Montana Standard* in an interview, "You've heard the expression 'rolling in the aisles'. Well, with Charlie this was literally true. I would have to say his act was the funniest I have ever seen. Chaplin already had developed some of his trademarks in Butte like wearing baggy pants, a derby and the use of a cane."

The Fred Karno London Pantomime Company played in Butte a number of times. Charlie Chaplin was with the group in Butte when he received a telegraph from Hollywood asking for his talents in a silent movie project which was the biggest break of his life and started Charlie Chaplin on a whole new career.

Charlie Chaplin's new career in silent movies was the start of the final act for vaudeville in Butte. As silent movies became more popular in the 1910s the vaudeville circuit faded away from the stage and the Butte theater scene.

Prior to its departure, there were many popular stage performers who appeared in Butte. The list included: Marian Anderson, Fatty Arbuckle, Adele Astaire, Fred Astaire, Ethel Barrymore, Wallace Beery, Jack Benny, Sarah Barnhardt, Fannie Brice, Billie Burke, Buffalo Bill, George Cohn,

Gary Cooper, Bing Crosby, Billy Dalton, Allen Dinehart, Melvyn Douglas, Marie Dressler, Douglas Fairbanks, W.C. Fields, Eddie Foy, Clark Gable, Louis Gossett Jr., Charlton Heston, Bob Hope, Huodini, Walter Huston, Burl Ives, Frank James, Al Jolson, Stan Laurel, Harpo Marx, Tom Mix, Chauncey Olcott, Pavlova, Enzio Pinza, Lily Pons, Anthony Quinn, Luise Rainer, Martha Raye, Tex Ritter, Will Rogers, Mickey Rooney, Lillian Russell, Beatrice Straight, Sophie Tucker, Mark Twain, Rudolph Valentino, Vivian Vance and Jon Voight.

The list is equally impressive when it comes to musical entertainers who performed on the Butte stage. Delighting Butte crowds were: jazz great Louie Armstrong, the singing cowboy Gene Autry, The Boys' Town Choir, Bing Crosby, Christopher Cross, Dana, Jimmy and Tommy Dorsey, Duke Ellington, Joe Feeney from the Lawrence Welk Orchestra, Arthur Fielder and the Boston Pops, Benny Goodman, Lionel Hampton, Horace Heidt and his Orchestra, Harry James and his Music Makers, Sammy Kaye and his Orchestra, Guy Lombardo, Glen Miller Band, New York Symphony Orchestra, Paddy Noonan, John Philip Sousa and the Vienna Boys' Choir.

In 1951, the Butte Symphony Orchestra was formed by piano teacher Eleanor McTucker and Mrs. Spencer Tripp. A number of local musicians joined in starting the orchestra. They played at the home of Al Kreitinger, but the group got too large to practice at the Kreitinger home and moved their sessions to the Crystal Room of the ACM Club on Broadway Street.

In 1955, the group received funds from the city council to buy additional instruments. This helped prepare the group for its first concert on May 4, 1955, at the Bow Theater. The first concert featured 38 players and was conducted by Anton Leskovar.

Leskovar was a Slovenian immigrant who came to America from Europe with the outbreak of World War I in 1914. He lived in Racine, Wisconsin, and played in the Chicago Symphony Orchestra. Anton joined a traveling troop that put on the show "*Birth of a Nation.*" He was in Helena, Montana, when the troop ran out of money and Leskovar had no job. Anton moved to Butte where he established an auto body and paint shop. He also got involved in the local music scene playing for a number of years in the Butte Mines' Band. Leskovar's vast experience in music made him an ideal first conductor for the Butte Symphony Orchestra.

"I think one reason why the Symphony was able to survive was the strong board of directors we appointed," according Fay Taylor, a Symphony member. "We always had non-musicians who had some clout and could get things done serving on the board. The members of the orchestra were too busy playing music to get involved in the politics of running the Symphony."

In addition to a strong board, the Butte Symphony Orchestra had top conductors leading the group. Fred Honeychurch served as the Symphony conductor for a number of years. Honeychurch , a music graduate of the University of Montana, was a music instructor in the Montana communities of Power, Dillon and Missoula before returning home to his native Butte to give lessons. Others who served as conductor included Ray Sims, Fay Taylor, Leo Medino and Matthew Savery.

Another key element which helped the Orchestra grow was the formation of a Symphony Guild. Taylor said, "The guild would host receptions at the Gold Hill Lutheran Church and did various other things to help the Symphony."

Dorothy Honeychurch, a former Guild member, recalled, "It seemed like we were always busy doing something to raise money for the Symphony. We had bake sales and other events to bring in revenue to keep things going."

The Symphony continued to grow in numbers and popularity through the years. A major growth period came in the 1960s when a Symphony Chorus was formed. "There were lots of choral instructors teaching in the Butte schools during that time," Taylor said. "It made the task of finding people for the chorus easy. We had quite a large group that would sing at Butte Symphony Orchestra performances. Once a year our group would have a solo performance without the orchestra. We had a Messiah Chorus and would sing Christmas and Easter hymns during the appropriate time of year.

"The chorus eventually died when the school district started eliminating choral instructors in the school system. We also were hurt when they cut the elementary band and strings program. It has made it difficult to get young, new talent working in the Orchestra."

Despite a drop in numbers, the Butte Symphony Orchestra has continued for almost 50 years. Each year the Symphony still gives four performances.

The Symphony has been a popular attraction in Butte theaters, but the main drawing card for many years was the motion picture industry. It took center stage especially after "talkies" were introduced in 1928. The Rialto Theater was the first place in Montana to show a "talkie."

Maurine Higman Dennehy remembers, "The best place to go to the movies was always the Rialto Theater. Of course, it cost more to go to the Rialto because they had the better shows. It was 40 cents at the Rialto and only 25 cents at the Park and Liberty."

The choice of theaters to go to in Butte slowly started to dwindle as vaudeville became a thing of the past and a declining population base forced the motion picture industry to reduce the number of places in Butte showing their product. Some of the grand show palaces were converted into other businesses, but some were destroyed by fire. The show palaces turned into ashes included the Family in 1907, the Peoples in 1920, the Empress in 1931, the Park in 1949 and the American in 1950.

When the Montana Theater came tumbling down in 1989, that left the Fox as Butte's only uptown theater. Rather than face the possibility of losing the Fox, an effort was made to save the theater in 1992. The drive to refurbish the Fox was headed by Bob and Pauline Poore along with Helen Guthrie 'Gus' Miller.

"It was vital that we try to save the Fox before it was tore down like the Montana Theater," Bob Poore said. "The theater has been a very important part of life for many Butte residents through the years.

"The first thing we had to do was form a committee which was originally called 'Save the Fox.' It would later be changed to the Butte Center for Performing Arts.

"The next step was approaching the folks in Billings at the Alberta Bear Theater to see how they were able to turn an old theater into a glorious entertainment center. We tried to copy a lot of their ideas because they simply worked. The Alberta Bear became a model for our group.

"Once that was accomplished we talked to the owners of the Fox, the Masonic Lodge, about working out an agreement for our committee to take over the theater. The Masons were super and told us if we fixed the roof and refurbished the front area by doing some painting, fixing the sidewalks plus a few other things that they would deed the property over to us. It took about $300,000 to accomplish all the necessary tasks, but some how we got it done and the Masons gave us the building."

The local committee had plenty of work ahead once they took over the theater. The most difficult challenge was getting the money. Bob and Pauline Poore were one of the first to donate a large sum of money. They also led the effort along with Helen Guthrie "Gus" Miller, vice-president of the organization, to raise capital for the renovation. When the fund raising effort was completed over $2.5 million had been received, an enormous amount of money to raise in a small town like Butte.

Bob Poore said, "The Butte people were absolutely super about donating to this project. They understand the value of culture and theater a lot more than folks give them credit for. I think many people forget that Butte has always been a strong theater town even in its early days. It was a very cosmopolitan community. When corporation people controlling The Anaconda Company came to town, a key entertainment source for them was the theater. They expected good plays with top performers which is what they saw here in Butte.

"In addition to major corporation people, the students from Montana Tech came here from all over the world. They know what good entertainment is and appreciate all the talented people who come here."

The Fox was completely refurbished with all the seats being taken out, sandblasted, redone by Bert's Upholstery, and put back into place. An entire new heating system was installed. The front entrance was completely refurbished. A major challenge was fixing the stage area.

Poore said the stage was "a major concern for me. People who come to the theater will never see it, but there is a huge 60-foot steel grid for sets, lights and other things that sits behind the stage. It was an enormous task to tear down the old wooden grid and build a new one. The company from Las Vegas who did it was excellent. They did a first-class job in building that new grid.

"Another important aspect on stage is the coding system.. All the ropes were color coded corresponding to similar systems that are used around the country. When a stage crew comes to town, they do not have to get familiar with the local theater's unique system. The system in place here is the same one they used at their last location.

Another concern of Poore's was the acoustics. "Prior to the renovation, the acoustics had always been good and with some minor tinkering we were able to continue that with the new theater." A major effort was made to develop a first-class lighting grid. When it was finished, everything was close enough to being done to attempt a performance at the newly named Mother Lode Theater.

The curtain came up on September 4, 1995, for the first Mother Lode performance, a concert by musician, John Michael Talbot. His performance was well-received, but what most impressed the audience was the incredible remodeling effort accomplished at the theater.

The Mother Lode Theater is a first-class entertainment center, site of performances by national touring companies and famous singers. The local theater has a constant stream of events.

The Mother Lode added another special element to their performing arts center when the Orphan Girl Theatre was opened in the basement. The theater is designed as a performing and learning center for the children of Butte. They get an opportunity to perform on stage, run equipment behind the scenes, develop publicity for their plays and run the concessions.

The Orphan Girl Theatre was completed through the help of Butte sisters, Ruth and Ann Busch. They gave the Center for the Performing Arts board a gift of $525,000 for development of a children's theater which, since it was opened in 1996, has held numerous performances for and by kids.

Bob Poore said, "The entire complex has far exceeded anything I could've imagined. There are almost 150 performances a year between the Mother Lode and Orphan Girl. It is an absolute joy to go into such a grand theater and watch a live performance.

"I have not heard one bad word said about the theater since it opened. That's unusual because normally no matter what you do someone always has a suggestion about how you could do it better. I think the reason for the success of the theater is that our committee put a lot of time and effort into making sure the Mother Lode would be something everyone could be proud of and that has certainly been the case."

Through the efforts of Bob and Pauline Poore, Gus Miller, plus hundreds of volunteers, the Mother Lode is indeed a pot of theatrical gold for every person who appreciates fine performance art.

Parades

Butte loves a parade.

The most colorful is the Fourth of July parade. Butte's first Independence Day parade took place on July 4, 1878. The grand marshals were Captain Shepard and Fred Joeber.

The route for the parade changed numerous times, but the event remained in the Uptown district for over 100 years. All that changed in 1983, when Butte Celebrations, the non-profit group operating the event, decided to move the event to Harrison Avenue. Celebrations' members made the change because of fear that one of the floats traveling on Montana Street would lose its brakes leading to an accident.

"The route on Montana Street was just an accident waiting to happen," said Art Korn, a Celebrations committee member. "One time a float got loose going down Montana Street and crashed near the Corner Bar. We had to use ropes to get the float to the bottom of the hill.

"The route on Harrison Avenue gave us a flat, straight surface to conduct the parade, plus the assembly area at the Civic Center parking lot was much easier to put every float, and group into place to start the festivities."

Other major parades were held for Memorial Day, Miners' Union Day, and Bohunkus Day.

The Miners' Union gathered annually on June 13, the day their union was formed in 1878, to march in solidarity as union members. In 1914, all that changed, when the march led to a riot pitting rival union factions against each other. Parade violence led to its cancellation from 1917 until 1935 for safety reasons.

The Bohunkus Day parade was an annual affair for Butte High School students through the early 1950s. The origins for the parade center around the term "Bohunk" which was used in a disparaging way to describe immigrants from the Austria-Hungary Empire. The high school kids dressed in unusual costumes to march in the parade. The event was canceled because students formed long snake lines, traveling off the streets and into large department stores. Store owners were helpless trying to stop the teenagers from grabbing items right off the shelf and marching outside without paying for them.

The one parade standing the test of time in Uptown is the St. Patrick's Day march. Butte's first parade on the Irish patron saint's feast day took place in 1882. The event became more than just an Irish celebration in 1915 when German and Austrian immigrants joined their Irish compatriots. The three groups protested the start of World War I which had the Germans and Austrians taking on the English. The Irish hatred of the English came forth with a massive demonstration against the war. Other political St. Patrick's Day parades revolved around the theme of making Ireland free from Great Britain.

Through the years, there were small St. Patrick's Day parades, but in 1981, the festivities were upgraded when Butte Celebrations decided to hold a large parade. Neil Lynch said, "By the 1980s, we didn't have many activities Uptown so I got together with Gary Gorsh, the president of Butte Celebrations, and talked about doing a St. Patrick's Day parade through Uptown Butte. This was a real project for us because, unlike the Fourth of July parade which we had done for years, we were not sure how to organize it and what kind of response we would get in the community.

"We decided it would be a fun thing to get kids from the various schools marching in the festivities. They could compete against each other marching and also create signs. The schools were really excited about the opportunity. Unfortunately, it snowed on the day of the first parade. It was a minor inconvenience for the kids, but we had a devil of a time getting the parade put together.

"I remember Carolyn Larson with her big, beautiful white horse was going to lead the parade carrying the Irish flag, however, with all the snow she couldn't get the horse trailer up to the starting point. She was able, though, to bring the flag up. Carolyn had like 28 different national flags and the Italian, Irish and Mexican flags all have the same colors. When I pulled out the flag for the parade I noticed the eagle and snake symbol in the middle of it; however, I never paid much attention because we had to get the parade going.

"I had to lead the parade carrying the flag. I went through most of the parade route almost unnoticed. I was walking over Galena Street near the end when a lady yelled out, 'Hey, Mister Lynch, why are you carrying the Mexican flag!' Right away I looked back up at the flag of the eagle and snake symbols then realized that there are no snakes in Ireland. St. Patrick had chased them all out. Here I was carrying the Mexican flag, instead of the Irish one, through the Butte streets on St. Patrick's Day."

Despite the problems with the flag, the initial 1981 parade was a major success. The reception to the event was a massive party in the business district. Each year the parade grew and so did the crowd. Butte Celebrations also got better organized, but there were still problems with the parade.

"I recall the second or third year we held the parade walking down Park Street," Lynch said. "I was leading the parade carrying the flag again. Someone asked me where was the rest of the parade? I looked back and noticed the police cars almost a full block away stopped in front of the First Bank Building. I went up there to find out what was going on.

"Sheriff Bob Butorovich was passing the bank in his car when his department got a report that a bank robbery suspect had been spotted inside the bank. Butorovich immediately stopped his vehicle and went running inside the bank with some of his officers to arrest the guy. He left the doors to his car wide open. I asked him if he could please close the doors and pull the car to the side so we could finish the parade. It was a wild scene."

Another parade incident that was not so pretty took place in 1997. As the parade was finishing on Wyoming Street, a horse carrying a wagon load of people was spooked and started jumping out-of-control. The horse narrowly missed hitting some young Irish dancers from Helena. The driver of the wagon, Robert Ricketts of Polson, was thrown from his carriage and received some injuries. The carriage was destroyed when it flipped over and smashed against the sidewalk.

Despite problems now and then, the event continues to attract large enthusiastic crowds every March 17. The parade has become the top event of the year in the Uptown attracting folks from Portland, Seattle, Calgary, Edmonton, Spokane, and Salt Lake City. Every motel and hotel in the town is booked weeks in advance of the big day. The number of revelers has grown to thousands.

The festivities actually begin on the Sunday before St. Patrick's Day with the Duggan Dolan Family Fun Day. The fun starts with the Blarney Stone Fun Run as competitors race to kiss a green stone labeled after Ireland's fabled Blarney Stone. Following the event, the Gathering of the Clans takes place inside the Knights of Columbus Hall. The family with the largest clan of members wins a cash prize.

During the festivities, music is provided by local Irish group, Dublin Gulch, with the Corktown Dancers also kicking up their heels before a large crowd.

The activities continue on the eve of St. Patrick's Day when the streets are painted with green shamrocks after the annual Friendly Sons of St. Patrick Dinner.

In addition to the parade and family activities, the bars are filled with revelers. The party goes on until the wee hours of the next morning.

"I love St. Patrick's Day," Mike Gribben, a member of the Ancient Order of Hibernians, said. "I love to see people have a good time and they really do in Butte on St. Patrick's Day. The folks from out-of-town bring a fresh, new spirit every year to the festivities."

Transportation

A major factor for growth of the business district and the city was transportation. The horse and buggy of the 1870s was replaced by the street car in the 1880s. The trolley system helped extend the city's boundaries far beyond its initial 42-acre town site. The street car allowed people to live in other sections of the Summit Valley.

The street car era began with the advent of the Butte Railroad Company in 1881. The company was formed after the arrival of the Utah and Northern Railroad's first entrance into the community.

The original idea behind the street car was to link its lines in the business district to the Utah and Northern operations on Front Street in South Butte. The Butte Railroad Company's plan was never completed.

A new firm, the Butte City Street Railway Company, was more successful. Formed in 1886, it featured horse car lines from the Montana Union Railway depot to Park Street, a distance of 1.5 miles. When the company purchased some steam engines the next year their lines stretched to Meaderville, expanding the system to 2.5 miles of track.

The next step by the Butte City Street Railway Company was to link its street car lines in the business district to Walkerville. The line was finished in 1887 with the tracks going straight up Main Street climbing the steep 17 percent grade. Even after the arrival of the city's first steam-powered trolley cars in 1887, it took 25 minutes to ride the trolley car to Walkerville. It was an unsafe system and was abandoned for an easier route up Excelsior Street.

The trolley cars were converted to electric power in 1890, making the system more reliable and safe. Each year the system grew as workers continued to lay down more track, enabling the street car lines to stretch further and further into the valley and allowing continued growth.

An important development occurred in 1899 when the street car system was purchased by the Butte Electric Railway owned by William Clark. The financial backing of Clark allowed the street car system to grow at a much more rapid pace. By 1908, there were over 25 miles of track with 39 motor passenger cars and nine freight cars. The system expanded to its peak in 1933 when 40 miles of track and 57 passenger cars were in service.

The system was safe, but there were some accidents. The most tragic occurred on August 20, 1905, when a trolley car loaded with people crashed into a freight train in the Warehouse District shortly after dark, killing 10 and injuring over 100 people.

The slow-moving street cars were also the target of robbers who jumped aboard and conducted their business while the car was in operation. Once they had finished taking money and valuables, the robbers would hop off the trolley.

In 1928, The Anaconda Company purchased the Butte Electric Railway Company which was a part of Clark's estate. One of the key elements in the sale was that The Company had to pay off two large loan notes of the trolley system in 1937. When it came time to pay, Company officials decided instead to sell the street car firm.

Company officials sold the street car system to National City Lines, a bus company. This marked the end of an era because the new owners shut down the street cars in favor of bus service. The final day of operations for the street cars in Butte was September 22, 1937.

Bus transportation did play a major part in the movement of Butte's residents to various sections around town with their fleet of 28 buses, but it did not have the same impact as the street cars. The reason was the emergence of the automobile as a main source of transportation for many American families.

The dependence on mass transit was no longer needed like in the times prior to Butte's first automobile in 1910.

The National City Lines developed a subsidiary called Butte City Lines which started its operations in 1937. During its two decades in business, the firm only showed a marginal profit at best and was finally discontinued in 1957. Several attempts were made between 1957 to 1961 to operate the bus lines in Butte. All efforts failed.

In 1962, a new company, Butte Bus Lines, took control of the operation with only two buses. The system ran in the black until 1969 when the Butte School District started providing school bus service for its students, eliminating a major source of income for Butte Bus Lines. The company was forced to discontinue service in 1976.

City officials decided to take over the bus system with the closure of Butte Bus Lines. Local officials were able to put new buses on the streets in the 1980s thanks to a large influx of federal money. This helped lure more passengers on the buses and insured a future for the transportation system in the community.

Columbia Gardens

Entertainment, transportation and Uptown Butte all had one common link: the Columbia Gardens. It was in the business district that passengers caught the trolley cars which took them to the amusement park located three miles east of town at the foothills of the East Ridge of the Rocky Mountains.

The property was purchased by William Clark in the spring of 1899. Clark bought the 21-acre site from Walter William Adams, a prospector who could not turn the William and Hillside Lodes into a profitable mining venture. In 1888, Adams leased his property to theater owners, John A. Gordon and Frederick Ritchie. The two men built a picnic grounds and added some recreational equipment, a restaurant and a dance hall. Grandstands were set up for horse racing and rodeos. A collection of animals were housed at a zoo in a shack near the picnic grounds.

Gordon and Ritchie thought the spot was ideal for recreational activities, but their park drew only a handful of people. The reason was a lack of reliable transportation. The street car system to the area was plagued with safety problems which forced city officials to discontinue trolley service to the site. The only other way up to the site was on horseback, horse buggy or on foot up the steep wagon road. A lack of people turned Gordon and Ritchie's dream of an amusement park into a beer drinker's haven.

Clark purchased the property through his Butte Electric Railway Company. He put the manager of that firm, Jesse Wharton, in charge of developing the Columbia Gardens. Wharton immediately decided to tear down all the structures at the site and start from scratch. After some initial work, the gates to the new Columbia Gardens opened for the first time on June 4, 1899. No admission was charged to park patrons, starting a tradition which continued throughout the 74 years of the park's operation.

One major advantage Clark and Wharton had over Gordon and Ritchie was transportation. Because Clark's company, Butte Electric Railway, owned the Columbia Gardens, it was important the firm capitalize on its investment. Within two years after purchasing the ground, the Butte Electric Railway Company put over $40,000 into the construction of a dual-track system to the park. Bigger and better trolley cars were also purchased.

In addition to the trolley system, Clark spent over $125,000 on more land and on construction projects. A grand pavilion was built along with a zoo, baseball grandstands, playground equipment and herbarium . Electric lights, a sewer and water system were also put into place.

The greatest improvement during the first three years of operation was the planting of over 250,000 trees, flowers and other shrubbery. A greenhouse was added at the 68-acre park. German native, Victor Siegel, was placed in charge of growing and planting. Siegel and his team of workers created flower gardens made into beautiful floral designs. Through the years, the workers developed designs featuring butterflies, anchors, stars, lyres and the insignia of the Butte Miners' Union. The workers used various types of geraniums, pansies and begonias. The tradition started by Siegel continued through various park supervisors, including Ted Beech who managed the Gardens during its final 25 years in operations.

The response to the park was overwhelming. By 1902, gate counts indicated that the park attracted over 375,000 visitors during the year. Visitor counts never again approached the 1902 numbers, but they remained high.

There were many reasons why the Columbia Gardens was such a popular place. The most obvious was the natural beauty of the area. Butte was an urban center with plenty of pollution generated by the mining industry. The Columbia Gardens was completely opposite of the mining camp with a lots of trees, flowers and lawns creating a peaceful feeling.

Carl Rowan said, "I can close my eyes and still see it today. It was the most beautiful place on earth. You would've had to see it in person to appreciate how fabulous a place it was for every visitor who walked through the gates at the Columbia Gardens."

Butte native Pauline Poore remembered the Columbia Gardens as "a paradise for birds. They were everywhere! I think all the wild flowers around the Gardens attracted them to the grounds."

Bob Kovacich said, "It was a unique place that any person who visited immediately fell in love with."

The Columbia Gardens had many things for the entire family to do. The parents could sit under a tree and have a peaceful picnic. The kids scattered off and enjoyed the cowboy swings or other pieces of playground gear. There was also the option of going to the Midway and riding the Pacific Northwest's only permanent roller coaster. In addition to the roller coaster, patrons could ride the carousel merry-go-round or bi-planes.

When the kids tired of the rides, they ventured to the arcade building which was constructed in 1910. Here visitors could stroll the boardwalk and stop at the ice cream parlor to get a soda or ice cream cone, get a burger or hot dog, or stop at the candy store.

Frank Panisko's "Paneek Carnival Emporium" was a favorite attraction for kids, with all sorts of games kids could play including the fish pond where they could win a treat by snagging a metal fish out of the water. Contestants could throw balls at milk bottles and Katzenjammer dolls. A popular attraction was the shock machine where kids put a penny into the machine and got a mild electric shock when they put a finger into a certain slot.

A short walk from the arcade building sat the dance pavilion, constructed and finished in 1909 just two short years after a fire destroyed Clark's first grand pavilion at the Columbia Gardens.

The pavilion was the site of many performances by the best of the big band era, including the Glenn Miller Band, Duke Ellington, Benny Goodman, Guy Lombardo and his Royal Canadians, Frank Yankovic's Band, Harry James and his Troubadours, Phil Harris, Tommy Dorsey's Band, Iysham Jones' Music Makers, and Glenn Gray's Casloma Orchestra.

The pavilion's unique wooden dance floor was touted as "the best in the Pacific Northwest," Jesse Poore said. "The floor had a lot of spring to it. It's really hard to describe the spring action. It was simply great to dance on."

Joe Yerkich explained the "springy" feeling. "There were rubber floaters built underneath the floor. A lot of old dance floors in Butte were constructed the same way. When a big crowd was dancing at the Gardens, the floor swayed back and forth. It was like dancing on an ocean and you never seemed to get tired."

The local high schools staged their annual spring proms at the pavilion, always drawing a large crowd. Alana Lecioni LaRock remembered, "The big moment of the night was the grand march. People from throughout the town came to the Gardens to watch the Senior Class officers lead all the young couples around the dance floor.

"Prom night was very special. Couples would ride the roller coaster and merry-go-round with their best formal dresses and suits on. It was something to see! Of course, many couples would stroll off into the park. It was a very romantic place to enjoy a prom."

Each dance at the pavilion provided special moments. So did many special days scattered throughout the years. The most important day of the week during the summer was Thursday, Children's Day. Every Thursday, kids 16-years-old and younger could hop aboard the trolley cars in Uptown Butte or in later years the city bus lines and come to the Columbia Gardens free of charge. Once at the Gardens, youngsters had lots of things to do including picking pansies late in the summer at the Children's Flower Garden. This tradition allowed kids five minutes inside a restricted garden area to pick pansies. Most took their bouquet of pansies home to give to their mothers. Parents never worried about sending their kids alone to the Columbia Gardens on Children's Day because the park provided paid playground supervisors who made sure all the kids were safe.

While Children's Day was the most special day of the week in the summer, the most special day was June 13, Miners' Union Day. Butte miners and their families flocked to the park. There were special mining exercises like a hard-rock drilling competition, mucking events and first-aid contests. The mining exercises pitted the best miners from the various underground operations.

The direction of the Columbia Gardens changed following the death of park owner, William Clark, on March 3, 1925. It took three years of legal battles to sort through his $49 million estate. Once the estate was figured out, all of Clark's Montana holdings were sold to The Anaconda Company for $5.1 million. A segment of the sale was the purchase of the Butte Electric Railway Company and the Columbia Gardens for $450,000.

During their early years of operation, The Company made many improvements to the park. They tore down the Ferris wheel ride and replaced it with the bi-planes. The Company installed a new carousel, replacing the one built by Clark. They ordered cowboy swings made by the Tracy-Dahl Company in Chicago, the first ever cowboy swings made by the Illinois' firm. Because the two-rider, push-pull swings were so expensive to manufacture, Tracy-Dahl officials decided not to construct any more cowboy swings once their order was filled with The Anaconda Company. Thus, the cowboy swings, now a part of Clark Park, are a one-of-a-kind piece of playground equipment.

As times changed so did the direction of mining. The Company replaced Butte's underground mines with the Berkeley Pit, leading to the end of a number of ethnic neighborhoods. The dramatic changes a few miles away had very little impact on the Columbia Gardens which remained the same green haven, year after year. That changed in the early 1970s when Chile dictator, Salvador Allende, took control of the valuable Anaconda Company mining properties in his country. The Company was forced to make drastic cuts in staff, production, programs and the Columbia Gardens.

Anaconda Company officials shut down the amusement park for good following the summer of 1973. The Anaconda Company tried a mining venture at the site which lasted only two years before it was discontinued due to a lack of ore plus water springs in the region. The springs made it nearly impossible for heavy equipment to operate.

The move to close the Columbia Gardens was opposed by civic leaders. A group was formed to try to prevent the closure; however, The Anaconda Company won and the final day at the Columbia Gardens was September 6, 1973.

"It was the worst thing that ever happened in Butte," said Norman Bone. "The Columbia Gardens was the only decent thing that came out of all the mining done here."

Alice O'Donnell said, "It was the best spot in Butte. It was a way of life. If you wanted to see someone, you went to the Gardens on Sunday. That's why it was such a shame to see it shut down."

Lyle Metz said, "It was heartbreaking to see the Columbia Gardens shut down. It was the only thing Butte had that was good."

The Anaconda Company donated money to a local group who tried to develop a Columbia Gardens II park at the Beef Trail ski area southwest of Butte. The funds provided by The Company were far less than what was needed to get the park completed. The Columbia Gardens faded away as another piece of Butte's past history.

The Future

Butte's Uptown has had a better fate than the Columbia Gardens. It survived despite pressure from The Anaconda Company in 1972 to move the business district into the valley in favor of open pit mining. In 1962, the Uptown was declared a National Historic Landmark District. The preservation of the district has become a major concern for many Butte people. The efforts to preserve the region allows one of America's most unique business districts to live on.

A Brief History of Butte, Montana by Harry Freeman published in 1900
A Brief History of the Columbia Gardens by Adolph Heilbronner published in 1902
Butte Metropolis of Montana written by John McIntosh published in 1915
Beautiful Columbia Gardens "Senator Clark'sMasterpiece" by the Butte Electric Railway Company published 1918
The last will of William Clark signed May 29, 1922
The Anaconda Company purchase agreement William Clark estate August 22, 1928
Inventory of the County Archives of Montana by Work Projects Administration published 1939
Butte Was Like That written by Joe Duffy published in 1941
Copper Camp by William Burke published in 1943
Anaconda by Isaac Marcosson published in 1957
Montana Trolley II by Ira Swett published in 1970
Sketches of Old Butte by Jacob Ostberg published in 1972
Memories of the Columbia Gardens by Frank Quinn published in 1973
St. Patrick's Parish 100 years written by Chris Daly published in 1981
Montana Magazine article by Dave Walter published in 1986
Butte, Montana 1923 by Frank Carden published in 1988
Tales of the Dumas by Zena Beth McGlashan published in 1991
The Montana Standard newspaper
West Shore newspaper
Butte Silver Bow Assessor's office
Mary Murphy's study on Butte women in the Red Light District
Butte's Pride - The Columbia Gardens by Pat Kearney published in 1994
Butte Archives
The Montana Standard interview with Sam Spiegel
February 23, 1991 interview Ruby Garrett for *The Montana Standard*
1994 interview Norman Bone
1994 interview Bob Kovacich
1994 interview Alana Lecoini LaRock
1994 interview Lyle Metz
1994 interview Jesse Poore

1994 interview Pauline Poore
1994 interview Carl Rowan
1994 interview Joe Yerkich
1997 interview Mike Gribben
1997 interview Bob Kissell
1997 interview Art Korn
1997 interview Dorothy Lombardi
1998 interview Dorothy Honeychurch
1998 interview Charlie Bugni
1998 interview Vince Downing
1998 interview Neil Lynch
1998 interview Bob Poore
1998 interview Fay Taylor

Butte prior to 1875
photo courtesy A Brief History of Butte, Montana by Harry Freeman

Uptown Butte - corner Park & Montana Street
Photo by Butte-Silver Bow Archives

St.Patrick's Church in 1896
photo courtesy St. Patrick's Parish 100 Years 1881-1981

Mountain View Methodist Church
photo courtesy Pat Kearney

Hilbour Block - left

Metals Bank Building - right
photos courtesy Pat Kearney

Hennessy's Building in 1900
photo courtesy A Brief History of Butte, Montana by Harry Freeman

Paul Cote serves a meal at Gamer's Cafe
photo courtesy Pat Kearney

Lunch time at the M & M Bar & Cafe
photo courtesy Pat Kearney

Butte Brewery in 1900
photo courtesy A Brief History of Butte, Montana by Harry Freeman

Venus Alley
photo courtesy World Museum of Mining

Dumas Brothel
photo courtesy Pat Kearney

Sutton Theater on Montana Street
photo courtesy World Museum of Mining

Mother Lode Theater - photo courtesy Pat Kearney

Butte's Fourth of July parade - photo courtesy Lou Kearney

Butte's Ancient Order of Hibernians lead the St. Patrick's Day parade
photo courtesy Pat Kearney

Edmonton, Alberta bagpipers marching in St. Patrick's Day parade
photo courtesy Pat Kearney

Street car in Uptown Butte 1913- photo courtesy World Museum of Mining

Roller Coaster and first Columbia Gardens pavillion prior to 1907
photo courtesy Jerry Bugni, World Museum of Mining

People at the Columbia Gardens
photo courtesy Jerry Bugni, World Museum of Mining

Chapter Three

A Land of Opportunity

The tremendous growth Butte experienced after the silver rush of 1875 can be directly attributed to the influx of foreign immigrants. The 1880s census revealed Butte's population increasing 218 percent in a ten-year period.

By 1890, records indicate 45 percent of the city's total population had been born in a foreign country.

Foreigners kept pouring into Butte as quickly as workers were shoveling out the copper from underground. The decade of the 1890s showed the city's numbers increased 184 percent.

Almost all the new arrivals were foreign born and ended up working in the mines. By 1900, records indicate there were 30,470 people living in Butte with 64 percent of the population stating their occupation as a miner.

The influx of foreigners remained constant, but the difference was their country of origin. Instead of the British Isles, the new immigrants were coming from the Scandinavian region and countries bordering along the Mediterranean Sea.

The community was also seeing more families rather than just single males arriving in town. In 1900, records reveal 57 percent of the workers were married which is a jump of 25 percent over data from 20 years earlier. The number of women in the city's population had climbed to 42 percent, an increase of 12 percent from 1880.

Foreign immigration remained constant through the end of World War I in 1918. The 1920 records show between 29 to 33 percent of the city's population were born in a foreign country.

In a short 50-year period, Butte became home to more than 25 nationalities: Irish, English, Cornish, Welsh, Scottish, Italians, Finns, Norwegians, Swedish, Danes, Swiss, Lebanese, French, Chinese, Serbs, Croats, Slovenians, Germans, Mexicans, Austrians, Africans, Greeks, Dutch, Korean, Japanese, Polish, Swiss, and Spanish.

"It was the type of town where you had to learn other languages and customs," recalled Al Niemi. "If a fellow miner said hello to you in his native tongue be it Gaelic, Italian, Serbian, Finnish or whatever you had to know how to make the appropriate response. If you did not the miner and his buddies would teach you a lesson down underneath the hill."

Ireland

One ethnic group stood out in Butte: the Irish. The seeds for the Irish roots were planted by Irish immigrant, Marcus Daly. He was born on December 5, 1841, at Ballyjamesduff, County Cavan, Ireland. Marcus came to the United States when he was 15-years-old, one of four million Irish who left their country after the 1845 potato famine outbreak. Once in America, he moved to California to work in the gold mines. Daly quickly became a mining authority after working at the Comstock Lode in Nevada where he met George Hearst.

His path to success led him to Utah to work for the Walker Brothers and then on to Butte. After purchasing and running the Alice Mine for the Walkers, Daly bought the Anaconda Mine and started his rise to wealth through copper.

Daly hired Irish foremen to run his mining properties. The Irish foremen hired mainly Irish immigrants to work at Daly's mines. A number of job openings were written in Gaelic, the national language of the Irish. This gave the Irish a huge advantage in seeking employment.

"There is no question that Marcus Daly was the key person in developing Butte Irish roots," said Bob McCarthy, a Butte historian. "He had a major influence in bringing lots of Irish workers from the Comstock Lode and from Ireland to come here to work.

"The impact Marcus Daly and the Irish had on Butte was enormous. Daly became the head of the largest copper mining company in the world. The Irish controlled city hall which meant jobs for their fellow immigrants as police officers, firemen and city workers. The Irish had an influence on almost every phase of life in Butte."

Immigrants from all 32 Irish counties flocked to Butte. The first major thrust came during the 1890s. By the turn of the century, 36 per cent of Butte's population was Irish. The percentage of Irish immigrants based on the city's population topped numbers of Irish strongholds in Boston, Chicago and Philadelphia. It made Butte, Montana, the most Irish city in the United States.

McCarthy said, "Butte was a popular destination point for the Irish. The new arrivals were told by relatives 'Don't stop in America come straight to Butte' and that's what they did in very large numbers. Port authorities knew where Butte, Montana, was when it came to the Irish."

Butte had Irish from throughout the tiny island; however, one small section of Ireland led the migration charge. The place was in the southwestern corner of County Cork on the Beare Peninsula. The small communities of Castletown Bare, Eyeries and Alliheis were the primary starting point for the long journey to Butte.

The two main sources of employment in the Castletown Bare region were fishing and mining. Castletown Bare's location is next to Beare Bay, a perfect spot to launch a boat into the Atlantic Ocean searching for fish. The mining operations were above the small town of Alliheis, a few miles over the rugged mountains from Castletown Bare. It was at the Alliheis' copper mines that many Butte citizens developed the skills to dig for copper.

The wage scale at the Alliheis' mine was only a few pence a day. Irish workers were looking for better conditions. The first miners to leave the Beare Peninsula settled primarily in the Keweenaw Peninsula in the upper Michigan mining region. After a short period of time, some Irish decided to travel further west. They landed in Colorado where they worked in local mines. Next came a chance to move to Butte, Montana, where jobs were plentiful and, more importantly, the Irish were welcomed.

The family name of Sullivan, Murphy, Walsh, Shea, Lynch and Driscoll all trace their roots back to the Beare Peninsula. At one time Butte had 1,500 Sullivans and 1,350 Murphys living in the city. Church records in Alliheis, Eyeries and Castletown Bare indicate 77 different Sullivan families sent at least one member of their family to Butte. In many cases, 10 or more siblings from the same household came to Montana.

Once in Butte, the new immigrants settled in areas like Dublin Gulch, Centerville, the Hub Addition and Corktown. In many cases, one relative came to Butte, saved enough money, and sent it back to Ireland, allowing another relative a chance to pay the fare to come across the sea. This system and the inter-circle of Irish already settled made it much easier for the new immigrants to adjust to Butte.

"A big factor giving the Irish an advantage was their ability to speak the English language," McCarthy said. "It made things easier on Irish immigrants than on other ethnic groups that came to Butte. The use of the English language allowed the Irish to gain employment in government jobs where the other groups struggled working underground."

The Irish were connected to their homeland through local newspapers. The first Irish newspaper was *The Rocky Mountain Celt.* It appeared briefly in 1899. Another paper was the *Irishman Corcoran.* The most popular newspaper was the *Butte Independent.* It was published by James Mulcahy with its first edition reaching the streets on January 22, 1910. Mulcahy continued to publish a weekly paper with Irish news and the advancement of his "American Ideals" for 24 years. The paper had subscribers from out-of-town, out-of-state and out-of-country. The final *Butte Independent* was published on January 20, 1934, as Mulcahy shut down the newspaper and returned home to his native Ireland.

The Butte Irish were supportive of the various causes to help liberate their country from British rule. Through the years large sums of money were collected for the Irish rebellion across the ocean.

Mike Gribben recalled that, "if a Butte Irishmen was asked to give money to the church he probably tossed 25 cents into the collection basket if he had it. Yet, if that same Irishmen was asked to give money to help the fight for Ireland's freedom he'd donate $100. The Butte Irish always had a strong commitment to a free state in Ireland."

During a 1920 fund raising drive for the Ireland freedom movement, organizers raised over $50,000 in Butte. That $50,000 was raised the year after the provisional president of the Irish republic, Eamonn DeValera, came to town. DeValera arrived in Butte on July 25, 1919, to a greeting befitting a United States President. Thousands of people welcomed the Irish president at the train depot.

DeValera delivered a speech on the steps of the Silver Bow County Courthouse. After a meal in the Finlen Hotel, the Irish politician delivered another speech before 10,000 people at Hebgen Park. His second talk pointed out the main themes of the time supported by the Butte Irish: self-determination for the Irish and denouncing the League of Nations agreement. DeValera said the League of Nations was a political ploy to protect the interests of the British empire. DeValera's visit was one of his key stops in this country on a visit attempting to gain recognition for his newly found republic.

The Butte Irish did not need a speech to rally behind the cause for a free Irish state. Irish Volunteers were formed in Butte prior to the start of World War I. They did military drills south of town at the Nine Mile. The group was training in case they were called back to Ireland to battle to free the country from England.

"There were a number of officers in the Irish Republican Army who came to Butte to hide," said John Shea. "There was a price on their head if they went back to Ireland so they came here where they knew it would be safe."

One group displaying the Irish colors was the Pearse-Connolly Fife & Drum Corps. The musical group formed in 1916 to promote a free Irish Republic was an offshoot of an organization by the same name called the Pearse-Connolly Irish Independence Club. The groups name came from two central figures in the 1916 Irish Easter Rebellion, Patrick Pearse and James Connolly. During the next few years, the Pearse-Connolly Fife & Drum Corps tried to lead Butte's St. Patrick's Day parade. In 1917, the group was told they could not march because local officials felt the Irish would demonstrate against American involvement in World War I. They marched despite the warning from city officials.

The next year, group members went to Captain Omar Bradley commanding officer of federal troops stationed in Butte. They asked for permission to march on St. Patrick's Day. Bradley said they could parade so long as the march was orderly and no unpatriotic demonstration took place. When city officials found out about Bradley's approval, they put pressure on state officials to stop the march. Through the help of state leaders, military officials ordered Bradley not to allow the parade. Despite the military orders, the Pearse-Connolly group tried to march; however, federal troops moved in, arresting 100 people in front of the Federal Courthouse Building.

The defiant actions by the Pearse-Connolly Fife & Drum Corps ended in 1920 when the Butte group disbanded. The Pearse-Connolly Fife & Drum Corps later resurfaced in San Francisco.

The Ancient Order of Hibernians, an organization set up to maintain Irish heritage, established their first local chapter in Walkerville in 1879. Later, in the 1880s, a Hibernian Hall was constructed in Centerville. It was here that traditional Irish dances and songs were kept alive. By 1907, there were three different AOH groups in Butte.

John Shea remembered the Hibernia Hall as "really something. It was three floors with the top one serving as the meeting and dance hall. There was also Casey's Bar inside the building and on the south side of the hall, kids could play handball on a two-wall court."

There was also a chapter of the Robert Emmett Literary Association. It was considered the most radical Irish organization in the community.

Irish politics had a direct bearing on Butte. In 1922, a peace accord was signed giving Ireland the status of being a free state. It was followed by a civil war between the Republicans who wanted one republic for the entire island and the Free-Staters who simply wanted peace even if it meant allowing the British to still rule the six northern counties.

The civil war in Ireland carried across the sea to Butte with the city's Irish divided into Free-Staters and Republicans. The Free-Staters or Pro-Treaty supporters were primarily members of the Hibernians. They were led by District Judge Jeremiah Lynch.

Father Sarsfield O'Sullivan said, "I think even the Pro-Treaty people were not really excited about the agreement reached in Ireland. If fact, a majority of the Irish folks did not like the treaty at all. The goal of the Pro-Treaty supporters was simply to try to stop the bloodshed and if the treaty was the answer then they were for it."

Across town, the Republicans were called the "Sarsfields" listed

 Father Mike Hannan of St. Mary's Church as their spokesperson.

Bob McCarthy said, "The two sides did not see eye-to-eye on anything dealing with Irish politics. They refused to meet together and refused to be buried next to each other. The Sarsfield's got their own cemetery plot at Holy Cross cemetery so they could avoid the Free-Staters."

The civil unrest between the Irish factions almost led to bloodshed. On New Year's Eve, 1922, the Hibernian dance at their Centerville hall was halted by a bomb blast in the back of the building. Six sticks of dynamite had been set off. Prior to the blast, some windows were opened because the hall was so warm that night. That was the main reason why the blast did only minor damage to the building and saved many people from being killed. No one was arrested for the bomb blast, but Hibernian members stated it was done by members of the Sarsfield group.

The 1922 New Year's Eve bomb blast forced some changes in future Irish celebrations. The Friendly Sons of St. Patrick Dinner became the primary St. Patrick's Day celebration for the Butte Irish with their annual parade being discontinued for a number of years in fear of problems developing between the two Irish factions. The deep divisions by the Irish were confined to the immigrants who came over on the boat. The first generation Irish-Americans had little use for politics from the old country. The division between the Irish plus a new generation wanting to be Americans first and Irish second did not help to maintain ties to the old country.

Father O'Sullivan said, "I think one of the things hurting the Irish heritage passing from generation to generation in Butte was the early deaths of miners. A lot of the Irish miners died at an early age and never had an opportunity to share their experiences of the old country with their kids. Children get their culture from their father and for many kids that was missing."

The interest in Irish heritage dropped off to a point where in 1954 the local Ancient Order of Hibernians chapter was discontinued. It was revived by Mike Gribben in 1985.

"I just felt that we were missing something in our schools," explained Gribben. "We were losing a piece of our past with Irish heritage. It was such a big part of Butte's past and I wanted it to endure." Since Gribben's efforts, the AOH has tripled its Butte membership and has a strong base to maintain the Irish heritage well into the next century.

A second development in preserving Irish heritage was started by Butte native, Tom Powers, in 1991. He formed a musical group called "Dublin Gulch." Powers was joined by Kevin McGreevy and Zoe Wood. Mick Cavanaugh replaced Wood in 1993 when Zoe moved to Missoula.

"I grew up listening to the old folk tunes of Ireland," Powers said. "Yet, every St. Patrick's Day in Butte it seemed like the only music being played was Irish-American songs like 'McNamera's Band.' There was a real void for old-time Irish folk music. When Dublin Gulch started playing we tried to fill that void.

"We were performing good material that dates back 100 years or more in some cases. We have a lot of fun doing it and I think we do a pretty good job because everyone who hears our music seems to enjoy it." When Dublin Gulch performs on or around St. Patrick's Day they pack bars, dance halls or motel ballroom where ever they're performing.

Powers said, "St. Patrick's Day in Butte has become a big spring break party for many college kids. I think our music provides local natives a chance to enjoy the day away from all the pushing, shoving and drinking done by the kids. It certainly has rekindled a new spirit of Irish heritage."

The efforts of Tom Powers and Dublin Gulch provide many Butte Irish with a chance to learn songs from the old country. In addition to their St. Patrick's Day gigs, the group has concerts a number of times a year at various locations around town.

Cindy Powers, Tom's wife, added to the heritage preservation by forming the Corktown Dancers in 1996. The group of foot-movers ranges from small children to grown adults. Since it was formed, the group quickly tripled in size in a few years.

In addition to their efforts to preserve their heritage, the Butte Irish are noted for their loyalty to the Roman Catholic Church and the Democratic Party. For years the Republicans seldom ran a candidate in local races because of the heavy Irish Catholic Democratic vote. Republican leaders realized there was little chance to win in Butte.

England

Although the Irish were Butte's largest ethnic population, they were not the first group to settle here. That destination belongs to the English or to be more precise the Cornish from County Cornwall in Southern England. The Cornish, known as "Cousin Jack's" came mainly from the towns of St. Austel, Red Ruth, Treverbyn, Henwood, Liverscoombe and Carthew.

The emergence of the Cornish in Butte can be partly attributed to copper king William Clark. Oddly, Clark's roots go back to Ireland not Cornwall. Yet, Clark was raised a Protestant and shared the same faith as the Cornish. He liked the work habits of the experienced Cornish miners and recruited them to Butte from Michigan.

Clark was born in Pennsylvania on January 8, 1839. Both his parents were born in Northern Ireland and came to the United States shortly after the Revolutionary War. The Clark family moved to Van Buren County, Iowa, in 1856. Clark was a bright student in school and followed up his prep classes by attending law school at Iowa Wesleyan for two years. After college, Clark moved to Missouri where he became a teacher.

In 1862, the urge to travel had Clark leaving the classroom for adventure west of the Mississippi River. He landed in Black Hawk, Colorado, a small mining camp 40 miles west of Denver. Clark worked at the Black Hawk mining operations for the remainder of the year. The next spring Clark and three other men left Colorado for Bannack in the Idaho Territory. The previous year gold had been discovered in the area. Once in Bannack, Clark would spend the rest of 1863 mining for gold.

Clark made a fortune in the territory which became Montana in 1864. His initial success was not in mining, but in hauling supplies from Salt Lake City, Utah, to the Montana mining camps of Bannack and Virginia City. Clark succeeded in other business ventures like transporting mail and banking before arriving in Butte in 1872.

It was through Clark's early success in mining that triggered the arrival of the Cornish to Butte in the 1880s. By 1890, they accounted for 26 percent of the city's population making them the largest ethnic group in the community. They found quick employment working in Clark's mines.

The Cornish were skilled miners who learned their trade working in the tin and copper mines of Cornwall. Prior to 1850, Cornwall produced most of the world's tin and copper. Figures from 1862 reveal that over 50,000 men and women worked in the 340 Cornwall mines.

The bright mining economy started to change around 1865 when copper ore operations got into full-scale production on the Keweenaw Peninsula in Michigan. The emergence of the Michigan Copper Range produced "the copper collapse" in Cornwall. Competition forced major cutbacks in the work force at the Cornwall mines. The layoffs forced many to look toward the United States and Canada for employment.

The Registrar General indicated Cornwall's population dropped 8.9 percent between 1871 and 1888 with over 24 percent of the mine workers leaving the country. By 1888, over 33 percent of all Cornwall miners had left in search of a better opportunity.

The Cornish who came to America first worked at the Michigan Copper Range. They were experienced with underground copper mining, making them a tremendous asset in securing the Keweenaw Peninsula as the world's largest copper producer from 1865 to 1883.

A number of Cornish eventually left Michigan looking for a new opportunity. They migrated to various western mining camps before settling in Butte. It was here that the Cornish again became a prominent part of a major copper boom with the rich discovery of ore. The experienced Cornish miners gave Clark a fighting chance to succeed in his mines against Daly's large Irish work force.

Beyond their mining experience, the Cornish had a lot in common with the Irish. They saved their money, sent the cash back to their homeland so more relatives could come try their luck in the local mines. The Cornish scattered throughout the hill working in the underground mines. The largest concentration of workers was at the Mountain View Mine. The Cornish followed the Methodist religion and the Republican Party which was in sharp contrast to the Irish who favored the Roman Catholic faith and the Democratic Party.

"I remember my grandmother talking about politics," laughed Maurine Higman Dennehy. "She would vote for a rat if the Republicans put it on the ticket rather than any Democrat. She was Cornish, Republican, Protestant and very proud of it!"

During Butte's early years, the Cornish and Irish immigrants were bitter enemies. It was common to see individuals from each side slugging it out with their rivals in Walkerville and Centerville. One noted fight began on July 4, 1894, and ended as a riot in the business district.

The American Protective Association, an organization supported by the Cornish and antagonistic towards the Catholic Church, displayed their bright orange colors and their sign in front of two Broadway Street saloons, the Hauswirth and Sazerac on America's Independence Day. The Irish Catholics, who favored the color green, were upset with this blatant symbol of the APA so they blew up the Association's flag with dynamite. The Irish tried to do the same thing to the APA signs, but did not succeed which led to an-all-out brawl between the two sides. Better than 2,000 men from all over town heard about the fight and came to join in. The fisticuffs lasted for hours in a two-block section. Attempts by the police and civic leaders to calm things down did little good. A military unit firing shots into the crowd finally ended the disturbance. Firemen also helped by washing down the APA banners. The final tally showed one person, police officer D.H. Daly dead; two others shot, hundreds requiring stitches and half the Butte police force ended up in the hospital.

About the Irish-Cornish rivalry Lee Masters remembered being told a story about "how my grandmother, Jesse, came home one night with a new green hat she bought. My grandparents were both Cornish and grandpa Will never liked the green hat because it reminded him of the

Irish. So one night when Jesse was sleeping, he got up, took the hat and burnt it in the stove."

Father Sarsfield O'Sullivan said, "My father got fired working at the mines because of the hatred between the two sides. The mine foremen kept putting up the Union Jack flag every day at the mine and my father, being a true Irishmen, promptly took the thing down every day in protest. Finally, the mine supervisor fired him for his actions."

The Cornish displayed their loyalty to their homeland in Centerville where they built the Sons of St. George Hall on the corner of Main and Center Streets. The hall served as a social center for the Cornish.

"St. George's Hall was just beautiful," recalled Evelyn Eva. "T. J. Bennett operated a dry goods store on the first floor of the building. The hall was upstairs and included the best dance floor in Butte. There were springs underneath the floor and it seemed like you could dance all night.

"There were always plenty of activities going on at the hall. People could play pool or cards and the men held their meetings at the hall. It really was a hub center for the Cornish."

Rich Holman remembered that "one of the activities they provided for kids was tumbling. Tubie Johnson taught tumbling classes in the hall after school during the 1950s."

The big day of the year for the Cornish was April 23, St. George's Day. A parade was staged with a march up Centerville's Center Street.

The organization provided its members with illness, injury and death benefits, which the mining companies never offered workers at the turn of the century.

The Cornish had their own newspaper called *Tribune Review* which survived longer than any other ethnic paper in Butte. It was published from 1893 to 1917. A lot of its content contained homeland accounts, "*Notes from Cornwall*" sent to Butte from Cornwall. The example of the newspaper points out an interesting Cornish trait: their ability to organize and communicate. They had a much better system of corresponding with folks back home than any other Butte ethnic group.

"My father always talked about Cornwall," Evelyn Eva said. "He use to get together with friends all the time and talk about the old country."

The Cornish were noted for their pasties. It was made up of meat, potatoes, onions and sometimes carrots, all encased in pastry. It was a meal other ethnic groups picked up and became a main-stay in many local households regardless of their nationality. In fact, its commom for former Butte residents returning here on a summer vacation to go back to their home with a bag full of pasties.

The Cornish were not the only English people ending up in Butte. There was a strong contingent of Welsh that came to the mining camp. The Welsh, like the Cornish, had a background in mining. A number of Welsh immigrants had experience working in the slate quarries, coal and lead mines at Carmarthen in an area called the Vale of Toweyand in Wales.

The Welsh also brought a skill and background the Cornish or Irish were not familiar with: smelting. A smelter at Swansea, Wales, was the only one of its kind in the world that could process raw copper ore prior to building a smelter in Anaconda, Montana.

The majority of Welsh who came to Butte in the 1880s were seeking smelting jobs. They had lots of places to pick from to practice their craft. During that time frame, Butte had nine different open-air smelters operating in town.

Once in town, the majority of the Welsh people settled in Central Butte located south of the business district. They built the Welsh Presbyterian Church on the corner of Aluminum and Dakota Streets in Central Butte. A feature at the church was the singing of the Butte Male Chorus consisting of 30 singers mainly Welsh with some Cornish members. Some Welsh folks called Meaderville their new home which was one of the bigger areas for smelting in Butte's early days.

A day of celebration every year for the Welsh was March 1, St. David's Day.

The Scots also played a role in the development of Butte. Unlike the Irish, Cornish and Welsh who had flocks of immigrants the number of Scots who came to the mining camp was small. The Scots also took a different route to get to the city through Canada rather than the eastern sea port cities of the United States. The Scots had little background in mining and smelting so their skills were limited in Butte's economic development.

Some other English people besides Cornish, Welsh and Scots lived in Butte. Their numbers were rather small. One of the few English families that had an impact were the Lutey's who operated a series of very successful self-service grocery stores. At one time, they owned 14 stores in town employing 350 people. The store empire came crashing down to nothing when the lone remaining Lutey brother still alive, William, refused to give a $150 donation to the free Ireland cause in 1923. The Butte Irish boycotted the Lutey stores and soon the company had to shut down their operations.

Finland

Another region with a major influence in Butte was Scandinavia encompassing Finland, Sweden, Norway and Denmark.

The most prominent Scandinavian ethnic group were the Finns. They were noted for being good farmers, but the change to a market economy in Finland in the 1870s eroded a farmers' self-sufficient way of life forcing many Finns off their property and into major cities like Helsinki. In less than 30 years, 34 percent of all the rural farmers were now living in Helsinki. These transplants discovered they could not make a living in the bigger towns so they got on boats and came across the ocean to America in search of a new beginning.

The migration of Finns to America began in the 1870s and continued until the 1893 depression which marked a slow down in the migration process. In 1899, the wave of immigrants intensified again as many Finnish people left to escape the brutal Tsar Nicholas II's Russian army. In 1902 alone, there were 23,152 Finns who left their home for good.

Once the Finns cleared their way through the large American cities, some settled in the Keweenaw Peninsula in Michigan. It was here the Finnish farmer was introduced to copper mining. Later, some Finns moved west to other mining camps in Colorado and the coal mines at Red Lodge, Montana.

Finally it was on to Butte's copper mines.

Records show only 96 Finns living in Butte in 1900. By 1910, that number had escalated to 1,239 with even more people coming during the next decade. By 1917, over 3,000 Finns were living in Butte.

Most of the Finns worked in the mines and lived in a section of the city called Finn Town just northeast of the business district. They were noted for keeping their homes and boarding houses spotless. Their church called Trinity Methodist was on East Park Street. The Finnish Workers' Hall on North Wyoming Street just below the Anaconda Road was a social and political center holding many plays, dances, dinners and political rallies. The hall was the site for the last political speech given by Wobbly officer, Frank Little, the night before he was killed.

A Finnish tradition maintained in Butte was the salma, which means bath or steamhouse. There were a number of them located in Finn Town. Even years after most of Finn Town has disappeared as a result of the Berkeley Pit expansion the salma remains alive in the rear entrance to the Helsinki Bar.

Al Niemi recalled as a kid going up to the steam baths in Finn Town every Saturday night. "A number of families did not have indoor plumbing so the steam bath was the next best thing to getting refreshed.

"You would pour water on hot rocks and sit back to allow the steam to build up all around you. There was one place where you just turned a certain valve and got instant steam. As a Finn I loved to take a steam bath or sauna. It was a great tradition and a lot of fun."

They were famous for their love of fishing. It was common to see many Finns leave the area during their days off to go fishing at either nearby Georgetown or Delmoe Lake.

The Finns were noted for getting involved in politics, especially when it centered around their mining employment. The Finns took bold, radical steps as members of the Butte Miners' Union to develop a better wage scale and working conditions.

They antagonized the Irish and Cornish by backing the Socialist Party and the Industrial Workers of the World. Both groups were looked down on by the conservative Irish and Cornish.

Norway

The number of people from Norway did not come close to rival the packs of folks from Finland who came to town; however, the Norwegians did make an impact here. The Norwegians migration to Butte occurred primarily between 1890 to 1910. The ethnic group never banded together in one section of town, but scattered throughout the city.

Many Norwegians worked for The Anaconda Company; however, most were not underground miners. They were revered for working in high places with little room for error. A number of them worked on sailing ships rigging and hoisting equipment near the top of the sails, in Butte, they turned that trade into being ropemen and riggers at the mine operations building steel head frames.

The Norwegians were noted as church-going people. Their national religion is Lutheran. The Butte Norwegians built their first house of worship at the corner of Alaska and Copper Streets below the Original Mine. The church was called the First Norwegian Independent Evangelical Church with services held in both English and Norwegian.

The church was the brainchild of Per Skorgen. He changed his name to Peder Pedersen when he became a United States citizen. Pedersen operated a shoe making shop on Main Street. During the week, the Norwegians gathered in the back of the shop to play a card game of pitch. On weekends the shop became a church until the church on Alaska and Copper Streets was built.

The Norwegians changed the name of the church to Gold Hill Lutheran in 1910, taking the name of the mining claim on which the church was built. The congregation built a new church on Placer Street in 1939, and, in 1958, an education center constructed next door.

A favorite day for the Norwegians was May 17, Norwegian Independence Day, a day they claim all the Swedes were chased out of their country. Norway did not gain its independence from Sweden until 1905 ending Swedish rule which began in 1814. That fact produced some bitterness and a rivalry between the two sides. Norwegians held dinners and drama plays to commemorate their Independence Day. They also got city officials to wave their national flag at the Silver Bow County Courthouse.

As part of their unique heritage, the Norwegians brought to Butte some of their favorite dishes like lutefisk and lefse. Lutefisk is a cod fish that is soaked in lye plus salt and left to air-dry. Once dry, its as hard as a board, but preserved for future use. When it comes time to cook, the lutefisk is first soaked in water for a few days to get rid of the lye. Its then placed in boiling water until cooked and ready for consumption.

Lutefisk is a Christmas dish made during the holidays. Each year Gold Hill Lutheran Church members hold a lutefisk dinner. The event is so popular that residents from Anaconda, Deer Lodge, Whitehall and Ramsay attend.

Lefse is a fried potato bread. When rolled out with butter and brown sugar it is a delicious meal especially for someone with a sweet tooth. Lefse is made annually at Christmas by the Daughters of Norway. The organization was formed in Butte on February 28, 1913, with 30 women signing the original charter. The purpose of the association was to promote the heritage of all the Scandinavian countries. Through the years, their annual sale of lefse helps raise money for college scholarships for women.

Sweden

Although few in numbers, the Swedes who came here mainly between 1890 to 1910 did have an impact on the town. Like the Norwegians, the Swedes did not congregate in one area. They were also similar because the Swedes were devoted church-going people. The first Swedish church was built near the Norwegian church on the corner of Alaska and Copper Streets. It was called the Swedish Methodist Church.

On February 1, 1896, the Swedish Lutheran Society was formed in Butte. Two years later, on January 25, 1898, the society voted to become a congregation of the Augustana Synod. There were 35 charter members of the congregation. They built a church on the corner of Montana and Silver Streets. It was called the Swedish Evangelical Lutheran Emanuel Church. The church built for $75,000 was completed in 1916 and dedicated the next year. Services were conducted in Swedish and English until 1926 when the congregation decided to use only the English language.

The congregation changed its name to Gloria Dei Evangelical Lutheran when moving into a new church at 2300 Florence in 1958.

Besides church, a gathering place for the group was the Runeberg Hall on East Galena Street. It was here that the youth of the Swedish Order of Runeberg staged plays, concerts and other social events.

The Swedes were noted for being good with wood. A role they played in Butte's underground mines was building timber shafts. They also were very civic-minded operating the Swedish Salvation Army for the homeless.

A big day for the Swedes was December 13, St. Lucia's Day. The tradition of the day was the oldest daughter serving saffron buns and coffee before dawn to her parents.

Denmark

The Scandinavian country with the smallest population in Butte were the Danes. They lived primarily in Central Butte near the Scandinavian Hall on South Main Street.

The Danes were different in a number of ways from many ethnic groups who came here. They were well-educated merchant-class people. A majority of Danes who settled in Butte had lived elsewhere in the United States before coming to the mining camp with only a small percentage coming here directly from their homeland.

There limited numbers reflect a very small influence in the development of the community. There were, though, enough Danes present here to create the fraternal lodge, the Danish Brotherhood and Sisterhood.

Italy

The mainland of Europe played a role in the development of Butte. The area along the Mediterranean Sea produced large numbers of immigrants to Montana. The most prominent Southern European nation to send immigrants to Butte was Italy. Some Italian families were here prior to 1900. The main flood of immigrants infiltrating the mining camp occurred just after the start of the 20th century. During a ten-year period, from 1900 to 1910, the Italian population in the town tripled.

The new immigrants were mainly from two regions: the majority came from the northern portion near the city of Turin and the second group came from the central section around the nation's capital of Rome. The Italians were lured to Butte by the prosperous copper mines. It meant jobs and a chance for a new opportunity.

The vast majority of them settled in the smelting community of Meaderville. In a short period of time, the Italians dominated the neighborhood. Others had an opportunity to settle outside the urban setting on farms in areas known as Brown's Gulch and Elk Park.

The majority of Italians were Roman Catholic. They practiced their religion at St. Helena's Catholic Church in Meaderville.

The Italians, like many Southern Europeans, had to struggle to get good jobs working in the underground mines. When they first arrived, Italians were assigned to work in the most dreadful mines which had extremely hot conditions with temperatures reaching over 100 degrees.

Although the Italians were not dominant underground, above the surface they were a cultural force because of their cuisine. Italians were noted for producing some of the city's finest foods and best restaurants. Their dishes included raviolis, polenta, spaghetti and breadsticks.

A favorite dish with Italian ties is the tamale. Tamales were made of chicken, turkey or other pieces of meat wrapped in a pasta corn meal. The pasta corn meal can be traced directly to the Italians while the ingredients inside can be credited to the Spanish. Tamales were wrapped so they could be heated in boiling water. Two major producers were Truzzolino's Tamales and Gus's Tamales both located in Meaderville.

The Italians had a number of newspapers published in Meaderville. The first was *The Montana Star Weekly* published by Joseph Civinini, Charles Grosso and Benedict Fresia. There was also *The Italian Weekly News* also called *L'Era Nuovo* which continued publication until 1923. The final Italian newspaper to appear was *L'Era Avaldo* which was published in 1926.

Besides newspapers, a strong tie to Italy was the fraternal group Christopho Columbo Lodge made up of Italians who tried to help each other. Christopho Columbo members paid dues and could draw sick or death benefits. A member received up to $120 a month for sick benefits. There was also a death benefit where the burial was paid for by the lodge.

Angelo Petroni, a member of Christopho Columbo said that the group "was great to maintain ties with Italy. It was also good for single men who were miners living in boarding houses. They had an extended family in the lodge."

Besides sick and death benefits, the Christopher Columbo Lodge held a big celebration every year on October 12, Christopher Columbus Day. During the early years, a parade through Meaderville was followed by a picnic at the Columbia Gardens. In later years, after Meaderville was destroyed by pit shovels, a large dinner banquet was held somewhere in the community.

Serbia

An important Southern European group to come to Butte were the Serbs from Serbia and Montenegro. They made their first appearance in Butte shortly before the 20th century. After 1900, Serbs started to come in large numbers to Butte. By 1910, there were over 2,000 Serbs in Butte.

The Serbs was not well-received by the established Cornish and Irish people. Both groups showed open hostilities to the new immigrants who could not speak English.

The Serbs settled in various sections of Butte with a majority on the East Side. Also, a good number found homes in the Irish strongholds of Dublin Gulch and the southern half of the Hub Addition.

Beyond the language barrier, there were other reasons for tension between the Serbs and the established Irish and Cornish. One of the biggest differences was the Serbs living under the Julian Calendar system. It was introduced in Rome in 46 BC establishing a 12 month year of 365 days. The Gregorian calendar was introduced in 1582 by Pope Gregory XIII as a revision to the Julian calendar. It was adopted by Great Britain and the American colonies in 1752. The difference between the two calendars is 13 days. The Irish and Cornish celebrate Christmas on December 25, and New Year's Day on January 1, while the Serbs celebrate Christmas on January 7, and New Year's Day on January 14. The Serbian New Year's Eve celebration was considered one of the best parties of the year with the celebration sometimes lasting for up to three days with singing, dancing and lots of food on hand.

A second major difference was their religion, Eastern Orthodox. Serbia was the dividing line between the Byzantine Eastern Orthodox Church with a base in Constantinople and the Roman Catholic Church of the West based in Rome. The division of the two sides came in 1054. Through the years, Serbia has seen numerous battles between various religious denominations.

An important day dealing with one particular battle every year for the Serbs is June 28 called "Vidovdan" or "Vision Day". It was on this date in the year 1389 that the Serbs stopped the advancement of the Turkish Army at Kossovo Polje in Serbia. Each year the Butte Serbian community celebrates with church services on their sacred day to give thanks to God.

The first Orthodox services held in Butte took place on August 28, 1897, by the Very Reverend Abbot Father Sebastian Dabovich, the first American born Serbian priest. Dabovich came to Butte four to five times a year from his base in Jackson, California, to provide services for Butte Serbian Orthodox members.

On January 7, 1904, during the Serbian Orthodox Christmas celebration, Father Dabovich urged his parish members to built a permanent church in Butte. The money was raised and by September 1904, the church was completed on the corner of Idaho and Porphyry Streets. It was called the Holy Trinity Church. The church was only the second Serbian Orthodox Church built in the United States. The next year, on June 28, 1905, the new church was consecrated by Russian Archbishop Tikhon.

The original church lasted until 1968 when it was torn down due to structural damage caused by an old mining operation located at the site. A new church on Continental Drive was built to replace it. The church was completed with the first services taking place on July 25, 1965. The Very Rev. Bishop Gregory of California along with local Rev. Dositel Obradovich presided over the consecration of the new church.

Through the years, 32 priests have served at Holy Trinity Church in Butte. The only priest serving the parish who was ordained at Holy Trinity was Father Bratislave Krsic. He was ordained a priest on September 15, 1996, by His Grace Bishop Jovan.

The Eastern Orthodox Church has been a main component of Serbian life in Butte. A number of Serbian organizations developed through the church. The Circle of Serbian Sisters was organized in 1934, the Church School Mothers Club was started in 1954 and the Serbian American Men's Club also called the SAM Club was organized in 1969. All three organizations have become the backbone of the church and the Church's Executive Council.

The Serbs were united by more than just calendar and religion. They were also bonded by a Serbian newspaper called *Slavenska Jedinsto* which means Serbian unity. It was published by Michael Chiuda and stayed in publication until 1904. A couple of years later *The Servian Voice* paper was being peddled on the Butte streets starting in 1908. It operated for less than a year. A final Serbian newspaper called *Norodna Misao* was published in 1912 by the Serbian Publishing Company.

Like the Italians, the Serbs had to prove their worth in Butte by working in the hottest mines underground before acquiring assignments elsewhere on the hill.

Austria-Hungary Empire

The Serbs were not the only Slavic people who settled in Butte. The city's language mix included people who came from what was known as the Austria-Hungary Empire, which, prior to World War I, was one of the largest nations in Europe. Located just north of Serbia the country was formed in 1867. Under a duel monarchy called Hasburg both sides shared an army, bureaucracy and most importantly the Roman Catholic Church. The Empire consisted of three main ethnic groups the Croatians, Slovenians, and Austrians. The Croatians were in the southern section of the Empire; the Slovenians settled north and west of the Croatians, while the Austrians were north of both groups.

All three groups both disliked and distrusted Serbians. The Austria-Hungary Empire annexed the Turkish states of Bosnia and Herzegovina in 1908. This infuriated the Serbs who were trying to include those two states in a southern Serbian country of Yugoslav. The hatred between the groups intensified on June 28, 1914, when Austrian Archduke, Franz Ferdinand, was killed in the Bosnian town of Sarajevo by a Serbian nationalist, an event which triggered the start of World War I.

The three ethnic groups came in vast numbers to the mining camp, following the same migration pattern as the Serbs arriving here after the turn of the 20th century. Yet, unlike the Serbs who came to work in the mines the Croatians, Slovenians and Austrians flocked to the area to work in the region's smelters. This led to a high percentage of these ethnic groups living in Anaconda.

In Butte, the Croatians, Slovenians and Austrians clustered together to became a major force in the sections of town called the Boulevard, Parrot Flat, East Butte, McQueen and Silver Bow Parks.

"The primary reason for living together in Butte was the language," Ann Simonich said. "The Irish and Cornish had a huge advantage because they knew English and were here first. They got the best jobs and forced all the Southern Europeans to work in the hottest mines and perform the dirtiest jobs. In order to survive, the Croatians, Slovenians and Austrians had to stick together. They needed each other."

A major difference between the three ethnic groups and the Serbs was religion. The Serbs followed the Eastern Orthodox faith, while the Croatians, Slovenians and Austrians were Roman Catholics. A symbol of that faith was established with the completion of Holy Savior Catholic Church in McQueen. Finished in 1902, Holy Savior was the first Catholic Church built in Butte that did not have ties to the Irish.

One unique experience in their faith that the Croatians brought to Butte was the celebration of Mesopust which in Croatian stands for meso (meat) and pust (fast). Mesopust was celebrated just prior to the beginning of Lent. Folks went around the Boulevard neighborhood collecting butter and eggs for the big event. They collected food and cooked a huge meal. Once all the food was ready, there was a parade to the Boulevard Hall and then a trial of Mesopust, a stuffed character who represented sins, grievances and scandals. Mesopust lost the trial every year and was burned in effigy.

Simonich said, "Almost all the celebrations by the Croatians, Slovenians and Austrians revolved around some type of celebration in the Catholic Church. Besides Mesopust, various feast days were commemorated with a mass followed by a family gathering at Holy Savior Parish Hall in McQueen. They celebrated the feasts of St. Martin, St. Philip, St. Jacob and St. Ann. All the various saints had lodges which people from Butte could join. The headquarters for most of the lodges was Cleveland, Ohio, which has a large Croatian and Slovenian population."

In addition to the lodges, another fraternal organization for the Croatians, Slovenians and Austrians was the Slovenian Sons Lodge. It held meetings at the Slovenian American Hall in East Butte. There was also the Croatian Fraternal Union and the Slovenska Narodna Podporna Jednota (Slovenian National Benefit Society). All the various lodges helped local members with sick and death benefits.

Easter was the biggest holiday of the year. One of the favorite treats for kids on Easter Sunday was not hunting Easter eggs, but collecting money through a game with adults.

"The kids held an Easter egg in the palm of their hand between the thumb and first two fingers," Cathy Brozovich James explained. "We went into the neighborhood and people threw coins at the eggs trying to get them to stick in your hand. If the coin stuck they kept both the coin and the egg; however, if the coins did not stick then you got to keep all the loose change. The game was a lot of fun and it was next to impossible to get a coin to stick in your hand so the kids made plenty of money."

Despite the Croatians differences with the Serbs, they shared some similar traits. Like the Serbs, the Croatians had their own newspaper which was called *The Croatian World,* a weekly newsletter which came out in 1908 and 1909. The language of the two groups was also similar unlike their Balkan neighbors to the north, the Slovenians.

The Croatian and Serbs also brought to town a lot of similar dishes which became household delights to the entire population. The dishes included kobase, sausages, suckling pig, rostula, pohanje, povitica and slivovitz.

France

Other nationalities came to Butte; however, their numbers were small and their impact only minor. One such group was the French. Their role belongs primarily to the early mining development period. The French were noted as wood-cutters and played a vital role in supplying wood to operate the various smelters and timber to support the underground mines.

A majority of the men were rugged French-Canadians from the timber country of Quebec. They lived in make-shift villages near their work on the outskirts of town. The small French communities were Stringtown north of Walkerville, Woodville northeast of Butte in the Elk Park valley and the Nine Mile in the southern region of Summit Valley.

The French population was small, but there was enough of an influence by them to have a weekly newspaper called *La Courie de Butte.* It was published in 1895 and came out every Friday for about a year.

The French supported the Society of St. John the Baptist.

A key day for them was Easter when a religious procession was held with a number of people participating in the event.

The use of coal to replace wood as a heat source for Butte smelters around 1890 was a turning point for the French. A majority left for wood-cutting jobs elsewhere in North America.

Germany

Like the French, Germans immigrants were few and did not play a large role in the development of the mining camp. Those who came here settled in Williamsburg, a small neighborhood in the southwestern corner of the valley and also in Rocker, a town three miles northwest along the BA&P railway.

The Germans were looking for other forms of employment besides mining. They took jobs as tavern owners, brewers, farmers, tradesmen and business people. The Germans displayed their business skills with numerous newspapers. The first was called *The Montana Journal* which was later shortened to *The Journal.* It was published by Herman Rosenweig and was found on the Butte streets from 1897 to 1904. A second newspaper, *Der Nordwesten,* came out in 1902, published by J.C. Martin. After the paper folded, a year later, Martin published *The Montana Volkszeitung* from 1908 to 1911.

The Germans did participate in their country's main religious faith by constructing the St. Mark's Lutheran Church in 1907 on South Montana Street. They also displayed their skills for singing in the German Lodge's Singing Society called "Der Butte Liederkranz."

Switzerland

A number of people from Switzerland came to Butte, mostly from near the Swiss and Italian border, from towns like Iragne, so they were labeled as Swiss-Italians. These immigrants spoke three different languages: Italian, French and German, a necessity because those three countries all were within easy distance of Switzerland and all conducted business in the tiny European country.

The Swiss settled outside of town on Elk Park dairy farms just like the Italians who were in the same occupation in Brown's Gulch. There were lots of dairy farms in the Elk Park region with some housing 75 to 100 head of dairy cows. Two-hundred gallons of milk were produced daily and taken into town and sold to the local creameries.

There were lots of big Swiss-Italian families in Elk Park with the Parini family the largest producing 17 children.

The Swiss were predominantly Catholics with their biggest celebration of the year being Easter Sunday.

Jews

Just as Jewish people were known to wander the earth, some were attracted to Butte in the early days. Many Jewish folks moved west to escape the anti-Semitism of the Eastern cities. They were immigrants from Holland, Denmark, Romania, Russia, Poland and other primarily European countries.

The first Jewish settlers were Sam Alexander and David Cohen in 1875. Alexander, a Polish immigrant, opened one of the city's first restaurants. Like Alexander, the Jewish people who came here did not become miners, but instead were the business life-blood of the town holding positions as jewelers, pawnbrokers, shoemakers, tailors, lawyers, doctors and junk dealers.

The Jewish community played a major role in Butte's early day political world. Butte's first mayor, Henry Jacobs, was Jewish as was Henry Frank, who became mayor in 1885.

The leadership displayed by the Jewish people was certainly evident in Joseph Oppenheimer who came here in 1881. He joined two brothers, William and George Symons, to form Symons' Dry Goods Store in 1897 on the corner of Dakota and Park Streets. The store became a key shopping center for many years in the business district.

In addition to his success in business, Oppenheimer was a major civic leader helping to lead the financial drive to construct the Butte YMCA in June 1917.

Helping others through civic projects was a trademark of the Jewish people; however, in 1892 troubles developed. The Jewish community divided when a younger segment of the congregation broke ranks from the Orthodox traditions to form a Reform congregation called B'Nai Israel. The Reform group was strong enough to have a full time rabbi M.

Eisenberg in 1897. By 1903, they built their own synagogue, the Temple of B'Nai Israel, on the corner of Galena and Washington Streets. The temple was formally dedicated on February 26, 1904, by Rabbi Jacob Melziner of Helena. It was only the second Jewish synagogue built in Montana with the first being located in Helena. The Butte synagogue was one of the first built west of the Continental Divide in the United States.

The Jewish Orthodox congregation called the Adath Israel also built their own synagogue on Silver Street near the Emma Mine prior to 1900; however, the synagogue lasted only a short time before closing.

There was also a Jewish Conservative congregation that met briefly in the Knights of Pythias Hall on South Main Street before joining together with the B'Nai Israel.

The Jewish people did not cluster in any one section of town, but were scattered throughout the community. The largest concentration of Jewish people was in Central Butte on Utah, Colorado, Wyoming and Platinum Streets. The peek of the Jewish population came in 1906 when 400 folks called the community home. Since then, the population has fallen off sharply especially after a dramatic drop in the copper prices following the end of World War I.

Despite the fact there are only 30 Jewish families living in Butte at the end of the 20th century, the B'Nai Israel synagogue remains open as a symbol of their faith. Through the years, there have been 21 different rabbis that have served at the Temple of B'Nai Israel. Some have only been present during High Holydays around the celebration of Yom Kippur which for the Jewish community is the Day of Atonement. The last full time rabbi serving in Butte was Ilene Melamed who left town in 1989. Since then, the Butte Jewish community has been served once a month by a student rabbi who comes to town from Hebrew Union College in Los Angeles. The student rabbi can perform every Jewish service except a marriage. The presence of a student rabbi has allowed the Jewish community to continue celebrating their faith. It also makes the temple of B'Nai Israel the oldest synagogue in the Western United States holding continuous services in the 20th century.

Greece

Only a handful of Greeks came to town. They avoided the mines and concentrated their efforts in operating local restaurants. The Greeks ran a number of places in the business district like the Lelland Cafe, State Cafe, Creamery Cafe and Carkulis' Hamburger Shop. Some Greek treats were lamb, bean soup, beef with onions and stuffed grape leaves.

They followed the Greek Orthodox religion and held services at various locations. One place of worship was in Central Butte at the former location of the Welsh Presbyterian Church on the corner of Aluminum and Dakota Streets. The Greeks took over the church in 1960 and held services at the location until 1977.

Lebanon

The number of people from Lebanon who came here was not large, but they did have an impact in the community.

The Lebanese, like the Greeks, avoided the mines and put their efforts into retail business. They were noted for selling vegetables, clothes and other items in carts that were hauled around town. The salesmen would go door-to-door selling their products.

Like a number of groups, the Lebanese stuck together. They primarily found housing on the East Side in an area referred to as Syrian Town on East Galena Street.

A binding force for the entire group was the formation of the Syrian Peace Society in June 1908. It is the oldest society of its kind in the United States. The goal of the group was to free their people from the rule by Syria. In defiance of the Syrians, the name of the organization was switched to Lebanon Peace Society in 1921 some 22 years before Lebanon gained independence from Syria in 1943. They held meetings in local homes until a meeting hall was constructed and put into use in May 1929 on East Galena Street. Once in operation, the Lebanon Peace Society Hall served as the site for meetings, wedding receptions, concerts and other events. The lodge hall was torn down by The Anaconda Company in the 1970s, but a second hall was built on Paxson Street on Butte's South Side.

A popular activity during wedding receptions was to do "al debke," a Lebanese dance entailing stomping your feet.

The Lebanese people were strong church-going people who followed the Roman Catholic faith.

Spain

The number of Spaniards was small. They were first recruited to work in Butte by William Clark at his smelter operations. Later, they labored in the underground mines.

The Spanish, like their Mediterranean neighbors the Italians and Serbians, were assigned to work in the hottest mines.

The influence of the Spanish is not great in Butte; however, the ingredients for one of the city's most popular dishes, the tamale, can be traced back to Spanish roots. The Italians are also given credit for the dish through the use of the pasta corn meal surrounding the ingredients.

Mexico

Mexicans played a significant role in Butte's development. A number of Mexican miners traveled north looking for work underground after the start of the 20th Century. Due to their late arrival on the scene, the Mexicans could only find employment in the hot mines like the Belmont.

Located on Butte's East Side, the Belmont Mine area served as one of the primary settlement locations for the Mexican people. A large number of Mexican families lived in Central Butte. By the 1920's, there were over 2,000 Mexican people in town.

The Mexicans brought a special religious celebration to Butte, the feast of Our Lady of Guadeloupe. The day is commemorated on December 12 every year with an elaborate Catholic mass said in Spanish. Our Lady of Guadeloupe is the patron saint of Mexico.

Africa

Two to three thousand African-Americans called the mining camp their hometown prior to 1900.

The local unions took whatever steps were necessary to discriminate against blacks and keep them from digging in the mines. Black people were not allowed underground, forcing them to take service jobs like hotel and railroad porters, coachmen, barbers, janitors, waiters and maids.

The black population had a pair of newspapers in the town. *The Butte Advocate* was published in 1896 by Frank Beach. There was also *The New Age* which began publication in 1902 and remained in business for a year.

The blacks had their own fraternal club, the Silver City Lodge No. 9 of the Masons which held bi-monthly meetings at the Bethel Baptist Church located on the corner of Idaho and Mercury Streets. Another church for the black community was a Methodist Church located on Arizona and Second Street.

The most popular black night spot was the Silver City Club operated by Frank Yarner on Main Street. Yarner was a key black leader in the community. He was instrumental in getting many high-profile black athletes like Satchel Paige to come perform in Butte. It was through his efforts other black folks got an opportunity to display their athletic abilities. The Colored Giants, a baseball team of black athletes with some Butte players, toured Montana and all corners of the region taking on all comers. They played a number of their games at Clark Park.

August Holtse, an African-American, became the head football coach at Butte High in 1913. He led the Bulldogs to the state title beating Billings 7-6 in a controversial championship game. After the contest, the Billings people called the Butte players "bullies" for their rough play during the title game. Billings school officials refused to play Butte High School for three years. One of Holtse's star players, Buddy Phelps, was also black.

The role of Butte's black population diminished in the 1920s. Jobs were scarce especially after the mines were shut down for nine months in 1921. It forced a large majority of the black population to leave town looking for opportunities elsewhere.

There was a major effort by The Anaconda Company to bring blacks back to Butte during World War II to work in the mines. The local unions blocked The Company's move and after a short stay the blacks were put back on a train and left town.

China

One of the most colorful ethnic groups in Butte were the Chinese. Chinese men first came to the United States in large numbers during the 1849 California gold rush.

The main group of Chinese were from the Pearl River Delta, primarily an agriculture region. Yet, not all the Chinese who came to this country were farmers. A number had worked in foreign mining ventures before visiting California.

The Chinese began appearing in the area shortly after gold was discovered in the valley. It was common for the Chinese to follow the various gold rush booms. Because white men usually left an area once the easily discovered gold was gone, this left the Chinese to rework claims and, in many cases, show remarkable results.

By the early 1870s, there were only 200 people in Butte with the Chinese making up half of the camp's entire population. In 1875, Butte's silver rush changed the role for the Chinese. They were kept out of the mines and were confined to service work cutting wood, cooking food and cleaning laundry.

The important role of cutting wood for the underground shafts came down to a confrontation between the Chinese and the French-Canadians. There was bloodshed between the two sides in the 1880s as both muscled for control of the timber industry. The French-Canadians won the battle and the Chinese were forced to give up the work.

The Chinese were resourceful in the laundry business with their "washee washee." It was a profitable industry because of all the single miners working in town. Rather than wash their own clothes, the miners found it much easier and more convenient to take their clothes to a Chinese laundry. They were spread out around the community with over 40 operations doing business prior to 1900.

The industry started to lose many of its best customers when the single miners got married. Only fifteen laundries were left by 1915 and only nine by 1930. The business eventually was washed out when the final Chinese laundry, Quong Fong, at 329 South Arizona Street closed in 1968.

The Chinese love for gambling was displayed in Chinatown. The game of "fan-tan" or dominoes was a favorite among the Chinese. There was also a contest called "Chuck-a-Luck" which was the early form of the modern day game of keno. While the games were being played shrill Chinese music could be heard in the background.

A number of the Chinese gaming houses were protected by hatchet men who demanded money to keep the gambling parlors open and free of law enforcement people. The hatchet men also protected business people who operated opium dens in tunnels underground below Chinatown.

The Chinese carried on many of their traditional celebrations including their annual New Year's party. The celebration in late January or early February included firecrackers, paper mache figures like dragons and dancers in the streets.

The Chinese built a joss house for meetings and ancestral worship. Some of their customs were unique to other Butte residents like a traditional Chinese burial. As the mourners carried the corpse to Mount Moriah Cemetery, people tossed bits of paper in front of the procession to ward off evil spirits. The streams of paper had lots of holes which were to force demons to go through the holes, thus keeping them away from the corpse. When the corpse was buried the Chinese placed food around the grave.

The height of Butte's Chinese population came around 1890 when 2,500 residents lived here. They settled Chinatown on Galena and Mercury Streets below the business district.

After 1890, the population slowly started to leave Butte. One reason for the decline was a labor union boycott in 1896 of Chinese businesses which forced Chinese merchants to lay off workers or close their business. By the end of World War I in 1918, there were only 300 Chinese still remaining in town.

The population was not large, but that did not stop a Chinese tong war from surfacing in 1922. The tong war broke out between the Bing

Kong and Hip Song tong groups. Tongs were business organizations largely developed along family lines. In a few short weeks, five people were killed in China Alley inside Chinatown. No one was ever convicted of murder during the war which spread across the country between the two groups.

Following the tong wars, the number of Chinese continued to decline with the few remaining working in restaurants.

The Chinese eating places survived numerous swings in the local economy. One establishment, the Pekin Noodle Parlor, started in 1909 still does business on South Main Street.

The Chinese were noted for their steamed pork, squab soup, eel, chicken, sweet ham, duck, chop suey egg rolls, sweet and sour pork plus fried rice.

Korea

A handful of Koreans and Japanese came to Butte. Of the two, the Koreans played a role in the mining camp. They lived and worked in the Flats near the Nine Mile. The Koreans were noted for creating elegant flower and truck gardens, irrigating from the vast water supply in the region. They made a living by growing and selling lettuce, onions, peas, radish and other vegetables raised at the Nine Mile.

"There were some large Korean families living in the Nine Mile area," Howie Wing said. "Some of the families had as many as 10 kids in a home. So they had lots of labor available to help them grow things."

The break out of World War II saw the Korean families leave the area for good-paying jobs at the shipyards on the west coast. They remained in their new locations after the War and thus the influence of the Koreans disappeared from Butte.

Native Americans

The first migration of people to Butte came from within North America. The American Indian did play a role in the Summit Valley before the white man found gold here. The Native Americans were roaming the region for years before the white man came into the valley. Elk bones were found near the Original Mine site by the first white man who came into the area. It was thought that the Indians had used the bones as tools for mining.

Once Butte started to develop, a tribe of Crees Indians established a camp in the valley near the city's original dump site. Later, the area was developed into the Stodden Park complex.

The Crees were joined by some Chippewa Indians. Yet, the Indian population never did grow in Butte like it did other parts of Montana. Many Native Americans were forced to live on one of seven Indian reservations developed in Montana. Thus, the Native American Indians played only a minor role in Butte's history.

The Next Step

It is remarkable to note just how many different ethnic groups came to Butte. It is even more remarkable how each tried to make a statement about their old homeland. The Lebanese developed the first Lebanese Peace Society in America. The Serbians built only the second Serbain Orthodox Church in the United States. The Jewish community constructed the first synagogue west of the Continental Divide. The President of the Irish Republic made Butte one of his key stops in building support for the Free Irish State. The Butte Croatians and Slovenians had one of the few annual Mesopust celebrations in the country. The Cornish could read "Notes from Cornwall" in the *Tribune Review* newspaper.

The ethnic display of the old homeland would eventually give way to the pride of being Americans as the various groups started to mesh together in Butte's neighborhoods.

REFERENCES USED IN CHAPTER THREE

1939 Inventory of County Archives of Montana by Work Projects Administration

US Department of Justice report on the investigation for the use of military force to quell domestic disturbances in Butte, Montana

Copper Camp written by Bill Burke published in 1943

Sketches of Old Butte written by Jacob Ostberg published in 1972

Butte Heritage Cookbook edited by Jean McGrath published in 1976

The Speculator Summer Edition 1984 written by Butte Historical Society

The Speculator Winter Edition 1985 written by Butte Historical Society

Champagne in a Tea Cup written by George Everett published in 1995

The Montana Standard newspaper

The Butte Daily Post newspaper

Butte Archives

1996 interview Maurine Higman Dennehy

1997 interview Mike Gribben

1997 interview	Cathy Brozovich James
1998 interview	Elelyn Eva
1998 interview	Rich Holman
1998 interview	Lee Masters
1998 interview	Bob McCarthy
1998 interview	Al Niemi
1998 interview	Angelo Petroni
1998 interview	Father Sarsfield O'Sullivan
1998 interview	Tom Powers
1998 interview	John Shea
1998 interview	Ann Simonich
1998 interview	Howie Wing

Holy Trinity Serbian Orthodox Church
photo courtesy Pat Kearney

Castletown Bere, County Cork, Ireland
photo courtesy Pat Kearney

Dublin Gulch Irish musical group
photo courtesy Pat Kearney

Irish dancers in Butte on St. Patrick's Day
photo courtesy Pat Kearney

St. Patrick's Day in Butte
photos courtesy Pat Kearney

Holy Savior Church - photo courtesy Jerry Bugni

Preparing lutefisk dinner at Gold Hill Lutheran Church
photo courtesy Pat Kearney

Serving Lutefisk dinner - photo courtesy Pat Kearney

B'Nai Israel Jewish synagogue
photo courtesy Pat Kearney

Chinese people in Butte
photo courtesy World Museum of Mining

Satchel Paige in Butte
photo courtesy
Martin Kearney

CHAPTER FOUR

Neighborhoods

Once they settled in Butte, it was common for people from the same country to locate in the same neighborhood. In many cases, relatives or neighbors provided the fare so new immigrants could come to Butte.

A majority of the new arrivals did not know the English language and were not familiar with American customs. So, for them, being around people they could talk to plus share similar experiences with was important. They also had to learn how to deal with other ethnic groups, some of whom were not friendly to the new citizens.

"It was like going into a different country every time you entered a different neighborhood," said Bob Kissell, a former driver for the Meaderville Mercantile Store. "Everyone was nice and friendly, but everyone had their own value system and way of doing business."

Each neighborhood had its own unique characteristics. Some were loaded with one dominant ethnic group, while others were tied together by a geographic region, a nearby mine or a common work place. The neighborhoods were where Butte developed its American roots. Many of Butte's neighborhoods are still active, while others have become a distant memory.

Big Butte is nestled at the base of the Big Butte overlooking the community and from which the city gets its name. The neighborhood was bordered on the north by Zarelda Street, the south by Caledonia Street, the east by the Syndicate Pit, Missoula Gulch, and Anselmo Mine, and west by the Big Butte.

Because Big Butte was a couple of miles northwest of the business district, it was a small neighborhood until local officials decided to construct a new street car line from the business district, west to Excelsior Street and north to Walkerville. The new line, built in 1897, replaced an unsafe system that went north to Walkerville up Main Street.

The trolley car was the key ingredient to growth not only in Big Butte, but in many other neighborhoods. Public transportation allowed people living in the business district a chance to branch out into the valley and the western section of the hill.

Once the trolley car was making regular runs up Excelsior Street, the Big Butte neighborhood grew rapidly. The construction boom period lasted 16 years from 1900 to 1916. During that short time, more than half the homes in the area were built. By 1920, the neighborhood stretched up the hill to Hornet Street. To keep up with the development, city officials installed a new water and sewer system for the region.

This hilly neighborhood provided some very interesting homes located on some rather unusual surroundings. Residential units on the north side of the street usually were 5 to 10 feet higher than the actual street level. Numerous retaining walls and stairways were constructed so residents could reach their front doors. Right across the street was the exact opposite problem with homes below street level, so stairs had to be laid down a slope to reach the front entrance.

The neighborhood was tied together by location. The area saw a wide mixture of working class people and ethnic groups. Miners occupied more than 50 percent of the homes; however, there were also doctors, lawyers, and other professional people who owned houses in the neighborhood. There were both multi-unit homes and single dwellings.

Even though Big Butte was connected to the business district by the trolley car system, it was a long ride downtown. And so, like many other areas, Big Butte developed its own trade center. At one time, the region had 10 different grocery stores, including Big Butte Grocery, Doran's, Aguirre's, Manion Dairy, Excelsior Meats, and the Eclipse Store There was also the Big Butte Tavern, the Centennial Brewery, and a bakery plus a fire station located at the corner of Excelsior and Caledonia Streets. The fire station would remain in operation until the 1940s.

In addition to nearby stores, work was within a short walking distance. Close by were four major mines: the Anselmo, Sulvadore, Hope and Mount Moriah.

A common trait other neighborhoods had which Big Butte lacked was a number of schools and churches. Big Butte was much different because the only church and school built in the region was the Immaculate Conception Catholic Church. The parish was formed in 1906. A church and school were constructed the following year at the corner of Western and Caledonia Streets. A parish hall and gym were built on Western Street in 1935 at a cost of $50,000.

A couple of years later, in 1938, construction on a new $200,000 church was started across the street from the parish hall by the John Link Company. The Immaculate Conception Church features a white pillar steeple towering 160 feet high. The white church on the hill became a prominent landmark. The old church/school building was remodeled and turned into a school serving in that capacity until the Butte Catholic School Board decided to close it in 1982. The educational center was turned into an archery range by a local group.

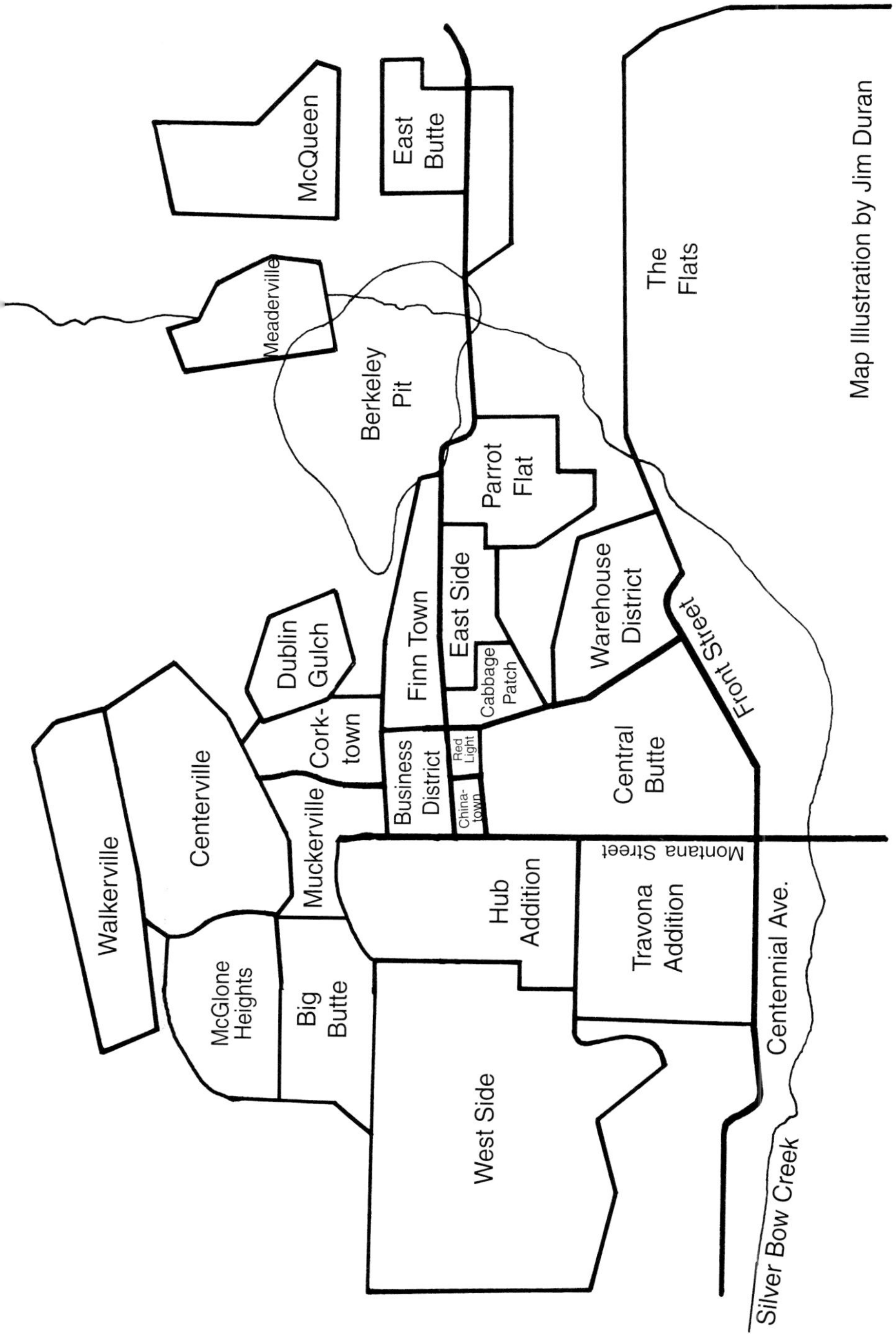

Map Illustration by Jim Duran

The Butte Public School Board did not decide to construct a school in the neighborhood until 1958. Big Butte Elementary School was built at the north base of the Big Butte. The name of the school was changed to the John F. Kennedy Elementary School on November 26, 1963, four days after the President of the United States had been killed in Dallas, Texas.

Another form of transportation, the automobile, changed the scope of the area just as much as the street car. The automobile allowed residents a chance to move more freely and not depend so much on local neighborhood stores. Big Butte saw its 10 area grocery stores dwindle down to 3 by the 1950s and be sliced down to a Town Pump convenience store by the 1990s. As the stores dwindled, so did the feeling of a united neighborhood, which became a common theme experienced by many neighborhoods in the city.

Boulevard located below Front Street along South Montana Street, was bordered on the east by swamp land, the south by Timber Butte and a series of cemeteries, the west by Williamsburg and the Colorado Smelter tailings, and the north by a number of railroad tracks and the Butte Reduction Plant.

The neighborhood started to develop roots prior to the turn of the 20th century. There were enough families and homes in the region to lead to the construction of a public elementary school, the Madison, in 1896.

The turn of the century in 1900 marked the start of a tremendous growth period for the Boulevard. Southern European immigrants were flooding into Butte searching for jobs and moving into the Boulevard looking for homes.

One main ethnic group, the Croatians, clustered into the Boulevard and dominated. The impact of the Croatians could be reflected in the local public school. The Madison School had to be expanded in 1916, just 20 short years after it was first built. The school underwent another expansion in 1955, but this was due to the World War II baby boom generation not the influx of new immigrants.

The Boulevard was a small neighborhood in terms of population and territory. The homes were simple in nature with the residents working mainly in labor-intense jobs like underground mining and at the Butte Reduction Plant, which later was called the Domestic Manganese Development Plant. The plant, built by William Clark in 1905, featured a stack which stood 352 feet tall. It was later reduced 105 feet in 1953 when cracks developed on the concrete stack. The plant closed in 1959 and was torn down.

A major recreational center, the Holland Rink, was located on the northern edge of the Boulevard. The rink was built and opened for the first time in 1889 by Jim Byrne. Later his son Paul took over the management duties. Through the help of A. E. H. Clarke, an early day organizer of skating, many activities like skating, hockey and speedskating were established for youngsters at the Holland Rink.

Tubie Johnson remembered, "We sure had a lot of fun playing hockey at the Holland Rink. All the kids rolled up *Life* magazines around their lower legs to use as protection when they got hit with the puck. We had no other type of padding or helmets to use. All we had was a stick."

A large wooden fence encircled the rink until 1946 when one side of the barrier collapsed. Rather than repair the structure, local officials elected to abandon the Holland Rink in favor of the facility at Clark Park.

The nearby ponds of the Colorado Smelter operations also attracted kids.

"I recall playing in those copper ponds as a boy and having lots of fun," said Art Korn. "Heck, we played there all the time. We also spent a lot of time at the Clark Mill up in Timber Butte. You know many of us lived to our 80s and they talk about how dangerous those places were because its a so-called health hazard."

The center of activities for adults in the neighborhood was the Boulevard Fire Hall which was built thanks to funds supplied by William Clark. The fire hall served Clark's needs well if a fire broke out at his nearby Clark Mill.

At the Boulevard Fire Hall, the Croatian people celebrated Mesopust just prior to Lent. The location of the ceremony had to be changed in 1962 after the hall was torn down to make way for a new Interstate highway.

The Interstate split the neighborhood into two sections and the area never was the same again. A number of longtime residents were forced to relocate because of the new highway, putting an end to the neighborhood feeling developed in the Boulevard. It was one of Butte's only ethnic neighborhoods disrupted not by Berkeley Pit shovels, but instead by the progress of interstate commerce.

Brown's Gulch is an agricultural region just northwest of Butte. The Brown's Gulch area, which spread for miles along dirt roads and through valleys, provided prime country for raising cattle and growing hay.

The lure of the farm attracted large Italian families to the region around 1900. The opportunity to get back to their roots suited the Italians because it allowed them a chance to do the same type of work they performed in the old country.

The main occupation was raising dairy and beef cattle, then bringing their products to market in Butte. The options for dairy farmers were sell their product to local merchants or deal with one of two co-op creameries. Both creameries, the Crystal Creamery and Western Creamery located on Main Street, had been established by local farmers. When ranchers brought their beef to town for sale, they had similar options, sell to local merchants directly or sell through the local stockyard.

Farming and ranching were time consuming and weren't providing the real cash crop for most farmers. "The real money for residents in Brown's Gulch was logging," said Dula Schonsberg. "It was tough making ends meet raising cattle and selling dairy products. So most of the farmers cut down logs on their property and sold them to The Anaconda Company for wood in the mines. Farmers made good money doing it and that allowed them to keep their ranches in operation."

Kevin Shannon said, "I recall as a child growing up in Brown's Gulch seeing how bare the hills were because of all the logging. The Italians were great for making logging profitable so they could spend more time in the dairy business."

Logging was not the only lucrative pursuit in Brown's Gulch. During Prohibition, the area became a haven for large moonshine operations. The Italians, experienced in making grappo, capitalized on that trade to feed their families.

"There were thousands and thousands of gallons of grappo and moonshine made in Brown's Gulch during Prohibition," said Al Hooper. "I recall one time workers were having problems with the pump on one of the bigger stills. They went into town and hired a guy who was familiar with pumps to come out and fix it. Before taking the man to their still, they blindfolded him until they got to their operation. Once he finished, they blindfolded him again and returned him to Butte. They were not going to take any chance of local authorities finding out where their still was located."

Federal officials were hard pressed to find the stills that were set up in Brown's Gulch. When they did discover a still, they normally had a gun battle with the moonshiners. One such gun battle took place in February 1923 when federal officials located a moonshine distillery 13 miles north of Butte. After a gun battle, federal officials seized a 50-gallon still, 20 gallons of moonshine and 1,500 gallons of mash used to make grappo.

Moonshine was taken to Butte in milk bottles that were painted white. One truck driver was picked up in September 1920 with a full load of moonshine. When federal officials were done investigating the truck driver's connections, they had seized over $65,000 in liquor and drugs.

Due to the distance from town, all the Brown's Gulch farmers had to be self-sufficient. The dairy and beef cows provided milk and meat. Farmers also raised some crops in the small valleys of Brown's Gulch.

The great distance between farms also made it tough on children trying to get an education and so three schools were established in the Brown's Gulch area: one in Flume Gulch, a second near the Pene ranch and the third near the Simon ranch.

The modernization of the beef and dairy industry had a severe impact on Brown's Gulch farmers. As the demand for their products decreased, so did the number of family farms in the region. It led to the closure of all three area schools. The dream of farming and raising cattle still remains in Brown's Gulch, but the glory days with lots of people and plenty of activity are long gone.

Burlington was a small mining camp just northwest of Butte and the Montana Tech campus. It was located about a mile northeast of Rocker.

Prior to 1900, the town of Burlington had over 700 residents. The Cornish dominated the town which featured a post office, general store, one-room school house and a number of bars. During its early days, a stage line transported residents into Butte.

A few boarding houses housed local miners. One of the boarding houses was operated by Will Masters who came to Butte in the 1880s seeking his fortune. Masters also ran a saloon with his brother-in-law called the Masters & Sampson Saloon.

The main source for employment was local mines in the area: the Bluebird, Great Republic and Black Warrior. The largest operation was the Bluebird, owned and managed by Frederick Van Zandt. Besides the mine, the operation had its own mill for refining ore.

Times were good in Burlington until the Silver Panic of 1893 which almost wiped out silver mining across the country. The Silver Panic had a tremendous impact on the community as the number one source of employment was gone and soon the people followed.

There was a brief hope for Burlington folks in 1906 when six local dairy farmers got into full production nearby. The dairy business was strong until 1915 when a slow down meant the end of Burlington. The last family left in 1937 and Burlington, the once bustling mining camp, became Burlington, the ghost town.

Butchertown was located north of Walkerville a short distance beyond the Alice Pit. The small cluster of homes were named after Rollo Butcher, the man who started the Alice Mine in the 1870s. He sold his mine interests to the Walker Brothers of Salt Lake City and their representative, Marcus Daly, in 1876.

The Alice Mine was a top silver producer in the 1870s and Butchertown grew as a result of the mine's success. The advent of copper mining in the 1880s turned the attention of many away from the Alice and Butchertown. The small group of homes continued to be occupied for a number of years, but continued on through other commerce. A number of families in the Butchertown area raised dairy cows and took their milk products to sell in Walkerville and Butte. Besides the dairy industry, Butchertown served as the home for a large slaughter house.

The small group of homes eventually disappeared with only the Pesanti ranch remaining. It was the last symbol of Butchertown which became just a memory to many residents in the region.

Cabbage Patch was just southeast of Butte's central business district. It consisted of the Hesperus and Hopkins Additions being bordered on the north by the Colorado Mine, east by the East Side, south by the Warehouse District, and west by Arizona Street.

The region was located on an old mining claim known as Mahoney's Lode. There were many people who claimed to own the surface and mineral rights to the area. Multiple ownership created problems in the neighborhood with constant battles between landlords over who legally owned a certain piece of property. Each landlord demanded the renters to pay them and not the other disputed property owner. It led to confusion for renters who many times refused to pay anyone. No money coming in kept landlords from maintaining their property and the numerous homes and other dwellings in the area were left rundown or vacant.

The Cabbage Patch was one of the first sections of Butte that was settled in the 1880s. It was a rundown eyesore because the common link among residents was poverty. The Cabbage Patch was filled with shabby shacks, shanties and unpainted dwellings. Some shacks were built from dry goods and grocery pine boxes. They were further eroded by people raiding local shacks, taking out all of the available wood so they could heat their own homes during the winter.

For many years there was no running water or toilet facilities in any neighborhood homes. There was a nearby spring, but residents refused to take water from the well because they felt the water was full of poison.

Matt Vucurovich recalled, "You tried to avoid walking through the Cabbage Patch if you could. It could really smell bad there because residents threw raw sewage out into the street. They had no plumbing or anything else there. It was a real mess."

The rundown conditions produced the poorest of the poor living in the Cabbage Patch. It was also home for bootleggers, dope peddlers, criminals and prostitutes who worked in nearby brothels. Crime was a major problem with numerous knifings and shootings. It was a haven from which criminals ran their operations, sheltered away from the police. Local law enforcement officials were busy all the time with activities going on around the Cabbage Patch.

"I recall lots of widows with very little money trying to raise their kids in those rundown conditions in the Cabbage Patch," remembered Bob Koprivica. "It was especially tough because they had no welfare or anything else to supplement their income."

The neighborhood dictated not only the type of residents it attracted, but also the quality of stores in the region. There were only a couple of second-hand stores, third-class restaurants and a Chinese laundry. One of the busiest stores was at the southern tip of the Cabbage Patch. It was called "the house of a million parts" because it was here that a person could get an auto part for almost any vehicle being driven in the 1920s and 1930s.

A major plus for the Cabbage Patch was a local fire station located at the northern edge of the neighborhood at the corner of Mercury and Arizona Streets. The fire house was one of four in Butte during the 1920s.

Local officials rejoiced when the Cabbage Patch came tumbling down during the spring of 1940. Workers destroyed 225 rundown units in the area. The region was taken over by the Butte Housing Authority who constructed the Silver Bow Homes. The housing project consisted of 225 individual apartment style units in two-story buildings, designed as housing for low income families.

The Silver Bow Homes Project resulted from the Federal Housing Act, New Deal legislation passed in 1937. The city received $1 million in federal aid to help destroy the Cabbage Patch and replace it with the Silver Bow Homes.

Esther Zanon Judd recalled, "It forced a lot of people to leave the area when they tore the Cabbage Patch down. Of course, it was a big improvement when they finished the Silver Bow Homes. They claimed the people in the Cabbage Patch were desperate which was not the truth. There were a lot of good families that lived in the neighborhood. I believe that people really got the wrong impression about the Cabbage Patch."

The Silver Bow Homes were completed in the spring of 1941, and the first residents moved into their new homes on May 9, 1941. Through time the units became rundown, but local officials were able to acquire funding to remodel the entire housing project in the 1990s.

The Silver Bow Homes provided the region with a cleaner environment, but it did not rid the neighborhood of trouble. Law enforcement officers had to consistently visit the homes through the years to take care of problems. Despite the constant troubles, the overall goal established by the Butte Housing Authority was achieved with the Silver Bow Homes. It provided low income families with better housing plus at the same time got rid of Butte's biggest eyesore, the Cabbage Patch.

Centerville north of the central business district on the Butte hill, is bordered on the north by Bennett Street and Walkerville, east by numerous mines, south by Boardmen Street and west by Missoula Gulch.

Centerville was in the heart of the mining district with many mines within easy walking distance of the neighborhood. The primary operation was the Mountain Con. Other mines in the region included the Mountain View, Diamond, Moonlight, Raven and Buffalo Mines.

"In its hey-day Centerville was filled with activity," remembered Rich Holman. "There were trains going day and night to the various mines hauling ore from Butte to the smelter in Anaconda."

The community grew with the expansion of mining. A cluster of homes during the 1870s silver boom turned into a vast well-established neighborhood in the 1880s with the advent of copper mining.

Centerville homes were simple in nature and built close to mines with little thought given to planning and street design. Homes were everywhere and resulted in lots of problems during Centerville's early development years. The most pressing problem dealt with health conditions. The scattered Centerville homes made it very difficult to develop a water and sewer system. For many years Centerville lacked both water and sewer lines which meant no toilet facilities. The outhouses in the area were still being used in the 1950s.

Lack of proper sewers combined with garbage piled up everywhere resulted in a foul odor throughout neighborhood. Despite the rundown conditions, Centerville was near work and so families tolerated the poor sanitary conditions for employment.

Because the area was home for the city's two largest ethnic groups, the Cornish and the Irish, ethnic pride was a dominant theme in the neighborhood. Neither group was fond of the other so the neighborhood was a war zone for ethnic superiority, especially in the early days. The ethnic clash could be illustrated in the various types of businesses located along Main and Center Streets. Each group supported its own barber shop, paint store, plumbing store, drug store, meat market, grocery store and clothing stores. It was an unwritten rule never to do business with the other side. An example was getting a haircut. The Irish went to Bill

McCarthy's shop, while the Cornish traveled to Jim Rowe's place.

Evelyn Eva said, "The one thing I liked so much about Centerville was you had everything you ever needed right there. You never had to go down the hill into Butte to pick up anything. You had places like T. J. Bennett's dry goods store on the first floor of the Sons of St. George's Hall where you could buy anything from cotton to whiskey."

Both sides displayed their heritage in Centerville with large massive halls. There was the Sons of St. George Hall on the corner of Main and Center Streets for the Cornish with the brick building being constructed in the 1880s. Less than a block down Main Street stood the Irish's Hibernia Hall for the Ancient Order of Hibernians. It was here the Irish carried on their traditions from the old country through song and dance. The Hibernia Hall had a saloon, store and a handball court.

Each group went out of its way to support political or religious holidays. St. George's Day on April 23 plus the Daughters of St. George Day on May 24 were always big events for the Cornish, while St. Patrick's Day on March 17 was the grand day for the Irish.

Religious preference was displayed through churches. In 1887, the Cornish constructed the Trinity Methodist Church on Main Street, while the Irish built St. Lawrence Catholic Church at the top of the hill just inside the Walkerville city limits in 1897.

"They can talk all they want about how the Irish and Cornish never got along in Centerville," said Eva. "That is simply not true. Our Cornish family lived next to a Sullivan family of Irish descent with 10 kids. We got along just fine. Oh, there was an argument once in awhile and maybe some fisticuffs, but for the most part the Irish and Cornish got along just fine."

Jim Hanley recalled, "I really think the hatred between the Irish and Cornish was confined to the immigrants and maybe the first generation of Americans. When it came to my era as a second-generation American, a lot of the bitterness between the two sides was gone. It was especially evident after the end of World War II when you started to see some intermarriages between the two groups."

Rich Holman remembered, "My father was Cornish and his best friend was Mike Harrington, an Irishman. They used to tease each other to death with my father calling Mike a 'Damn Wop' and Mike countering by calling my dad a 'Cousin Jack Bastard.' It looked like they were always mad at each other, but they were the best of friends. I mean either man would go into a burning building to save the other."

John Shea said, "If there was any trouble up in Centerville, it was not between the Cornish and Irish. The real trouble was between the kids from Centerville and Walkerville. There were lots of problems when those two groups got together. The Centerville kids went to the Dream Theater in Walkerville on Saturday afternoon. Once that show was over, you were expected to get back over that hill where you belonged. If you didn't, there'd be trouble brewing with the Walkerville gang and the local sheriff, Mike Peters."

When the Centerville kids were not mixing it up with the Walkerville bunch, they enjoyed activities like clubhouses. They built a couple of large cabins called the Snakehouse Clubhouse and Decker Stadium. The clubhouses were decorated with movie posters obtained from local theaters.

Mullen Field offered kids a chance to play at night because the street lights were turned on around the field. The kids could also watch the Centerville football team practice in the fall prior to a match in the Independent Football League.

Centerville was one of the main neighborhoods in town where miners lived in boarding houses. One of the largest boarding places in the district was the Mullen House operated by Paddy and Nora Harrington of County Cork, Ireland.

"Paddy and Nora Harrington were my grandparents," Hanley said. "It was a lot of work for them to run that place. As a kid I had to help them by feeding and milking cows every day. The cows were kept behind the boarding house. During the winter time, I was required to haul coal and wood to the upper floors to help keep the place warm. There was just a ton of work that went into keeping up that place. They had lots of cooks and other workers who were always cooking something or making lunch buckets for the miners which was part of the rent. It was like operating a large-scale hotel."

Constructed by Pat Mullen in 1888, the three-story building was located at the corner of Main and Mullen Streets. Mullen House served as the home for hundreds of miners at one time. The boarding house had 125 rooms with over 300 miners calling it home during its peak operation period. In addition to serving as a boarding house, the first floor of the Mullen House was home to a branch of the Hennessy's Store.

Emmett Cronnelly recalled, "Nora Harrington really ran a tight ship at the Mullen House. A number of the miners could not read or write, so they did what was called a 'sign over.' The miners at the Mullen House signed over their checks to Mrs. Harrington. She collected their wages in cash at The Anaconda Company pay window every week. When the miners came to get their money, Nora took so much out of their pay for rent and other things that they owed her for. She got their rent money before the miner could take off and spend it at a bar or somewhere else in town. There were a lot of landlords of boarding houses who required miners to do a sign over as part of their condition to stay at a certain rooming house."

The Mullen House primarily catered to Irish miners, but there were also a few Italians, Greeks and Finns who stayed at the place.

Cronnelly said, "A big difference between the Irish and Cornish miners in Centerville was their marital status. A lot of the Irish were single men who stayed in boarding establishments like the Mullen House, while the Cornish miners were mainly married with families and homes in Cousin Jack Gulch or near Sutter Street and Tin Can Alley behind the Sons' of St. George Hall."

All the miners and boarding houses made Centerville a prime location for bars. There were plenty of watering holes, like the Klondike, Boyle's Eagle, Buckley's, Casey's and Paddy the Dig within easy walking distance.

Because Centerville was one of Butte's earliest developing areas, it has the distinction of housing one of the city's first public schools, Adams School, on Center Street.

Centerville remained a major neighborhood until many of the underground mining operations were shut down. The closure of the Mountain Con in 1975 was a crushing blow to Centerville.

"Centerville was always a mining haven," said Holman. "I believe everyone thought mining would last forever. It was a real shock and blow when they shut down the Mountain Con."

A lack of work in the area forced many residents to leave the neighborhood and the community for good. As people left, so did much of Centerville's flavor. The local stores and bars closed, and the two massive ethnic halls were both torn down. The neighborhood still remains, but the colorful heart and soul of its past is now just a distant memory.

Central Butte located below the main business district, is, in terms of territory, one of Butte's largest, bordered on the west by Montana Street, south by Front Street, east by Arizona Street, and north by Mercury Street.

The neighborhood was filled mainly with working class people. Many residents were miners; some worked in the business district, while other labored in the Warehouse District just east of the neighborhood. There were some stores and a couple of warehouses in the region. The Emma Mine was also here located on Dakota Street. The mine's unusual location in the middle of a large neighborhood forced The Anaconda Company to build an ore train line up Montana Street to get to the site.

Railroad lines were a key feature in the neighborhood with a majority of the lines running along Iron Street through the mid-section of the neighborhood. The trains were the main means of transportation for many hobos during the Great Depression. They jumped off the locomotive near Iron Street in search of a meal at nearby homes.

The region included many simple homes and a large number of four-unit apartment buildings, as well as large apartment buildings such as the Tripp and Drastedt.

Central Butte with its large size provided plenty of room for numerous ethnic groups, including the Welsh, Irish, Jews, Africans, Chinese, Mexicans, Norwegians, Finns, Swedes and Danes. The influence of the Scandinavians - the Norwegians, Finns, Swedes and Danes was reflected in the Scandinavian Hall built in 1898 on South Main Street. The Scandinavian impact was also evident in the Gold Hill Lutheran Church on Placer Street and the Emmanuel Lutheran Church constructed on South Montana Street.

The Welsh had a strong influence especially near Iron and Aluminum Streets. They built a Welsh Church on the corner of Aluminum and Dakota Streets.

The Irish had a dominant cluster of folks living along Second Street between Main and Arizona Streets. A symbol of their strength was the St. Joseph's Catholic Church and School built on the corner of Arizona and Second Streets in 1907. The church/school building was destroyed by fire on February 1, 1911, and a new church plus separate school building were later constructed.

The Jews and Mexicans never had one large concentrated group of people in a particular area, but rather they were spread throughout the region.

A reflection of the growth in Central Butte can be directly traced to the school system. The Garfield School was built in 1892 and enlarged in 1907. Among its students from various ethnic groups, the school at Colorado and Porphyry Streets served many Chinese families that lived nearby.

The Garfield School closed in 1949 to make way for the new $680,000 school, the Webster-Garfield. The elementary center on the corner of Front and Montana Streets was south of a section of Central Butte called the Rowe Addition. The new school served students from the Garfield School of Central Butte and the Webster School from the Travona Addition. The grade school was later converted into an alternative school for students.

The neighborhood changed enormously thanks to education. A new Butte Public High School was built, opening in 1937 on the corner of Wyoming and Gold Streets. The funds for the new $800,000 school were obtained through a local tax bond issue and federal money obtained from the WPA program.

The history of Butte High School dates back to 1884. The first lessons were taught in some temporary classrooms in the business district. The first graduation ceremony took place at the Miners' Unions Hall on Main Street in 1886 with student, P. W. Irvine, receiving a diploma.

Classes for high school students were moved into the newly built Washington School in Finn Town prior to 1890. By the fall of 1892, overcrowded conditions at the at the Granite Street school forced officials to rent classroom space in uptown office buildings. The overcrowded classrooms resulted in officials pushing for the construction of a new high school building.

In 1895, school officials began plans for a new high school at the corner of Idaho and Park Streets. The cornerstone for the new complex was laid on December 12, 1896. The school was completed in 1897, with students experiencing their first classes in the new building on January 3, 1898. John McKay served as the first principal at the new school, and the first graduation class of 1898 included 32 seniors. They wore purple gowns, the color of kings, during their graduation ceremonies. The color purple became a symbol of the school that was carried on through the decades.

Improvements were made to the high school building through the years with additional classroom space being constructed for manual and domestic arts. An auditorium, gymnasium and swimming pool were built at the school prior to 1915. Student numbers continued to increase through the years making the school overcrowded.

The new high school building became the main focal point for Central Butte. The new school was great for neighborhood business people. One of the popular spots for students to visit was the McGree Ice Cream Store at 500 South Main Street. It was a favorite place for students to get an ice cream cone, a pasty lunch or another meal.

An athletic complex was also constructed at the same time and completed in 1938. The football field, north of the high school, was called Butte High Stadium. The name was changed to Naranche Stadium on October 15, 1943, to honor former Butte High football player, Eso Naranche. Naranche grew up on the East Side. He was a two-time all-state football player for Butte High in 1936 and 1937, leading the Bulldogs to the state title in 1937. Eso went on to star for the University of Montana and played for the West team in the 1942 Shrine football game.

After football, Eso like thousands of other able-bodied young men during World War II, went into the Army. He was noted for his bravery while serving his country during the North African campaign. His military career came to an end on March 28, 1943, when Eso Naranche was killed trying to defend and hold a mountain pass.

Naranche Stadium held 10,000 fans for a football game and served as the home for high school, college and independent league games for many years. It was common to see thousands of cars parked in Central Butte during athletic events. Fans walked from their cars for blocks to get to the stadium.

Unfortunately, the wooden beams holding up the north grandstands of Naranche Stadium rotted away, making the stands unsafe. Officials decided to tear down rather than fix the grandstands following the 1973 football season. A major attraction for Central Butte was gone.

The same thing almost happened to the high school building. Butte High School became rundown from years of use and neglect. There was some discussion about building a new school on the Flats where a majority of the population was now living, but remodeling the existing structure won the debate. Butte High received new life after a $9 million bond issue was approved by voters in 1988. The entire school was remodeled and upgraded.

The high school building was saved, but the neighborhood surrounding it suffered through tough times. Central Butte lost a good share of its population as some people moved into better homes in other sections of town or through a lack of jobs and opportunities left Butte for good. The neighborhood became rundown with many old houses and apartments in desperate need of repair. The neighborhood once vibrant with various ethnic groups, schools and churches changed into an area just trying to survive.

Chicken Flats was located in Walkerville from the 500 and 600 blocks of Daly Street west to the town's edge at Dewey's Point. It was just a extension of Walkerville and even old-time residents are not sure why Chicken Flats got its name.

"They raised a lot of chickens and rabbits in the area," said Maurine Higman Dennehy, a Walkerville resident. "I guess that's why the area got its name."

Chinatown located just below Butte's business district between Main and Montana Streets, was, in terms of land mass one of the city's smallest, but one of the most crowded.

In 1876, the first Chinese cabin was built in the neighborhood. Other small huts followed in the tiny four-block area on Galena and Mercury Streets. In a short 20-year period, Chinatown grew to over 2,500 residents by the 1890s.

Because of the distinct culture of its inhabitants, Chinatown was much different from any other section of Butte with noodle parlors, laundry shops, herb shops, silk stores, opium dens, firecracker stores, underground tunnels, plus a flourishing drug trade. Its population prior to 1900 made it the second largest Chinatown west of the Mississippi River behind only San Francisco.

Residents retained the dress and customs of their homeland with braided queues, baggy trousers and blouses of silk or cotton. There was also colorful decorations on the brick buildings which replaced crude huts during a construction boom in the 1910s.

A favorite place for the Chinese was the joss house, a two-story pagoda-roofed building covered with elaborate embellishments. The first joss house, a place of meeting and worship, was constructed in 1886. One of the most elaborate joss homes was in China Alley between Galena and Mercury Streets.

China Alley was the heart of Chinatown. It was here you could see little old Chinese men sitting smoking pipes or witness the sale of almost anything, vegetables, fruit, poultry and opium.

Yet, the real live action of Chinatown was not above board, but actually underground. Law enforcement officials discovered many tunnels used for gambling and opium dens below China Alley. One raid by authorities on October 15, 1920, resulted in the arrest of 14 people for gambling. The tunnels connected various buildings along the alley.

At one time, there were a number of restaurants serving meals in Chinatown. One of the most famous was Mai Wah Noodle Parlor at 15 West Mercury Street operated by Quong Loy, the self-proclaimed "Mayor of Chinatown." The Mai Wah building was constructed in 1909 and was connected to the Wah Chong Tai Company which was Chinatown's version of a mini-shopping mall. The Wah Chong Tai mercantile store opened for business in 1899 with the completion of the building. The first floor of the building carried stock of imported Chinese items. There was also a herbal shop, restaurant, post office and lodging area inside the Wah Chong building. Both the Mai Wah and Wah Chong buildings shut down their operations in the 1940s after the end of World War II. A reason for the closures was the declining Chinese population in Butte because many had left the area during the war to seek employment on the West Coast.

Another Chinese restaurant stood the test of time, the Pekin Noodle Parlor. It was opened for business in 1909 by Chinese physician Hum Yow Wong. The restaurant business was passed down through the years to other members of the Wong family who still operate the Pekin Noodle Parlor.

The decline of the Chinese population in Butte after 1900 eroded the neighborhood. Many of the buildings were torn down because they did not meet safety codes in the 1920s. The joss house temple in China Alley met the fate of a wrecking ball in 1943.

Better than 100 years after its beginnings, little remains pointing to the flourishing activity that once radiated in Chinatown. The Mai Wah and Wah Chong buildings were taken over by a local group called the Mai Wah Society in 1992. They turned the buildings into a Chinese cultural center. It is through this center and the local organization that Chinatown will retain a lasting fame in Butte.

Columbia Gardens was a small group of homes just outside the fence of the amusement park east of town at the base of the East Ridge of the Rocky Mountains. The series of homes began at the base of the hill leading up to the park at a location called "Five Cent Limit" or, in early days prior to 1890, as Park City. Beyond that location, a person encountered houses driving up the road leading to the Gardens and beyond to the far backside of the amusement park.

The cluster of homes became a reality shortly after the land was purchased for a park by William Clark in 1899. Clark hired a massive team of workers who would turn the park into a paradise of trees and flowers. The original flower garden crew had 15 members, led by Victor Siegel. Because transportation to the park was a slow-moving trolley car, the workers elected to build homes near their place of employment.

The neighborhood featured a machine and carpenter shop behind the Gardens' greenhouses on the eastern edge of the park. There was also a dairy farm nearby. A fire station was built. Volunteer firemen were kept busy because many wooden homes went up in flames. Columbia Gardens' residents believed The Anaconda Company, the longtime tenant of the park, was the culprit. Company officials were not fond of people living close to the park.

Despite the constant problem with fires, the neighborhood had many features that Butte citizens did not enjoy. There was fresh air, abundant wildlife, clean running spring water, and lots of shrubbery. Of course, having one of the top parks in the Rocky Mountain region just outside your doorstep certainly did not hurt either.

"It was a wonderful place to live," recalled Pauline Poore. "Right out our backyard was this immaculate playground area. It was just grand."

June Wilson remembered, "The Columbia Gardens was a tremendous place to raise a family. They had so many things for the kids to do, like visiting the zoo or going to the playground area.

" I remember the wonderful water we had. It was pumped over the mountain from the Elk Park reservoir into the Columbia Gardens. The water was so crystal and pure."

Guido Bugni said with a laugh, "Yes, the water was good, but the service was lousy. The wooden pipes that funneled the water down the mountain had rings around them. The pipes were always breaking down and workers were constantly repairing the system. There were many days when the water to our house was shut off while they fixed the line. Of course, I can't complain too much because the water was free."

Jesse Poore said, "We had a large apple orchard in our yard. Later, we added a flower bed and other things. It was just an unbelievable place to grow up."

Besides the park, other summertime activities for neighborhood kids included playing tennis on courts built just southwest of the Columbia Gardens. A number of tournaments were held on the courts. There was also a large baseball diamond to play softball or baseball near the tennis courts. Activities never ceased once winter set in; the Columbia Gardens made an ideal location for sledding.

"The Gardens' staff use to plow the road for us from the herbarium down to the pavilion," recalled Alana Lencioni LaRock. "The park crew had a specially designed flat device they used to pull behind the truck to compact the snow. It was similar to a Zamboni you see them use to redo the ice at the Sports Center here in town.

"Once they were finished, you had wonderful conditions to sled down. You zipped down from the herbarium, past the playground area, down the hill past the bi-planes and merry-go-round. Here you had to make a sharp turn to the left to make it past the arcade building down to the pavilion. The only ones who could make that sharp turn well were the kids living at the Gardens. I remember most kids plowed into the steps of the arcade building because they were going too fast and never knew how to make that turn. Boy, it was about a mile-long ride down to the pavilion and was wonderful fun."

All the "wonderful fun" at the Columbia Gardens for nearby residents came to an abrupt end in the fall of 1973. The Anaconda Company elected to shut down the park to make way for a new mining project in the area. The days of the family homes near the Columbia Gardens grew to a select few once the shovels moved in and the residents were finally moved out for good five years later in the fall of 1978.

Corktown was located south of the Butte, Anaconda and Pacific Railroad tracks above the Anaconda Road. Situated near where the Kelley

Mine complex is located, it was bordered on the west by Main Street, north by the BA&P Railroad tracks leading to the Mountain Con Mine, east by the bridge near the Kelley Mine, and the south by the Anaconda Road and Dublin Gulch.

The name Corktown reflected the strong influx of residents from County Cork, Ireland. A majority of the people were from the small strip of land on the Beare Peninsula around Castletown Beare.

Kevin Shannon said, "The Irish, especially in Corktown, were great in exercising their right to vote. It's simply not true that the Irish voted early and often. What is true is that they voted Democratic and made sure everyone in Corktown got to the polls. Corktown carried lots of political clout because it was the largest voting precinct in Montana prior to World War II."

Dan O'Gara remembered, "The entire neighborhood was almost all Irish. If you went up North Wyoming Street there were maybe three families at the most who were not Catholic or Irish."

The strong influence of the Irish resulted in St. Mary's Catholic Church becoming a main focal point in the region. The church was founded in 1902 by Bishop John Brondel, the first bishop of Helena. A wooden church was built in 1903 with the first services held inside in October of that year.

In September 1904, a school run by the Sisters of Charity of Leavenworth opened in the basement of the church. The temporary school was replaced by a three-story brick school house in 1906. The school was the center of attention for neighborhood families. By 1916, St. Mary's School had 726 pupils. A favorite subject taught was the Gaelic language with Sean O'Sullivan conducting classes in the basement of St. Mary's. A new St. Mary's Elementary School was dedicated and put into service on September 28, 1952.

The original wooden church at 713 North Wyoming Street was destroyed by fire on August 31, 1931. O'Gara remembered, "The fire at St. Mary's Church was horrible. There were people on top of their roofs with hoses trying to save their homes."

Father Sarsfield O'Sullivan said, "It was a bad fire. When it was over, there were five or six homes destroyed besides the destruction done to the church. The only thing that saved our home from the flames were a series of trees next to our house. I recall the Delaney family was losing their house. They kept running into our home throwing their clothes in our living room because they were trying to save as much as they could.

"One of the things saved in the devastation was Our Lady of Victory statue that was in the church. It's remarkable to note the statue came to

St. Mary's after Sacred Heart Church was destroyed by fire, but somehow the statue survived that blaze too."

Father J. M. Nolan quickly began the task of starting a new church. A brick structure was constructed on Main Street with the cornerstone laid on December 20, 1931. The Catholic Church abandoned the brick building in 1986 due to a lack of priests in the diocese. Rather than face destruction, the church was purchased by the local volunteer group, Our Lady of the Rockies, in 1989. The church became the headquarters and visitors' center for Our Lady of the Rockies.

One of the more popular Irish traditions in Corktown took place on St. Stephen's Day, the day after Christmas. Vince Downing recalled, "The kids in the neighborhood would form a group and go sing songs at all the homes in the area. It was a sign of good luck if we came to your home and sang the 'wren bird song.' The neighbors always appreciated our efforts and would give us nickels and dimes."

Shannon said with a laugh, "That was a fun time. When we went around singing, we brought along a Christmas tree with the head of a turkey on top of it which represented the wren bird. There were lots of different versions of the wren song."

Another popular tradition for the Irish took place on the day after Easter. "All the kids in the neighborhood went to church the day after Easter wearing a cardboard Easter Lily," said Father O'Sullivan. "The lily was a tribute to the 1916 Easter Rebellion in Ireland. It was the way the Butte Irish showed their appreciation for the efforts of the rebels of 1916."

Corktown had a number of little neighborhood stores to serve the people. One of the favorite spots was Harrington's Grocery on the corner of Woolman and Main Streets.

The homes in Corktown were simple, housing mostly miners and their families. The men were close to large mining operations like the Steward, Mountain Con, Neversweat, St. Lawrence and Anaconda.

The hazardous occupation of mining had a devastating impact on Corktown. O'Sullivan says, "They called Corktown the parish of widows. If you went up Wyoming Street a number the families were run by the mother because the father had been killed in the mines. The sad part of the whole ordeal is very few families knew exactly how their fathers were killed. The Company put very little information out about accidents. One of the few ways you knew the exact cause of death was through word of month by the various miners located in the operation where the accident took place."

The demise of the underground mining industry with the advent of open pit mining had a direct impact on Corktown. A large segment of the neighborhood's population left the area in search of new opportunities. As people left, so did the flavor of the neighborhood with only a few homes and apartment buildings remaining in one of Butte's biggest Irish's neighborhoods.

Corra Terrace was located east of Walkerville over the hill from St. Lawrence Catholic Church near the Granite Mountain and Speculator Mines, at the top of the Anaconda Road and Hungry Hill. The neighborhood consisted of some miners' homes. There were both Irish and Cornish families living in the area. A future Anaconda Company president, Con Kelley, and his family lived in Corra Terrace while he was growing up.

Like many Butte neighborhoods, Corra Terrace served its purpose allowing miners to be close to their work. The small neighborhood remained until the start of the Berkeley Pit operations in 1955. When the digging began the neighbors sold their homes to The Anaconda Company and moved. The region around Corra Terrace was turned into an early viewing stand area for the Berkeley Pit.

Country Club is on the Flats some five miles south of the Butte business district. The neighborhood sat at the base of the East Ridge of the Rocky Mountains with the Bert Mooney Airport located just southwest of the Country Club.

The area had two distinct periods: the Lake Avoca era prior to World War II and the Butte Country Club Golf Course years following the great war. Lake Avoca was a man-made lake developed by Butte businessman, Wallace McClintock White, the president of the Tidewater Investment Company. The lake was 15 to 20 feet deep and was formed by a man-made dam near two ravines.

White invested large sums of money planting trees and other vegetation in the area to turn barren land into a pleasant surrounding. His grounds were finished in 1911 and called Luna Park.

Lake Avoca became a first-class lakeside resort and amusement park. It was a wonderful place for fraternal organizations to hold large-scale picnics. The small group of families living in the Lake Avoca area also enjoyed the park because there were loads of recreational opportunities just a short walk away from their homes. There was swimming, sailing, canoeing, or riding the steam boat during the summer, while speedskating and hockey were dominant activities during the cold winter months. In addition, a dance hall and pavilion were located near the shore line, as well as a picnic facility, playground equipment, and steam locomotive, all operated by the Luna Park Amusement Company.

A landmark at Lake Avoca was a German village which served as a favorite beer-garden spot for many who ventured out to the lake. It was destroyed by fire on September 25, 1922. No other buildings were damaged.

In addition to entertainment during the summer, White's investment had a winter aspect: the sale of ice from the lake to the Butte Ice Company. This business venture was left out in the cold when refrigeration was developed in the 1920s, causing White to lose a major source of income. This led to financial trouble, and so White sold his property to Butte businessman John Burke in 1928. Burke, the president of the Lakeshore Development Company, turned the pavilion into a clubhouse for a 12-hole Lakeshore Golf Course which was built around the lake.

"The golf course was a great place for kids to make some money," said Howie Wing. "A lot of kids caddied to make a few coins. Everyone started out as a 'B' Caddie and worked their way up to being an 'A' caddie which meant you knew how to sweep the sand greens just right."

The prominent Lakeshore Country Club building was destroyed by fire on October 24, 1937. The next year, Butte businessmen Bob Corette talked Burke into donating his land for the development of Montana's first all-grass golf course. Once an agreement was reached in the fall of 1939, workers began draining water from the lake. It took two years to complete the project. The 18-hole golf course was completed and dedicated on August 2, 1941, as golfers from around the state came to play on the new links.

Prior to the new golf course, there were enough families living in the area to support the construction of the Hawthrone School on White Boulevard and the Cleveland School on Elizabeth Warren Avenue in 1918.

Only the Hawthrone School was considered a neighborhood center because the Cleveland replaced the Whittier Elementary as the home of the industrial trade school for the Butte School District. The Cleveland School served as an industrial center until it was torn down in 1969. It was replaced by the Butte Vo-Tech Center which was built next to the public high school building on Arizona Street.

The small group of homes in the area prior to the construction of the Butte Country Club golf course was filled with large families operating dairy farms. Wing recalled, "It took a lot of free labor to run a dairy farm. I guess we were the free labor because there were four kids in our family and we all had to work at the dairy farm."

The dairy business in Butte was very competitive with 56 different dairies in the area at one time. There were nine different dairy farms in the Country Club region alone: the Rocky Mountain, East Side, South Side, Pine Tree, Rainbow, Daisy and Pierce Dairies.

The time frame following the 1941 golf course dedication saw a continuous growth in the Country Club area with a wide variety of homes. There were some expensive new homes built, along with older more modest houses and even a few rundown trailer homes. All the construction in the area produced lots of new families. The growth eventually led to the region's second elementary school, the Hillcrest, in 1969.

An aspect of the growth was the building of a large stake house by the Church of Jesus Christ of Latter Day Saints on Continental Drive. The Mormons' roots in Butte date back to at least 1910 when the Relief Society, a women's group, met to determine how many people of their faith lived in the mining camp. The eight women were able to locate sixteen other Mormons. They met for services in the Scandia Hall and Knights of Pythias Hall, both located on Main Street, prior to building a Mormon Mission Church on Florence and Massachusetts Streets. The construction of the new church started in 1940 and was completed in 1945. Through the leadership of men like Edgar Henderson, Charles Hanni and Mel Peterson the church membership began to grow. It allowed the church to branch off into two wards. Besides serving as a church, the building on Florence and Massachusetts also included a large gymnasium and a cultural hall.

As the Mormon congregation grew, it became evident to local leaders that they needed a larger church. The new building in the Country Club was finished in 1976 and serves as a Stake House for Butte, Anaconda, Dillon, Philipsburg and Deer Lodge.

The building boom in the Country Club continued when the United States High Altitude Sports Center became a part of the neighborhood in 1987. It was located a short distance down the road from the Mormon Church. Also, the Roman Catholic community built Holy Spirit Church on Continental Drive in 1992.

There is still plenty of room for more building. The Country Club promises to only continue growing for some time into the next century.

Dublin Gulch was located northeast of the central business district on Anaconda Road with its heart situated where the Kelley Mine Shaft now rests. Dublin Gulch extended up the hill to the southern edge of the Mountain Con Mine.

Dublin Gulch was Butte's first neighborhood. The first house built in Butte was in Dublin Gulch on East Quartz Street. It was home to Butte's first settlers, G. O. Humphrey, William Allison, Dennis Leary, George

Newkirk and H. H. Porter. They found the first gold nuggets in the valley in 1864.

The area was called Town Gulch during the gold rush days. The name changed to Dublin Gulch after the influx of Irish miners came here. The main reason for its early development was its location in the heart of the mining district. The first mining efforts were all concentrated around Quartz Street. Dublin Gulch was encircled by highly productive mines like the Anaconda, Neversweat, St. Lawrence, Mountain View, High Ore, Tramway and Parrot Mines. The underground operations were all within easy walking distance for miners who built homes next door, or across the street, or just down the block from their places of employment.

"There were benefits for kids living so close to such a large mining district," recalled Bob Koprivica. "As kids we went up near the mines when a shift got off where miners gave us fruit from their buckets."

President Warren Harding was driven through Dublin Gulch on June 29, 1923, to see the mining operations.

Aside from employment, residents did not benefit from the riches being pulled from the hill. The mines in Dublin Gulch and throughout Butte were not in the city limits because Company officials gerrymandered boundaries so Anaconda could avoid paying property taxes. This was done despite the fact that neighborhoods like Dublin Gulch were located less than a mile from city hall.

Koprivica said, "The Anaconda Company lied and cheated the people of Butte. If The Anaconda Company had been forced to pay property taxes like everyone else, they could've paved the streets with gold rather than asphalt. Instead, they were a bunch of thieves and allowed to get away with it. All the real money left town for some big, fat cat's wallet back East."

Jack Harris said, "The Anaconda Company not only controlled Butte, but Montana as well. Hell, they could do anything they wanted here and get away with it because they owned everyone."

Avoiding city property taxes was a great deal for Anaconda, but tough on local residents who did not enjoy the privileges of many city services. As late as 1929, Dublin Gulch residents were passing out petitions around their neighborhood trying to get city officials to install a fire hydrant.

Fire was a constant threat due to the flimsy nature of the wooden homes. One of the more prominent boarding houses, the Duggan House, was destroyed by fire on April 15, 1903. The O'Brien Boarding House was engulfed in flames on September 30, 1923. A blaze on May 5, 1924, disabled five homes. Another three homes on Ridgeway Avenue were destroyed by fire on April 10, 1930.

The Company also avoided paying a net proceeds tax on the minerals taken out of their ground until 1924. A state-wide initiative that year, led by Senator Burton Wheeler, passed, forcing Anaconda to pay a net proceeds tax.

One of the few items The Company did pay taxes on was the surface equipment at their mines. Anaconda was forced to pay 40 percent of the value of their surface equipment; however, the vast majority of their machinery was underground and did not fall under tax laws.

Dublin Gulch was purely residential with wooden cottages and houses. The business district consisted of a neighborhood store and a pair of saloons. A number of residents referred to this section of Butte as the place where "the shanty Irish" lived or "the hard boiled Irish" because the neighborhood was loaded with great fighters.

"Boy, there were a lot of tough kids in the neighborhood," remembered Ed Crnich. "They knew how to fight in Dublin Gulch!"

The nature of the area changed after the turn to the 20th century with the introduction of immigrants from Southern Europe into the neighborhood. Dublin Gulch became a primary battleground between the established Irish and the new arrivals. The new immigrants heading up the hill looking for work had to pass through Dublin Gulch to get to the mining operations. It was in here that the new immigrants were greeted with open hostility by Irish miners and their families.

The situation only got worse when mine bosses who owned property in Dublin Gulch started renting their holdings to Southern Europeans at high rates in return for their services in the mines.

The neighborhood changed again with the start of the Greater Butte Project in 1947. The plan had an immediate impact as The Anaconda Company decided to center its hub around the new Kelley Mine. The operation meant the beginning of the end of Dublin Gulch. Butte's first neighborhood became the first to feel the sting of the Greater Butte Project.

The Company project led to the Berkeley Pit. As it started to expand in the late 1950s, Anaconda officials started to buy out many homes in Dublin Gulch to have more room for the Pit and their warehouse operations. Some families stayed to the bitter end, but when it was over the final residents sold their property in 1973. It put an end to Butte's first neighborhood.

East Butte was located on the eastern edge of the city at the base of Woodville Hill. It was one of three neighborhoods on the eastern edge of Butte, along with Meaderville and McQueen. Of the three, East Butte was the first to develop prior to 1890. A primary reason for its early development was the Pittsmont Mine which was located in East Butte. It was the first section of Butte that a traveler encountered by car coming south down Highway 91 into the city from Elk Park. Besides Highway 91, which ran right through the neighborhood, the only thing even near East Butte was McQueen which sat north and east of the area.

The location of the highway provided the neighborhood with a good spot for motels with three situated in East Butte. In addition, the neighborhood featured a pair of gas stations.

East Butte consisted of 20 blocks of homes mainly filled by Croatian and Slovenian families. Some English and Swedish families lived in the area. A school, the Harrison, was built in 1901 and expanded in 1917 because of a large population growth. Many kids from nearby McQueen, Elk Park and the Columbia Gardens attended the Harrison.

"The school was like the dividing line in East Butte," said Carl Gergurich. "All the Swedes and English lived on one side of the school and the Croatians and Slovenians were on the lower side of the neighborhood on Cherry and Plum Streets."

Ted Leskovar remembered, "We called each other the uppers and the lowers. All the Slavic people below Harrison School were the lowers while the English and Swedes above the school were the uppers."

Cathy Brozovich says, "The thing I remember most about East Butte were all the bars. It seems like they had a bar on every corner like the 156 Bar and the Hi-Ho Bar."

One of the more popular attractions in East Butte was the Slovenian American Hall which also was called Narodni Dom hall translated from Slovenian means National Home. There was a banquet room on the first floor and a dance hall of the second floor. The Slovenians held a Mesopust celebration at the hall on a number of occasions. Its main attraction was a weekly dance and some extra-curricular activities which developed after too much vino (wine) or piva (beer) flowed.

"They called it the Bucket of Blood," said Michael Muffich with a laugh. "That's because they always seemed to have a fight there. If it were not the Croatians fighting the Slovenians, then it was the Croatians fighting the Serbs or the Serbs battling the Slovenians or the Italians were mixing it up with someone. Every nationality seemed to tolerate the other, but there was always a simmering boiling pot underneath, which led to fights. One thing was certain the Bucket of Blood earned its name well."

Gergurich also remembered, "a lot of fights there. In fact, we had a name for it in Croatian called 'Boob ni ga' which means 'hit'em.' They had a dance at the hall every Sunday night and during all the dancing tempers flared leading to fights."

There were other forms of activities besides fighting in East Butte. Kids had great hills for sledding in Highway 91 and the slag piles at the Pittsmont Mine. A second form of winter fun was ice skating.

"We had to make our own ice rink every year," said Leskovar. "We used hoses from the Northern Pacific Railroad to flood the rink. It took a long time to flood, usually into the night. Once it got dark, we alerted drivers with flash lights to slow them down so no one got hit by a car. It was a lot of work, but we sure had a lot of fun."

In the summer, the kids played a lot of baseball. Like winter skating, the East Butte kids had to create their own playing field.

"It was much different back then," recalled Gergurich. "We never had a regular field with bases and a pitcher's mound like today. Before playing, we had to mark out our own field. There was also no funding from the city or a league for equipment like today. We never had much, but we sure had a lot of fun playing."

The neighborhood had some boarding houses; however, unlike similar facilities around Butte, instead of miners, it was for railroad men who worked on the nearby track and the Northern Pacific Roundhouse where engines were repaired.

Besides the railroad, another form of employment nearby was the Pittsmont Mine. There was also Jerry's Distributing which sold Blue Bell Potato Chips. In the 1950s, a favorite place to quench your thirst was the A&W Root Beer Stand.

The neighborhood started to change when the shovels from the Berkeley Pit moved closer to the area. A crushing blow came when Highway 91 was shut off to make way for mining.

Gergurich said, "When they shut down the highway, it was only a matter of time before everything else went also. My father's grocery store lost its main customer base in the travelers. The three motels quickly went out of business and the A&W Root Beer Stand moved to Continental Drive."

East Butte, like other neighborhoods, could not avoid the Pit shovels. The area was chewed up by The Anaconda Company's aggressive Pit expansion in the 1970s. The Harrison School, one of the final buildings in East Butte, was destroyed by Company officials on August 29, 1974.

East Side was situated just east of the central business district with boundaries of Park Street on the north, Arizona Street on the west, Mercury Street on the south and mining operations on the east.

It was a true melting pot of Butte consisting of Serbians, Finns, Lebanese, Mexicans, Croatians, Slovenians, Chinese and some Irish. Due to the international mixture, it was a tough neighborhood for a youngster to grow up.

"I remember the first day my family moved down to the East Side from Dublin Gulch," recalled Bob Koprivica. "I got into a fight with four different kids in one day. I found out very quickly on the East Side you did one of two things, either you fought or you ran like hell.

"It was a tough neighborhood, but after being there I discovered the East Side had the most beautiful people in the world. They were willing to do anything to help you. It was through this spirit of cooperation that America became such a great country."

Jim Carden said, "Everyone seemed to look out for each other on the East Side. My mother was sick a lot, and when she was down, neighbors brought cooked dinners over to the house. They also sent their daughters over to clean the house and make sure everything was in order. When you were down, your neighbors really watched out for you."

Matt Vucurovich remembered, "When I went to the Grant School, it seemed like every nationality you could name had someone in the school. It was different from Sacred Heart Catholic School which mainly catered to the Irish and Lebanese."

George Krstulich added, "There were also a lot of Croatians and Slovenians who went to the Sacred Heart School too besides the Irish and Lebanese."

Some buildings were in the area prior to 1900 when the region was called the Moonlight Addition, but the main push for development came shortly after 1900 when loads of Serbians, Finns and Lebanese came to Butte looking for work. Better than half the homes and business establishments in the area were constructed between 1900 and 1920.

A reflection of the enormous growth can be traced to the schools built in the region during a short three-year period. There were two schools constructed between 1899 and 1901; the first was the Grant Public School on Kemper Avenue built in 1899. A couple of years later, in 1901, the Sacred Heart Catholic School was completed.

Sacred Heart consisted of both a school and a church. The original building was destroyed by fire on November 17, 1912. Both the church and school were replaced with separate buildings. The church on East Park Street had Spanish-style architecture, the only one of its kind ever built in Montana.

There were other churches in the neighborhood. The Finns held services at the Trinity Methodist Church on East Park Street. A few blocks away on Warren and Mercury Streets sat the home of the St. Paul Episcopal Church.

The homes built in the neighborhood were simple in nature. There were also a number of boarding houses for miners like the Braund House on Galena Street.

The only nationality that clustered together in one section on the East Side were the Lebanese. They lived in an area called "Syrian Town" on East Galena between Oklahoma and Ohio Streets.

A center of activity for kids was a place called "the neighborhood house" on Atlantic and Galena Streets.

Vucurovich recalled, "The neighborhood house was quite a place for all the kids. The boys played in the gym upstairs. During basketball games, the out-of-bounds was the wall. We never had a lot of room. The girls had a sewing room on the second floor and the adults played cards downstairs."

Milt Popovich said, "The neighborhood house really was some place special. We sure had a lot of fun there."

Howie Wing said with a laugh, "It was fun, but it also could be very rough. Our Lake Avoca Cowboys' basketball team used to go up and play against the East Side at the neighborhood house. The brown spots you saw on the wall was the dried blood spilt by the various players who got shoved into the wall during the heat of the action."

The residents of the East Side had lots of opportunities to do business within their own neighborhood. There was Manx Bakery, Sewell's Hardware, the Butte Casket Company, Thomas' Family Apparel, American Swiss Dairy Products, Metropolitan Meats, Abbe Hotel, Driver's Drug Store, Harrick's Store & Ice Cream Parlor, Summers' Gas Station, Colorado Cash Grocery and the COD Laundry.

The East Side Athletic Club on East Galena Street was also a favorite destination for people looking to "wet their whistle." The 200 block of East Park Street had seven bars located on the same block. The two featured joints were the COD and Kirk's Bar.

Life and times for the working people of the East Side were not easy, especially during the Great Depression years of the 1930s.

Alex Koprivica recalled, "I remember as a kid taking my little red wagon and going with my brother George to the business district. We collected as many cardboard boxes as we could for resale at two cents a box to the merchants in the fish market. It was one of the few ways to make money in those days. The wooden boxes we found were taken home to use as firewood. It was not an easy time for anyone."

Despite the tough times, the East Side continued to grow as its schools were expanded to meet the needs of more students. The Grant School had a facelift done in 1958. The expansion came right when The Anaconda Company had started to greatly enlarge its Berkeley Pit operations. When the Pit was started in 1955, the shovels were well over a half-mile away from East Side. Yet, that quickly changed with each dig moving closer and closer to the neighborhood.

By the early 1960s, Anaconda Company officials started to buy homes from residents. Company officials wanted to eliminate the residential neighborhood and create a buffer zone for the Berkeley Pit. Some East Side residents got good deals and moved elsewhere in the community, while others reached a deal with Anaconda, then repurchased their homes for a dollar so they could move the dwellings to a different section of town. Some could not reach an agreement or refused to deal with The Company and were left with property that went down in value when each home around them came tumbling down.

"It was very sad how The Anaconda Company bullied residents out of their homes," recalled Jimmy Shea. "In many cases, The Company paid for only the market value of homes rather than the replacement value. If your home was anywhere near the Pit your home's market value was next to nothing. What Anaconda should've been giving people was the replacement value of homes which was much higher than the market value. It would've given people who lived for years in the same house a better chance to relocate without going broke."

Bob Koprivica said, "When the Anaconda Company started the Berkeley Pit, I thought it would be great because the miners no longer had to go underground. However, as the Pit got bigger and bigger it destroyed some of the finest history this town has to offer. It just shows you what greed without conscience can do to people like officials from The Anaconda Company."

The Company got its way with residents and as the Pit expanded, fewer and fewer people lived in the area. The results could be felt on the local neighborhood schools. Sacred Heart Catholic Grade School was closed for good in 1967. The Grant School shut down and was destroyed by Company officials on July 21, 1975.

The symbol of faith, the Sacred Heart Church, held its last mass on July 27, 1970. The Spanish-style church was torn down by The Anaconda Company in 1974.

The East Side became exactly what Company officials intended, a buffer zone for the Berkeley Pit. The neighborhood, its schools, and much of its flavor were gone and now just a distant memory.

Elk Park is located northeast of Butte just beyond the Continental Divide. The large mountain valley was a perfect place for raising dairy cattle with numerous dairy ranches housing 75 head of cows or more on their property. The hundreds of gallons of milk produced daily in Elk Park were taken to Butte to sell at one of the various creameries. By the 1920s, Crystal Creamery sent a pick-up truck out to Elk Park every day. Farmers could now take their milk to the highway which ran right down the heart of the valley instead of traveling all the way into town to deliver their product.

The dairymen and their families in the region were primarily Swiss-Italian immigrants who came here from near the Swiss-Italian border shortly after 1900.

Besides the dairy industry, large herds of sheep were raised in Elk Park.

When it was time to take a break from work, a favorite spot for the people in the region was the Elk Park Inn at the northern tip of the valley. Locals gathered at the Inn for "basket socials."

"The basket socials were very popular with the people," remembered Jenny Serich. "The single gals made up these elaborate baskets filled with home-made jams, bread, bakeries, cookies, meats and other things. The baskets were decorated in ribbons and flowers. On the night of the social, the single men who won the raffle for the various baskets also got the gal who made up the gift as a dance partner for the night. It was a lot of fun for all the hired-hands working and a great way to meet people."

Elk Park had plenty of timber, so the logging business was good. The community of Woodville on the southern edge of the valley served as the center of logging activity. During its boom time, Woodville had a number of residents and served as a train stop for the railroad in its route between Helena and Butte. The loggers in the Woodville area supplied the Butte mines with over 100,000 cords of wood for the underground operations.

The lumber industry gradually diminished and the number of large families in Elk Park dwindled to only a few as the need for dairy and beef products were reduced. The Elk Park area today has just a few large ranches and little activity.

Englewood was located on Butte's Flats with its center being on Harrison Avenue just south of Grand Avenue. The Englewood Athletic Club was located in this area along Harrison Avenue.

The neighborhood developed shortly after 1900 when lines from the Butte trolley car system were built. The homes in the area were bigger and more elaborate than similar workers' homes constructed on the hill.

A major development for the region took place in 1905 when William

Clark bought some land for $6,000 near the Englewood-Racetrack junction for his Butte Electric Trolley Car system. Clark pumped another $4,000 into land development. The area became Clark Park and was dedicated on December 13, 1905. The park became the focal point for the entire neighborhood. Clark gave the new park to the city, but he retained ownership of the 11 acres just in case a profitable body of ore might be discovered underneath the surface. In 1928, The Anaconda Company took over ownership of the land when they bought out Clark's estate. Company officials finally agreed to turn over the land ownership of Clark Park to the city of Butte on May 11, 1938.

The park was expanded into an athletic complex in 1921. By 1922, a major wooden grandstands had been built, allowing 6,000 fans to watch football and baseball games. During the next few years, the local high school teams, Butte High and Butte Central, played all their home games at Clark Park. College teams like the Montana School of Mines, Montana Grizzlies, and Montana State Bobcats competed at the complex. The annual Bobcats-Grizzlies football clash was held at Clark Park from 1926 to 1937. The showdown was then moved to Naranche Stadium in Central Butte until officials from the two schools elected in 1950 to move the annual game to either Bozeman or Missoula every year.

"Boy, let me tell you, the town was roaring when the Bobcats and Grizzlies came to town to play," Mary Gassino Mencarelli said with a laugh. "There was activity everywhere you went in this town. It was like a three-day party."

Jenny Serich recalled, "It was New Year's Eve rolled into an entire weekend. There were people everywhere in town enjoying themselves getting ready for the big game."

The annual Bobcat-Grizzly game was not the only contest moved to Naranche Stadium when it opened in 1938. The high school teams also moved their games to the new complex. The change of locations did not, however, mean the end of activities at Clark Park. For many years speedskating meets were held during the winter time while baseball was the main activity of the summer as the Butte Copper League held games at Clark Park through the 1956 season.

A fire destroyed the Clark Park grandstands on May 1, 1957. The first alarm for the fire came at 8:40 P.M. with the blaze starting in the press box area. In a short time, flames were ripping through the old wooden bleachers and in less than one-hour, the grandstands were completely destroyed. Firefighters spent almost their entire time trying to save homes on Wall Street rather than battle the hopeless cause of saving the grandstands. A strong south wind helped push flames near the homes on Wall

Street. One lawn caught on fire. So did a nearby tree, but both were put out before the inferno could spread.

"Boy, that was a hot fire at Clark Park," remembered Bus Stuart. "It got so hot that it blistered the paint off of homes at Wall Street, which was a couple hundred feet away from the grandstands."

Local officials decided not to rebuild the grandstands. Clark Park was converted into a softball field for awhile. Once the softball players left for a new complex at Stodden Park, the area remained quiet for a number of years. The park received new life in 1987 when Columbia Gardens' playground equipment was placed in Clark Park.

"It was a very positive step for the neighborhood when the Columbia Gardens' playground gear was relocated to Clark Park," Mike Gribben said. "It added a new life to the park and brought more families back into the neighborhood."

Gribben grew up in Englewood when sections of the neighborhood were being transformed into a commercial center. From 1940 through 1970 a number of businesses located their shops in the Englewood section of Harrison Avenue. The businesses included Gribben's Plumbing and Heating, Downey Drug, Ann's Fabrics, South Side Hardware and Walsh Plumbing. There was also the addition of Luigi's Bar in 1964 after the famous musician was forced to leave the East Side due to the expansion of the Berkeley Pit.

By the 1970s, Harrison Avenue had completely became a commercial center. Many of the remaining homes on Harrison Avenue were turned into commercial offices. It is one of the few section of Butte that was dramatically changed, not by mining, but by growth.

Finn Town was situated just northeast of the business district. The neighborhood was bordered on the north by Dublin Gulch, the east by mining properties, the south by the East Side and the west by Arizona Street.

The neighborhood grew enormously after 1900 with the arrival of Finnish immigrants to the mining camp. The area on East Granite, Broadway, and Park Streets consisted mainly of Finns with some Irish living in the district.

The primary feature of Finn Town was the number of boarding houses. There were 18 different boarding houses on East Broadway Street between Arizona and Oklahoma Streets.

One boarding house run by Mrs. Riipi called the Broadway Dining Room served 600 meals a day to hungry miners. There was also the Kingston House operated by Fanny Tuomala; the Central House run by the Kauhanen family, and a house directed by Mrs. Souminen on Covert Street.

The boarding houses served excellent meals around the clock because some miners were always just ending their shift. One favorite dish of boarders was "stir-about," better known today as oatmeal. The mush was very filling and was served at all times of the day. All the food being cooked and served was a boom for the local economy because the boarding houses provided many women and girls with jobs as cooks, waitresses and bucket girls.

The boarding houses catered to more than just the residents in the building.

"I recall our entire family going up to the Finn Town boarding houses from the East Side on Sunday for dinner," recalled Matt Vucurovich. "We could eat a big meal for only 50 cents and the food was out-of-this-world."

One of the more famous Finn Town boarding houses sat at the 300 block of East Broadway Street across the roadway from the Washington School. It was the Florence also nicknamed "the Big Ship." The name was coined by house manager John O'Rourke who said, "There was enough liquor consumed here in a weekend to float a ship. A mighty big ship at that."

The Florence was home mainly to Irish workers. A drill was located in the basement of the complex so new Irish immigrants could practice their skills at drilling before trying to rustle a job working in the mines. The Florence served more than just the Irish. In April 1920, "the Big Ship" was turned into an army barracks when federal troops were sent to town to halt a strike by union members. The strike turned ugly with union member Thomas Manning being shot and killed the day before the troops arrived. The Florence had to be used by the troops because their main headquarters in previous trips to Butte, the Pennsylvania Mine, was housing numerous gunmen brought to town by The Anaconda Company.

Except for the Irish and the occasional presence of federal troops, Finn Town was just that: a neighborhood filled with Finns. The neighborhood was noted for its bars and sauna baths. There were plenty of places to catch a drink or take a sauna. The first sauna in the neighborhood was Isan's Sauna on the 700 block of East Broadway Street. There were five bars all on the south side of the 400 block of East Broadway Street. The joints were called the Corner later renamed the Helsinki, Moonlight later called the Red Front, Broadway, Alaska and the Alley bars.

A tradition carried on for years at the five Finn Town bars was serving miners right after they got off shift. A miner had to display his lunch bucket which was called a "pie can" to get a glass of beer for a dime and a free shot of whiskey.

There was also another bar in the neighborhood, the Yellowstone, which was located at the corner of Covert and Granite Streets.

The Broadway Bar had a second business situated in the basement of the building: a bakery operated by Matt Lampi. Other businesses in the neighborhood included Pera's Store on Covert Street, Jarvela's Barber Shop and Maki's Store.

The neighborhood was the site of Butte's first high school building on the corner of Granite and Arizona Streets. The school served that function until a new learning center was completed in 1897 on the corner of Park and Idaho Street.

The school in Finn Town became the Washington School and was later converted into a junior high. It served that function until 1957 when a new school called Butte Junior High was completed and opened in the Racetrack area. The Washington School was then changed into an elementary center.

The Washington School had served as a temporary hospital during the 1918 Spanish Influenza epidemic. During a four-month period, from October 1918 to January 1919, over 1,000 Butte residents died from the disease.

By the time the Washington School was torn down in 1976, Finn Town had all but disappeared from the Butte landscape. The emergence of the Berkeley Pit in the early 1960s had a major impact on the region. Residents sold their homes to The Anaconda Company and pulled out of the neighborhood. Only a few homes remain today with only one operating bar, the Helsinki, which still has saunas available for patrons. The only time the neighborhood comes alive today is on March 16, when Butte citizens overflow the Helsinki Bar to celebrate St. Urho's Day.

The Flats also called "South Butte" begins where the hill ends on Front Street. The Flats extends over nine miles out into the valley all the way to Thompson Park to the south and the East Ridge of the Rocky Mountains to the east. Of course, the Flats can be subdivided into numerous neighborhoods like the Boulevard, Country Club, Englewood, Floral Park, Racetrack and Terra Verde Heights.

During Butte's early days, the Flats was primarily a spot for Native American Indians to live once the first miners came looking for golden nuggets. All the miners and their families lived in housing above Front Street while the Indians occupied the region below Front Street. It remained that way until officials started to stretch the boundaries of the city through the construction of the Butte Electric Railway trolley car system. When tracks were built below Front Street, housing soon followed. The first major construction project was the Silver Bow Addition south of

Silver Bow Creek near the present day Civic Center.

As the rail system moved further out onto the Flats, so did the construction of more homes and more neighborhoods.

A major development helping spur even more growth on the Flats was the introduction of the automobile to Butte in 1910. The new form of transportation allowed folks to build homes even further and further out in the valley.

The Flats were primarily working class neighborhoods during the early days of mining. Unlike other neighborhoods where ethnic groups clustered, the vast space on the Flats resulted in a mixture of ethnic groups. There were also a number of boarding houses. One of the landmark boarding houses was the Balkovetz Boarding and Rooming House which was destroyed by fire on February 10, 1933.

The major push for housing in the Flats area took place shortly after the announcement of the Great Butte Project in 1947 by The Anaconda Company. Less than a year after that announcement, the Butte Development Association was formed under the leadership of Tim Sullivan. Through the efforts of the Butte Development Association, major housing districts were established primarily around the "Old Circus Grounds" near St. Ann's School. During its first five years of operation, the Butte Development Association helped in the construction of over 400 homes on the Flats.

"When I moved out on the Flats in 1956, there was still lots of wide-open space," said George Krstulich. "I could see St. Ann's Church off in the distance which was five or six blocks away. Now that entire area is filled with houses."

A reflection of the growth on the Flats can be traced to the various schools which were built and later expanded as more people moved into the region. The Emerson and Greeley Schools were both built in 1901. The original Emerson was demolished in 1962 and replaced with a new structure. The Greeley underwent a new look in 1917, 1957 and 1962. The Whittier School, built in 1903, was first used as an industrial center for students. After the original school was destroyed by fire on February 2, 1953, a new school was built and later expanded in 1962. During the construction of the new school, students were transported to the Butte Civic Center to attend class in one of eight emergency classrooms set up at the arena.

The Longfellow School constructed in 1917, was destroyed by fire in 1937. The Longfellow was rebuilt and expanded in 1949, 1957 and 1967.

Two Catholic grade schools, St. Ann's and St. John's, were started in 1917 and 1918. St. John's got a new $50,000 school building in 1938. Both

Catholic schools were used until the parochial grade schools were shut down in 1969. St. Ann's School was converted into South Central Junior High serving in this role until 1982 when the school was shut down and students were shipped to Butte Central Junior High in the old St. Patrick's School building in the Hub Addition.

The Hawthorne and Cleveland Schools both came on line in 1918 with the Cleveland taking over the task as the industrial trade school for the district. The Butte Junior High, now East Middle School, first started accepting students in 1957. The Hillcrest was built in 1969 and the Margaret Leary was constructed in 1975.

People moving to the Flats produced more than just schools. A major commercial district developed along Harrison Avenue. A few grocery stores and other mercantile shops were the first signs of the business expansion. In addition, there were three early-day theaters built on the Flats: the Acme Theater on Rowe Road and Holmes Avenue, the Harrison Theater on Harrison Avenue and the Englewood Theater also on Harrison Avenue.

The commercial district along Harrison Avenue really started to boom after the end of World War II. The growth hit a milestone in 1968 with the completion of Butte's first major shopping mall, the Butte Plaza. There were other major shopping centers constructed along Harrison Avenue after the Butte Plaza. In addition, numerous fast food restaurants emerged along the roadway, making it look like many other cities in America. There were major motels built along Harrison Avenue and large-scale night club restaurants. The most famous of these was Lydia's which was constructed in 1964.

Commerce was not the only thing to develop on the Flats. A major dump along Rowe Road and Holmes Avenue was given to the city by former mayor, Thomas Stodden, who acquired the land prior to 1919. The donation of the land was done through the help of the Butte Exchange Club in 1927. The dump was converted into a recreational center through the development of the public Highland's View Golf Course. In 1968, the golf course was included as a segment of Stodden Park. Stodden Park features a swimming pool, softball fields, tennis courts, horseshoe pits and playground equipment.

The Butte Civic Center was another major recreational complex built on the Flats. Local voters passed a bond issue for $1 million during the 1948 November general election. Once the money was approved, city officials received 45 acres of donated land on Harrison Avenue from The Anaconda Company for construction of a multi-purpose sports complex.

Prior to the Butte Civic Center, a multi-purpose complex had never been built in Montana. Local officials hoped the money approved was enough to build a complex that could house both football and basketball plus also construct a new baseball diamond and grandstands just north of the main arena. When the construction bids came in, the lowest bid was $1.4 million so officials had to scale back their efforts. The baseball diamond was cut, and the arena was built to only house basketball.

A ground breaking ceremony for the multi-purpose arena took place on May 8, 1950. J. G. Link served as the architect, while Cahill-Mooney was the general contractor. Over 300 yards of cement in one continuous pour of 26 hours straight completed the floor. Laid underneath the concrete was 54,000 linear feet of coil, which was connected to an ice machine, allowing the Civic Center to feature hockey, figure skating and ice shows.

Construction work was finally completed in 1952. On Sunday, March 16, 1952, the general public got a chance to tour the new sports arena during an open house. More than 17,000 people walked through the doors on that first day to see Montana's first multi-purpose sports complex. The facility could house 4,270 for hockey, 5,380 for basketball with an additional 3,000 portable seats being placed down on the floor to push the seating capacity to over 8,000 fans.

The seats to the new complex quickly came into use. Two days after the grand opening, the Butte Civic Center hosted the Class A state basketball tournament. The event drew over 31,000 fans, a state tournament record. The championship was won by Kalispell.

Besides basketball, the Civic Center has played host to various events like rodeos, ice hockey, wrestling tournaments, horse shows, boxing, concerts, conventions, pro wrestling, ice shows, ice motorcycle racing, monster trucks, professional basketball, Olympic ice hockey, speedskating, religious services and dinners. Through the years it has been well used by the community.

There was also a major medical center built on the Flats in 1902. The hospital was for poor families and people who could not afford hospital treatment. The fact that Butte had such a facility made it a leader in medical service in the region. It served as a hospital center until July 11, 1960, when a $2.5 million facility was opened on Continental Drive. The old hospital for indigents eventually became the home of the National Center for Appropriate Technology.

The new hospital was operated by the local government. Due to the rising cost of health care, local officials sold the medical center in the 1980s to the Sisters of Charity at Leavenworth who turned the facility into an outpatient care center.

The one event which shaped the Flats and the city forever occurred on July 2, 1912, when Terah Maroney flew his Curtiss flying machine into the community. It was the first airplane flight into Butte. Maroney received headlines in the local newspapers for flying his bi-plane into town from Gregson, a distance of 17 miles, in just 14 minutes. The previous day Maroney had left Butte by automobile loaded with aviation fuel for his historic flight. The auto trip with gasoline to Gregson took 90 minutes. The successful flight triggered the aviation age for Butte.

The first airport, the Butte National Airport, was laid out just south of Elizabeth Warren Street.

In 1926, construction for a more permanent air strip began with a plane hangar being put up in a cow pasture field at the site. The field and terminal were completed in 1927 and the complex was named the Butte Municipal Airport just a few short months before Charles Lindbergh's appearance in the city in September 1927. Lindbergh flew his Spirit of St. Louis airplane, the same plane he used a few months earlier to cross the Atlantic Ocean. "Lucky Lindy" spoke to 10,000 people at a gathering held in his honor at the Clark Park ballfield. Lindbergh insisted that the front rows of seats be reserved for young children because he was determined to bring them the message on the future of aviation.

A year after Lindbergh's appearance in Butte, the National Parks Airways began air mail service between Butte and Salt Lake City on August 1, 1928. One of the first pilots to fly from Butte for National Parks Airways was native son, Bert Mooney. He served for many years as a pilot for National Parks Airways which was bought out by Western Air Express in 1937. The new company later changed its name to Western Airlines. The Butte airport changed its name to Bert Mooney Airport in honor of the pioneer aviator in May 1972.

The airport was in Silver Bow County, but was being operated by the local city government. In 1956, control of the airport changed hands from the city to county. The switch was made because the county government had access to more federal grant money. That grant money plus the passage of a successful $500,000 bond issue allowed county officials to construct a new terminal and runway at the airport in 1962.

The completion of the new airfield helped pave the way for the only Presidential visit at the Butte airport. On October 12, 1964, President Lyndon Johnson arrived in Butte aboard Air Force One for a campaign rally at the Butte Civic Center.

"It was a real madhouse at the airport the day President Johnson came to town," recalled Angelo Petroni, then the airport manager. " I remember we had to install over 200 phone lines at the terminal building just to accommodate all the press people who covered the stop. Of course, they also had the place crawling with Secret Service agents."

The new additions at the airport went far beyond just a Presidential visit. Western Airlines, a long-time carrier in Butte, added jet service to the community on September 7, 1968. Northwest Airlines flew its first jet service into Butte on December 18, 1970.

More construction work completed in the 1970s added more taxiways plus sophisticated landing equipment. Almost all the work was done through federal grant money. Despite the improvements, Bert Mooney Airport was in for major changes over which local officials had no control because of the deregulation of the airlines industry by the federal government.

After deregulation, Western Airlines with its north-south routes merged with Delta Airlines in 1987. Delta would eventually turn its Butte routes over to Skywest Airlines, a Delta link in Salt Lake City. Northwest Airlines, with its east-west routes maintained service until January 1984, when the airline elected to discontinue flights into the community. The service left behind by Northwest was picked up by a Montana-based carrier Big Sky Airlines and Cascade Airlines. Later, in 1989, Horizon Airlines took over the east-west service routes.

The changes at the airport just reflected the ever changing times on the Flats, the section of Butte which is seeing more development than any other region of the community.

Hub Addition located northwest of the business district was bordered on the east by Montana Street, the south by Platinum Street, the west by Alabama Street and the north by Woolman and Caledonia Streets.

The Hub Addition was much different than many of the Butte neighborhoods. The reason was the mixture of working class folks with the wealthy. It was common to see a number of simple, working class homes in the same block with elaborate mansions built for wealthy people.

A symbol of the wealth in the Hub Addition is the Clark Mansion at 219 West Granite Street. William Clark began the magnificent palace in 1884, bringing European craftsmen to Butte to help complete the project which took four years. When it was done, the Clark Mansion was one of the most elaborate buildings in the West prior to 1900. The home included white oak wood stairways, wood floors in each of the 30 rooms, 13 fireplaces, fresco paintings on the ceilings, stained-glass windows and a dance hall on the third floor.

After Clark's death, in 1925, the mansion was passed on several times before becoming the home for the Sisters of Charity at Leavenworth.

 In 1953, the home was purchased by Butte businesswomen Ann Cote Smith who turned the mansion into one of the city's top tourist attractions. Through the years, Smith collected many antiques which she put on display at the Clark Mansion, creating one of the largest antique collections in the Northwest.

The Clark Mansion represented the copper king's wealth. The building right next door was suppose to reflect the hatred developed between William Clark and Marcus Daly. After Clark built his magnificent palace, legend has it that Daly bought the land just east of the mansion and ordered the construction of the five-story Leonard Apartments in order to block Clark's view of the East Ridge.

"It has never really been proven that Marcus Daly bought the land next to William Clark's mansion," said Bob McCarthy. "If he did not actually buy the land himself, Daly might have still financed the project through someone. There certainly was a big division between the two copper kings.

"You can only trace some of the actions that Daly did during his life. A lot of the things Daly might have done can't actually be proven because he had his wife burn all his personal papers shortly before his death. There is even some confusion as to when Daly was actually born in Ireland."

The legendary Butte story of Marcus Daly buying the land next to the Clark Mansion to build the Leonard Apartments is simply not true. Daly died in 1900. The Leonard Apartments were not built until 1906.

A couple of blocks from the Clark Mansion sits another grand building constructed by Charles Clark, the copper king's eldest son. Completed in 1898 at a cost of $260,000, the four-story home, a replica of a French castle, features stained-glass windows, 26 rooms, seven fire places and a ballroom. The architect for the Clark Mansion was Will Aldrich of Massachusetts.

Charles Clark and his wife Katherine only lived in the house three years. They left Montana in 1901. The building was sold a couple of times before landing in the hands of the Fez Club, a Butte Shriners' organization in 1949. They sold it to the Butte Bi-Centennial Commission in 1976 for $40,000. The organization soon changed its name to the Silver Bow Arts Foundation which turned the castle into the Arts Chateau, giving the city an art museum and gallery, housed in a one-of-a-kind architectural gem.

The Hub Addition, one of the first neighborhoods, was primarily an Irish stronghold, and their symbol of strength was the construction of the city's first church called St. Patrick's Catholic Church. It was a simple-framed wooden structure which was finished in 1879.

A couple of years after the new church was built, Father John Dols became the first pastor of St. Patrick's in March 8, 1881. Prior to Dols' arrival, Father Remigius de Ryckere had been traveling to Butte since 1866 providing church services. His main station was in Deer Lodge, the biggest city in the region at the time. A few years after Father Dols' arrival, a second more permanent brick church was finished on the corner of Mercury and Washington Streets. It was dedicated on September 17, 1884.

St. Patrick's parish developed a special place in Butte's history becoming the cornerstone of Catholic faith in the community. By 1885, St. Patrick's parish had 2,500 parishioners which represented 60 percent of the town's population.

St. Patrick's also served as the cornerstone for Catholic education in the town.

The Sisters of Mercy operated a boarding school for girls in a large house near the corner of Washington and Park Streets in 1886-87. The male students were taught lessons in the original wooden-framed church.

Father Henry Van de Venn started a permanent St. Patrick's Grade School in 1887 with the Sisters of Charity replacing the Sisters of Mercy as classroom instructors. The cornerstone for a new school was laid on September 15, 1888, at the corner of Washington and Park Streets. The school building was opened for classes in the fall of 1889. In 1892, the Sisters of Charity began providing high school classes as well as teaching the elementary students. The first graduating high school class from St. Patrick's High School was in 1896.

The demand for educational opportunities continued to grow as quickly as the population. Less than 15 years after St. Patrick's started offering high school classes, the Butte Catholic community had grown to seven other parish churches and schools. High school students were moved to Butte Central Catholic High School, a separate building on Quartz Street in September 1908. The first graduation ceremony was held the following spring with five students receiving diplomas. Members of the Class of 1909 were Jane O'Brien, Grace Crunnican, Agnus Foley, William Silver and Angela Durack.

"The high school was an old boarding house," remembered Millie Boyle Moriarty. "Our study hall was a big, old room that once served as a dining area for miners. It was not the best building, but we sure had a lot of fun at that school."

Having a separate high school allowed church officials to turn St. Patrick's School into strictly elementary instruction.

The Hub Addition's strong ties to Catholic education continued beyond St. Patrick's in 1924 with the completion of Boys' Central High School, next to St. Patrick's Catholic Church on Mercury Street. The high school was operated for boys by the Irish Christian Brothers.

"The Irish Christian Brothers really taught you about respect for others and about authority," Mike Gribben said. "You never got the leather unless you deserved it. The last thing you ever did was go home and tell your parents you got the leather that day because then you really would be in trouble. We need more educators like the Irish Christian Brothers today who teach you a lot more than just what's inside a book."

Jim Carden remembered, "I'll tell you when you got the leather across your hands it hurt like hell. You made darn sure never again to do what led to the leather exposure. It was a way the Irish Christian Brothers taught discipline and, trust me, the message got through loud and clear. If the leather did not provide enough of an incentive, then the Brothers took you down to the handball courts and beat the hell out of you. Some today might call that cruel and unusual punishment, but there were a lot of valuable lessons the Irish Christian Brothers taught. They drilled into you how to be a man and how you should behave yourself. It was a real solid education and I would've never traded it for anything in the world."

Vince Downing said, "If you wanted an education, the Brothers could certainly supply it. All you have to do is look at all the professional people like doctors, lawyers, dentists and others who graduated from Boys' Central. They had a very solid educational system."

The girls attending the Catholic High School remained at the building on Quartz Street until April 1951 when they moved into Girls' Central High School, a new $800,000 building on the corner of Idaho and Park Streets, a short block up the street from Boys' Central.

The situation of boys being educated in one building and girls in another structure remained until the spring of 1969 when Catholic officials decided to make some major changes in their Butte Catholic School System. The enrollment of students in the Butte Catholic school system had gone down considerably from a high of 3,353 students in 1954. A pair of lengthy mines strikes in 1959 and 1967 diminished enrollment, which, in turn, hurt the finances, forcing school officials to eliminate all the first grade classes at Catholic schools in 1967. A couple of years later, in 1969, school officials elected to shut down all eight Butte parochial grade schools. The two high schools, Boys' and Girls' Central, were merged into one coeducational facility, Butte Central Catholic High School in the former Girls' Central building. St. Patrick's School was converted into an annex building of the high school. The Boys' Central building was closed and was later converted into the Butte Business Development Center.

The reduction of Catholic schools did little to help stabilize the enrollment in their overall system. By 1976, the overall student enrollment was down to 1,000 students. As enrollment continued to drop, school officials elected to convert the St. Patrick's School building into Butte Central Junior High School in 1982, eliminating North Central Junior High located in the Immaculate Conception School and South Central Junior High in the St. Ann's School. Those two schools had been created in 1969 when the parochial grade schools were closed.

A blow for the system took place at the conclusion of the 1986 school year. The Irish Christian Brothers decided to leave the community for good after teaching in Butte 51 years. The Irish Christian Brothers had experienced a dramatic drop in their numbers due to fewer men entering their vocation. Because they were running 13 schools from Michigan to Hawaii, they were forced to make cuts. Officials of the brotherhood said that leaving Butte was one of the most difficult choices Irish Christian Brothers officials had to make.

Despite the departure of the Irish Christian Brothers, Butte Central High School lived on and eventually started to grow with the rebirth of a local elementary school in 1986. Since the elementary school opened its doors, the Butte Catholic school system has experienced a gradual increase in its enrollment. Student numbers are not near the peak period of the 1950s, but they are climbing.

The public school system also played a major role in the Hub Addition. The first public school was the Lincoln Elementary in 1892, on the corner of Clark and Broadway Streets. It was renovated in 1958. The school was eventually shut down and served a number of different functions after its closure.

The main public school developed in the Hub Addition was Butte High School, built and open for students at the corner of Idaho and Park Streets in 1897. The building served as the public high school until a new school was constructed in Central Butte on Main Street in 1938.

"The old high school was a very adequate building," recalled Bill Antonioli. "I remember it had a large gym. The facility was made of stone. In Europe, that type of building still would be in use today, but here in America we're always looking for something new.

"When we went down to the new high school on Main Street it was sure exciting for everyone."

The old high school building was converted into a multi-purpose complex with the Montana Recruiting and Induction Center housed in the annex and students from Webster Elementary School placed in the main section of the school. It served in that capacity until the building was destroyed by fire on April 10, 1946.

The Hub Addition was also a major location for medical care. In 1881, two years after the town was incorporated, the Sisters of Charity at Leavenworth built their first hospital on Idaho Street. Through the years, there were a number of construction projects undertaken to enlarge the hospital from its original two-story brick structure. The most ambitious expansion took place in 1943 when major improvements were made in the surgery room, laboratory and pediatrics departments of the hospital. The hospital was expanded to include 210 beds.

In addition to the hospital, St. James started a nursing program in 1906 which continued until 1970 when the program was disbanded. During its 64 years of service, the hospital graduated over 1,000 students into the field of nursing.

"The nuns were great teachers," said Millie Boyle Moriarty. "They were very strict but always knew exactly what they were talking about. It was a good solid three-year education."

The hospital on Idaho and Silver Streets served as a center for health care until August 3, 1962. Two years before, the Sisters of Charity at Leavenworth took over the Community Memorial Hospital which was built in 1951 by The Anaconda Company at a cost of $4.4 million. The nuns renamed their new building St. James Community Hospital. The transfer of ownership took place on February 1, 1960.

The new medical center was located on South Clark Street at the southern edge of the Hub Addition. Prior to 1900, the area around the hospital was actually called the Stevens' Addition based on the operation of the Stevens' Mine. The mine was located around Jackson and Washington Streets directly behind the hospital grounds. The Sisters of Charity at Leavenworth operated two hospitals for a couple of years before electing to shut down their medical center on Idaho Street in 1962.

Since taking over the Community Memorial Hospital in 1960 and renaming it St. James Community, the Sisters of Charity at Leavenworth have undertaken numerous construction projects at the hospital including the development of a cancer treatment center.

A location where many Butte youngsters parked was a hill south of St. James Community Hospital. Called "Lover's Roost," the hill overlooked the city lights.

The Anselmo Mine on the northwest tip of the neighborhood north of Caledonia Street off of Excelsior was the industrial focal point of the Hub Addition

"The mine was right next to our home on Edison Street," recalled Shirley Niemi. "As a kid I'd be in bed at night and could hear the trains passing in the tunnels underneath our home. They made a lot of noise."

Bus Stuart said, "We rustled wood at the Anselmo during the winter time. The miners used to haul wood out of the mine every day. It was primarily scrap wood that was left over from the new timber shafts being built underground. The wood was beneficial in keeping our home warm in the winter."

Wood and coal from the mine yards were not the only things residents acquired from the underground mines. If Butte people, in all neighborhoods and from all walks of life, needed something for their homes, there was always a way to get it from the mines.

"I'll bet you half the homes on the hill got the pipe for their plumbing from workers taking the material from The Anaconda Company," Evelyn Eva said. "Everyone in town did it and, hell, the Company didn't miss it!"

Hub Addition residents, like many Butte neighborhoods, was served by numerous local grocery stores including Crystal Grocery on Crystal and Granite Streets, Finley's Grocery on the corner of Jackson and Quartz Streets, and two larger stores on Granite and Alabama Streets, Driscoll Drug and Ashford Grocery.

The Hub Addition playground area next to Copper Street served as a place for kids to participate in baseball, football and basketball during the summer and fall months. It was also the home practice field of the Hub Addition Independent League football team. During the winter, the kids converted the playground into an ice rink where hockey and skating were the favorite activities.

"We had a great time skating at the Hub playground," recalled Carol Gilmore. "All the kids in the neighborhood skated during that time. A big thing to do was to steal Christmas trees from the Gagnon gang. They had a rink a few blocks up the street at the Gagnon Mine. We were always taking Christmas trees from each other to light a fire and keep warm during the winter. It was all done in fun."

Another key spot for kids centered around a baseball diamond next to Caledonia Street at the base of the Anselmo Mine. Called the Northwest Little League, it was later renamed the Jim Scown Field in honor of a longtime president of the league. The field was the scene for many great games and lots of fun. It also had some strange adventures like the time a game was halted when a kid crawled out of a manhole located in left field. The manhole became a thing of the past when a grass field was put down at the complex.

Stuart said, "We had great times in the Hub Addition. One thing about our neighborhood was the togetherness we had for one another. We were a close-knit bunch that stuck together well and we all respected one another. It was a great place to live."

The Hub Addition underwent many changes through the years. The decline in Butte's overall population had a dramatic impact on the Hub Addition as a number of residents left the area. As the neighborhood changed so did the Irish influence in the area. St. Patrick's Church still remains as a pillar for the Catholic faith in Butte, but the strong Irish ties have long since passed away.

McGlone Heights is a neighborhood of homes above the Big Butte area and west of Walkerville with the Syndicate Pit situated southeast of the area. The region was named in honor of a longtime Anaconda Company official Ed McGlone. The name "McGlone Heights" became official at a dinner honoring McGlone on August 18, 1952, at the Finlen Hotel.

McGlone came to Butte as a graduate from the Colorado School of Mines in 1923 where he was a star football player. He continued to shine on the gridiron as a member of the Hub Addition football team in the Butte Independent Football League.

His real claim to fame, though, came in mining. Starting out as a miner at the Tramway Mine in 1923, two years later McGlone was a shift boss at the Tramway. By 1930, he had worked his way up to be the Tramway Mine foreman. In 1946, Ed was put in charge of western operation for The Anaconda Company. The next step up came in 1952 when McGlone was named a vice president of The Anaconda Company at their corporate headquarters in New York.

In terms of years, McGlone Heights was a late developing neighborhood. After World War II, the 125 home units were constructed under the direction of Tim Sullivan. All the homes were the property of Kenwood Realty.

The destruction of neighborhoods like the Parrot Flat, East Butte, McQueen and Meaderville in the early 1960's was a benefit to McGlone Heights. Many residents from those destroyed areas were relocated in McGlone Heights. The relocation formed a common bond for residents in the new neighborhood. In fact, when they moved to McGlone Heights, some residents insisted that their next-door-neighbor be the same folks they had in their old section of town.

During the time of the Berkeley Pit's expansion in the late 1950s and early 1960s, Anaconda Company officials watched closely to see if a home became available in the McGlone Heights area. When there was a vacancy, Anaconda officials would buy the home, then went to a person still living in places like Parrot Flat, East Butte, McQueen or Meaderville and trade the person's home for the one purchased in McGlone Heights.

McGlone Heights is much different from early developing neighborhoods. The emergence of the automobile did not require McGlone Heights to develop local stores like other places. It was purely a neighborhood filled with homes.

McQueen was a small neighborhood nestled at the base of Sunflower Hill and the Continental Divide on the northeast edge of the mining district. A short distance north of McQueen was the neighborhood of Meaderville.

McQueen was named after a McQueen placer mining claim that had been located at the town site. The small community was started in 1891. By 1901, the area still had only 15 homes. The region soon changed with the enormous influx of Southern Europeans coming into Butte looking for work. McQueen became a home mainly for Slovenians, Austrians and Croatians. There were also a few Italians, English, Swedes, Norwegians, Germans, Scots and Finns.

The old country traditions of the Slovenians, Austrians and Croatians were very evident in McQueen. During the early days, residents raised their own animals like hogs, chickens and rabbits. They also had their own smokehouses to cook such food as sausages, ham and strips of pork.

The people in McQueen were simple folks living in basic workers' homes. A unique feature of the neighborhood was the absence of boarding houses. McQueen was strictly a district filled with single-family homes. The majority of residents were miners who toiled their labors in nearby mines like the Leonard, London, Butte, Six O'Clock, Greenleaf and Sinbad.

"One thing about the people living in McQueen is they really kept their homes clean," said Ed Bartoletti. "They never possessed much money, but they were proud of what they had and took care of it."

Bernice Favilla Maki recalled, "It was a wonderful place to live. Everybody really watched out for each other and helped out in any way possible."

Michael Muffich said with a laugh, "Well, that was true except for three families. Those three families were always looking for a fight. If you fought one of them you had to fight them all which made it a tough neighborhood!"

Residents did not have an abundance of money which led to desperate acts by many families to maintain a living. During the winter months, it was common to see mothers and their kids raiding coal trains near McQueen to heat their homes. The mothers hopped aboard a train car and tossed coal down to their kids.

The only winter sport for kids was sledding.

"I recall hooking on the back of semi-trucks that went up the highway leaving town," Charlie Bugni remembered. "We hooked on the back with our sleds and went all the way to the top of Woodville Hill. Once there, it was time to turn around and sled all the way down the highway from Woodville Hill. It was quite a ride and you could really get going fast."

Muffich said, "I was a member of a group called the Al Capone gang. We used an empty house in McQueen as our meeting place. We stole some grappo and drank it at our club. It was all done in fun. We never meant to really harm anyone."

Religion was important for McQueen residents. Holy Savior Catholic Church was started by Jesuit missionaries in 1901. The next year a wooden church was completed which was replaced by a brick building in 1927. Prior to 1920, Holy Savior Church served residents from McQueen, Meaderville, East Butte, Silver Bow Parks, Racetrack, Woodville and the Columbia Gardens.

Besides the church, the Jesuits constructed Holy Savior Catholic Elementary School, opened in 1904. Prior to the new school, students walked to Meaderville and went to school at a boarding house near the Rocky Mountain Cafe. One of the key advocates of the new school was Father Michael Pirnat who served in the parish from 1907 until his death in 1953.

The Catholic faith was not the only form of religion practiced in McQueen. A number of folks went to the Unity Methodist Episcopal Church in nearby Meaderville.

McQueen's location on the northeast edge of the mining district made it an isolated community until the street car system finally laid tracks to the neighborhood in 1909. During the early years, McQueen residents lived a rugged life. There was no water system in place, so residents had to go to a community well at the northeast corner of Oak and Hayes Streets. McQueen folks aggressively sought to upgrade their small area of town. They were one of the first Butte neighborhoods to put in sanitary sewers and street lights.

McQueen's isolation forced residents to be self-sufficient within their own area. The first grocery store was built in the region in 1907. Other stores followed like Cesarini's, Lutey's, Grosso's, and Merzlak's. The Crnich family ran the Tipperary Candy Store. Another favorite spot for kids was Nettie's Super Ice Cream. The Petritz family operated a shoe repair business. The Tomich's had a barber shop.

In addition to all the stores, there were numerous bars located in McQueen, such as the Brozovich's, Jurnich's, Petrovich's, Raenovich's, Krizman's, Alder's, Baldy's Place, and the Castle.

Another kind of entertainment was offered by the Crystal Theater built in 1916.

McQueen grew to a peak of over 1,200 residents in the 1930s. After the 1930s, as the local economy fluctuated, the neighborhood slowly started to lose residents. When the Berkeley Pit started in 1955, there were 276 residential homes in McQueen, a number which dropped sharply as the Pit grew and moved ever closer to the neighborhood.

Maki said, "When the Pit started, things got pretty rough in McQueen. One of the first dumping sites used by The Anaconda Company was right by McQueen. The trucks used to come within 20 to 30 feet of homes. It was terrible. There was always so much noise and dust. It made life really miserable for residents."

The end of McQueen began in 1973 when The Anaconda Company spent over $800,000 to acquire Holy Savior Church and various properties. Within five years, Anaconda owned everything in McQueen. The neighborhood was eliminated to make room for shovels, trucks and the expanding Berkeley Pit.

"The move out of places like McQueen and Meaderville was especially hard on the older people," Maki said. "My mother never did learn how to speak English. She only knew Italian. One thing she shared with neighbors was her language. When she was forced to move, my mother lost a major component of her life. It was extremely hard on her and the others who only had each other to rely on. Now they were scattered throughout the town."

The neighborhood was gone forever, but a symbol of it remains today on Continental Drive. The McQueen Club was built in 1977 after it closed up shop in the old neighborhood. The area might be gone, but the memories of the place called McQueen will last.

Meaderville was situated on the eastern end of Butte at the base of Hungry Hill, the main mining district in town. Besides Hungry Hill, the neighborhood was bordered on the east by McQueen.

The close proximity to Hungry Hill made Meaderville a mining neighborhood. The mines located in the area included the Leonard, West Colusa, Black Rock, East Colusa and Minnie Healy. The Minnie Healy, with one of the richest deposits of copper ore, was the focal point of F. Augustus Heinze's battle with The Anaconda Company over the apex mining laws.

Besides the mines, Meaderville served as the home of numerous mine dumps and lots of smelter operations. At one time in the early days of the community, four smelters were pouring sulfur into the air, killing all the vegetation and making breathing very difficult especially in the wintertime. The open-aired smelters were called "stink pots" by Meaderville residents. The various smelters included the Boston and Montana plus the Montana Ore Purchasing of Meaderville. There were also the Parrot, Colorado and Bell Smelters plus the Butte Reduction Works in other sections of town.

Bill Donati told *The Montana Standard* newspaper in an interview, "You could put your hands up like that and could barely see them. Sometimes it made your nose bleed and it stunk like everything."

Meaderville was not the only area impacted by smelters. The entire community suffered with the "stink pots." The ore was roasted outside, with arsenic and sulfurous matter rising in the air. When there was little or no wind to push the poisonous gases out of the valley, the clouds settled over the community. The smoke was so dense at times that streets lights had to be turned on in the middle of the day. Trolley car conductors blew their whistles at every corner to alert people they were on the move. There were numerous attempts in the 1890s to filter the smoke out of the various smelter operations. None of the ideas provided a solution and the smoke only continued to be a nuisance for local residents.

The problem of the smoke-filled city was so bad that the local professional baseball team was known as the "Smoke Eaters" prior to 1900.

Besides smoke, there were also environmental concerns in Meaderville over the polluted Silver Bow Creek which ran through the northern section of the community. When large thunderstorms pelted down on Meaderville, many times the water from Silver Bow Creek overflowed its banks. On numerous occasions large-scale flooding took place in nearby homes. A 1936 storm resulted in over $75,000 in damage to Meaderville dwellings. A couple of years later, in 1938, another storm caused over $10,000 in damage.

Residents put up with the problems because mining and smelting meant jobs. After all, the reliance on mining is how Meaderville got its name. Charles Meader was one of Butte's pioneer miners. He came here in 1876 following his adventures in California during the 1849 gold rush days. Meader purchased the East and West Colusa Mines from William Clark who had bought the mines four years earlier. Meader would also purchase the Bell-Diamond Mine.

Meader constructed a smelter as the manager of the New York Copper Company which later became the Montana Copper Company in 1880. The smelter was located in a section of town called "Gunderson" after two brothers, Al and Lou Gunderson, who operated a grocery store in the region. Once the smelter was in place, the small township called Gunderson became known as "Meaderville."

Meaderville certainly had a long, colorful mining history, but the small community with the winding roads is best remembered as the home of

Italians, wide-open gambling, and first-class restaurants.

The Italians dominated the neighborhood for years, but they were not the first major ethnic group to settle in Meaderville. The Welsh moved into the area first to work in the four smelters operating at one time in the community. When the smelters shut down, most of the Welsh moved out of the area.

It was after the start of the 20th century that many Italians came to Butte and settled in Meaderville. In a short time, they became the dominant ethnic group with a few Cornish and Welsh families living in the northern section of the community and some Irish blending in with the Italians on the east side of the district.

Meaderville was the home of the Italian/American Society headquarters on Main Street between Noble and Leatherwood. There was also the Christopho Columbo Lodge and so it was natural that Meaderville became the center of the annual Christopher Columbus Day celebration every fall on October 12. A parade in Meaderville was followed by activities at the Columbia Gardens.

Italian was commonly spoken in the homes around Meaderville. It made life difficult for children of Italian immigrants.

"My brother Joe and I really struggled in school," said Mary Gussino Mencarelli. "All my mother and father spoke at home was Italian. Yet, when we went to the Franklin School all the teachers allowed us to speak was English. When we came home at night to do our homework we could not receive any help from our parents because they did not know the English language. Joe and I were always shuttling between Italian and English."

Jenny Serich said, "When I started school English was a foreign language for me. All we ever spoke at home was Italian. Once school started, I had to make an adjustment, but it did not take long to learn English."

The neighborhood was called "Little Monte Carlo" due to the gambling that was a fixture in "the Night Club Mecca of the Rockies." Club patrons could enjoy a variety of games of chance playing craps, blackjack, poker, slot machines, roulette and a variety of sports pools.

Grappo, a famous potent Italian wine, was served in the bars even during the times of Prohibition. Some of the bars included Horse and Jockey, Fred's Place, Rex's, Sam Fian's, the Brass Rail, the White Front, Union, Salot's, Grosso's, Mike Salot's, Vegas Club, Bertoglio's, the Sump, and the Colusa Bar.

"It seemed like everyone was a bootlegger making grappo and moonshine in Meaderville," remembered Ed Bartoletti. "I recall old women walking back from mass in the morning with their long coats and a little flask of grappo tucked away under their coats."

Al Hooper said, "Meaderville was really a mecca for making grappo. Every fall the Italian people pooled their money and got a train load of grapes sent to Butte from California. They hauled the grapes in refrigerated box cars. Even the poorest of poor Italian families some how managed to scrape enough money together to buy grapes for making wine. Some people were buying a couple of tons of grapes at a time."

Gambling or drinking went hand-in-hand with great food at such places as Teddy Traparish's internationally famous Rocky Mountain Cafe, the Golden Fan, the Aro and the Savoy. Italian dishes such as raviolis, spaghetti and chicken were favorites among patrons.

"During the summertime, we kept our windows open," recalled Pauline deBarathy. "We could smell the delicious food from the restaurants across the way and also hear the people enjoying themselves."

Emily Sherman said, "One thing all the night clubs and casinos provided was lots of jobs for the local residents. It took a lot of people to make those night clubs tick and it was a tremendous benefit to the community."

Emily's brother, Bob Sherman recalled, "The night club action was really confined to the southern end of Meaderville. The northern area was pretty much residential and the folks going to the night clubs stayed in the commercial section. They never wandered into the northern section of Meaderville."

Emily added, "We always felt safe in Meaderville. Why, you could leave your house for a week and never have to lock the doors because you knew the neighbors would be watching over the place."

Not all of the action was confined to the saloons and restaurants. One of Meaderville's most popular activities was fighting. It was common for Meaderville folks to team together to battle guys from Dublin Gulch and other ethnic neighborhoods who came to Meaderville looking for trouble.

Meaderville certainly had its unique characteristics with wide-open gambling, restaurants and bars. Yet, it also had many things common with other neighborhoods. There were a number of boarding houses for miners. The houses were run by people like Annie Lazzari, Philomena George, Ghella Gianino, Rochina Calvetti, and the Francesconis.

"Those boarding houses were a big plus for kids trying to earn some money," Bob Sherman said. "I would leave the Franklin School during a break, go over to the boarding house and pack a couple of lunch buckets up to the mines for the workers. The buckets contained tea in the bottom with a meal and pie above it. After school, I went back up to the mines to retrieve the buckets. I got paid 5 cents for every bucket I delivered which was big money in those days during the Depression."

Meaderville residents, like other folks, relied on stores right in their own neighborhood for all their shopping needs. A grocery store was run by Bertoglio and Grosso. Mike Ciabattarri and Joe Stefani operated Meaderville Groceries. There was Guidi's Meat Market. One of their specialties was Italian sausage. The Meaderville Bakery was noted for its French bread and breadsticks. There was also Rossellini's Eatery. Martin Favaro and Dan Stefani had the Meaderville Mercantile store which was famous for selling Thanksgiving turkeys that came off the Guy George Ranch at Waterloo near Whitehall.

"The Meaderville Mercantile Store was the real hub of activity for the region," said Jenny Serich, a former store employee. "We sold every type of grocery you could think of at the store. There was nothing packaged like today and the only thing modern was a large cooler where we stored meat. We had no freezers.

"Our store attracted people from all over town. The wealthy folks from the West Side always made trips to the store to purchase the best cut meats in town at the Meaderville Mercantile Store."

Other businesses provided necessities. Fred Orso had a barber shop. The Sutey and Ossello families operated gas stations, while the Butori and Borini families had a coal shop. The Fagan family operated a pharmacy. A movie house, Mission Theater, served the community.

During the early days, residents even had their own hospital operated by the nearby Boston and Montana Copper Mining Company. Doctor H. J. MacDonald served as a surgeon for the hospital while William Brule was the nurse.

The first school in the area was in the IOOF Hall on Main Street. The upstairs of the two-story structure was used as a lodge. It also served as a place of worship for the Methodist faith. A permanent church was later built on Leatherwood Street.

In 1902, the Franklin School replaced the make-shift classroom. The Franklin survived until an earthquake in 1959 when tremors caused enough damage to close the school. A couple of years later, the building was destroyed by a fire on January 23, 1961.

Catholics in Meaderville traveled just east to McQueen to attend services at the Holy Savior Church. The route to the altar became much shorter after 1920 when St. Helena Catholic Church was built in Meaderville.

"They built St. Helena's Church because of World War I," said Bartoletti. "The Italians fought on one side of the battle, while the Croatians,

Slovenians and Austrians were on the other side. The division created a lot of animosity in Butte, even though we were thousands of miles away from the battlefield. When the War ended, the Italians wanted to build their own church rather than travel over to McQueen and go to the Holy Savior Church with their 'enemies.' There was really a lot of bad blood developed over that War."

Bernice Favillia Maki said, "It was really puzzling for me as a child growing up. I could not understand why as a kid I had to go to St. Helena's in Meaderville when Holy Savior Church was only a block away from my house in McQueen. It was only later on did I realize why as an Italian I had to go to St. Helena's rather than Holy Savior because it was the proper thing to do."

Once St. Helena's Catholic Church was finished, it was classified as "the Italian Church." The few Italians living in McQueen like the Favilla family were strongly encouraged by the Croatians, Slovenians, Austrians and even the parish priest to go to St. Helena's rather than Holy Savior Church.

"There was some bitterness between the various nationalities who were first-generation Americans," Neil Lynch said. "Yet, all that bitterness was gone by the time I was growing up as the next generation. All the various nationalities got along just fine on the east end of town. In fact, I only discovered all the prejudice and bitterness groups had for each other after I left Butte."

Bob Sherman said, "One way to end all the bitterness between ethnic groups was better education in the school system. Every time there was an ethnic holiday we celebrated it at the Franklin School. It forced all the students, regardless of their nationality, to learn about and respect the heritage of their fellow classmates."

One of the favorite games brought to Meaderville from Italy was bocce. A local alley served as the court for the game which involved four balls for each team plus a smaller pallino ball. The game had similar characteristics to the Scottish game of curling and the American game of bowling. First, the smaller pallino ball was rolled on the court by one team. The same team followed up by rolling down one of their own balls toward the pallino. The other team was then allowed to roll a ball toward the pallino. The team with their closest ball to the pallino was awarded a point. The first team to achieve 11 points won the match.

Bartoletti said, "I remember them having lots of fun playing bocce next to homes and restaurants. They started playing bocce and drinking a little grappo and pretty soon the game went on all night. The more they played, the more they drank. It got to be amazing entertainment just watching them."

Angelo Petroni said with a laugh, "It seemed like every bar in Meaderville had a bocce court. It was a lot of fun and I know the Italians really enjoyed playing the game."

Besides playing bocce, kids went to the local mine yards to rustle copper wire and other pieces of junk they felt had any value. On Saturday, various junk men came to the area to buy the merchandise. The junk man inspected a kids' junk pile and then offered him a price for the stuff. Once a price was determined and paid, the kid hauled the junk out to the man's wagon.

When the kids were not finding junk in the mine yards, they were stealing wood and coal from the local ore trains just like their neighbors in McQueen. The wood and coal were used as fuel to heat their homes.

"I recall going over the mine yards with a wheel-barrow," said Mary Gossino Mencarelli. "We loaded railroad ties onto the wheel-barrow and hauled them home for firewood. It was a lot of work, but we needed to stay warm in the winter."

The lure of the mines being so close did cause problems. Youngsters tried to break into the mine property to take explosives. This led to the death of six youngsters at the Meaderville ballfield on the early morning of July 4, 1932, the worst Fourth of July accident in the city's history. The six boys had stolen some caps and other blasting equipment the night before from the Black Rock Mine.

"Actually, all the kids killed were from McQueen," remembered Michael Muffich, who lost his brother in the accident. "After they took the primers and caps, the group wanted to set them off north of McQueen. This did not work very well so they went to the Meaderville baseball field. I told my brother it was time to get away from the gang and go home before something happened. He decided to stay and the next morning we found him and the five others dead on the baseball field. They had laid out the explosives in a circle and some how it ignited at once and killed them all. It was really a sad deal."

Charlie Bugni recalled, "We lived about a block away from the ballfield. The blast really shook our house. I looked out the window and commented to my mom that I could see all sorts of paper flying around at the ballfield. When the sun came up, we went over there. The paper was actually body parts that went flying everywhere from the explosion. It was a real mess."

Ice skating was a favorite activity for youngsters during the winter. The rink was just across the street from St. Helena's Church. Some kids also skated on Silver Bow Creek which froze over during the cold months. It was not as wide or as big as the rink near St. Helena's Church, but it did provide enjoyment for Meaderville children.

"We used to find blades and wire them to the bottom of our shoes," recalled Bartoletti. "We laced the blades tight and went skating. The Meaderville people were real poor and could not afford skates so we had to make do with whatever we could find."

In addition to ice skating, the winding hills and streets of Meaderville made sledding a joy. A favorite spot was Davis Hill which was one of the steeper inclines located in the community.

A highlight during the cold season was the annual Christmas display at the Meaderville Volunteer Fire Department. The tradition was started at Christmas time in 1945 by Gary Gorsh, the Meaderville Volunteer Fire Chief. Gorsh recalled that two local merchants from the Meaderville Mercantile asked him if the fire department could build some type of Christmas display. The decoration was a fabulous success and lured hundreds of people to the neighborhood to see the lights.

The volunteer fire department took on the challenge of a new display every year and worked for months getting the Christmas showcase ready. Each year the display got more elaborate, often featuring animated parts along with the Christmas light show. When patrons watched the display, they could also hear Christmas music coming from nearby speakers.

"The Christmas decorations were always fun to work on," remembered Petroni. "It was sure satisfying to watch the people enjoy all the hard work we put into each display.

"Each year it got a bit tougher to do because we had to go out and raise the money for the project. The businessmen chipped in financially at the beginning, but eventually they backed out. So we had to raise money by doing things like charging people to park their cars on a lot that was formerly the Rocky Mountain Cafe. It was a good source of income because on the weekends there were so many cars in Meaderville, it was tough walking across the street."

Esther Francone said, "Everyone in Meaderville lived to just get a glimpse of the annual Christmas display. The display brought people from all across town to Meaderville and it was extra special the night every year when Santa Claus handed out presents."

When the Meaderville volunteer firemen were not preparing for Christmas, their attention turned to the Fourth of July. The organization was noted for designing some of the most elaborate floats in the annual parade. It normally took the volunteers up to eight weeks to construct their float. The theme and design of the float were kept secret by the volunteers until the day of the parade. The float was built right inside the fire station. The volunteers received assistance from The Anaconda Company who provided the necessary materials needed without charging the volunteers.

A number of the floats had animated parts like Ferris wheels, merry-go-rounds, airplanes, eagles, bucking horses and one year the float had an operating water fountain.

The Meaderville Volunteer Firefighters float was always one of the highlights of the Fourth of July parade, usually receiving a prize for its decoration and creativity.

Music was also a special characteristic of Meaderville even in its early days. Sam Treloar, a native of Cornwall, got together with six friends on December 21, 1887, at a log cabin in Meaderville. Treloar and the five other musicians formed the Boston and Montana Band. As the band got bigger, their practice sessions moved to the Knights of Labor Hall on Meaderville's Main Street. The band was extremely popular during its day and was especially a treat to hear at the Columbia Gardens on a Sunday afternoon. Besides delighting Butte residents, the band took its skills on the road, playing at the 1896 Democratic National Convention held in Chicago and the 1900 Democratic National Convention in Kansas City.

The band took the name from the local mining company in Meaderville, the Boston and Montana. Prior to 1915, the name was changed to The Anaconda Company Band and later the Butte Mines Band.

A second band developed later was called Fanfora. It was not uncommon to see the band parading through the streets of Meaderville after a jam session at the Old Sam's Club.

The Fanfora was a popular treat for residents during the annual Christopher Columbus Day parade in Meaderville.

All the music came to a halt and the Christmas tree lights went dark in 1963 in Meaderville. Anaconda Company officials came into the neighborhood to purchase everything in site. The town was gobbled up by the shovels from the Berkeley Pit. One of the last remaining buildings in the neighborhood was St. Helena's Catholic Church. The final mass said at St. Helena's took place in 1964. The church building was then uprooted and placed at the World Museum of Mining west of the Montana Tech campus.

"Everyone in town knew something was up when The Anaconda Company started buying up property all around Meaderville," Emily Sherman said. "They really kept their plans hidden from the people for quite awhile."

Petroni said, "The Company did not give a damn about the people of Meaderville when they began open pit mining. They started digging at the

West Colusa Mine which is on the edge of Meaderville. Company officials told us at a number of meetings that its Skyrme Pit was strictly experimental and that it would take 25 years to become very large. Why, the Skyrme Pit was followed by the Berkeley Pit nearby and they accomplished in five years what they said would take 25 years for them to do.

"When they started blasting at the West Colusa, there was rocks flying everywhere in Meaderville. One time a lady was using a phone inside a bar and a rock came crashing through the roof and landed next to her as she was talking on the phone. The rock was large enough to kill her if she had been hit."

John Orizotti said, "Boy, it was noisy and dusty when Anaconda started hauling dirt from the Berkeley Pit. Those trucks were going all day and all night. There was no let up on the noise or the dust and all the residents had no choice. We had to move."

Al Hooper said, "The thing that made it hard was that everything in Meaderville was on Company ground. We paid a dollar a month in rent to keep our home on Company ground. When the Pit came along, the Meaderville residents had no choice. They had to move because they did not own the ground."

Pauline deBarathy recalled, "It was a very difficult time for everyone living in Meaderville. We were forced to abandon our security which was our neighborhood and try to find a new home that fit our budget. A majority of the Meaderville residents ended up in either McGlone Heights or the Drives."

Emily Sherman remembered, "It was a very difficult process for us relocating. I looked for two years trying to find a house I could afford on a music teacher's salary. I finally located one on Floral Boulevard, but my goodness, it was not easy. There were so many people out looking for homes that it really became a seller's market. We had no choice. We had to find a new place to live."

Petroni said, "Every time I think about what The Anaconda Company did to the people of Meaderville, I get a sour taste in my mouth. They screwed the people of Meaderville like you can't believe. They brought a man in who wrote every one a letter stating that land rent on Company property would go from a dollar a month up to 100 dollars a month if they did not sell out to Anaconda. Why, some poor old widows didn't get enough money from their settlement with The Company to live in Silver Bow Homes.

"In many cases, people got a settlement that was not even close to the value of their homes. A number of people had to resettle in sections of Butte that were being developed, like McGlone Heights. The newly developed areas needed sewer and water lines put in that the taxpayers of Butte paid for not The Anaconda Company. We really had to pay twice for things like water and sewer, once in Meaderville, and a second time in the new developments. The Company property was always kept out of the city limits so they never had to pay for such infrastructure projects.

"We tried to get some State Senators to come to Butte and see what The Anaconda Company was doing to our neighborhood. When they finally agreed to come, Company officials grabbed them before we could and they were entertaining them at the Rocky Mountain Cafe. We never had a chance with Anaconda because they controlled everyone including the legislators."

Pauline deBarathy remembered, "What soured the whole process even more was someone would torch abandoned homes once the families left the area. We no sooner left Meaderville when our home went up in flames. It really made you feel sad."

Francone said, "We were the last family to move out of Meaderville and it came just in the nick of time. The day we moved out our yard caved in because of the underground mines. Thank goodness we got out of there before my daughter fell in that hole. It was a very difficult situation."

The citizens of Meaderville did hire an attorney to try and stop the growth of the Berkeley Pit, but that did not work. Slowly, the population of Meaderville was reduced to a few souls until no residents remained by 1964.

The final symbol to fall from the small community of Meaderville took place in 1972. The Leonard Mine head frame was destroyed by dynamite charges set off by Company workers. It was a sad time for many who had wonderful memories of one of Butte's most colorful neighborhoods, Meaderville.

"Meaderville was a lot of fun with all the gambling and fine restaurants," recalled Dick Skates. "Frankly, Butte has never been the same without Meaderville. It was really a special place."

Petroni reflected, "I was born there and lived in Meaderville all my life. If I had my way, I'd still be there. It was a great community. The entire neighborhood was close-knit just like one big family."

Mencarelli said, "It really hit me when we had to leave Meaderville. I cried for days because it had such a major impact on my life. I loved the place and wish it were still around today."

Bartoletti explained, "Anyone who loses their roots will find it tough as hell to get going again. It was tough on the residents of Meaderville because it was such a grand neighborhood to live in. Meaderville was really something!"

Muckerville was a series of homes in the heart of the mining district on the Butte hill. The southern edge of Muckerville began on Woolman Street across the street from the Original Mine. It was bordered on the west by Montana Street, the east by Main Street and the north by Summit Street.

The neighborhood was confined to working class homes with primarily Irish residents and a few Cornish families. The vast majority of workers were miners. There were no mines in the immediate neighborhood, but the Original, Steward and Buffalo were all within easy walking distance of Muckerville.

The area was unlike many Butte neighborhoods because Muckerville did not include a large number of local stores or bars. One main bar on Montana Street, the Goodwill, was operated for years by Mike O'Leary and Jerry Shea. The Dineen family ran a small grocery store next to the bar. A small candy shop was managed by the Sheehy family right out of their home just below the Goodwill.

A favorite activity for area kids during the winter was to walk a few blocks west to the Gagnon Mine area where an empty lot served as an ice rink.

The name Muckerville came from the various athletic teams that competed from the residential neighborhood. The local teams called themselves "the Muckers" and thus their neighborhood became Muckerville. The kids played in the Unemployment Boys' Football League during the Great Depression. They also played in various local baseball and basketball leagues.

Parrot Flat was located just south of the Belmont Mine below East Mercury Street. The East Side sat directly northwest of the Parrot Flat; Meaderville was a short distance away to the east, and Butte's Flats was off to the south.

The Parrot Flat was the home for many Croatian families. There were some other ethnic groups like Cornish, Finns, Slovenians and Austrians in the area, but Croatians dominated.

The neighborhood was named after the Parrot Smelter which operated in the area prior to the start of the 20th century.

A neighborhood school, the Jefferson, was constructed in 1902 and later expanded in the 1930s.

There were a number of local bars in the neighborhood like the Parrot, Evatz's and Koochy's, that served as much as community centers as they did places to buy a beer.

"They had barbecues all the time at Evatz's," remembered Cathy

Brozovich James. "It was like a neighborhood party. They also had polka music and dancing all the time. I think we learned to polka before we learned to walk."

Mary Evatz said with a laugh, "Yes, we had plenty of polka music at our bar. We always seemed to have accordion players around and boy could they play!

"Of course, our barbecues were also popular with the neighbors. We cooked just about everything pork, chicken, lamb, turkey, beef, steak and, once in awhile, goats which we purchased from Whitehall. It was always a lot of fun."

James said, "Koochy's was noted for having the most vicious pinochle game in town on Saturday afternoon with the miners who were off shift that day. Koochy's also was a place where you never needed much money to get a beer or drink. There were people who went in there with less than a dollar in their pocket and came out loaded with still some change in their pockets because they would buy you back drinks."

George Krstulich recalled, " I remember a glass of beer only costing a dime in Koochy's. They kicked back a beer after every third drink. So you really never needed much to have a good time in Koochy's."

The neighborhood had plenty of things for kids to do; however, not everything would've gained the approval of their parents. Some kids tied ropes around the nearby Belmont Mine gallows frame or the bridge on East Park Street leading into Meaderville. Once everything was in place, the kids hung on tight to the rope and swang high off the ground, a dangerous precursor to bungee jumping with no safety harness.

Some folks who grew up in Parrot Flat remember the Friday night potato roast where the Weed Concentrator is now located. The kids would start a fire and, once the blaze had gotten down to coals, they buried potatoes under the coals until the spuds were cooked. They uncovered the blackened potatoes and ate them. Ice skating was a big activity during the winter months. A rink was built for the kids at the Shields Street ballfield, now called Parrot Field.

The neighborhood had lots of railroad activity. A favorite form of recreation for kids was hooking rides on the "Put-Put" pulley cars used by crews to fix and inspect the lines.

The Great Northern Roundhouse, where all the engines were repaired, was a hub of activity. The railroad tracks also attracted activities in the Parrot Flat that few Butte neighborhoods got to experience. Railroads were the main form of transportation for hobos who got off the trains near the Parrot Flat and searched for a meal.

"There were many times when hobos would come to our door looking for a meal," said James. "My mother always gave them something, but never let them in the house. She wanted them to eat it away from our home.

"One of the reasons why so many hobos came to our house was that they marked the fence. When a hobo got a meal from a home, he had a way of marking a fence so the next time a fellow hobo came along he knew which homes were handing out meals. The funny thing is the hobos never asked for money, only a meal and actually they were real gentlemen about it."

Krstulich said, "The hobos had a camp right below the Great Northern Roundhouse. As kids we went down there all the time. The hobos had an open fire going and were trying to cook something up. They were actually people you could trust, although, I do remember one time my mom baking some loaves of bread and leaving them on the porch to cool. When she came back, a few of the loaves were missing. She knew that some hobos had wondered along and took the freshly baked treat for themselves."

Al Niemi recalled, "We called the camp 'hobo jungle' because of all the people who lived there. They were good people and really pretty harmless."

The hobo camp was similar in nature to Indian camps that were developed in the Parrot Flat shortly after the white man first settled in the valley. The Indians set up camp in the Parrot Flat area and traveled up the hill to the business district looking for hand-outs.

The Parrot Flat had a number of local stores like Peterson's Meat Market. There was also Ray Reynolds' Warehouse which sold Great Falls Beer. F&S Construction had a large warehouse in the area, and Western Iron Works was located just on the edge of the Parrot Flat.

A favorite time of the year in the Parrot Flat was wine-making season. Croatians were used to having wine or what they called in Croatian "vino" as part of their daily meal. They had grown grapes in the old country and carried on that tradition of serving wine. Wine-making season took place in the fall. The Croatian families filled their porches with stacks of wooden crates of grapes. A number of families made vino while others took another step making some potent grappo.

"There was one person in particular who always made grappo," said James. "Heck, you could smell the odor. It was so strong when he was cooking, but he never opened the doors to his garage while making it in fear that federal agents might bust him. All the kids in the neighborhood were told never to talk to a stranger about it. If someone asked you about the strange odor, you were to tell them nothing. It was like a neighborhood secret."

George Krstulich said with a laugh, "Everyone in the neighborhood knew when my grandmother was making moonshine. She put newspapers over the windows thinking that might conceal her efforts of brewing the stuff right in the kitchen. Why, everyone knew what she was doing."

The advent of the Berkeley Pit just north of the Parrot Flat in 1955 signaled the beginning of the end for the neighborhood. Before it was gone, the residents in the neighborhood had to withstand the grim reality of the powerful Anaconda Company's control over the town.

"When the Company started blasting in the neighborhood, it was absolutely terrible," James recalled. "They blew off a whistle before a blast took place. Many times the blasts knocked pictures off our walls and caused things to fall off shelves and break. One time they almost destroyed everything in our house. It caused cracks in the walls and our home quickly lost value because of all the structural damage being done."

The blasting took its toll in a quick hurry. By 1965, many of the residents in the Parrot Flat had left the area for another place to live. The Jefferson School was torn down. The Parrot Flat would be lost forever.

"It was heartbreaking when the neighborhood was broken up," remembered James. "No one really wanted to leave the area. We had such a tight-knit neighborhood, that was safe and people watched out for each other. There were a lot of tears shed as each family left the area. We had something that was lost forever and will never be the same again."

Racetrack is a neighborhood located on the Flats just east of Silver Bow Creek and south of Meaderville. The Silver Bow Addition was directly north of the Racetrack, with the Hamilton and North Pacific Additions sitting east of the neighborhood.

Racetrack got its name from Marcus Daly who built and maintained a large horse racetrack in the area prior to 1896. Daly turned the track over to a new management team in 1896. The grandstands could seat more than 2,000 racing fans at one time. The 60-day race season saw thousands of visitors bet enormous sums of money at the track. The 60-day season continued until 1912 when laws forced the track to be opened for only 30 days during the summer. Horse racing was eventually put out of business when lawmakers ended the popular sport in the Racetrack area. The owner of the track, W. I. Wilson, sold the racetrack ground and divided the section into lots in September 1915.

The ponies were gone, but the neighborhood grew with the emergence of the trolley car system in the area. The region was not heavily populated during the early days and featured plenty of wide-open space.

"I remember going over lots of open field just to get to the Greeley

School," said Emma Strike Smith. "We were a long way from the mainstream of uptown Butte. The neighborhood was a mixture of many different ethnic groups. It was a section of town for the working class.

"I recall my parents paid seven dollars in rent during bad times that increased to fourteen dollars a month when times were good. We were a poor family like many of our neighbors.

"Times were especially tough during the Depression. I used to take a lard bucket and walk a number of miles to the business district to get some skim milk. Once in awhile, they gave you grapefruit and other things. It was a tough time trying to make a living."

The neighborhood continued growing once the automobile was introduced to Butte in 1910, growth which is reflected in the emergence of the school system within the region. The Greeley Elementary School was built in 1901 and later expanded in 1917, 1957 and in 1962. A second school, Butte Junior High School, was constructed in 1957. The name of the school changed to East Junior High in 1969 when a second junior high was completed across town. It was changed to East Middle School in 1986 when the two junior high schools in town combined into one.

A baseball field was built just east of the Junior High building in 1957 shortly after the Clark Park grandstands were destroyed by fire. The land for the ballfield was donated by Jack Duggan. When it was completed, the ballpark was called Duggan Memorial Field. It was used for a few years as the site of American Legion and Copper League baseball games. The ballfield was eventually torn down after the games were moved to the new multi-purpose stadium at Alumni Coliseum on the campus of Montana Tech in 1965.

A second sports complex, the East Junior High Stadium, was added in 1976, becoming the site for high school football games plus local and state track meets. The stadium would later be renamed Bulldog Memorial Stadium.

The growth of the neighborhood with schools and stadiums was a far cry from the early days when the Racetrack section of town had few activities for kids.

"It was a neighborhood with not a lot to offer kids," Smith remembered. "We played ball in our bare feet on an open field near where East Junior High is now located. No one could afford shoes in those times during the Depression. We were always trying to heal our feet because they were always sore from walking around barefoot.

"I guess the most excitement we had was trying to stop one of the street cars which came down to our neighborhood. We saw the street car off in the distance and a bunch of us kids tried to find something that forced the street car to stop. One time we hauled an old box-spring mattress over and laid it on top of the tracks. The street car was forced to stop. At the time there were some cops on board. They hopped off the track and started chasing us, but there were so many kids that they never could figure out who exactly put the box springs on the track.

"Of course, that was not the only trouble we got into. We used to let air out of car tires and soap windshields. My father told us to not let all the air out of the tires or soap the drivers' side window just in case there was an emergency and the car owner needed to make a quick trip to the hospital or something."

The mischievous deeds of young Racetrack area kids during the early days was replaced with many constructive activities for kids with the emergence of the Junior High School and the various fields surrounding it. The practice fields behind the school are used for soccer, baseball, softball, rugby and other activities. There was also some outdoor handball courts constructed next to the school.

The Racetrack area started off with horses and wide open spaces. Today it houses a major school and sports complex, and is one of Butte's core neighborhoods.

Rocker, about three miles northwest of Butte, served as a railroad stop and switching point for the Butte, Anaconda & Pacific Railroad.

It was also the home of a large logging operation, the Rocker Mill, that helped form timber for the mines. The Rocker Timber, Framing and Treatment Plant employed 50 to 60 workers at one time in the 1950s. Workers took long 90-foot strips of lumber and prepared the wood for support timber for the underground mines.

"Many pieces of timber were not even treated," recalled Lee Masters, a former mill worker. "They sent the lumber off, bark-and-all, to the mines. This timber was mainly used in dry sections of the mines. The timber we did treat was soaked with arsenic and water. Once properly treated, it was sent to a wet underground section of the mines. Moisture normally rotted timber, but once it was treated at our mill the lumber could withstand the wet conditions and thus provide support for the underground operations."

The timber plant was shut down in 1957. Four decades later, Atlantic Richfield was forced to come into the region and clean up because the arsenic in the area was threatening to intersect with the local ground water. ARCO spent over $5 million cleaning up the material with an innovative method to immobilize the arsenic using a combination of ferrous sulfate and calcium carbonate.

Prior to its days as an industrial center for railroads and timber, Rocker was a town dominated by one ethnic group, the Chinese. They tried to change the name of the small community to "Foochow" after the capital of the Fukien Province in China. When the name switch was made, the Chinese did not alert local post officials, so the name Rocker survived the Chinese theme and lives on with a few homes in the area plus the It Club and Bluebird Bars. In recent years, Rocker has become a major stopping point for truckers with two mega-stations, Town Pump and Flying J, serving their needs.

Stringtown was located a short distance north of Walkerville and Butchertown.

The small group of homes in Stringtown was built in a string-type formation and thus the name of the town. It was inhabited mainly by French-Canadian woodcutters who chopped down timber for the Butte mines, a major business employing over 1,600 men in the early 1880s. The loggers hauled thousands of wood cords a month into town for use in the mines.

The only real sign of community development in Stringtown was a small school built in the neighborhood which eventually closed as students went into Walkerville for their education. The small group of residents also left for good as Stringtown turned into a ghost town.

Timber Butte is a small group of homes located at the base of a hill called Timber Butte, just south of Montana Street beyond a series of cemeteries. Now, there are only a few working class homes in the neighborhood. Prior to the turn of the 20th century, the area was mainly a center for smelting activity with the featured attraction being the Clark Mill, a remnant of which can be seen on the side of the butte. The mill is now a private residence.

Travona Addition also known as "Sleepy Hollow" was a collection of small residential and industrial additions located on Butte's lower West Side, situated south of Platinum Street down to Centennial Avenue, bordered on the east by Montana Street and the west by Excelsior Street.

The Travona Addition got its name from the Travona Mine constructed in the area by William Farlin in 1876.

"I remember friends who lived right next to the Travona telling me how they could hear the miners yelling at each other underground at night," recalled Bev McClafferty. "We lived a couple of blocks away from the mine, so I never did hear the workers down below, but my neighbors swear they could hear lots of talking, blasting and other activities from underground during the still of the night."

A mixture of many different ethnic groups lived in the area. The Serbians had enough people around the neighborhood to lead to the construction of the Holy Trinity Serbian Orthodox Church on Idaho Street in 1905.

The Travona Addition had a neighborhood school, the Webster, built in 1897 at the corner of Idaho and Aluminum Streets and remodeled in 1908. The immediate area around the Webster School was a beehive of activity. In a two-block radius around the school, there were ten different small grocery stores. The Webster School was closed by city officials who condemned the building in the early 1940s. Students were moved to the vacated old Butte High School on the corner of Park and Idaho Streets. When that building was destroyed by fire on April 10, 1946, upper level students were sent to Butte High School where classes were conducted on the third floor of that building and lower grade students were sent to the McKinley School. This arrangement continued until 1949 when the new Webster-Garfield School was opened on Front Street in Central Butte.

A neighborhood center was the Dexter Addition located just below Iron Street. The area featured simple homes for local miners. The name Dexter comes from the nearby Dexter Mill that was built by William Farlin to smelt silver from the Travona Mine.

Industrial activity east of the Dexter Addition revolved around a series of warehouse buildings which stretched down Montana Street to Centennial Avenue. A main staple among the warehouses was the Montana Hardware Company in the Storey Addition. The store eventually closed. Rosenberg's Furniture took over the building in 1976. Rosenberg's was one of Butte's most successful family-owned furniture stores. It was started by Edward and Anna Rosenberg in 1934 in the central business district. The business was in operation 64 years under the guidance of Jack Rosenberg Sr. and his son, Jack Rosenberg Jr.

The Milwaukee Railroad Depot was another major feature in the warehouse section. When a train came into the area, it had to be backed in the final half-mile to park the passengers cars next to the depot. Near the depot, the Milwaukee Railroad had a wooden trestle crossing which was the site of the lynching of Wobbly leader, Frank Little. The train depot later became the studios of KXLF-TV.

When mining activities were in full swing, the Washoe Sampling Center behind the Milwaukee Railroad Depot was where ore was sampled before being shipped to Anaconda for smelting. "I remember as a kid watching the miners take manganese ore right out of the Travona and hauling it by truck a couple of blocks to the Washoe Sampling Center," said McClafferty. "It was a very busy time and the entire neighborhood was filled with activity."

Like other sections of town, the neighborhood was hurt when mining jobs became scarce for various reasons and a lack of employment opportunities forced many residents to leave the Travona Addition for good.

People still live in the small neighborhood and there is still industrial activity in the region. In fact, the 1990s saw new development in the area with the remodeling of a building into the Rocky Mountain Clinic on South Montana Street. This has given the region new hope for more growth in the future.

Walkerville is located just over the summit of the hill above Butte some 6,172 feet above sea level. The community is referred to as "Hill City" or by some local residents as "God's Country." Due to its location above the Butte city limits, Walkerville enjoys much warmer temperatures during the winter some ten to twenty degrees warmer than Butte and the Flats. The reason for the dramatic difference is cooler air getting trapped in the valley while the hotter air rises to the upper extremes of the hill.

The town developed after Marcus Daly persuaded the Walker Brothers of Salt Lake City to purchase the Alice Mine following his visit in 1876. Walkerville grew up around the mine with the town being named after the Walker brothers.

Mining activity was everywhere around Walkerville with over 60 mines in operation at one time. The list of prominent mines in the area included the Alice, Badger, Moulton, Lexington, Granite Mountain, Speculator and Diamond.

Two years after the Walker Brothers purchased the Alice Mine, the city of Walkerville had 364 residents and was growing almost daily. The various mine properties allowed the community to grow at a much faster pace than Butte. At one time, the city of Walkerville had a population of 4,000 residents.

Walkerville became an incorporated city in 1890, with municipal codes written and agreed upon in 1891. One of the most unique laws was city ordinance Number 38 which reads, "no burial or interment shall be lawful in the city of Walkerville." Despite its lack of a cemetery, the city certainly had its own identity with its own post office, liquor store, fire hall and entertainment center called the Dream Theater where at one time you could go to a Sunday matinee for a nickel.

There were local stores operated by the Broughton, Driscoll and Fasso families. The Dunovan's ran a drug, photography and shoe store. Felix Osier was in charge of a dress-maker shop. Charlie Beeley ran the Walkerville Bakery. The Walkerville Coal Company was operated by T. J. Bennett. Manza's Market served the region for over 70 years. In addition, Walkerville was home for three Chinese laundries and two newspapers, *The Walkerville Telegraph News* plus *The Walkerville News.*

Prior to 1940, Walkerville had no sewer system. Water was provided by local wells. Residents used cesspools, septic tanks and outhouses. It made for less than satisfactory sanitary conditions.

"It was common for water running in the kitchen sink to go under the house, under the wooden sidewalks and out onto Daly Street," remembered Maurine Higman Dennehy.

A sewer system was put in through the WPA Program in 1941, thanks to the efforts of Walkerville mayor, Jimmy Shea. The federal government provided 75 percent of the funds for the project. Shea acquired the other necessary funds through grants he obtained from large companies like the Montana Power and The Anaconda Company plus a 20 dollar connection fee for residents.

All the mining activity in the region required lots of housing for workers. Walkerville featured a number of boarding houses for miners to live in when they were not beneath the surface. The houses included the American, Walker and Martin plus the Palace Hotel.

When miners wanted to quench their thirst, they had lots of options in bars like the Atlas, Matthew's, Prize, Hilltop, Hitch n Post, Friendly Tavern and Schonsberg's. Even during Prohibition Days in the 1920s, miners never had to look far for a drink. Walkerville became a haven for bootleggers with seven different moonshine companies.

"There sure was a lot of bootlegging during Prohibition Days in Walkerville," said resident Rudy Tomazich. "The key was who paid off the local and federal agents and who did not. I remember a lady up on Toboggan Street getting busted with booze that her son made out near Bernice. They took all the booze out on the street and busted it up. On the other hand the guy who lived next door to me was one of the biggest bootleggers in Walkerville and he never got busted once. I am not sure how he was paying off the federal agents, but I know he was doing it."

The dominant ethnic group in Walkerville was the Cornish. There was also a handful of Irish, Italians, French, Austrians and others mixed into the neighborhood.

"It was a grand place to grow up," Carol Wyatt Maunder said. "Unlike Centerville, where the Cornish and Irish used to fight a lot, everyone seemed to get along with everyone in Walkerville.

"Of course, Walkerville was not without its problems. Most of the trouble I remember always happened around Halloween. The kids pulled old outhouses onto Daly Street. They set them on fire and created quite a stir.

"I recall one time the kids stole the old Model T truck the sheriff of Walkerville rode in. They went up and down the street in the truck with the sheriff running desperately trying to catch them. It was wild!"

During the winter, kids could enjoy skating on one of three ice rinks: one was on Daly Street, a second was located east of the Sherman School and the third was at the present site of the Blaine Community Center.

Dennehy remembered, "Of course, when you went skating at the various rinks you had to bring a shovel. Before you could skate you had to clean all the snow off the ice. The local firemen flooded the rink with their hoses early in the winter. It was then up to the kids to maintain the rink for the rest of the winter."

Another favorite winter sport was sledding. "We used to start our ride on Fourth Street," Dennehy recalled. "You went down Fourth Street, under the railroad tunnel and finished up on Missoula Avenue. It was a long way down the hill and my mom never liked us riding down there because you went over some sewer water. Of course, the water was frozen and it made your sled go faster. You really went like the devil there. Boy, it was a great ride down, but a long trip back up the hill hauling your sled."

The dominance of the Cornish can be found in the first church built in Walkerville in 1883, the Mount Bethel Methodist Church on Daly Street. George Stull served as the first pastor.

The Irish countered with their own church, St. Lawrence O'Toole Catholic Church, built through miners' donations of $25,000. The land was donated by the Butte and Boston Mining Company at the entrance to Walkerville on Main Street. The parish was formed by Bishop John Brondel in 1897. He named the church after being moved by his visit to the shrine of St. Lawrence O'Toole in Ireland.

The church remains one of the most colorful in Butte with decorated frescos on the ceiling that were completed in 1906 through the work of Mr. Tolston. He painted 40 different frescos. St. Lawrence, Butte's second Catholic parish, remained a pillar of the Catholic strength on the hill for many years. Catholic Church officials finally closed St. Lawrence for good in 1986 due to a lack of priests in the diocese.

Church officials wanted to tear down the structure; however, a group of local residents won a battle with church officials in June 1987 to save the church. The structure was turned over to the Save St. Lawrence Committee. In the agreement between the Church and the committee, all liturgical items such as chalices and vestments were taken from the building by Roman Catholic Church officials. The second condition for turning over St. Lawrence to the local group was that the committee never try to return the property to the Church. The building was turned into a museum/church with weddings and other non-Catholic services being held in the St. Lawrence Center.

The first school built in Walkerville was Jeffers School located on Academy Street. Next came St. Joseph's Catholic School on Daly Street. Nuns from the Sisters of Charity of Leavenworth who were stationed at St. Patrick's School in Butte traveled north to Walkerville to conduct classes at St. Joseph's. The Blaine School was built on Main Street just north of the Trinity Methodist Church on the corner of Main and Bennett Streets in 1890. A few years later, St. Lawrence Catholic School was constructed near the Blaine building and St. Joseph's School was shut down. Another public grade school, the Sherman, was finished and opened for students in 1902.

The school encountering the most problems was St. Lawrence. It was destroyed by a series of fires in both 1908 and 1936. Both times the school was rebuilt. After the 1936 blaze, during reconstruction, a gymnasium was put in the school building, the first gym located high on the hill. School officials allowed students from both the Blaine and Sherman to practice and have a night of their own in the facility.

St. Lawrence survived the fires, but could not live through a dwindling student enrollment. Catholic school officials were forced to shut down St. Lawrence in 1967. Students were sent down the hill to merge with St. Mary's elementary pupils into a new school called St. Raymond's.

The Blaine and Sherman Schools suffered the same fate as St. Lawrence. A new Blaine School was built across the street from the original building in 1959. The Blaine was shut down for good in 1982 and converted into a Community Center. The Sherman closed a couple of years later, leaving the incorporated town of Walkerville with no neighborhood school. The Sherman building became a center for a local gymnastics club.

Walkerville's long history of mining was not without its problems. The community became one of the first test sites for the new law called Superfund. State officials came to the community in April 1986 and conducted tests in the neighborhood. Ground samples revealed that some yards had high levels of toxic materials.

The Sherman baseball field just north of Daly Street had high levels of lead and mercury in the soil, levels that were over one hundred times higher than soils tested elsewhere in Butte. Two years later, in 1988, the

60-year-old ballfield was cut off from recreational use when state officials put a fence around the field and did some reclamation work on the soil.

Atlantic Richfield gave the community $100,000 in April 1998 for a new ball diamond near the old Ryan Mine shaft just northwest of the community.

The Alice Pit and mine dump posed a clean up challenge. Atlantic Richfield officials finally decided on June 24, 1998, to take the tailings from the dump and place it inside the old open pit mine. It would reduce the dump by 30 percent plus scale down the steep walls of the open pit to a 17 degree slope.

The issue of Superfund and clean up put a cloud over Walkerville. The community's future revolves around state and federal officials as clean up from a century of mining now becomes the center of activity in the town.

North Walkerville also called "Seldom Seen" was a cluster of homes north of Walkerville on the far side of the large mine dump. Three streets running north and south connected to Williams Street which went east and west.

North Walkerville was inhabited by Cornish descendants who lived in simple workers' homes. The main place of employment during the early days were the Alice and Moulton Mines. When the Alice opened in 1877, the Walker Brothers who owned the property wanted to provide some protection for workers. The Walkers built their own hospital in the area in the early 1880s. Doctor George Wells served as the surgeon with Mrs. D. Veen acting as the matron.

Besides the hospital, a school, the Jefferson, was built in the area.

The Alice Mine was later replaced by the Alice Pit which was started in 1955. The shovels at the Alice dug up over 5.5 million yards of dirt and ore.

"Our home was right across the street from the Alice Pit," Carol Wyatt Maunder recalled. "The thing I remember most was The Anaconda Company always blasting inside the Pit. There were many times when we picked up rocks in our yard that ended up there from a dynamite blast at the Alice. We had to dodge flying rocks numerous times following a blast.

"I remember a neighbor, Gene Kuhn, came running into our house because he wanted to use our phone. He was mad as hell and called The Company up to claim that his kids almost got killed from flying rocks after a blast. Company officials told him they didn't care if his kids got hurt or killed because of the blasting. They had enough money to pay for any health problems or funerals. Well, of course, Kuhn was furious over Anaconda's response. A short time after the incident Kuhn packed up his family and left town for good."

City officials in Walkerville were upset with the blasting being done by The Anaconda Company. Walkerville Mayor Jimmy Shea ordered town marshall, Oral Rickey, to arrest workers from The Company who were digging up public streets and alleys for the pit. The workers were arrested and taken to the county jail. The Anaconda Company and its workers had to go to court where a legal ruling forced Company officials to take a different approach to blasting and digging activities in the Alice.

"The Anaconda Company was a big bully in North Walkerville," Jimmy Shea said. "The Company felt they could do anything they wanted at the Alice. Our only protection was the city laws governing streets and alleys. You needed a permit to dig up the pavement. We used that against Anaconda to slow down their progress at the Pit. They wanted to build a dump that extended all the way down to Daly Street. We were able to stop that expansion with our laws.

"I'll tell you, it was a tough fight battling Anaconda. They had control of everything in town. I remember going to Jim Dickey, the head of all the Company-run newspapers in the state which included *The Montana Standard.* I asked him why he would not put some news in the paper about our sheriff arresting Company workers for digging up our streets. He said the incident was controversial to The Company position so no story would ever make the paper. I rebutted by asking about the freedom of the press and the First Amendment. Dickey told me, "Well, we have freedom of the press because our newspaper has the freedom to put anything in the paper that is not controversial to The Company position."

The Anaconda Company, through their Fairmont Corporation, controlled the newspapers in Butte, Helena, Missoula, Billings, Livingston and Libby until Lee Enterprises bought them out on June 2, 1959. At the time of the sale total circulation of Company-controlled newspapers in Montana was 89,934. The total circulation of all other non-Company independent newspapers in the state was 69,552. The Company used a heavy hand in controlling its newspapers, ignoring such stories as labor unrest, mine accidents, digging up streets, and legislative matters which impacted Anaconda.

"I remember Jimmy Shea paying to have an advertisement run in *The Great Falls Tribune,*" recalled Rudy Tomazich. "It was one of the few state newspapers not controlled by the Company. Once that article hit, *Life* magazine rushed to Butte to do a story on what The Anaconda

Company was trying to do to the residents of Walkerville."

Shea remembered, "The fact that The Company controlled all the newspapers forced me to go out of town to radio stations in Missoula and Billings to get the truth out about what Anaconda was trying to do in Walkerville. I guess all the fighting was worth it, though, because if you look today Meaderville, McQueen, Parrot Flat, East Butte and the East Side are all gone because of the Berkeley Pit. However, Walkerville is still here and that's because we went eyeball-to-eyeball with The Company and would not let them do anything they wanted to."

The efforts of Shea and others forced The Anaconda Company to build a fence around the property and construct wooden sidewalks along side the Alice Pit. The ability of Walkerville officials forced Anaconda to continue digging straight down rather than spread out the operation. It was the main reason why Anaconda suspended its operation on February 27, 1959. The incline inside the area became too steep for the large Pit trucks to move ore out of the mine.

The small community of North Walkerville survived the pit mining operations and still has a few families calling the small neighborhood their home.

Warehouse District is located south of the business district. Originally, it was bordered on the north by the Cabbage Patch and East Side, the west by Central Butte, the south by Butte's Flats and the east by Parrot Flats.

The Warehouse District was just that: a series of warehouses used for both commerce and mining, providing major industrial employment area for hundreds of people. Newbro Drug, Christie Transfer, City Transfer, Railway Express, Butte Produce and Bertoglio's were some of the large warehouses.

"I can remember the Warehouse District as always being a beehive of activity," said Bob Koprivica. "As kids we'd go down to the Warehouse District where sometimes workers gave us fruit they were unloading."

Besides all the activities at the large warehouses, the district featured a number of very successful family-owned businesses including Bob and Joe's Wholesale, Montana Broom & Brush, Quilici Glass, Thompson Distributing, Butte Produce, Butte Floral, J&J Floral, S. J. Perry, R&R Electric, A&M Fire Supply, Morris Marketing, Furniture Factory Outlet, Rosin Brothers, Ward Thompson Paper, Evans Transfer, Steele's Warehouse, Whalen Tire and Ossello's.

The family-owned businesses were one unique element of the Warehouse District. Another key factor of the district was it served as home of the Great Northern Railroad Depot, one of the city's more popular destinations during the railroad era. The Great Northern Railroad Depot, along with the Union Pacific Railroad Depot a couple of blocks south on Front Street, served hundreds of passengers on a daily basis. Arizona Street was constantly busy with people coming and going to the train depots.

The Great Northern Depot yards served as more than just a popular place for an arrival or departure. It was here and at nearby coal plants that local residents rustled coal and wood to heat their homes.

The Warehouse District did have an excellent location for kids to play: Hebgen Park on Second Street. One of Butte's first parks, it served as one of the home fields along with the Columbia Gardens for Butte's professional baseball teams prior to 1920. Hebgen Park was used for football games and soccer matches. It was also the site for a political rally for Irish President, Eamonn DeValera, during his visit to Butte in 1919.

The large park was renamed Koprivica Park in 1995 in honor of longtime Butte supporter, Bob Koprivica. He helped improve the park through money out of his own pocket and funds he received from friends throughout the community.

As kids everywhere will do, youngsters created their own fun, too. "We built a little three-hole golf course behind the Warehouse District in the mine yards," recalled Matt Vucurovich. "We used regular balls with two and five irons plus a putter we got while caddying at the Country Club. The holes were no longer than 100 yards, but we sure had a lot of fun."

For adults, a favorite entertainment spot was Boyle's Bar at 632 South Utah Street. Green beer, one of many traditions on Butte's St. Patrick's Day, began at Boyle's.

Millie Boyle Moriarty remembered, "My father, Jim Boyle, started serving green beer on St. Patrick's Day in the early 1940s. He was from Donegal County, Ireland, and felt as long as he was going to celebrate St. Patrick's Day he should do it in grand style. So, he got some coloring dye and turned the beer green. It was a big hit. After that first year, the Butte Beer Company started supplying green beer every March 17.

"Boyle's was the place to be on St. Patrick's Day in Butte during the 1940s and 1950s. My dad along with his brothers, Bud and Jack, were busy all day on St. Paddy's Day. The place went 24-hours straight with music and dancing. The place was absolutely jammed. It was a lot of fun!"

A couple of other watering holes dotted the neighborhood. There was the Scoop Bar on East Second Street. A block from the Scoop was a bar which changed hands a couple of times with the Wedlake brothers, Bob and Joe, owning it for awhile. Jim Hill had control of the bar at one time and later the establishment became known as Klapin's Korner named after owner, Joe Klapin.

The Warehouse District featured one of the best neighborhood groceries stores in Butte: Lenz Grocery which opened for business in 1909 on Utah Street. Another local store in the neighborhood was Bob's Market which was located next to Klapin's Korner.

The neighborhood offered Butte travelers one of the city's best hotels, the National Hotel, on Utah Street which was a stop-over spot for many professional people. The hotel had a pharmacy located on the first floor along with an ice cream parlor.

The Warehouse District lacked the flavor of other neighborhoods due to its limited residential population which was mainly Austrian, but it can't be ignored in the history of Butte. It was in the Warehouse District that two of the city's worst disasters took place.

A fire at the Kenyon-Connell Warehouse on January 15, 1895, led to the death of 62 people, with 57 of the victims being firemen. They were killed after numerous explosions occurred from dynamite stored inside the warehouse. A train wreck involving passengers returning from the Columbia Gardens resulted in 10 deaths and over 100 people injured on August 20, 1905.

The Warehouse District also can be noted for housing one of the city's first schools. The Monroe School was built in 1890.

The commerce of the Warehouse District still carries on today; however, the amount of activity and the volume of goods being moved has been greatly reduced from earlier days with the Great Northern Depot now an office and the Northern Pacific Depot, a warehouse.

West Side is located on the western edge of the town, south of Caledonia Street, west of Alabama Street, and north of the Interstate Highway.

From its beginnings it was a neighborhood filled with a diverse number of ethnic groups and housing arrangements. Some of Butte's wealthiest residents like John D. Ryan, Con Kelley, Charles Virden and William Symon built massive mansions on the West Side near or along Excelsior Street. The mansions were located on the same block or very close to simple one or two-bed working class family homes.

The Paul Clark Home on South Excelsior was completed in 1900, thanks to a $50,000 donation from William Clark. The home was named after Clark's son, Paul, who died at a young age. The home was originally built to help families during a time of need after arriving in Butte. It later was used to help young mothers with their new infants. The home was then converted and served its primary purpose for many years as an orphanage.

"I remember the generosity of William Clark quite well," Dula Schonsberg recalled. "He always bought at least one new, nice thing for every child in the home every Christmas. Clark was very kind to all the kids."

Kay Kosmack remembered, "Christmas was a great event for us. About a month before the holiday the matron took our orders for presents. Each child was allowed two presents, one being clothing, a coat, dress or suit. The second present was always a toy for the younger kids while the older ones got anything they wanted. All the presents were brought through the trust fund established by Clark."

A second big holiday for all the kids occurred on January 19 every year. It marked the birthday of Paul Clark. A large party took place on the second floor recreation room with dancing, entertainment and outside guests coming to honor the late son of William Clark.

The orphanage could house up to 60 kids at one time. The children ranged in age from four- to eighteen-years-old. The sleeping quarters for all the kids was on the third floor of the home. The home featured a large dining room plus kitchen and pantry on the first floor. Each week 24 loaves of bread were made three times a week with some of the older girls helping cook the bread. All the children were required to do chores and pass inspection every day before going off to school. There was also room in the home for a small infirmary. The sick children of the orphanage were isolated there to limit the spread of various diseases.

"I recall the hospital room well," said Kosmack. "I spent two weeks there trying to fight off scarlet fever. Late one night, I recall a little boy was near death and everyone in the house prayed until the crises was over and he started to get better.

"One thing about the orphanage was all the kids stuck together. We were loyal to each other and tried to keep each other out of trouble. I developed some life-long friends from my stay at the Paul Clark Home."

The orphanage was in operation through the 1950s before closing. The building sat vacant for a number of years before becoming a Paul Clark Home/McDonald's Family Place. Prior to the conversion, the home underwent a four-year remodeling project. The renovation work went forward when enough funds were raised for the project. The McDonald's Corporation gave a grant to start the project with the rest of the money for remodeling coming from fund raising projects spearheaded by Lowell and Susan Bartels who operated the local McDonald's Restaurant in town. The project was called Butte's own "House that Love Built." A major fund raising project for the Paul Clark Home every year is the Festival of Trees during the Christmas season when a number of individuals and businesses decorate trees which are auctioned.

When the Paul Clark Home/McDonald's Family Place was reopened in October 1992, its primary purpose was to provide temporary lodging for families of patients receiving treatment at a Southwestern Montana Hospital. It is designed to provide affordable, comfortable and convenient housing for out-of-town patients and their families.

A dominant segment of the West Side is the Montana Tech campus located on the far west edge of the neighborhood. Established as the Montana School of Mines in 1893, the campus received its first students on September 11, 1900. Two majors, one in mining engineering and the other in electrical engineering, were available to the 37 male and 2 female students in the fall of 1900.

Main Hall, the first building, was financed through a bond issue of $120,000 and completed in 1897. The college was small, but soon grew with more students and more buildings. One thing that grew quickly was the outstanding quality of education students received from the school on the hill. The Montana School of Mines was soon the top mining and engineering school in the country.

As the student population grew, the campus took on a new look. On January 25, 1965, the name of the college was changed to the Montana College of Science and Technology or Montana Tech for short. The curriculum was expanded to include more liberal arts and business courses.

The college climbed to a population of over 2,000 students in the 1970s. A full century has done little to change the high quality of education the school offers its students. Every year a very high percentage of graduating students receive excellent paying jobs when they receive their diploma.

School of Mines students developed one of the city's landmark symbols: the M on Big Butte. In 1910, three Tech students hauled 44 tons of rhyolite rock to the Big Butte site which was 6,369 feet above sea level. They constructed an M that stood 75 feet wide. Next, the students got other classmates to help whitewash the M on May 20, 1910. A couple of years later, the M was widened to 90 feet. A major addition took place in 1962 when 130 light bulbs were wired at the site so the M glowed at night. Later, students rewired the light bulb system at the M so it glowed in a V when their school wins an athletic contest.

Another symbol of Butte stands at the entrance to the campus: the statue of Marcus Daly by sculptor Augustus Saint-Gaudens. The statue was made from stone obtained at a quarry run by James Welsh near Homestake Lake 16 miles southeast of Butte. The statue was originally built and placed on Main Street near the Federal Building in 1906. Butte citizens contributed more than $5,000 to help complete the statue. Daly's image was moved to the top of Park Street at the entrance of the Montana Tech campus in 1941 for safety reasons after a number of cars had run into the base of the statue on Main Street.

The West Side had neighborhood schools, too. The McKinley Elementary School, constructed in 1903, was destroyed by fire on December 13, 1919, and rebuilt in 1926 using some of the same stones from the original building. The school was shut down in 1986 and later became a church center, the Park Street Baptist Church. West Junior High, built in 1969, was converted into an elementary school in 1986 after the McKinley closed.

A source of recreation for kids in the neighborhood was a tennis court complex located just below the corner of Excelsior and Platinum Streets. Next to the courts on Emmett Street was a large field used as a football practice facility by both high school teams. The field added a running track when West Junior High was completed in 1969.

When the recreational activities were over, folks could quench their thirst at a root beer stand on South Excelsior Street.

There were a number of businesses located on the West Side. They included The Party Shoppe convenience store at Park and Excelsior Streets. On South Excelsior Street is Driscoll's Pharmacy, Al & Ray's Body Shop, Buttrey's and the Dairy Queen.

The West Side continues to thrive as a neighborhood in Butte. The 1990s started to see an expansion of new housing in the area which means the West Side will continue as a dominant region for the city of Butte.

Williamsburg is located in the southwest corner of the city. It also was called "Dogtown" by many people. The community was named after Henry Williams who was a manager of the nearby Colorado Smelter.

Williamsburg was like a small peninsula surrounded completely by industrial activity. North of the community was the Colorado Smelter operations which was started by William Clark in 1879. East of the small neighborhood sat the Montana Pole Plant, a pressured treatment facility for utility poles that was in operation from 1947 to 1983, plus the Butte Reduction Works, a plant which processed manganese, a material to strengthen steel.

Other industry jobs could be found at two breweries located near the neighborhood. They were the Centennial and Tivoli Breweries. The prominent work force at the breweries was German immigrants. Many brewery workers lived in Williamsburg, so the community of Williamsburg has strong ties to the Germany. The influence is reflected in the name of the streets in the small community. The list includes the street names Baden, Baveria, Berlin, Dresden, Frankfort, Munich, Nassau, Vienna and Stuttgart. It is the only neighborhood in the entire community where city names from Europe are prominent in street names.

Besides Germans, there were a few English families located in Williamsburg.

The industrial activity surrounding Williamsburg ended after the Interstate Highway System was built north of the neighborhood in 1962. When the area plants shut down, major cleanup work was needed through the Superfund program. The Colorado Smelter, Montana Pole Plant, Butte Reduction Works and Montana Pole Plant all underwent a major cleanup facelift. It clouded the future of the tiny neighborhood known as Williamsburg.

REFERENCES USED IN CHAPTER FOUR

Butte Was Like That written by Joe Duff published in 1941
Sketches of Old Butte written by Jacob Ostberg published in 1972
Sketches of Walkerville written by Beverly Brothers published in 1973
St. Patrick's Parish 100 Years written by Chris Daly published in 1981
The Speculator Winter magazine 1985 by Butte Historical Society
Butte's Big Game written by Pat Kearney published in 1989
Butte's Pride - The Columbia Gardens written by Pat Kearney pubished in 1994
The Butte Chinese written by George Everett published in 1997
Butte Archives
The Montana Standard newspaper
Alex Koprivica notes
1994 interview Guido Bugni
1994 interview Alana Lencioni LaRock
1994 interview Jesse Poore
1994 interview Pauline Poore
1994 interview June Wilson
1996 interview Maurine Higman Dennehy
1996 interview Bob Koprivica
1996 interview Dula Schonsberg

1996 interview Jimmy Shea
1996 interview Emma Strike Smith
1997 interview Ed Bartoletti
1997 interview Charlie Bugni
1997 interview Mike Gribben
1997 interview Jack Harris
1997 interview Al Hooper
1997 interview Esther Zanon Judd
1997 interview Bob Kissell
1997 interview Art Korn
1997 interview Kay Kosmack
1997 interview Bernice Favilla Maki
1997 interview Kevin Shannon
1998 interview Bill Antonioli
1998 interview Jim Carden
1998 interview Ed Crnich
1998 interview Emmett Cronnolly
1998 interview Pauline deBarathy
1998 interview Vince Downey
1998 interview Evelyn Eva
1998 interview Mary Evatz
1997 interview Esther Francone
1998 interview Jim Hanley
1998 interview Carl Gergurich
1998 interview Rich Holman
1998 interview Cathy Brozovich James
1998 interview Tubie Johnson
1998 interview George Krstulich
1998 interview Ted Leskovar
1998 interview Neil Lynch
1998 interview Carol Wyatt Maunder
1998 interview Lee Masters
1998 interview Bob McCarthy
1998 interview Bev McClafferty
1998 interview Mary Gassino Mencarelli
1998 interview Millie Boyle Moriarty
1998 interview Michael Muffich
1998 interview Al Niemi
1998 interview Shirley Niemi
1998 interview Dan O'Gara
1998 interview John Orizotti

1998 interview Father Sarsfield O'Sullivan
1998 interview Angelo Petroni
1998 interview Milt Popovich
1998 interview Jenny Serich
1998 interview Bob Sherman
1998 interview Emily Sherman
1998 interview Dick Skates
1998 interview Bus Stuart
1998 interview Rudy Tomazich
1998 interview Matt Vucurovich
1998 interview Howie Wing

Finn Town - photo courtesy Butte-Silver Bow Archives

Immaculate Conception Church
photo courtesy Pat Kearney

Art Chateau
photo courtesy Pat Kearney

Silver Bow Homes - photo courtesy Pat Kearney

Burlington - photo courtesy Ruth Otto

Browns Gulch's
Louie Pene moves
dairy products
photo courtesy
Sharon Metz

Frank Gozzano
ready to deliver
dairy products in
Joe Martina truck
photo courtesy
Sharon Metz

Surviving in Butte
photo courtesy Butte-Silver Bow Archives

Centerville in 1900
photo courtesy A Brief History of Butte, Montana by Harry Freeman

Mountain Con Mine in Centerville - photo courtesy Pat Kearney

Mormon Church in Country Club - photo courtesy Pat Kearney

Butte High School - photo courtesy Pat Kearney

Naranche Stadium photo courtesy 1988 Hall of Fame calendar

The Wah Chong Tai Company store in Chinatown
photo courtesy World Museum of Mining

Columbia Gardens floral crew - photo courtesy June Wilson

East Butte - photo courtesy Jerry Bugni, World Museum of Mining

Washington School - photo courtesy World Museum of Mining

Jenny, Jim Ronco
at Elk Park Inn
photo courtesy Jenny Serich

Bert Mooney Airport
photo courtesy Pat Kearney

Skating at Clark Park - photo courtesy Butte Silver Bow Archives

Clark Mansion
photo courtesy
Pat Kearney

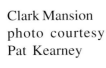

St. Patrick's School in 1890s photo courtesy <u>St. Patrick's Parish 100 Years 1881-1981</u>

Butte Central Catholic High School - photo courtesy Pat Kearney

Hub Addition - photo courtesy Pat Kearney

St. James Community Hospital - photo courtesy Mike Kearney

Holy Savior School and Church - photo courtesy Jerry Bugni

McQueen Market - photo courtesy Jerry Bugni, World Museum of Minir

Meaderville photo courtesy Jerry Bugni, World Museum of Mining

Meaderville with Rocky Mountain Cafe Leonard Mine in background photo courtesy Jerry Bugni, World Museum of Mining

Rocky Mountain Cafe party photo courtesy World Museum of Mining

Italians playing bocce in Meaderville
photo courtesy Jerry Bugni, World Museum of Mining

Meaderville Market photo courtesy Jenny Serich

Meaderville
Christmas display
in 1960
photo courtesy
World Museum of
Mining

Meaderville Fire Department float in 1956 Fourth of July parade
photo courtesy Jim Michelotti

Marcus Daly's race track - photo courtesy World Museum of Mining

Walkerville in 1900
photo courtesy A Brief History of Butte, Montana by Harry Freeman

Jimmy Shea shows broken car glass from Alice Pit blast
photo courtesy Jimmy Shea

Brekey's Bar
in Walkerville
photo courtesy
World Museum
of Mining

Montana School of Mines Main Hall in 1900
photo courtesy A Brief History of Butte, Montana by Harry Freeman

Marcus Daly statue
photo courtesy Pat Kearney

Montana Tech campus - photo courtesy Pat Kearney

Paul Clark Home
photo courtesy
A Brief History of Butte, Montana
by Harry Freeman

McGlone Heights - photo courtesy Pat Kearney

A cold day on Butte's West Side photo courtesy Tom Mulcahy collection Butte-Silver Bow Archives

Sacred Heart Church as it was being torn down
photo courtesy Jenny Serich

CHAPTER FIVE

People

The various ethnic groups and neighborhoods provided Butte with its character. Yet, individuals made Butte a place enriched with a lasting memory. "One of the things that struck me the most when I came to Butte in 1985 was all the self-made people," said Doug Smith. "The playing field here was level for everyone which was not the case in the various towns I called home. If you worked hard in Butte, you could get some place. A number of people I know came from the lowest of the low on the society chart and made a success for themselves. It really is a town where you can make it if you really try."

Butte produced a wide variety of people. Some were great leaders, others humanitarians, coaches or heroes, and others were just plain characters. Here are just some of the folks who made Butte unique in its own style.

The date was December 27, 1979. The place was the Butte-Silver Bow Council of Commissioners Chambers inside the County Courthouse. The commissioners were facing a difficult assignment: Butte-Silver Bow Chief Executive Mike Micone had recently resigned his position to take a state job in Helena. The local lawmakers needed to pick a new leader. The choice was Don Peoples, the Public Works Director. The commissioners' decision was one of the most important ever made in the community.

Don Peoples was born in Butte on August 26, 1939, to James and Marie Peoples. He went to Emerson Grade School and later graduated in 1957 from Boys' Central High School where he participated in wrestling and football. His love of athletics directed Peoples' college choice to became a teacher and coach. He did both at Boys' Central from 1967 to 1969, but bigger hurdles lay ahead for Don. He became the City Recreation director and served as the Industrial League's president during the 1968 baseball season. Next came the assignment of directing the efforts of the Model Cities' Program, and finally the job as Public Works and Community Development Director before his appointment as the new Butte-Silver Bow Chief Executive.

"When I took the job never in my wildest dreams could I have imagined what a difficult challenge it would be," he said.

The new Butte-Silver Bow Chief Executive quickly took steps to improve the community after officially taking over the local government on January 15, 1979. In his first year, he helped secure federal money to renovate the Butte Civic Center, the first substantial work done on the Civic Center since the building was first opened back in 1952. Peoples also was involved in the creation of the Urban Revitalization Agency in 1979 to help improve the Uptown business district.

"When I was with Model Cities, it became clear to me that much of the value in Butte was its historical Uptown district," recalled Peoples. "We needed to do something to protect the area.

"When the Butte Forward plan to move the business district was discussed in the early 1970s, people kept saying they did not want to move the district. They wanted the area renovated and restored. I got that message loud and clear which is why I created the URA district. My hope was the URA would improve the area and hopefully bring new companies into the district."

Both the renovation of the Butte Civic Center and the URA were successful ventures. Yet, the biggest challenge for Peoples and the city was still a couple of years down the road.

The year 1983 became a time of great need in Butte. It was also a time of great sorrow.

Peoples remembered, "I recall driving through Idaho on a January day. I stopped and called my office. My secretary, Meg Peters, told me ARCO had been calling all day for me. They were going to hold a news conference at 4 o'clock and they wanted to know if I could attend. I asked Meg if she had heard anything on the street and her reply was that the rumors were ARCO was ready to shut down their whole operations.

"It was absolutely devastating news. Of course, as I look back the handwriting was on the wall. They say the greatest sign of illiteracy is you can't read the writing on the wall. We should've seen it coming especially after ARCO had closed the Berkeley Pit the year before. Yet, even if we knew beforehand about their intentions there was really very little we could do about it at the time."

Don Peoples made it back to Butte in time for the closure announcement which came on January 6, 1983. Six months later, Atlantic Richfield suspended their operation on June 30, 1983.

"I never had time to sit around and feel sorry for myself or the city," said Peoples. "We had to do something and do it in a quick hurry. We could not quit because there was way too much at stake. We had to explore other options and get ready for the impact of having no mining in Butte."

When the trucks, shovels and other mining gear went silent, Butte was without mining and, for some people, without hope.

"I think we had to express to the folks a positive attitude all the time that things were going to get better," said Peoples. "It was very difficult to do because during that year the Safeway Warehouse closed, Stauffer Chemical shut down one of their furnaces and Northwest Airlines decided to leave town for good. We lost over 1,000 jobs in one year. It was very depressing getting up every day and opening up the paper to find more layoffs. It seemed like we were in a prize fight getting knocked all over the ring with no hope at all of surviving"

To use the old cliche' when the going gets tough the tough get going. Don Peoples was indeed tough, learning his competitive spirit in athletics as both a player and coach. During one of the roughest times in the city's history, Peoples got up off the canvas and started swinging back at the potential knock out.

Peoples put 17 different volunteer groups together trying to determine what new industries could be attracted to Butte, what impacts the lose in taxes might have on the town, and what needed to be done to lure a new company to reopen the Butte copper mine.

Peoples remembered, "We started having little things go right for us. Any time there was positive news for the city we jumped on it and started cheerleading how our community was coming back. We had the theme of 'City of Champions' where both our high schools were enjoying a lot of success. They both won the wrestling championship in 1983 and both won the state basketball titles in 1984. So that was a positive message we could start telling our citizens.

"We started to witness more construction in both Uptown Butte through the URA and down on the Flats with new stores and businesses. We took those developments and tried to tell the world that Butte, Montana, was coming back.

"The local government also pushed to settle a long-term court dispute over the gross proceeds tax between the State of Montana and The Anaconda Company. The two sides finally agreed on a settlement which has been a financial benefit for the city every since the agreement."

Even with all the positives, behind the scenes the future of Butte kept slipping and no one knew that better than Don Peoples.

"The real low point came long after they shut down the operations," remembered Peoples. "Frank Gardner, the president of the Pit operations, came to me and said ARCO had decided they were going to do one of two things. They were either going to sell the property to another mining firm or else they were going to mothball their concentrator and sell the metal as scrap. If they mothballed the concentrator it would've meant the end of mining forever in Butte. The concentrator not only was the key to a mining resumption, but also it made up about 20 percent of Atlantic Richfield overall tax base in Butte. Both the city government and school district would've faced major cutbacks with the loss of that money."

Peoples redoubled his efforts with the various committees to land a potential new mining firm. The efforts paid off when Missoula businessman Dennis Washington purchased the mining properties from Atlantic Richfield in December 1985. The trucks were back in service again in July 1986, just three years after they had been shut down.

"I always felt confident that someone could come into this community and reopen the mine," Peoples said. "The mining committee did a tremendous job staying at it until we finally got someone to come in here to get the trucks rolling again."

That accomplishment was a major one, but Peoples was not just satisfied with a resumption of mining. He wanted to make sure that the community could diversify its economy to the point where mining was no longer the only major industry in town.

"I was a member of the National League of Cities and Towns," explained Peoples. "The position allowed me to travel around the country and see what other communities were doing for economic development. One concept I saw in Indianapolis and later in Pueblo, Colorado, really intrigued me. It was the idea of a business incubator. I came back home and decided let's see if we can copy that idea in our town."

Through his efforts a business incubator was established in the old Boys' Central High School building. This incubator concept provides start-up small businesses an opportunity to share office help and managerial expertise which gives them a better chance to survive. The incubator was a success creating numerous jobs in the community. New jobs also came from a grain terminal Peoples pushed for at Silver Bow, three miles northwest of town.

In addition, Peoples was involved in major civic projects that became successful. He was instrumental in the movement of the Columbia Gardens' playground equipment into town from the Columbia Gardens' II site near the Beef Trail Ski Area. Peoples and the local government helped get the United States High Altitude Sports Center off the ground and rolling. He also came up with the idea for the Butte Sports Hall of Fame in the Civic Center.

As one successful accomplishment followed another, Peoples' efforts gained notice in the community, state and nation. In 1987, *US News & World Report* magazine named Peoples as one of the 20 best mayors in the entire country. He also received the 1987 Spirit of Enterprise Award from the Montana International Trade Commission. The individual awards were not quite as exciting to Peoples as the news in 1988 from the National Civic League that Butte was selected as an All-America City.

"We went from a plant-closure city to an All-America City in a five-year period," said Peoples. "That was quite an accomplishment for the city. There were a lot of people that worked very hard to achieve that goal."

Butte becoming an All-America City was Peoples' final major accomplishment as chief executive. He resigned in September 1989 to join Montana Technologies as CEO. His duties changed from running a local government to operating a private firm, but his mission to improve his hometown only continued.

Peoples negotiated to have his firm move into the private sector from the federal government. He expanded Montana Technologies into new areas. His firm took over the Butte Water Company and put the utility back on its feet before turning it over to the local government. His company came up with a concept for a potential Butte Gardens project on the east side of town. The company grew to an annual payroll of $15 million with 380 employees nationwide.

Peoples reflected, "As I look back, there are two reasons why I have been able to get things done. The first is hiring good people. You're only as good as the managers you hire and frankly I've hired good people like Gary Rowe, Jim Kambich, Janet Cornish and Ron Kenison. They were put in critical positions where they had to get things done and they did.

"The second and most important reason for my success is my wife, Cathy. She has always been there especially during the tough times. People always tell me how competitive I am, but I'll guarantee you my wife is more competitive than me. She absolutely hates to lose at anything and I get some of my competitive juices from her. She really has been an inspiration to me."

Don Peoples' determination to bring Butte back from the disaster of a mining closure in 1983 will make him one of the most important figures in the history of the community. He is one of Butte's all-time champions in the "City of Champions."

A favorite item on the Christmas list is Shepperd's Candy. The delicious delights of caramel fudge, cherries and chocolates makes former Butte people feel like they our back home for the holidays.

The man who began Butte's favorite candy tradition, Bruce Shepperd, started working at Gamer's Confectionery on the corner of Montana and Park Streets in 1910.

Shepperd grew up on a homestead near Moscow, Idaho. After local schooling, he enrolled at the University of Idaho and then took business college classes in Spokane where he learned the specialized craft of making ice cream and candy.

After coming to Butte, Shepperd made candy for store owner, Walt Gamer. He stayed at Gamer's through 1918 when he decided to branch out on his own. Shepperd established a business in Cardwell, Idaho, and later in Billings, Montana. In Billings, Shepperd encountered Gamer again, and Walt persuaded Bruce to return to Gamer's Confectionery in 1927.

The arrangement between Walt and Bruce worked great until October 31, 1932, when Gamer's Confectionery was destroyed by fire. Shortly after that, Gamer died. Shepperd was without a job and, with the Great Depression in full swing, without a lot of hope.

Gamer's sister-in-law, Sophia Gamer, took over the business. Nine months after the fire, she opened a new Gamer's Confectionery in the Curtis Music Hall on Park Street. Shepperd was back making candy in the basement of the new restaurant. In 1933, shortly after Gamer's reopened, Shepperd's son, also named Bruce, joined his father to learn the candy-making business at the age of 15.

"My father was incredible making candy," said Bruce Shepperd. "Mrs. Gamer always wanted a new special candy put in the front window every week. My dad was able to make just about any thing. All the candy he made came from his own hand-written recipes. He was always studying confectionery magazines on making candy and other things. When my father went around town picking up samples of candy, he tasted it to figure out what ingredients went into making it. He came back to Gamer's and tried to develop a recipe for making that same type of candy. My dad absolutely loved making candy."

The two Shepperds worked at Gamer's Confectionery for Mrs. Gamer and the new owners she sold the business to in 1944, Carl Rowan and George Schotte. Ten years later, rather than retire, Bruce decided to open his own candy store with his son.

"My wife, Irene, kept encouraging us to start our own business," remembered Bruce Shepperd Jr. "She even found a location for us down on Harrison Avenue.

Shepperd's Candy opened for business in 1954 at 2405 Harrison Avenue. In a few short years, Bruce and his son had a prosperous business.

"It took a lot of hard work to get that business off the ground," said Bruce Shepperd Jr. "We were just coming off a miners' strike in 1954 which did not help at all. In order to make it, we were opened seven days a week. The only days we shut down were Christmas and Easter. Through our reputation for making quality candy at Gamer's, we had some very loyal customers who purchased nice orders from us helping get the business started.

"One of the things you must remember about our business is that 50 percent of the total volume is done at Christmas time. We have to begin preparing for the holidays in September. During the early days, all the boxes had to be specially wrapped in ribbon to be mailed off. There was no tape or other things allowed on the packages. We had to work very late at night to box up all the candy that needed to be shipped out of town."

Bruce Shepperd and his son continued working side-by-side until 1973 when the senior Shepperd retired from the business at the age of 93. His health forced him to move to Spokane to live with his daughter who was a nurse.

"My dad just loved the business so much he'd be there all the time at the shop if you let him," recalled Bruce Jr. "If he had a choice, my dad would've made candy until the day he died he loved it so much."

Bruce Shepperd died six years later, gone, but certainly not forgotten. The people of Butte remember him through his candy. Bruce's son carried on the business through 1983 when he turned over the duties of candy-making to his daughter, Roberta, and son-in-law, Dave Egedahl. Since taking over the business, Roberta and Dave have been able to expand the operations.

Throughout the year, Shepperd's Candy has a steady steam of customers. But, at Christmas time, the shop is flooded with people looking to fill that special holiday request from out-of-town natives, "Just get me some of that Shepperd's Candy."

In *The Wizard of Oz* Dorothy encounters many unexpected twists and turns on her way to the Emerald City. One person who has lived through many twists and turns in her life is Judy Morstein Martz. During the winter, Judy used to skate the creek beds near her home in the Roosevelt Drive area with her sisters, Penny and Carol, and her brother, Joe. Judy was a gifted athlete, but in the 1950s women had very little opportunities in athletics. One of the few sports with a chance for women was rodeo, an activity Judy loved so much that she was allowed to move to Wilsal during her junior year in high school so she could compete in the sport.

On a visit back home in Butte, she went out skating with her friend, Sylvia White, who was a reigning national speedskating champion. The two had a race, with Sylvia just barely beating Judy. Local coaches were impressed with Morstein's performance and encouraged her to come back to Butte to try speedskating. Judy came home and started to practice. After graduating from Butte High in 1961, Judy put two long, hard years into training which were rewarded when she made the 1963 United States speedskating team. Judy and Sylvia White both competed for the USA at the world championships in Japan.

The next year both Judy Morstein and Sylvia White again made the United States team. This time, they traveled to Innsbruck, Austria, where the two Butte natives became the first Montana women ever to compete for the United States at the Winter Olympics.

Morstein placed 15th in the 1500-meter event, while Sylvia was 24th overall in the 3000-meter race.

Less than a year after that Olympics thrill, Judy lived through one of the low points in her life. Her boyfriend, Wayne Estes, was killed in a tragic accident in Logan, Utah. Estes, an Anaconda native, was a member of the Utah State basketball team and the school's all-time leader scorer. Wayne had just finished a game and was going out for something to eat when he and his teammates came upon an car accident. As the players checked out the scene, Estes grazed his head on a live electrical wire and was killed instantly.

"I remember the night as if it were yesterday," said Judy. "I was waiting for him to call me after the game. When the phone finally rang it was Wayne's high school coach, John Cheek, from Anaconda. He told me how Wayne had been killed in a freak accident.

"It was absolutely a devastating period in my life. I went to Anaconda and lived with Wayne's folks, Joe and Carol, for three months. It was not easy at all."

A few months after Wayne's death, Judy rekindled a relationship with her old boyfriend, Harry Martz. The relationship turned into marriage. In 1971, they acquired a commercial garbage business which she remembers as "a real tough business. We were told the gross income potential of the business could be $24,000 a year. It sounded like a lot of money to a new couple trying to make a living. Yet, we never figured all the expenses that went into the business like gas, equipment and parts. It took nine years to get the business solvent enough so we started to make some money.

"I drove the dump truck during the grave yard shift at night while Harry was home trying to get some sleep so he could do the morning route. During the night shift, my first child, Justin, slept on the truck seat next to me while I finished my pick-ups.

"You had to lift 50-gallon drums filled with garbage into the truck and once in a while clean out the containers. It was not easy at all, but I look back and cherish the struggle Harry and I went through to make a living at the commercial garbage business.

"As a small business person you never get too cocky because one false move or one major breakdown could mean the end of your business."

Judy Martz drove truck for 13 years for the family-owned company, as well as keeping all the books. She became a good business person which came in handy when Martin White, the founder of the United States High Altitude Sports Center, asked her to become the Executive Director of his non-profit organization in 1985. Judy helped get the speedskating oval off the ground.

"That was an exciting and challenging job," Martz said. "As a former skater, I just knew the concept could work in Butte. Some people doubted we could even get the rink built let alone hold an international meet. It took a lot of hard work, but we got it done. Its something that Butte and the state can be proud of."

Judy continued working at the United States High Altitude Sports Center until 1989. She left the position to take a job as the field representative for US Senator Conrad Burns. Martz had been active in Republican political campaigns and volunteer committees for many years. Yet, her job with Senator Burns was her first real taste of political life.

Martz said, "I have always enjoyed serving people. Its a challenge to try and make a difference in a person life. You can do that in politics and working with Conrad Burns was a good opportunity to serve people."

Her work with Senator Burns impressed many people in the state. With the 1992 election season approaching, three different people from three different sections of Montana urged Judy to seek the nomination as the Lieutenant Governor candidate with incumbent Governor Marc Racicot.

"After that, I went home and talked with Harry and my two kids, Justin and Stacey, about it," recalled Judy. They were all in favor of me asking Marc if he'd consider me for the job. Finally, one day as I was driving to Dillon, I pulled off to the side of the road and called Marc Racicot. I asked him to consider me to be his running mate. At the time, he had 25 different people on his potential list of candidates. After a couple of interviews with a group of people, Marc selected me to run with him. It was a great thrill and honor."

Racicot won the 1992 Governor's election easily and Judy Martz became Montana's first female Lieutenant Governor. It is the highest political office ever held by a woman in Montana.

"People ask me a lot what its like being Montana's first women Lieutenant Governor," Judy said. "I just tell them I'm very proud to serve. During my tenure, I have worked very hard to show that a woman can get the job done at a high-level political office. I put in 15-hour days on the job. Governor Racicot has given me a lot of responsibilities that previous Lieutenant Governors were never involved in."

Judy Morstein Martz has indeed lived through an adventure with a lot of turns in the yellow brick road. One bend took her to the Winter Olympics, another crossing involved a tragic death, an uphill climb took her and husband, Harry, to business success, a twist involved starting a world-class speedskating rink, a curve put her into politics which led her to the second highest office in the state.

Martz reflected, "My success can be traced back to Butte. There is the Butte mentality that if you want something bad enough you can achieve it, but don't expect to get it free. You have to work at it and, if you do, good things can happen to you. Its been a town with great family values, a wonderful heritage and a work ethic that is second to no where in the world. Butte, Montana, will always be some place special for me."

Callahan "the Bum" was one of Butte's more popular characters around 1900. He was simply that: a bum. He applied his trade well especially when it came to bumming a drink. Callahan claimed he knew 57 different ways to bum a drink. He was famous for yelling at a bartender, "Give us another!" Up came the drinks and whomever was around "the Bum" ended up paying for the next round.

Callahan was a well-educated man who could recite Shakespeare and Psalms. It was told that Callahan at one time studied to be a priest, but his curse of hard liquor ended up settling him down in front of a bar rather than an altar.

The police had to constantly deal with Callahan. In one year, he was arrested and locked up under the big clock at Butte's City Hall (the jail was located in the basement) 114 times. One time "the Bum" was arrested at nine o'clock in the morning. Callahan was taken before a judge to explain his condition. Callahan said, "Your honor, I just went into the place for an eye-opener. Its too bad I came out blind." The judge had a tough time trying to stop laughing after hearing Callahan's explanation. Finally he let "the Bum" go free.

Callahan "the Bum" had his troubles with alcohol, but he made up for it with a generous heart. When Sacred Heart Catholic Church came up $200 short in funding for a bell to complete its newly constructed church, it was Callahan who raised the necessary money. He organized various groups of other transients who went out bumming money for the church.

In one day the group raised enough money to buy a bell.

Callahan left the Butte area some time around 1910. It was rumored he was sent back east by relatives to try and dry him out. He was never heard from again by folks in Butte.

The backbone of success for over 100 years in Butte's Catholic educational system has always been volunteer lay people. The need for additional assistance became even more apparent when the ranks of the sisterhood, priesthood and Christian Brothers began to shrink in the 1970s.

No lay person has done more to keep the doors to Catholic education open for students than LaVerne Combo. Her tireless efforts for many decades to help in numerous ways has been a remarkable achievement.

LaVerne graduated from Girls' Central Catholic High School in 1946. The next fall, she traveled north to attend school at the College of Great Falls. Her mind and body were in Great Falls, but her heart was back in Butte. Combo returned on weekends and got involved in helping the drill team at Girls' Central. LaVerne had an interest in drill team since she starting taken dance lessons as a small child so the assignment was a natural for her.

A lack of money forced LaVerne to drop out of college. One dream of obtaining a college diploma was gone, but the dream to be around children only grew with her return to Butte. Combo became even more active in affairs at Girls' Central. Besides her duties as the drill team instructor, she also started to choreograph the musicals put on by students every year. Starting in 1951, the productions got bigger and better when the girls moved into a new high school building at Idaho and Park Streets. LaVerne choreographed 34 different musical performances through the years. In addition, LaVerne spent 19 years as the head of the drill team, giving that assignment up to take charge of the cheerleaders, a duty she performed for another 12 years.

In 1965, when the sisters needed office help at the high school, they asked LaVerne if she could give them a hand. This started a whole new career for LaVerne. Her duties in the office expanded with each passing year. She carried on the assignments for no pay until Father John McCoy arrived in 1972. When McCoy, the new principal, saw all the things LaVerne was doing he insisted that she have a salary. LaVerne was given the title of administrative assistant. She set up all the classroom schedules, completed all the registration, and handed out discipline to students who were late or skipped school. More than anything, though, she acted as a second mother to every high school student in the building.

"I have heard just about every story you can think of especially when it comes to being late," LaVerne said with a laugh. "The rule is pretty simple. If you're late or miss school its detention. That's just the way it is no matter what the excuse.

"I find kids don't realize it, but they really do have a simple life compared to adults. They break up with their boy friend or girl friend and think its the end of the world. The kids think the problem will never go away, but it does and its important to talk them through their mini-crises. I have found if you pay attention to a kid and listen to them things will work out. They just need someone to talk to because I believe the kids of today are just as good as the kids of 20 years ago."

LaVerne has seen lots of changes in Catholic education. The most trying time for her was the school year of 1969-70 when Girls' Central and Boys' Central were combined into one school for the first time.

Combo remembered, "That first year was an absolute nightmare. I especially recall Sister Bridget and Brother McCormick going at it all the time. The nuns felt the boys came in and took over their school while the brothers were upset because their school had been shut down. It was a real challenge especially for the Christian Brothers because they had never taught girls before. They had to run things a little differently than at old Boys' Central. I have been told about their trips down to the handball courts with kids who got out of line. Well, that type of discipline along with the leather had to be replaced with other measures now that the girls were present. In the long run, the combination of boys and girls into one school I think is the best thing going. There is a lot more unity by both sides today than when I went to old Girls' Central over 50 years ago."

The person who has provided more unity to the school than anyone is LaVerne Combo. A parent who graduated from Central 20 or 30 years ago can still feel at home inside the building because of Combo. She is the one person that was there 30 years ago and is still there at the end of the 20th century.

"The position of working with kids has just been a blessing for me," said LaVerne. "The kids have touched me in so many ways. The benefits I receive from their love and friendship far exceeds any type of money I get for this job. It has been a real joy in my life."

If ever a section of town needed help and leadership it was the Butte business district which was ravaged by fire throughout the 1970s. Hope and leadership came in October 1979, when Janet Cornish was selected as the director of the newly created Urban Revitalization Agency.

Cornish had a bachelor's degree in political science from the University of Wisconsin and a master's in environmental studies from the University of Montana. She used both well in her new position.

The idea of an urban revitalization agency was not new, having been used in various communities around the country. It was new to Butte, though, and that by itself led to mistrust by many of the Uptown business district merchants.

"The first real test was trying to change attitudes," Cornish said. "Besides being destroyed by fires, the Uptown business community had to fight off an attempt by a proposal called Butte Forward which tried to move the business district down on the Flats in the early 1970s. Butte Forward had lots of money behind it in the form of The Anaconda Company who wanted to mine in the area. Somehow the Uptown business owners fought off that plan, but the memories of that idea were still fresh in their minds when we launched the Urban Revitalization Agency.

"There was certainly a reserved feeling about what we were attempting to do to their central business area. We needed to turn things around because the only way the URA plan was going to work was through the investments of the business people in the district."

The mission of Cornish and her agency was to clean up the Uptown district through building improvements. The additional tax money generated by the improvements were put back into the agency rather than the local government to provide for more capital to make even more improvements. In addition, Cornish tried to recruit more business people to relocate in the district. She also wanted to add more life back in the district through various events.

Cornish remembered, "Due to the fact the urban revitalization agency was so new, we had to search elsewhere to figure out where to begin. The city of Missoula had already began a plan to upgrade their downtown area so we tried to learn from their efforts and put them to use in Butte."

The first major step in the revitalization of the district came in a facade program. Through the help of low-interest money, a number of business people were able to refurbish their store fronts. This helped to create a better looking business district, but even more importantly provided the area with additional revenue from higher taxes generated through the improvements.

"The facade program was just one phase of the improvements necessary to revitalize Uptown Butte," said Janet. "Another key factor was a lack of parking spaces for customers. It was very unattractive for a person who wanted to construct a new building in the Uptown area. The reason was they had to provide parking for the new store. There simply was no real space available unless they tore down some buildings. So through some of the money generated in the improvements we created a parking district on the outer edges of the business area. This eliminated the pressure on business people to create parking spaces Uptown without forcing them to tear down buildings. It also gave us a chance to design parking areas which were both attractive to the district and to customers."

The improvements were also attractive to potential business people. Through the work of the URA, almost every store front in the district was filled.

Besides store facades and parking spaces, the URA money helped in the construction of bus shelters, improvements to Mural Park on Park Street and repair of some local government buildings. Brick and mortar were not the only things that Janet Cornish wanted to accomplish. She also spent time creating more activities in the district. One of her first events was the development of the Christmas tree lighting ceremony. It took place at Heritage Park, an area created through URA money on the corner of Park and Main Streets. The event attracted hundreds of residents Uptown with dignitaries like Governor Ted Schwinden leading the festivities by lighting the tree.

Another popular event pushed by Cornish was an arts festival every year Uptown. She was also instrumental in producing an annual stop by the Shakespeare in the Park troupe at an Uptown location. All the activities helped to create traffic in the district and sparked the attitude of a new life for the area.

New life in the area resulted in a tax base increase of over $1 million in the business district through the URA during the nine years that Cornish served as head of the agency. Janet stepped down from her position in November 1988 to take a job in the private sector.

"I think the most important thing Janet Cornish did was get people to listen," said Chuck Richards, an Uptown business owner. "Janet could see the enormous historic value the Uptown district had on our community. She did a wonderful job in educating people that we have a treasure here that is unique and needs to be preserved."

Cornish reflected, "It was a very rewarding experience turning that whole thing around. There were a lot of hurdles to overcome, but we met the challenge and I think we succeeded in our mission."

Don Peoples said, "Janet really had a gift for being able to work with people. She also had a good sense about history and what was really valuable to the city. She is one of the best people I ever hired while serving as chief executive."

Ernie Richards, a business owner said, "There is no question in my mind that Janet Cornish was the key person to revitalizing Uptown Butte.

She was always coming up with new ideas, events, plans and other things that really put a new spark into Uptown Butte. Through it all she had such a great attitude that things could be turned around and she was able to do it. The Uptown area will always be grateful for her efforts. Janet Cornish left a mark on the Uptown area that few people could ever equal."

When Butte people referred to "the coach" only one name ever came to mind: Harry "Swede" Dahlberg who was the pillar and foundation of Butte High athletics for more than four decades.

Dahlberg began his career as an athlete at Butte High School. He played all sports and was especially good at football. Dahlberg was a member of the 1914 and 1915 Bulldog teams that won the Intermountain Regional title. Following his days at Butte High, the man referred to as "Swede" went to the University of Montana in Missoula. He played football for the Grizzlies. Dahlberg was a member of the 1920 Grizzlies' team which beat the University of Washington 18-14. It was Montana's only victory ever over the Huskies.

After his playing days, Dahlberg began a life-long career as a coach. He accepted his first job coaching in Hamilton in 1921. The next year he came back to his old home town of Butte to coach the Bulldogs in all sports. When Swede started to practice his team in the fall of 1922, he became the 13th straight first-year head football coach at Butte High. Every previous Butte High skipper since 1910 had spent one-year at the helm and then left. All that changed when Swede Dahlberg arrived at Butte High.

His first year of coaching the football, basketball and track teams was uneventful, but within a couple of years Swede had built up a tremendous program in all three sports which dominated in Montana.

" I remember when Swede Dahlberg became the coach at Butte High" recalled Chuck Davis, a former Bulldog player. "We use to practice at the old field on Emmett Street where the West Elementary School is now located. Our school was located where Butte Central sits today. Swede made us run all the way down to practice with all our gear on every day. He insisted we'd be the best conditioned team in the state. You ran down to practice and you ran back to school. Swede had this paddle he used on anyone he caught walking. It did not take players long to figure out who the boss was at Butte High."

Bill Hawke, a former player and assistant coach remembered, "Swede was a real bugger about conditioning. There was a saying that if Butte High could stay with you the first half they would beat you in the second half because Swede had his teams in such good shape. He always ran with the first unit right down to the practice field. If you slowed down even a bit Swede nailed you with the paddle. It was not easy running especially coming back up all those hills. All that running paid off because the 1929 undefeated team I played on was in much better shape than any of our opponents."

His first state championship came with the 1924 Butte High basketball team. He followed that up in the spring with a state track title, then captured the state football crown in the fall. The next winter and spring, the basketball and track teams repeated as state champions, marking five straight state championships in three different sports, a feat that has never been duplicated.

Dahlberg coached all three sports for 30 years up through 1951. He turned his duties as basketball coach over to longtime assistant Bill Hawke in 1952. Before turning over the reigns, Dahlberg had led his Butte High hoopsters to six state championships: 1924, 1925, 1928, 1932, 1933, 1941.

Swede continued as head football coach through the 1955 season. He posted ten state titles in football: 1924, 1927, 1929, 1930, 1931, 1935, 1937, 1940, 1941 and 1951. His overall record through 34 years as head skipper of the football team was 221 wins, 81 losses, and 18 ties.

Dahlberg remained as the head track coach through the 1966 season. His final squad fittingly won the state track championship for him. Dahlberg enjoyed his most success with his track teams which won twelve titles: 1924, 1925, 1927, 1928, 1931, 1933, 1935, 1936, 1937, 1938, 1963 and 1966. His 1964 cross country team also won the first-ever state meet.

His teams won 29 state championships, the most by any one coach in the history of athletics in Montana. Dahlberg was a joy for those athletes who had a chance to compete for him. "Swede Dahlberg symbolized what coaching is all about," recalled Sam Jankovich, a former Bulldog player. "He was firm, but fair and led by his clean example of living. I think any kid who was coached by Swede Dahlberg left the locker room a better person."

The adventure began when Dallas Doyle left his hometown of Washington DC in March 1959. He wanted to see the country and for the next seven years that is exactly what he did hitch-hiking and bumming his way around America.

In March 1966, Doyle got a ride into Butte, Montana. He was left off at the OK Bar on Arizona Street. Dallas, guitar in hand, went inside and began to play for both beer and money. For some reason Butte was different. Doyle liked the friendly people and so he started calling the town his new home.

During the next few years, Doyle played in every joint in town by himself or with his band called "The Trail Riders." The money was good and getting the booze was simple with the bar patrons normally ordering one for Dallas.

Doyle was enjoying his passion for drinking on the cold winter night of February 16, 1976. He left an Uptown bar and started to sleep off the alcohol in a nearby alley. After he had fallen asleep, Doyle was shaken by a large man carrying a Bible.

"The man asked me 'What on earth are you doing here?' recalled Doyle. "I saw he was carrying the Bible and cussed him out until he went away. Then I went back to sleep. The next day the words from the previous night kept coming back to me. What am I doing? I just knew God had a purpose for me. I needed to find out what was my calling."

Doyle soon found his calling shortly after his night visit from what turned out to be a Pentecostal preacher. Dallas was walking up Main Street during a cold spell in the winter when he saw two men walking back and forth between the M&M and Sportsmen Bars on Main Street. He asked the two what in the world they were doing, going back and forth between the two joints. The men told Doyle they had no place to go and were simply trying to keep warm. Doyle invited the two men to his place on Copper Street where they slept on the floor. Little did Dallas Doyle realize that night his calling had arrived. His mission was to help the needy and homeless.

Less than a year after he had been awakened in a Butte alley, Dallas Doyle had given up liquor for good and started the Butte Rescue Mission. The purpose of the mission was to help the homeless and needy by providing shelter.

Doyle was helped by a pair of sisters, Michele Ryan and Linda Kendrick, who donated their apartment complex on Second Street free of charge to the Mission. Once he had a permanent location, Dallas developed one of the best Rescue Mission's in the entire country. In a few short years, the Mission was expanded as more and more people came to Dallas' place for a hot meal and a warm bed.

Doyle held Christian services nightly for the patrons staying at his Mission. Instead of preaching, Dallas felt the idea behind the service was to help people find guidance. Doyle talked about his own background as an alcoholic and transient. His message was easy for the Mission folks to relate to because, in many cases, the story of Dallas Doyle was their story.

In the first 20 years of operation, the Butte Rescue Mission served the needs of over 27,000 people. The visitors were mainly transients on the move from one place to another. Yet, some were local people simply seeking shelter until better times came along for them. The facility was so successful that Doyle expanded the Mission a number of times. The Mission could sleep up to 42 people a night and feed 62 people a day.

The transformation of Dallas Doyle from a drunken bum to a preacher did not go unnoticed. In 1982, Doyle was one of a handful of people in the country who received the National Jefferson Award for community service to their hometown. It was a proud moment for Doyle, for Butte, and for Montana.

The calling began on a cold February night in a dark alley in Butte. Dallas Doyle had a mission to perform to help the homeless and needy. He served as head of the Butte Rescue Mission until September 10, 1997.

It was like any other night on the Friday evening of June 8, 1917, when 28-year-old Manus Duggan kissed his young wife, Madge, and left their home at 1010 Zarelda Street. His wife was expecting their first child and Manus was reluctant to leave his bride of two years at home with her being so close to giving birth.

He went up the hill to the Granite Mountain Mine just east of Walkerville. The mine was owned by the North Butte Mining Company. The complex was the best ventilated operation on the Butte hill and had just received an award. The Granite Mountain had a downcast air current through its 3700-foot shaft, the deepest mine on the Butte hill. The system delivered 60,000 cubic feet of fresh air a minute to the men working in temperatures 100 plus degrees underground. The air pushed to the Speculator Mine some 800 feet south of the Granite Mountain. Through the Speculator shaft, the air came out of the underground operation. It was an elaborate system and served its purpose well until this fateful night.

Duggan was just one of thousands of miners working on the Butte hill in 1917. All the local mines were running full capacity since the United States had entered World War I on April 6, 1917. The month of May 1917 saw the payroll for Butte miners hit a record $2.5 million. Times were good with copper selling at a robust price of 32 cents a pound and miners made $4.75 a shift. Copper from the mines was a vital metal for the Allies in their battle to win the war in Europe.

Manus was a nipper which was the assignment of handling tools underground. Duggan, who had been a Butte miner for 10 years, came to Montana from Coatesville, Pennsylvania, where he was born and raised.

That night, Manus was assigned to the 2400-foot level, one of 410 men lowered down underground to begin the night shift.

Prior to the night shift's arrival, a safety crew began lowering a cable down the shaft at around 8 o'clock. The three-ton electrical cable was needed to complete a sprinkler system. The cable slipped and broke through its clamps, crashing down below the 2400-foot level. During the fall, the lead covering the cable was ripped apart exposing oily, fabricated, flammable insulation.

Three hours after the cable crashed, four men went down to inspect the material to see if it was still useful, but the workers did not realize the protective lead cable covering was torn away. When they reached the cable one of the four men, Ernest Sallau, accidentally ignited the oily, frayed cable with his carbide lamp. Flames quickly rushed up the oily cable and the shaft timbers ignited on fire.

Ironically, the Granite Mountain's outstanding ventilation system now became an enemy rather than an ally for miners. The forced air from above helped spread the fire in seconds. The flames also created numerous deadly gases beneath the surface. It was a combination that spelled one word: disaster.

Smoke and gas spread quickly throughout the mine. Some workers were able to escape through connecting shafts. Elmer Miller was one of the few who was lucky enough to escape before the fire spread too far. "A whole gang assembled near the Granite Mountain shaft," recalled Miller in an interview with *The Montana Standard.* "We had to get out of there! A couple of us knew the way through the High Ore, but it had been partly blocked with small cave-ins, but some how we managed to get through and make it out through the High Ore."

Six different mines connected to the Granite Mountain. If a miner could reach the Badger, Black Rock, High Ore, Diamond, Speculator or Elm Orlu, they were free from the deadly gases. Miller and his party were fortunate to find their way out. Manus Duggan and others did not have the same luck.

The fire soon reached the 2400-foot level where Manus Duggan and others were working. The wildfire and the spread of gases forced the men around him to react quickly. Gathering 28 other men in the area around a crosscut at the 2400-foot level, Duggan organized the men in the construction of a bulkhead. It took 30 minutes to make the barrier.

Manus was one of the few men at the site who knew how to build such a blockade. The men used available timber, canvas, clothing and dirt to build the bulkhead. The workers also placed a keg of water inside their make-shift quarters. Once behind the safety of the bulkhead, Duggan ordered the men to construct another barricade ten feet beyond the first one so the workers were safe from the harmful gases and flames.

Duggan commanded two men at a time to spend short periods between the two bulkheads piling dirt into seeping holes to keep the deadly gas from entering their confined quarters. It was time to wait and hope they would be found. The 29 men, some who were now completely nude, were trapped inside. They took turns beating on air pipes hoping that rescue workers would hear their cry for help.

The lack of good air inside their protected barricade forced some strict rules for all 29 men. Duggan told the others they could not smoke and they could only take rations of the keg water so it could last for some time.

Meanwhile on the surface, rescue workers were almost helpless trying the pull out their fellow workers. The electrical power to the mine was shut down to stop the forced air from infiltrating the operation. The deadly gases underground forced the 150 helmet workers on the surface to concentrate their rescue efforts from the nearby Speculator.

Rescue workers had to wait until some of the gas fumes subsided before going down the Speculator shaft. The first bodies were hauled out of the mine at 1:30 in the morning, a couple of hours after the fire had ignited. Some of the dead bodies were not identifiable because they were bloated and disfigured by the gas and flames. By morning, it was clear to the rescue party that almost half the night shift crew was still trapped underground.

A morgue was set up at a nearby barn. Troops were assigned to encircle the mine property and keep people from interfering with rescue efforts.

As time passed, the men trapped with Duggan became more impatient, but Manus was able to keep everyone in check. He did not want anyone to try break the bulkhead and search for freedom until the deadly gases had gone away. During one episode, two men wanted to break down the bulkhead and try their luck outside. Manus stepped in front of the two and did not budge until they returned to their seats and waited. It was all Duggan's men could do, wait and pray for what seemed like an impossible dream, life back on the surface.

A full day passed and still there was no sign of rescue crews. The patience of the men began to wear thin. The air inside their confined chamber was only getting worse with each passing breath of air being taken by the miners. Well into their second day of their entrapment, Duggan and the others decided it was time to take a chance.

Duggan broke the bulkhead and went looking for a way out of hell. Duggan and three others headed away from the main shaft where the fire originated. Manus felt the passage way to safety was in the Rainbow Drift. They got about 1,000 feet away from the bulkhead where they tried to climb a ladder to the 2200-foot level and gain a passage way to the Rainbow Drift. The deadly gases overcame the four men, who collapsed and died. Duggan's body was one of the last dead miners hauled out of the shaft on June 14.

The remaining 25 men from Duggan's party took a different route and made it to the Speculator shaft station. It was now 38 hours after the fire had turned a mine into hell. They rang the bell from the 2400-foot level. Rescue workers were startled. They felt all remaining workers alive had been taken to the surface.

Two members from the rescue crew, Martin Howard and Ed Rucker, were lowered in the cage to the 2400-foot level where to their amazement they found 25 living souls. They got nine men inside the cage. They rang for the hoist engineer to take the cage to the surface. Rescue workers on top were stunned when nine men from Duggan's party came to the surface. The cage was lowered again and sixteen more souls long thought dead were now back to life. Some of the survivors could not walk while others were so shaken they could not talk.

Duggan was not the only hero during the tragic turn of events. James Moore, a shift boss, set up a bulkhead and helped save the lives of six men. Unfortunately, Moore was overcome by gases and died shortly before his party was rescued some 55 hours after the blaze had started.

The final count was 168 men dead, the worst hard-rock metal mine disaster ever recorded. Seven working horses were also killed in the inferno. The tragedy might have been much worst if it were not for the heroic efforts of men like Manus Duggan and James Moore. Through their leadership and courage, 31 men survived a black moment in the history of Butte.

A packed Sacred Heart Catholic Church attended Manus Duggan's funeral on June 15. At the end of the service the song "Nearer My God to Thee" was sung as everyone in the church cried over the loss of a brave fallen hero.

On July 7, 1917, some 27 days after the fire, Madge Duggan brought a young girl into the world. She was named after her hero father, Manus Duggan.

The fallen miners were never forgotten by the Butte people. A memorial tombstone was built at the Mountain View Cemetery. Then 80 years to the date of the tragedy on June 8, 1996, a Granite Mountain Memorial was dedicated to the men who never came out of the hole alive. The shrine was made possible through the efforts of VISTA volunteer, Gerry Walter, and hundreds of people who donated labor and money to the effort. The cost of the project was over $100,000. A federal grant of $50,000 plus community members purchasing bricks that are laid down at the Memorial helped pay for the project. The memorial overlooks the Granite Mountain, the last place of life for Manus Duggan, James Moore and 166 other brave miners.

A key connection for Butte's Catholic Church has been its ties to Ireland. During the course of many years, numerous priests born in Ireland served the various Butte parishes. The one Irish priest who did more than just serve his parish, but also became a prominent figure within the city was Monsignor Michael English.

English was born in County Limerick, Ireland, on November 13, 1890. After his initial studies at St. John's Academy in Hospital, Ireland, he came to the United States at the urging of his uncle Father James English. His uncle was the first Irish native priest ordained in the Diocese of Helena. He helped establish St. Mary Catholic Church in Butte. Through his uncle's encouragement, Michael English went to St. Paul Seminary in St. Paul, Minnesota. He was ordained a priest on May 31, 1913.

After his first assignment at St. Mary's Church in Butte, English served as a parish priest in Whitehall and Hamilton. When Irish president Eamonn DeValera came to Butte in 1919 Monsignor Michael English was one of the featured speakers at a political rally held at Hebgen Park.

He returned to Butte in 1930 to serve at St. Ann's Church. When he arrived at St. Ann's, the area was using old sewer and water lines. Setting to change this, English lobbied the federal government for help asking for WPA money to make the necessary improvements. The federal government told English the improvements would be made if the necessary number of picks, shovels and other tools needed could be found. English located the equipment and a $1 million construction project was completed to bring new sewer and water lines to the Flats.

English knew how to get things done. He was well-read and purchased major national newspapers like the *Los Angeles Times.* If there was one trait which separated him from other priests it was his ability to make massive sums of money through solid investments.

"Monsignor English had a keen sense for investments," said Carol Gilmore, a former parish member. "He owned a toy store in Butte and was a silent partner in many businesses here and also in Great Falls."

His financial acumen and the ability to get things done only increased when English was transferred to St. Patrick's Church in December 1942. Once at St. Patrick's, English took on additional duties as the dean of the Butte Conference of Catholics. He started a financial drive to build a new Catholic high school for girls with a goal to raise $1 million. English succeeded and on May 16, 1949, ground breaking ceremonies took place for the new school at the corner of Park and Idaho Streets which was completed two years later.

Monsignor English never ran Girls' Central on a daily basis, but it was clear if he wanted something done, especially for members of his own parish, he always got his way.

"I recall one time missing a photo session for the school annual," Gilmore said with a laugh. "I was head majorette and was suppose to have a full page photo. Well, Sister Mary Seraphine just about had a heart attack over it. She was not happy with me at all and told me there would be no photo in the annual. I was naturally heartbroken. I told my father what happened. He was good friends with Monsignor so he called him up. The next thing I know they were taking my picture and the photo was in the annual. I guess Monsignor called up Sister Mary Seraphine and told her to get my picture taken or else he'd cross the street from his rectory and show her who really ran Girls' Central. Of course, Sister was not too happy and never spoke to me the rest of the year. It just shows you, though, how much influence Monsignor English had over the Butte Catholic Community."

Bob McCarthy recalled, "The nuns were absolutely scared to death of Monsignor English. You always did it his way or else there would be consequences to pay and yet there was also a very gentle side to the man. Every year we got to celebrate his birthday with a day off from school."

Besides a new high school, English found the necessary funds to refurbish St. Patrick's Grade School in 1954-1955. A total remodeling project was completed and a gymnasium was added. He also had the St. Patrick's rectory redone and twice made major improvements to St. Patrick's Catholic Church. His last renovation included a Carrara marble altar that was purchased in Europe. Several beautiful statues were also added.

"The people of St. Patrick's took a lot of pride in their upgraded church," said McCarthy. "All the buildings were well-maintained and St. Patrick's was without question in the best financial shape of any Catholic parish in Butte thanks to Monsignor English."

Gilmore added, "Monsignor English took care of the people in St. Patrick's parish. We never had to pay tuition at the elementary school until 1957 because Monsignor underwrote the bill. It was the only Catholic school in Butte that was able to do this. Even when we started paying tuition it was only two dollars a month.

"When a strike took place, he went to every classroom at St. Patrick's

School. Monsignor found out which families were impacted with their fathers out of work because of the strike. He took care of the kids by providing them lunches and other things to get by during the walkout. He was a very generous man in a lot of ways and the people at St. Patrick's were extremely loyal to him because of it."

McCarthy recalled, "There was a deep loyalty to him because he did so many things for the people of St. Patrick's. I remember my father was dying and Monsignor made sure one of his parish priests came to see my dad every day. When you receive that kind of religious care its easy to see why people were so loyal to him."

The loyalty to Monsignor ended on October 4, 1967, when Michael English died of a heart attack. His accomplishments were both good for the city of Butte, St. Patrick's Parish and the Catholic Community.

The power Monsignor Michael English had on the Butte Catholic Community and the Diocese of Helena is remarkable. That power was revealed not during his life, but after his death. Less than two years after his death, the Catholic elementary schools in Butte were eliminated, two junior high schools were established plus Boys' and Girls' Central united into one school.

"I know they would've never shut down the grade schools especially St. Patrick's if Monsignor English were still alive," Gilmore said. "He put the fear of God into everyone including the Bishop in Helena at the time, Raymond Hunthausen. In fact, English and Hunthausen did not get along at all because the Bishop's brother, Father Jack Hunthausen, performed a marriage ceremony involving Monsignor's Irish niece while English was away from Butte.

"Monsignor English would've kept St. Patrick's School open. Anyone who knew him realized he meant business and ran the show."

A man who always seems to be in motion, Steve "Shoeshine Faulkner is constantly in a running stride, looking for his next assignment shining shoes. Steve has patrolled the Butte streets going from bar to bar for over 30 years.

Steve began shining shoes at the age of 12. He wanted to be on his own and get away from all the teasing he received from former school classmates. The reason for the verbal jabs was his big head. Steve suffers from hydrocephalus, which is characterized by an abnormal increase in the amount of fluid in the cranium, leading to an enlarged skull.

"One look at Steve made people assume that he was stupid," said Charlie Bugni, owner of the M & M Bar. "However, that's not the case at all. He's a bright guy."

Bugni hired Steve to do various odd jobs at his bar, one of many positions that Steve has labored at while living in Butte. Yet, it was shining shoes that made Steve a familiar face in Butte bars especially on weekends.

Through the years, Steve had some competition in the shoeshine business. He was always able to outlast the others and remain in business.

Steve married Bessie Caddy on March 12, 1976, some 14 years after they first met. Bessie died in 1985 from complications with diabetes. It was a crushing blow to Steve, but somehow he survived and so does his shoeshine business.

A Butte tradition during the holiday season is to light up the tops of the mine gallows frames in the form of a Christmas tree. The bright lights add a special touch to the meaning of Christmas for Butte folks. It seems only fitting that the Christmas tree has such a prominent role in the community because one of its own residents was a pioneer in developing the Christmas tree as a symbol of love and peace.

Her name was Alma Higgins who came to be known as "the Christmas tree lady." Through her efforts, the White House had its first Christmas tree lighting ceremony in 1924 with President Calvin Coolidge flipping the switch to ignite a new holiday tradition in our nation's capital.

Higgins was born on July 15, 1874, in Deer Lodge. She was educated in local schools and attended the College of Montana at Deer Lodge. Alma moved to Butte with her husband who had a number of mining claims in the area. Shortly after her arrival here in 1904, Higgins began her devotion to conservation efforts, becoming a pioneer in forest conservation and one of the country's leading environmentalist.

Higgins was one of the founders of the Rocky Mountain Garden Club in Butte in 1921. Alma also started the Floral Art Division and served as the club's president for over two decades. Higgins came up with the idea of a "garden week" long before it became a national project.

She was noted for maintaining an elegant garden at her Broadway Street home next to the First Presbyterian Church. Yet, it was the Christmas tree that earned Alma Higgins everlasting fame. She did special studies on the Christmas tree, examining its history, origins, legends, symbolism and ornaments. Her idea of the living tree was to portray the nativity scene at the birth of Jesus. Through her studies, Higgins became one of the leading national experts on the Christmas tree.

Alma was asked to give lectures about the Christmas tree all over the country. She also wrote numerous articles on the subject for national magazines. An article in December 1923 edition of the *American Forest* magazine sparked the idea for a national Christmas tree. This led to President Coolidge's first tree lighting ceremony in 1924. Since that first ceremony, the event has become a major event in Washington DC. The Christmas tree lighting ceremony at the White House led to other communities around the country doing the same thing. Now it's common for communities large and small to have a Christmas tree lighting ceremonies marking the start of the holiday season.

A nickname in Butte sometimes can fit a man to a T, however, other nicknames are a source of wonder. Such was the case with Fat Jack Jones. The nickname of "Fat Jack" invokes a picture of a big, burly man, but Fat Jack Jones was anything, but fat. He was tall and slender standing over six-feet tall. If he turned sideways people swore he looked like a utility pole he was so skinny.

Fat Jack Jones was one of Butte's first great characters. His real name was John Codman Jones and how he received the name Fat Jack is a mystery. There was no mystery, though, about Fat Jack's occupation: he was a hack driver, the most famous one of early Butte.

Jones transported people around town on his hackney, the name of a carriage for hire, which was pulled by a team of horses. When a celebrity came to town, Fat Jack was always called upon to haul the dignitary around the city. During his career, Jones had the honor of transporting presidential candidate William Jennings Bryan, actress Sarah Bernhardt, boxing champions Bob Fitzsimmons, James Corbitt and Jim Jeffries, plus President Theodore Roosevelt and President William Taft.

Jones tried to put a scare into Roosevelt during his visit to Butte on May 27, 1903. When he took the chief executive to the Columbia Gardens for a speech at the ballpark, Jones got going so fast around a turn the hack went up on two wheels. Instead of getting frightened, Roosevelt loved the experience and said so to Jones.

Fat Jack had a quick wit as passengers found out shortly after climbing aboard his hack wagon for a trip from the train depot to a hotel in the business district. He transported people from all walks of life around the community.

Jones did have his problems on the job. His horses got away from him once and trampled a man to death. Another time, after the car had been introduced to Butte, Jones hit and killed a women who stepped suddenly in front of his vehicle.

Driving was not the only trouble Jones got into. He was a hard drinker and loved any game of chance. Fat Jack enjoyed gambling so much that legend has it he once bet his false teeth in a game and lost.

After his wife Maria died, in 1915, Jones' health started to decline. He went to California to the Soldiers and Sailors' Home in 1919. Jones had been a veteran of the Civil War serving as a drummer boy. After spending some time at the Soldiers' center, he moved in with William Clark, the son of copper king William Clark. It was at Clark's home in California on December 16, 1920, that Fat Jack Jones died. Butte had lost one of its famous early-day characters.

Butte's Santa Claus was Charlie Judd. If there ever was a man both children and adults in the community adored, it was Charlie.

Judd operated the New Deal Bar on South Arizona Street, a business he took over from his father-in-law, Simon Zanon, in 1942 shortly after Charlie married Simon's daughter, Esther.

The New Deal Bar is located right across the street from the Silver Bow Homes, a Butte residential area confined to low income people. The children of the Silver Bow Homes had very little money, but they were not without entertainment. Charlie started a Halloween Party at the Silver Bow Homes in 1941 for the local kids, providing every kid with treats. The event became so successful that Charlie moved the activity across the street to his bar in 1951.

Once the Halloween party was inside the bar, the treats were not just confined to neighborhood kids, but any Butte child who wanted candy, popcorn, apples and pop. A kid picked up more in ten minutes inside the New Deal Bar than they could trick-or-treating for two or three hours in residential neighborhoods. All the treats were supplied by Charlie or donated by local business folks.

Of course, getting inside the New Deal Bar on Halloween night was a trick in itself. So many kids lined up at the front door that Charlie had to hire a police officer to control the crowd.

"Halloween was my dad's favorite time of the year," said Mike Judd, his son. "He would start about a month before the party, making popcorn at the bar. His excitement for the big day only grew as it got closer and closer to Halloween. The bar patrons helped by doing various things for my dad to get ready. The patrons also helped support the party financially because when my dad received tips at the bar he put the money in a large glass behind the bar. During the course of a year, the glass got pretty full and it helped a lot in providing necessary things to make the party a success."

A unique feature of the party was the bar remained open; however, no one could get a drink because alcohol was not served during the kids' party. The end of the festivities was the release of balloons from the ceiling. The balloons had coins inside and, once a kid had a hold of a balloon, they popped it to get the change. The annual party was given for over 40 years.

"One thing many people don't realize is that my dad held Halloween parties outside of Butte," Mike Judd said. "He used to take my brothers, Steve, Marty, Mark and myself to the orphanages in Twin Bridges and Deer Lodge. We helped him threw a party for those kids then we came back at Christmas to have another party where my dad handed out presents."

Although noted for his grand Halloween party, Charlie's generosity was not just confined to the end of October. Judd was a man who was always there to help out the youth of Butte. Charlie helped sponsor numerous athletic teams. He also was instrumental in helping young athletes acquire college scholarships around the country.

One of Charlie's more popular efforts was establishing and sponsoring of the Butte Buzzies' Independent football team. Formed in 1949 some eight years after the Butte/Anaconda Independent League had suspended its operations due to World War II, the Buzzies played games against regional teams from Seattle and Denver, competing until 1952.

Charlie's love of young people and athletics was not just confined to football. He was an avid Chicago White Sox baseball fan. When the White Sox won the 1959 American League pennant, Charlie threw a city-wide party at his bar. His place was jammed and the party easily rivaled any celebration taking place in Chicago. Judd and his wife, Esther, along with fellow White Sox follower, Marty Kearney and his wife, Louetta, went back to Chicago to watch their beloved Sox lose in six games to the Los Angeles Dodgers.

Undaunted by the loss Charlie came back to Butte and placed two Texas gallon-size bottles of whiskey over the bar. The signs said folks could drink free from the bottles when the White Sox repeated. They never have and to this day the bottles sit collecting dust.

Charlie Judd died on May 16, 1981. His efforts to help the Butte youth through the Halloween Party, sponsorship of various teams and the Butte Buzzies led to his induction into the Butte Sports Hall of Fame in 1993.

Plenty has been written about the Copper Kings Marcus Daly, William Clark and F. Augustus Heinze, who all played a major role in Butte's early mining development. Another man who made just as big a contribution to mining here was Cornelius F. Kelley, a leader and pioneer for The Anaconda Company throughout the first half of the 20th century.

Kelley was born in Mineral Hill, Nevada. In 1883, he came to Butte with his parents Jeremiah and Hannah Kelley from San Francisco. His father once owned a mining claim in Nevada where he became friends with Marcus Daly. The friendship between the two men continued in Butte and was helpful in young Con's first job as a water boy on Daly's Butte, Anaconda & Pacific Railroad in the early 1890s. Con Kelley did other jobs for Daly including working with The Anaconda Company's engineering department underground during the summer.

After his graduation from Butte High School in 1892, Kelley went to the University of Michigan where he received a law degree in 1898. Kelley returned to Butte and practiced law for a few years as both a deputy county attorney and as a private attorney.

He joined the legal department of The Anaconda Copper Mining Company in 1901 beginning a long career working for the mining firm. Kelley was thrust right into the battle shortly after joining Anaconda's legal team. In 1903, he was involved in litigation against F. Augustus Heinze over the apex mining law. Thanks to Heinze's control of judges, Kelley and his partners lost their courtroom case. The Anaconda Company shut down its mines in protest of the legal decision against them until legislation was passed in Helena allowing The Company to remove local judges from cases where the judge might have a vested interest.

In 1906, Kelley was responsible for signing a new contract with local unions which determined wages on a sliding-scale based on the price of copper. The five-year working agreement was hailed as a victory by conservative Irish and Cornish union members. Others, like the Finnish workers, felt the sliding-scale worked in favor of Anaconda and, in the long run, they were right. The price of copper went up slightly after 1906, but then fell and forced the miners back to a wage of $3.50 a day which is the same amount they earned back in 1878. The contract worked out by Kelley became the backbone of similar agreements throughout the United States.

In 1908, Con was put in charge of The Anaconda Company's legal department. Two years later, in 1910, he worked out a deal to purchase a majority of William Clark's mine holdings in Butte. By the start of World War I in 1918, Kelley had consolidated most of the Butte mining holdings under the umbrella of The Anaconda Company.

Con Kelley took another step up the corporate ladder in 1918. He was named president of The Anaconda Company when John D. Ryan left his post to become Assistant Secretary of the War for the United States where his assignment was to be in charge of airplane manufacturing.

Once the head of The Company, Con Kelley took bold steps to improve the firm. He was instrumental in Anaconda acquiring some rich copper mines in Chile in 1923 for $77 million. A few years later, in 1928, he helped secure almost all of the property estate of William Clark's Montana holdings. One feature of the estate was the Columbia Gardens. Kelley had his workers upgrade sections of the park and provided new rides and a new carousel.

Kelley kept the Butte mines opened during the Great Depression of the 1930s despite the fact that his Company was $105 million in debt. The price of copper hit an all-time low of 4.7 cents a pound, but some how Kelley managed to keep the mines partially in operation.

Con was named the Chairmen of the Board for The Anaconda Company in 1940, becoming the first chairmen of the board since the death of John D. Ryan on February 10, 1933.

After the end of World War II, Kelley was again taking bold steps to improve Butte's mining district. He unveiled the Greater Butte Project in 1947 which led to block cave mining and ultimately the Berkeley Pit in 1955.

Shortly after the shovels started digging the Berkeley Pit in 1955, Kelley stepped down as chairmen of the board. He had spent 54 years working for Anaconda. During his time with The Company, Kelley helped consolidate the Butte mines into one unit, worked out a pioneer labor deal, upgraded the Columbia Gardens, maintained the Butte mines during the Great Depression, helped lead the way for the construction of a $5 million hospital which was turned over to the community in 1951, and developed the Greater Butte Project which led to the Berkeley Pit.

His accomplishments reflect his enormous influence in Butte during the 20th century. Con's achievements can be reflected in corporate dollars. When The Anaconda Copper Mining Company was incorporated in 1895, it was worth $30 million. When Kelley stepped down as board chairmen, The Company was worth $673 million.

Two years after retiring, Cornelius F. Kelley, the ultimate company man, died on May 12, 1957.

The word "daredevil" in the dictionary means, " reckless and often ostentatiously daring, adventurous." If ever there was a person who fit the word "daredevil" it was Robert "Evel" Knievel.

Bobbie Knievel showed signs of his daredevil ways early in life. He liked to pole vault on the Butte High track team and enjoyed ski jumping at the Beef Trail Ski Area south of Butte. He also played hockey for the Butte Copper Kings.

As a youngster Bobbie Knievel was always in trouble. He was given the name "Evel" during a stay one night in the local jail. Bobbie was put behind bars with Bill Kanofle. The jailer that night, Maurice Mulcahy, said, "Well, here we are, we've got Awful Kanofle and Evel Knievel located up in the same jail." The name stuck and his legend soon grew.

His wild ways could be illustrated on his engagement to Linda Bork. He kidnapped her aboard his motorcycle and off they went to get married in 1959.

Evel tried to make a living by selling insurance in Chicago. Selling did not appeal to him so he went into motorcycle racing which did not pay much. He came up with an idea to try motorcycle jumping as a way to earn a paycheck. His first jump came in 1965 in Indio, California, near Palm Springs. He cleared two trucks and thus started an entirely new profession, motorcycle daredevil jumping. Such a sport demanded exact timing and precession or else the consequences could be deadly.

In all, he jumped over 300 times in his career which ended in 1980. At one time he held the world record for jumping over 21 cars. People never seem to remember all the successful jumps he accomplished as much as the ones in which he failed. Evel crashed eleven times resulting in over 50 separate fractures. By the end of his career, he had 14 steel plates in his body and needed the use of a cane.

The first major crash of his career took place on December 31, 1967. Knievel tried to jump the fountains at Caesar's Palace in Las Vegas. Evel came up short on his 150-foot jump and went head-over-handle bars off his bike. He suffered a crushed pelvis and numerous other injuries, and spent 67 days recovering in a hospital.

His most creative jump attempt took place on September 8, 1974. Evel tried to jump over the Snake River Canyon in his rocket Sky-Cycle X-2. Knievel had wanted to jump the Grand Canyon, but he could not get permission from the federal government to try such a stunt. So he spent $37,000 to lease some Snake River Canyon land near Twin Falls, Idaho, to attempt his leap.

A 108-foot long steel ramp was built at a 56 degree angle to launch the Sky-Cycle with Knievel on board. When the launch took place, the Sky-Cycle only made it part way over the canyon and the rocket crashed on land down below on the edge of the dangerous Snake River. Knievel survived the mishap and his legend as a stuntman only grew.

"I called the Skycycle a loaded bomb," said Jack Ferriter. "All the electrical instruments were of no value to him. He had to try and do everything manually which was almost impossible. But give him credit, he tried rather than walk away."

The failed stunt was witnessed by thousands at the Snake Rive Canyon and many more on a pay-per-view television put on by Top Rank Incorporated.

Another spectacular mishap occurred on May 26, 1975, when Knievel tried to jump over 13 double-tiered buses at Wembley Stadium in London, England. The crash resulted in fractured pelvis, crushed vertebrae and hand injuries.

A bizarre accident took place in 1977 when Knievel was attempting to jump a pool of man-eating sharks. His cycle crashed on the runway and he was in a coma for 30 days at a Chicago hospital.

All people wanted to talk about were his crashes, but they fail to mention how he came back every time to try something even more dangerous. A case in point took place on October 25, 1975, at King's Mill, Ohio, where Evel soared over 13 buses. It came just five months after his crash at Wembley Stadium in London trying to clear the same number of buses. The jump at King's Mill, Ohio, produced the highest rated program during the first 25 years of ABC's Wide World of Sports. Knievel's popularity for attracting an audience in the 1970s was only rivaled by Muhammad Ali. His attempted leap over the Snake River Canyon was the third most-watched show for the popular sports program during its first 25 years. He was dubbed "the white Muhammad Ali."

His fame produced plenty of wealth for Knievel. He claims to have made $50 million in a 15-year period as a stuntman. One of his key sources of income came from the Ideal Toy Company. The firm estimated they made over $100 million during a five-year period on Evel Knievel Toys. Evel received a royalty payment of between 2.5 to 10 percent on everything sold.

Knievel was paid a reported $6 million by Top Rank Incorporated in his failed attempt to rocket over the Snake River Canyon in 1974. Yet, on August 9, 1980, Evel filed a suit against Top Rank and their promoter, Bob Arum, because he felt the company still owed him $300,000 for close-circuit television and radio rights plus other obligations.

Knievel found himself in court a lot once he got money. Fame and fortune can also produce problems and Evel had his share. He was ordered by a South Florida Federal District Court to pay $187,000 to the Transit Charter Company for his purchase of a 116-foot luxury yacht called "Claybeth" which he bought on March 8, 1977.

In 1980, he lost his $187,000 home in the Butte Country Club area for not paying on the mortgage. He also owed the Internal Revenue Service $709,713 in back taxes in 1980. By 1987, the back taxes had climbed to $4.8 million. Knievel claimed a 1972 investment in a coal deal in Montana was a tax write-off that was not allowed thus the dispute over his taxes. On November 5, 1988, Federal District Judge Paul Hatfield ruled Knievel and his wife owed $5.3 million dollars to the IRS for taxes from 1972 to 1976. This included arrears taxes, interest and penalties.

Besides his money problems, Evel also had his run-ins with the law. In 1978, Knievel was found guilty of assaulting his former press agent, Sherman Saltman, with a baseball bat the previous year in California. Knievel spent six months in jail for the guilty verdict. What hurt even more was the decision by Ideal Toy Company to discontinue its sale of the Evel Knievel toys in the United States because of the assault verdict.

Knievel certainly had a wild side. He was noted for betting $1,000 on a hole of golf and once reportedly spent $5,000 on drinks one night in New Orleans. Yet, he also had a very kind side to him that few people ever knew about. Evel brought national celebrities to Butte to play in the annual Labor Day Golf Tournament for charitable causes in town. Evel cherished his role as host for many big-name people.

Ferriter said, "He was proud of Butte, Montana, and did what he could to help the town."

Evel Knievel attempted to give something back to the community where he grew up. He wanted to open the Evel Knievel and Friends Museum at the vacated Webster-Garfield School. Knievel announced his plans for a 25-room museum in March 1987. The museum idea was to showcase Evel's life plus the 30 different motorcycles and numerous toys with his name.

He needed $2 million for the renovation of the 70,000-square foot project, but Butte school officials were cautious about giving him the school building based on projected future enrollment figures for the city. An agreement between the two parties was finally reached on October 19, 1987; however, plans for the complex fell through when Evel did not come forward with the $30,000 in rent, a performance bond of $10,000 and a $1 million liability insurance policy. The agreed 30-year lease was declared null and void.

Knievel pushed for motorcycle safety on a national level. In 1987, he appeared before the California State Legislature in favor of a bill requiring helmets for motorcyclists. Knievel did this despite the fact that over a thousand motorcyclists had come to Sacramento to protest the piece of legislation.

Knievel tried various thing after his jumping career was over. He was helped in the art business by local artist, Jack Ferriter. A 90-minute video was made on Evel called "The Last of the Gladiators - Evel Knievel."

"Knievel was one of the last of the gladiators," said Ferriter. "He should've been killed nine or ten times when he crashed, but some how he always survived."

Butte provided people with an opportunity. The immigrants who came to the community were looking for a chance to better themselves and their families. People could come from the poorest of poor families and through hard work, dedication and will power, better themselves. Such was the case of Bob Koprivica.

Koprivica was the youngest of five children of Petar and Stane Koprivica. They had come to Butte from Yugoslavia. Petar was a Serb while Stane was a Croatian.

Petar Koprivica ran a grocery store called the Gem Market on Anaconda Road in Dublin Gulch. Times were tough in 1921 when the mines were shut down for a nine-month period. Petar allowed many local families to buy groceries on credit which led to the failure of his business because few families could pay him back. The Koprivica family was left with very little. They had to do various things to make do and put food on the table.

When the Great Depression came in the 1930s, young Bob Koprivica had to quit school at 16. He got a job working in the Montana Market on East Park Street. Bob had to learn the Finnish, Greek and Italian languages along with Slavic and English so he could deliver to families on the East Side. His six years of labor at the Montana Market plus serving as a salesmen for both the Sweet Brothers and Miller Produce prepared Bob for a crack at running his own business.

Koprivica joined three other partners in buying out the business of the Sweet Brothers. His new company was called Montana Wholesale with the firm selling beer, produce and canned goods. The company fell into deep financial trouble. In a short time, the company was $50,000 in debt and creditors and lawyers wanted the four men to file for bankruptcy. Koprivica refused and told the creditors he would do whatever was necessary to pay off the bills. Only one of the four men, Joe Keefe, decided to stick it out with Koprivica. They changed the name of the company to Bob & Joe's and elected to sell only beer and drop the produce and canned goods departments.

Many of his creditors said Koprivica and Keefe would be completely out of business in six months. Yet, in three years through a lot of hard work, dedication, some luck and a partnership with God, the $50,000 in bills were paid off by Bob Koprivica.

"There are two reasons how I turned it around," remembered Bob Koprivica. "First , I made God a partner in my business. I could do nothing without his help. He helped lead me to deals with Safeway, Brown Derby Beer and Miller Produce which all helped make the business profitable. Secondly, I had a motto I always stuck to which was good for my business. It read 'If you would win a man to your cause first you must convince him that your are his friend.' I had to go out and make friends first before I could sell my products. It was very important."

The motto worked quite well for Koprivica. In a short few years, he had a flourishing business. Yet, what made Koprivica a special human being was not his achievements as a businessman, but his incredible generosity.

"I always felt it was important that I give something back to the community," Koprivica said. "Its like growing a garden. If you keep taking carrots out of the ground and don't replace them sooner or later you will have nothing left. I wanted to make sure I gave something back so when I die my little corner of the world would be a better place than when I was on it."

Koprivica became one the most generous people in the community. During the summer, he supported as many as 35 softball and baseball teams. If there was a cause you could count on Bob Koprivica to support it.

One of Bob's biggest contributions came at one of Butte's lowest points, the 1959 Anaconda Company strike. The walkout lasted for almost a year and caused unbearable hardship on many families. Koprivica heard school kids were passing out in the classroom because of a lack of nourishment. When he questioned school officials and discovered the story was true, Koprivica took immediate action.

He told school officials he'd provide free lunch meals to kids through his company. Bob got a list of kids who were struggling because their father was out on strike. Koprivica started supplying daily lunches to the kids in all the schools around town. During the first day of his lunch program, 325 meals were served.

When other business people heard of Koprivica's generosity, they quickly chipped in to help. The Safeway stores provided lunch meat for the sandwiches, Crystal Creamery gave milk and Eddy's Bakery came through with bread. Other financial donations came in for the cause including a large sum of money from the Butte Teachers' Union. Soon, every student in Butte was receiving a solid lunch meal at school regardless of their conditions at home.

When the strike finally ended, Koprivica received letters from people around town thanking him for his efforts in feeding hungry school kids. With the money left over from the School Lunch Fund Bob started another charitable operation to help needy families. The next winter, he initiated a Christmas Program. Through his financial support, needy families were allowed to go to major department stores like JC Penney's to pick out new clothes which were delivered to their homes the day before Christmas.

Koprivica recalled, "I saw some families sleeping on the floor because they could not afford beds. The Christmas program was our way of helping because whatever was needed in our town we wanted to be there to help."

Bob helped play a key early role in the development of Our Lady of the Rockies statue. When the group held their first meeting on April 19, 1981, it was Koprivica and Joe Roberts who each gave $1,000 to the project to help get it off the ground.

Koprivica was more than just generous. When the Butte YMCA was ready to shut down its operations for good in the spring of 1982, Koprivica stepped in to help. In the past, the annual spring drive netted the YMCA around $35,000. Koprivica said shutting down the Y would be the worst thing that could happen to Butte kids. He set a goal to raise over $100,000. Through the help of his son, Bob, and many others, Koprivica took in over $125,000. It was more than enough to keep the doors open for many years to come at the YMCA.

As Koprivica got older his challenges started to come from beyond Butte. He tried to make peace with the Russian people long before the breakup of Communism and before it was popular to be friends with Russians. He made numerous trips around the country to meet with Russian diplomats to try and establish peace.

When the Bosnian War broke out in his former parents' homeland of Yugoslavia, Koprivica made numerous trips and phone calls trying to bring peace back to the region.

Koprivica's contributions both at home and around the world did not go unnoticed. He was elected to the Butte Sports Hall of Fame for all his generous support of many athletes and teams through the years.

Koprivica's last major project was turning the five-acre Hebgen Park into a refurbished activity center for the community. The complex was renamed Koprivica Family Park, featuring the newest playground equipment for kids and families, a lasting legacy for a man who started with almost nothing, but was given an opportunity.

"Hubba! Hubba! Its time for the dancing dolls." The words come from Butte's original one-man band, Ludvig "Luigi" Jurenic, whose show, complete with dancing dolls, instruments and lots of fun was an unforgettable part of Butte's night club scene for many years.

Ludvig Jurenic was born and raised in Eveleth, Minnesota. His parents came from Czechoslovakia where his grandfather, Paul Jurenic, had been the leader of a city marching band. The entire family of twelve kids followed Paul's footsteps by playing some type of music.

The large family and the Great Depression forced young Ludvig to do many things to help make ends meet for the family. He often went to the dump to salvage junk to sell which enabled Ludvig to purchase his first instrument. Ludvig bought numerous instruments in his youth. He was determined to learn how to play them all. His favorite was the accordion.

Ludvig left home at 16. After traveled around the country looking for work, he landed in Butte where he worked in the mines. A number of miners started called Ludvig by "Luigi" and the nickname stuck.

After living in Alaska with his wife, Pearl, for three years, Luigi returned to Butte in 1949. Blessed with musical talent, Luigi started to do the thing he absolutely loved, playing music as a one-man band. He wanted some company during his entertainment so he cut out a paper doll and made it a part of his act. Luigi practiced his dancing dolls show playing at various street dances in Meaderville.

The next year, Luigi started a new musical career when he purchased the Arc Light Bar on East Park Street. Luigi turned the establishment into a musical doll house. Over the next 12 years, he built up a strong, loyal following. Luigi entertained the crowds with his dancing dolls shows. When he took a break his brothers, Bernie and Tony Jurenic, stepped forward and played dance music.

"The place was always packed," remembered Tony Jurenic. "We use to get bus loads of people coming into the place because they heard how much fun they could have in Luigi's. It was really a unique place."

The music and dancing dolls on East Park Street were cut off in 1964 when Luigi was forced to sell his property to The Anaconda Company for the expansion of the Berkeley Pit. Luigi bought a place on Harrison Avenue and turned the place into an entertainment center. Luigi's was the same in many ways with dancing dolls, snakes and other things everywhere, but it was also different because his brothers, Tony and Bernie, went elsewhere to work and Luigi was now all by himself.

Luigi said in an interview once, "When your playing alone you've got to have some company and the dolls are my company."

One of his favorite tricks was playing music with various liquor bottles. He lined up a number of small bottles on the bar and filled each one to various levels, thus creating a different tone with each bottle. Luigi started the juke box and played along, tapping on the bottles. During his regular route, Luigi started playing music and suddenly puppets danced, spiders fell, and the whole place was alive with movement. The entire bar was controlled by Luigi with his instruments, and strings.

Luigi could play 24 different instruments and sometimes he got the crowd involved by forming a circle on the dance floor. The patrons used various pipes and other musical items to create their own music. It was not always the most pleasant sounding, but where else could a patron suddenly become a member of the band? Luigi was the conductor and everyone in the bar was in his orchestra. He had a special way of bringing the child out in every adult.

"The whole place was insane," recalled Bob Kearney. "When someone walked in the door, a huge ax swung in unison with the motion of the door. During his show, the same thing was true, only magnified 20 times over. No matter where a person sat in the bar, when Luigi played, the whole bar was jumping and dancing. Everything was interconnected by strings of wire, magically hooked up to the 10 to 15 instruments Luigi played at one time.

"A classic by Luigi was dropping spiders from the ceiling and having them dance on the floor. My favorite, though, was the dummy sitting at the table near the bathrooms. The dummy was activated to life as people walked by scaring some folks half to death. Luigi's was a wild place!"

Luigi's antics led to numerous articles in national magazines like *Good Housekeeping* and *The New Yorker* plus a segment on the television show "Real People" in February 1981, a couple of years before his death.

He was more than just a character. Luigi was a unique blend of entertainment, style and grace impossible for any person to match. His musical show came to en end on May 31, 1984, when he died of cancer.

Meaderville was noted for its wide-open gambling places and fine restaurants. The thrill of playing blackjack or the experience of eating delicious Italian food in Meaderville was wiped out by the shovels from the Berkeley Pit. The neighborhood was gone, but the taste of Meaderville is still alive today through the efforts of Lydia Micheletti.

Lydia was one of five children born to Dave and Attila Micheletti. Like many Butte immigrants the Micheletti family struggled to survive. Dave became a miner who worked in the Butte underground operations and also tried his luck at a claim he owned near Elkhorn. Poor health due to a bad heart forced him to give up mining and also forced the hand of the Micheletti family. Attila could only speak Italian and with five youngsters, it was impossible for her to go out to find a job. So the three oldest daughters - Mary, Connie and Lydia - had to leave school to find jobs to help support the family. Mary worked in a boarding house, Connie at a local ranch and Lydia as a dishwasher at a Meaderville restaurant. All were working when Dave's health turned worse and he died. Mary, the oldest, was only 16.

The death of their father only brought the Micheletti family closer together. They were poorer than poor, but they had each other and like many Butte families without a father that was the most important key to survival.

Lydia's job as a dishwasher started to take a new direction when she became friends with the restaurant's cook. Lydia became the cook's helper beginning a career that one day made her famous. She learned the art of cooking and through the years acquired many of the Italian recipes that made Meaderville's food world-renowned. Lydia built her reputation as a cook while being employed at the Rocky Mountain Cafe for Teddy Traparish. While Teddy was entertaining guests in the dining area, Lydia was running the kitchen.

Lydia wanted to be more than just a cook. She wanted to run her own place so she joined forces with Sonny O'Day and Marko Lean to open the Savoy Club in Meaderville. The business relationship between the three did not last long, but that did not discourage Lydia.

On March 17, 1946, she opened her own place on Harrison Avenue in a roadhouse restaurant/bar called the Casino. A few months later, her younger brother, Dave, fresh out of the service from World War II joined her. Later, her sister, Connie, joined them to work at the restaurant they renamed Lydia's in 1948.

The family bond developed early in life through the loss of their father now led Lydia and the Micheletti family into the night club restaurant business that became the most successful in town.

"I think Lydia's success can be traced to hard work and the dedication that she put into the place," said Dave Micheletti. "She never took a day off and was absolutely a fabulous cook.

"We made it a point to treat everyone as if they were the most special person in the world when they came into Lydia's. Through that extra care and service we provided the place developed a good reputation." The reputation led to the construction of a new building in 1964 next to the original Lydia's restaurant. Once the new building was finished, the old roadhouse restaurant was torn down. The new place added a special atmosphere to a Lydia's dining experience and, with Meaderville almost gone now through the development of the Berkeley Pit, the new restaurant building became a setting to remember the famous Meaderville dinners.

"We serve a Meaderville dinner today with chicken, steak and raviolis the same way they did in the old days," said Dave Micheletti. "The sad thing is today when you say Meaderville no one knows what you are talking about. Many people who come in the restaurant today were not even born when Meaderville was destroyed. They have no clue about Meaderville, but they know what a great meal is and they know what good service is which is what my sister expected us to provide at her restaurant."

Lydia started to back out of the restaurant business after the new building was put up in 1964. Her brother, Dave, took over the day-to-day operations and later Mark Sanderson oversaw the business. The change of hands maintained the first-class atmosphere and fine meals featured nightly at Lydia's. Its considered a Butte landmark and a place many former residents will visit when they come back to their old home town.

Lydia Micheletti died in 1989, but her name and her reputation live on through her restaurant and her family.

A pioneer is a person who leads in some way. Such was the case for Butte's Mary MacLane. She was a pioneer women's author.

Mary was born in Winnipeg, Manitoba, in 1881. Her family moved to Minnesota, then Great Falls and finally arrived in Butte in 1896. MacLane attended Butte High School where she was the editor of the high school newspaper. It was her interest in writing that soon captivated the world. She began writing a book while still in high school.

After graduating in 1900, Mary began the process of completing her first book, *The Story of Mary MacLane* about a youthful revolt against the moral values of her time. The book was a frank, honest, passionate look at men, morals, customs and events through the eyes of a young woman. Mary was successful in getting the Stone Publishing Company of Chicago to take her manuscript and publish her book in 1902. When it was released, *The Story of Mary MacLane* became a top seller in the country. Radical for its time, the book was praised for its unconventional ideas and originality. However, it was also not appreciated by many, especially some living in Butte. The Butte Library refused to put the book on their shelves which only produced more interest and sales.

The amount of criticism MacLane received resulted in her departure from Butte. She lived in New York for ten years where she wrote her second book *My Friend Annabelle Lee.* She also appeared as a guest speaker around the country.

Her third book was published in 1917 called *I Mary MacLane.* The book was an update of her inner thoughts from the first book. The book was published in 30 different languages; however, it did not provide the same type of shock value as her first publication had 15 years earlier.

MacLane also branched out as a screen writer and actress. She appeared in or wrote such plays and films as *Men Who Have Made Cove to Me* in 1918, *Which Shall It Be* in 1924, *The Night Ship,* in 1925 and *Sparrows* in 1926.

Mary MacLane came back to live in Butte where she worked for the *Butte Evening Post* newspaper. Her literary work lived on long past her death which occurred on August 6, 1929, in Chicago.

Every community in this country needs a champion for the handicapped, a person who takes up their cause and works for a better tomorrow. In Butte, that champion was Mary Mollish.

Mary and her husband, Frank, moved to Butte in 1960. Frank was a recruiter for the United States Army. Butte was a long way from the couples' home state of Missouri and neither was overly fond of coming to Montana.

Once in Butte, Mary Mollish started to help Irving Jacobs, a blind man who ran a store in the business district. Jacobs had lost his sight through diabetes. Mary soon realized the needs of the blind community.

Soon after helping Jacobs at his store, Mary Mollish took it upon herself to do everything in her power to help the blind. She started creating fund raising projects for the blind. One of her most successful projects was selling Christmas wreaths that were made by the blind. She received lots of help with her wreath project from businessman Joe Roberts. Mollish soon had blind people doing things they never thought possible a few years before, like snow skiing.

"I have always enjoyed fund raising very much," said Mary Mollish. "It's always a challenge raising money because there is always someone out there who tells you it can't be done."

When Mollish took a group of severely handicapped people on a picnic, other people in the area were making fun of one of the most handicapped people. The incident mad her mad enough to do something about it. Mollish recalled, "When that took place, I got real angry. Here we were trying to help this people and others were making fun of us. I wanted to do something so the handicapped could enjoy the benefits of Montana's great outdoors just like anyone else."

She wrote a letter to Montana's Senator Mike Mansfield asking for help. Through his efforts, a number things were done at Homestake Lake to make it more user-friendly to handicapped people. But, the picnic grounds were near a major restroom area on Interstate 90 and soon some travelers were causing problems for the handicapped.

Mollish wanted to move the location for a handicapped park away from the main steam of the traveling public. She heard the Lowland's Picnic area near Elk Park north of Butte might be available for development. Once again, she wrote to Mansfield requesting help. Mansfield came through with funds and through the help of the US Forest Service and the Anaconda Job Corps the Sheepshead Picnic Grounds was developed. The entire area was built with the handicapped in mind and represents a major victory for handicapped people who now had the pleasure of enjoying the outdoors like everyone else in society.

Mollish saw more than just the needs of the handicapped in Butte. She also felt something had to be done to help families who were enduring a medical crises in their family. She wrote to the corporate headquarters of the McDonald's Corporation asking them to construct a McDonald Family Place in Butte. At the time, Butte did not have a McDonald Restaurant. So the company replied that they only built a McDonald Family Place in a community where one of their restaurants was located.

Soon after Mollish's request was denied, a McDonald's was built in Butte. Mary took her cause to the local owner, Lowell Bartels. She told him about the need to help families during medical emergencies in town and how much it would help to have a McDonald Family Place in town. Bartels joined Mollish in the cause and the process began for the new house at the vacated Paul Clark Home. The Paul Clark Home/McDonald's Family Place, involving many volunteers and donors was completed four years later. Mollish's efforts to help the needy had paid off again.

Mollish has been involved in many projects for many different organizations in the community. Yet, her favorite mission revolved around a need she never even knew existed until 1971. That year, Frank and Mary Mollish lost their son, John, to death through a rare disease.

As a youngster John enjoyed ski racing; however, there were few opportunities for area young kids in the sport. That changed with the establishment of the John Mollish Ski Races in 1972.

"Actually, we never started the race," said Mollish. "It was Bob Leipheimer of The Outdoorsmen and Joe Stimpson who got things going. They provided all the trophies and ran the races. We simply helped out where we could."

Bob Leipheimer said, "Mary and Frank did more than just help out. They went out into the community and promoted the race. Those two did everything possible to make sure the race was successful. Each year they hand out the trophies to all the winners. You never saw two people who are more proud of something than Frank and Mary Mollish are about that race. Its written in their eyes. They have done so much to help develop ski racing for youngsters throughout the region.

"Both my sons were involved in ski racing and their first real taste of competition was in the John Mollish Ski Races. As a parent I am very grateful for everything Frank and Mary have done to promote the sport and I know there are hundreds of other parents who would say the same thing."

Because of her efforts of helping the blind, the handicapped, the needy, the youth of the region many will always have a soft spot in their heart for Mary Mollish.

"You know when Frank was assigned to Butte, Montana, we did everything we could to keep from coming here," Mollish said with a laugh. "You know what, though, I am sure glad we came here. It sure has been wonderful."

Leipheimer added, "Boy, I tell you it was a major blessing to Butte that Mary Mollish came to town. She has really touched the lives of many people here in this community."

Jerry "the Wise" Murphy was a big man, standing over six-feet tall and weighing better than 200 pounds, making him an imposing figure for anyone. His duties as the chief of police in Butte from 1911 to 1935 made him a major player in the city's early history. Murphy served as police chief for 16 different mayors in Butte.

Jerry Murphy was born in Kilkenney, Ireland. He came to the United States as a lad of 16 and lived for a short time with an aunt in Virginia. In 1888, Jerry arrived in Montana working first at the Anaconda Smelter. During his stay in Anaconda, the future police chief of Butte became friends with Marcus Daly. One of the reasons for their friendship was Murphy's efforts to throttle an attempted plot by some to kidnap Daly's son, Marcus Daly Jr. Murphy got an ex-convict to tell him about the plan and was able to stop the scheme before it was executed.

Murphy moved his family to Butte and operated a boarding house. He joined the Butte police force in 1893. During the next 18 years, he was on the force for various lengths of time depending on who was the mayor of the town. He was finally promoted to chief of detectives in 1909 and was named Police Chief by Mayor Louis Duncan in 1911, a position Murphy held until death.

Murphy was well-respected in the underworld and was given the name "the Wise" by them. For some reason the tall Irishmen could get information on just about anything and could spot trouble even before it took place.

He found out some known gangsters had come to Butte and were at a local hotel. Murphy went to the hotel and knocked on their door. When it was opened he said, "My name's Murphy. There's a train leaving town here at 3 o'clock. See that you are on it." Murphy never had to explain to the gangsters who he was because they already knew it was time to leave.

One of Murphy's best investigations involved a man who left town with another fellow's money. He was picked up for the crime by Canadian authorities, however they released him after not locating any money on him. When Murphy found out, he had officials pick up the man again. This time he told Canadian officials that the man had the money in the back of his shirt in a two-layered piece of cloth. The Canadian officials followed his instructions and sure enough they located the cash.

One time a man came to Murphy complaining that someone would not pay him for a cabinet he built for the person. The man also told Murphy how the cabinet moved when a button on the opposite side of the room was pushed. Murphy got the man his money, but he also took federal authorities to the house in question. The officials were there numerous times before looking for a potential bootleg operation. Once inside the room with the cabinet, Murphy walked over to the button on the opposite side of the room and pushed it. The cabinet moved to the side and officials discovered a large room which housed the bootlegger's equipment.

Murphy had a great memory for faces. He drove around the town and spotted people he knew were not right for "our village" as he liked to call Butte. He had his driver pull the car over and talked to the undesirable about leaving our village.

There were countless stories about how Murphy solved situations without even pulling out the gun out of his holster. Many times quick actions with his fists rectified a dispute. Yet, it was Murphy's reluctance to use a gun that ultimately cost him his life.

He went to the Montana Power Company building alone on Broadway Street to stop a crazed World War I veteran, William Lombardini, who was terrorizing the office with a gun because the utility clerks refused to give him money for bonds he had purchased. Murphy tried to grab the gun from the 44-year-old Lombardini. It went off twice with the bullets hitting the ceiling. Murphy and Lombardini continued their struggle for the weapon until Murphy's knee collapsed as both men fell to the floor. Murphy banged his head off the tiled floor.

The police chief suffered a severe head concussion. Murphy was rushed to St. James Hospital where he went into a coma. A few days later, Murphy died on September 20, 1935.

Everyone in Butte knew Margaret English by her nickname, "Nickel Annie," because her famous line was, "Five cents please." She never asked for more and said that line everywhere she went in the community.

Nickel Annie, wearing her black-faded dress and carrying an old umbrella, roamed Butte streets begging for 45 years. Although a mystery to most people, Nickel Annie came to Butte from a prominent St. Louis family. Her first job was working as a housekeeper for William Clark. She had other jobs with all her employers praising her as an excellent cook and a great house keeper.

When and why she took up begging on the streets is a mystery to everyone. When she was not walking the streets, Nickel Annie lived and worked at Mrs. Butcher's house at 903 South Nevada Street. She moved into the Butcher home in 1916 and stayed there a number of years.

In 1933, as her health started to fail Nickel Annie moved to the county home on Continental Drive. She turned over every nickel she had begged for to authorities to help pay for her keep at the home. The total came to over $300. A few years after turning over all her precious nickels, she died at the age of 80 in the county home on April 27, 1936.

The first stop many college students make when they come back to Butte is not home, but John's Pork Chop Sandwich Shop. Only after they have bitten into one of their delicious pork chop sandwiches does the student feel like they are truly home.

The pork chop sandwich and the Cornish pasty are two favorites for Butte patrons and newcomers alike. A large reason for the success and the growth of the pork chop sandwich in Butte is John Orizotti.

The Meaderville native did not invent the pork chop sandwich; that distinction belongs to John Burkland. Burkland used to prepare the pork loins in his special batter at his home on Crystal Street. Once everything was ready, Burkland went down to the corner of Mercury and Main Streets where he stood on the corner and sold the chops until they were gone. Burkland began selling pork chop sandwiches in 1924. Three years later, city laws forced him to rent a small shop at 8 West Mercury in the Doyle Hotel. It was here that the pork chop sandwich found a permanent home.

In 1932, Burkland sold his business to his son-in-law, Bernie Semmons, who eliminated the bone in the pork chop. The move helped transform the pork chop sandwich into a favorite Butte meal.

The pork chop sandwich shop became a solid business, as John Orizotti witnessed first-hand as a meat cutter working for his future father-in-law,

Dan Piazzola, at the Better Meat Market. The store was located right around the corner from the pork chop sandwich shop. One of their primary customers was Bernie Semmons. Orizotti pounded the pork loins into the pattie shape Semmons needed.

"We had to pound everything by hand which was a great deal of work," recalled John Orizotti. "Yet, it also gave me an opportunity to see how Semmons ran the business. In fact, I use to help him quite a bit at the sandwich shop."

By the 1960s, the Better Meat Market had moved a block up Main Street to become the Main Public Meat Market. The market was struggling through tough times especially with the nine-month miners' strike in 1967 and 1968.

Orizotti remembered, "When that strike was over, we almost went under. We had a lot of Company workers on what we called 'customer wage assignments.' When they got their check from Anaconda, so much had to go to their bill at the meat market. After the strike, the Company only hired back workers with 20 years seniority which meant we lost every customer wage assignment client we had except one, Darrell McBride. I had to do something because I had a large family to feed."

What Orizotti did was approach Bernie Semmons about trying to buy the pork chop sandwich business. A number of Orizotti's friends thought he was crazy attempting to buy the operation. The city had just come off the long strike and the prospects of future walkouts were very real. Orizotti was also told he could never make it because the price of a pork chop sandwich was only 65 cents. He had to sell a lot of pork chop sandwiches to pay off the note.

"I just had a gut feeling I could be successful at the pork chop shop," recalled Orizotti. "First of all, I knew the meat business because I had spent the last 17 years working in the trade. I also could see the potential and using the right marketing tools I just knew the pork chop sandwich shop could be a great business for my family.

"I worked out the deal and took over the business in 1969. Right away I did a number of things to help improve things. Previously, they only had two people working at the place. There was one person at the counter and another in the back preparing the sandwiches. We needed more people and we also needed to take a more personal interest in each customer. Right away you could see a difference."

In the first year of business, Orizotti topped sales from the previous year when it was owned by Semmons. A year later, Orizotti realized his gut feeling might work.

"We had such a good location I just knew the thing would fly," said

Orizotti. "I just could not wait for Friday nights to come especially during the fall. We were located just a block up from Naranche Stadium. After the high school football game, the fans overwhelmed us at the shop. It was absolutely wonderful. We took care of our customers and in a short time we had a booming business.

"A good business is not without its sacrifices, though, because when my kids played for Butte Central I could only watch the first three quarters of the game. I had to leave and get up to the shop before the crowd came and we got real busy.

"The other great time for us was during the Fourth of July. The parade use to be in Uptown and just after the marching was over we were swamped with customers. I recall spending 18 to 20 hours of a Fourth of July at the shop making sandwiches, and serving people. It was a lot of work, but we were successful."

Orizotti brought a whole new dimension to the pork chop sandwich through new marketing ideas and the mass production of the pork loins in the manufacturing area he established in the back of his shop on Mercury Street.

A few years after taking over the business, he purchased property to build a second sandwich shop on Harrison Avenue. The new facility was opened and serving pork chops for the first time on June 18, 1975. The first day was the biggest sales day in over two years for the business.

The move to Harrison Avenue was just the first in a series of moves Orizotti made to expand his business. He established pork chop sandwich locations in Billings and Bozeman. The pork chop sandwich had grown far beyond just the small shop on Mercury Street.

John Orizotti spent 18 years serving pork chop sandwiches before retiring on April 1, 1987. John turned the reigns of the business over to his sons, Ed and Tom. The two sons expanded the business even more by setting up a contract with Sysco to distribute their pork chop sandwiches on a state-wide basis. Each month the plant on Mercury Street prepares pork chops that are shipped to various parts of Montana. A contract has also been set up with the local school district so school kids can enjoy pork chop sandwiches.

Orizotti reflected, "The pork chop sandwich business has been great for my family. I really believe the Lord gave it to me and any time the good Lord gives you something in life you better take care of it."

A by-product of the automobile is the gas station. The motor buggies needed fuel to keep going and the gas station was the meal ticket for filling up a starving engine. The early-day gas station became a one-stop shopping place for gas, oil, tires and service. But, with so many gas stations around, it was a tough way to make a living.

Such was the situation facing Guy Ossello when he took over a gas station on Highway 91 on the northern edge of Meaderville. Ossello was handed a gas station from the previous owner who had gone bankrupt with the outbreak of the Great Depression.

Guy's formal education only went through the eighth grade because his mother told him that high school was a waste of his time. So instead of heading to the classroom, Guy become a miner in the nearby Leonard Mine where he served on the first-aid team. The Great Depression forced The Anaconda Company to implement layoffs; single miners like Guy Ossello were the first to be let go.

Ossello enjoyed mining, but he was also interested in business. Despite the advise of his mother about further education, Guy started taking business correspondence classes. The more he read the more interested Ossello become at running his own business. When the Meaderville gas station become available in 1930, Ossello, now an unemployed miner, jumped at the chance to operate his own business.

Life at the gas station meant long hours, seven days a week.

Stella, Guy's wife remembered, "After we got married, in 1935, the only time I really saw Guy was when I went down to the station. He had to work many times from six in the morning until midnight just to keep the place going. It was long, tough work changing tires, fixing cars and other things."

Guy Ossello Jr. added his memories, "A lot of people could not pay for the gas. My dad used to do a barter system with many people. He pumped them gasoline and, in turn, he was given a pig, chicken or whatever the customer had that was of value. A lot of folks simply did not have money during the Depression and bartering with my father was the only way they could fill the tank. He was very good dealing with people. He was honest and went out of his way to help people. Folks never forgot his kindness during tough times."

The nature of the service station and his business life started to change when Ossello purchased of all things, a refrigerator.

Guy Ossello Jr. recalled, "My dad always had a lot of salesmen trading with him at the station. One of his better clients was Marshall Wells, a Billings salesmen who sold products for Philco. Shortly after World War II ended, Wells walked into the station one day and sold my dad a refrigerator. Before my dad could get the refrigerator out of the box and take it home, someone walked into the station. They wanted to buy the refrigerator. My dad sold it and made a profit on it. Right then, my dad realized he could pump hundreds of gallons of gas and not make the same profit as he just achieved selling the refrigerator."

It might have been a degree of luck or fate, but the first refrigerator sale launched Guy Ossello into a whole new business opportunity. He started to purchase more refrigerators, along with other appliances like washers, dryers and stoves that he sold right out of the gas station. Gus Ossello's gas station became Guy Ossello's gas station/appliance store.

Times were changing in Meaderville and Ossello had to change directions too. When The Anaconda Company started buying up property in Meaderville for its Berkeley Pit expansion, Guy Ossello had to figure out what to do. He sold his station to The Company in 1960 and purchased a warehouse from Jim Fleming of Ellis Paint on South Arizona Street. Ossello moved his appliances into the new building. Through the encouragement of his son, Guy Jr., the senior Ossello took on electronics; in 1963, furniture and carpet departments were added.

His years of serving people in a gas station plus his extensive study of business had Ossello convinced if you treat people right, they became customers for life. That was the way he succeeded during the tough times of the Great Depression at his Meaderville gas station, and was the way he turned Ossello's store into one of Montana's largest appliance and furniture stores.

Guy recalled how much he appreciated the breaks that were given to him by many thoughtful people as a youngster growing up in a poor Italian family struggling through the Depression. Ossello transferred that type of generosity into his own business. Guy went out of his way to establish credit for Butte families to purchase things. The credit was available even during the tough times of strikes and other problems in Butte.

"You can never image just how many people he carried financially just so they could have a washer, dryer or refrigerator," said Guy Ossello Jr. "He always did business with a handshake and never used a contract. My dad always felt a person was as good as their word. They may not be able to pay much on a bill, but they felt an obligation to him because he had treated them right. People never forgot that and through that he developed a very loyal customer base."

Gus was also very generous outside his store. In 1980, he was approached by a group of men who wanted to build a statue on top of the East Ridge. They wanted to purchase the land that he and his son, Guy Jr., owned at Saddle Rock. After they heard about the project, Guy Ossello and his son turned over the land to the group called "Our Lady of the Rockies" for no cost, a early step in the development of the statue project.

Some five years after the Ossellos provided their land, the statue was completed on December 20, 1985. A one-hour video tape about the project was produced and sponsored by Ossello's Furniture Store.

A few months after Our Lady of the Rockies was finished, Guy Ossello died on February 26, 1986. Guy Ossello's generosity to people is remembered every night when a person looks up at the lights shining on Our Lady of the Rockies.

If entertainment, fun and eating could all be combined into one delicious dish then only one place in Butte would do, Gamer's Cafe. The taste of the unusual began the moment a person walked through the doors.

"Hello there darling! How are you!" or "I've been saving this place just for you. Its got your name written all over it." The comments came from Gamer's owner, Carl Rowan.

Rowan was a "blueplate special" himself, entertaining patrons throughout their visits to the restaurant he purchased with local businessman George Schotte in 1944. Carl bought out Schotte's share of the business in 1954.

For five decades Carl Rowan entertained and served meals at his cafe, gaining local, national and international acclaim. The food at Gamer's was not particularly different than any other eating establishment, but the entertainment, the hugs, the kisses, the pats on the back, the handshakes, the greetings and oh yes, the cash register, were all pure and simple Carl Rowan at his best.

Rowan was like a loose chain-saw stuck in a wood pile. He went buzzing from place to place greeting everyone with a hug or kiss, doing a little dance for some or reciting a menu in less than a minute for others. He had it all down pat and the patrons loved it.

"I think people without doubt are friendly and congenial if you make the first effort to make them feel so," Rowan said.

Carl established an unusual, but friendly "open shop." If someone needed coffee, another soda, or some extra food, Carl encouraged and expected them to help themselves. Gamer's was his home, but the customers' home too. Patrons felt free to go behind the counter, pick up the coffee pot and refill not only their own cup, but those of all the other patrons. A person could be sitting at the counter or in one of the small old-fashion wrap-around booths listening to a Carl story while a local bank president or perhaps an electrician from the Montana Power Company went around warming up your coffee cup.

When it came time to leave, the cash register faced toward the public. Carl had more important things to do than to ring up your bill. Patrons were expected to pay their own bill right at the till, putting in dollars and taking out their correct amount of change. It was the open cash register started in the 1950s that made Carl Rowan a famous man. National broadcasting television networks came to Butte to see the man's operation and his cash register.

"At the end of the day I know the money is there," explained Rowan. "I know everyone will be honest with me. If I didn't think people were honest, then I'd quit doing it."

His method of an open cash register worked wonders for better than 30 years. Carl talked to a women once who claimed her two sons in college both learned how to make change at Gamer's Cafe when they were kids. This type of story made Carl Rowan feel proud. Rowan had a good, unique system and he knew it.

In 1993, Rowan sold his business to Paul and Pam Cote. It marked the end of 50 years of entertaining and feeding people in Uptown Butte.

"Carl was really an amazing guy," said Paul Cote. "Years after he left this place, tourists still come in every summer looking for him. I think he really went out of his way to know people and they appreciated that very much. You might visit here once and meet Carl and come back five years later to discover he still remembered you. He might not know your name, but he might recall what you did or where you were from and in that way people always felt they had a friend in Carl Rowan."

For those lucky enough to visit Gamer's Cafe and see Carl Rowan in action he was unforgettable.

Shoestring Annie was a large women who carried quite a wallop in both of her huge forearms. She weighed over 200 pounds and was not only strong, but had a vicious tongue.

Shoestring Annie came to Butte with her husband from Colorado in 1910. Her tongue-lashing and other activities one day landed her husband at the State Hospital in Warm Springs.

Shoestring Annie wore a plain dress and always carried a cigar box filled with shoe strings. She appeared weekly at the local pay office of The Anaconda Company as workers filed in to receive their pay checks. Shoestring Annie held out her cigar box and shouted, "Buy a pair of shoe laces, you God damn cheap skate!" If a miner refused, the large women called him every name in the book and walloped the guy with a crutch she carried with her. Miners usually relented and gave her some cash for some shoe strings.

Shoestring Annie made no bones about what she wanted and was especially harsh with police officers. She spent plenty of time in jail for her outlandish antics.

Shoestring Annie lived in a cabin at the edge of Cabbage Patch. During her final days, police officials had to take the poor lady to the hospital. All her medical expenses were paid for by local officials; selling shoe strings had never paid well.

The Great Depression was certainly not the best of times, especially for someone trying to start a new business. Yet, that is exactly what George Steele attempted to do in 1934.

Steele was born and raised in North Dakota. He came to Butte looking for work during the Depression. George found a job as a salesmen for the Intermountain Maytag Company out of Salt Lake City. The Utah firm had a tough time selling products in Montana during the Depression years so it decided to close its shop in Butte.

George Steele asked Intermountain if he could take over as the distributor for Maytag products in Butte. Naturally, to get started Steele needed money. He formed a partnership with Doctor Jack Kirby to get the business off the ground. Steele realized trying to make a living simply selling Maytag products would not work, as Intermountain of Salt Lake City had found out. So in addition to selling appliances at their store on West Broadway Street, the partners developed a company to also sell propane, an industrial gas.

After working together for eight years, George Steele bought out his partner in 1942. The business became known as George Steele's Warehouse in 1942 and since then has developed into one of Butte's largest family-owned stores.

"It was very difficult getting the business going," recalled Oliver Steele, George's son. "People had very little money during the Depression to buy appliances and propane was a tough sell because it was something new to Montana. The core business for propane in the early days were the ranches around the state. My dad went from ranch to ranch selling the industrial gas. He loved to sell and he worked very hard at building up a solid business. He always maintained that success is something you work at and no one worked harder than him."

Steele continued to sell industrial gas until 1957 when he sold the distributorship to Petrolane Steelgas Services out of Long Beach, California. He retained the appliance segment of the business and decided to add furniture, bedding and other products.

In time, George Steele developed a solid business in furniture and appliances. Times became so good that he needed additional warehouse space. In 1968, he decided to purchase the Ryan Grocery Store building on South Wyoming Street. He used that facility as a storage area until

1972 when he remodeled the building to become the new home of George Steele's Warehouse.

"I think one reason my dad was so successful is that he took care of people," said Oliver Steele. "He always felt every person was honest especially if you treated them right. He was always very willing to give back to the community by supporting various fund raising efforts. My father maintained if you are good to people they will remember and be good back to you. He had a heart of gold when it came to helping folks."

George's gamble to start a business in the Depression had paid off. The company continued to grow after he retired under the leadership of his two sons, Oliver and Clifton. In 1989, Oliver's son, Dan, took over the business.

The ownership change has done little to alter George Steele's philosophy of treating the customer right and giving back to the community. George Steele's Warehouse became one of the pillars of strength in the Butte business community.

Character builds champions and for Butte no coach displayed more character than Jim Street. He built a dynasty in wrestling at Butte High School that has not been matched by any coach in any Montana high school sport. His Bulldog wrestling teams won a state-record 13 straight state championship between 1980 to 1992. During an 18-year period, Butte High came out of the state finals with the first place trophy 15 times.

Street built his program the same way Butte built itself into the copper capital of the world with lots of hard work.

His habit of learning how to win began as a student at Butte High.

"There were three people at Butte High who really shaped my coaching philosophy and what it takes to be champion," said Jim Street. "They are Swede Dahlberg, Bill Hawke and Sam Jankovich.

"Swede was the type of individual who never asked you to do something he could not do himself. In his PE classes, despite the fact he was in his later years of life, he showed you how he wanted a push-up done and then he expected you to do the same. Swede's lesson was if you want something done make sure you can do it yourself.

"Bill Hawke was simply a classy individual. He always carried himself in such a way that you respected him. In good times and bad, Bill always acted with class and dignity. Its an example that I have always tried to follow.

"Sam Jankovich taught me that to achieve something you have to work harder than the next guy. Hard work and determination can go along way and Sam had a lot of both of those things."

The lessons at Butte High paid off for Street as an athlete for the Bulldogs from 1962 to 1965. Jim was a starting running back and cornerback on the 1964 Bulldogs' undefeated state championship football team coached by Sam Jankovich. In wrestling, he placed second at the state finals his junior year. Jim also participated for Swede Dahlberg and Bill Hawke on the track team.

His first love was football, but wrestling also held his interest and, when Robert Lee of Eastern Montana College told Street he could compete in both sports, Jim jumped at the opportunity.

After playing football and wrestling for the Yellowjackets, Street transferred to Montana State University, which he felt had a better wrestling program. He wrestled for two years in Bozeman until back and shoulder injuries sidelined him for good as a competitive wrestler.

His days of competing were over, but his driving spirit to remain in athletics was still very much in his blood. Once he received an education degree from Western Montana College, Jim was hired as a teacher and coach at Butte High School.

He served as an assistant football and wrestling coach at Butte High for a number of years. His own success on the gridiron as a prep athlete carried over to his coaching ability on the sidelines. Street was the defensive coordinator for the 1977 Butte High football team which allowed only 20 points all season as they went undefeated winning the state championship. The team set a Montana High School Association state record recording eight shutouts.

In 1976, Jim was named head wrestling coach at Butte High. He told the Butte School Board that if he could not win the state championship within four years he'd resign and give the job back to the board. It was a bold statement to make because Butte High's wrestling program had never been very competitive.

"When I was wrestling for Bulldogs in the 1960s, the sport only seemed to be used by Butte High athletes to get into shape for football," recalled Street. "In three years, we had three different coaches Sam Jankovich, Howie Johnson and Bert West. There was no real pride in the wrestling program because as a team the Bulldogs had never been very successful. I intended to change that, but I knew it would not be easy.

"The first thing that had to change was attitude. I had to get the kids to believe in themselves and take pride in the sport. There was a wrestling camp set up here in town and I managed to get Tom Chesbro the head coach at Oklahoma State University to come in to help me run the camp. I started taking money out of my own pocket to truck kids around the country to wrestling camps and tournaments. The kids needed to be exposed to the sport year-round. The young men also needed to start working harder. I began opening up the school's weight room at six o'clock in the morning for the kids. If you work harder than the next guy you can be successful and that's what we started to do."

Even with all the hard work and wrestling camps it took time for Street to build the program at Butte High. The fruits of his labor started to show in 1979 when Street produced his first state champion, heavyweight Tom Konen.

In 1980, the individual success was following by team success when Butte High won their first state wrestling title in school history. The momentum of the program was evident when his club won the state title for a second straight year in 1981. The string was started and now the Bulldogs would roll to 13 straight wrestling crowns.

Street remembered. "When we won it the first time, many people were amazed that Butte High could take the state wrestling title. I had all sorts of people come up and congratulate me for winning state. As we continued to win it year after year fewer and fewer people came up to shake my hand. We were now the team to beat and everyone started gunning for us. It forced us to work harder just to stay on top."

Shooting to knock the Bulldogs off of the top spot on the awards stand had become the main mission of every wrestling program in the state. The Havre Blue Ponies came close at the 1983 state finals held at the Butte Civic Center, losing to the Bulldogs by only a half point. The Kalispell Braves also were within striking distance at the 1986 championships, losing by 2 1/2 points.

Street and his Bulldogs were there to meet every challenge. They became the most dominant high school athletic program in Montana. The pride developed in the Bulldogs and their wrestling streak became the talk of the town every year during state tournament time, even for folks that were not wrestling fans.

A cornerstone of the success for the Bulldogs was their effort in duel matches. Butte High won 112 straight duel events over the course of a number of years, a state record that may not be broken. Street's record overall in duel meets was 229-40.

"There were a lot of reasons why we stayed on top for so long," said Street. "First of all, we had great kids who were willing to pay the price to be a champion. We had outstanding assistant coaches who worked hard to make sure we were ready for every match. My assistants included Gene Fogarty, Fred Jozovich, Steve Stosich, Bob Liva, John Connolle, Ken Carver and Dan Liva. We also got help from the Butte AAU free style wrestling program. When we first started the program, we had maybe three or four kids each year in our program who competed in free-style. Today, most of our wrestlers have free-style experience."

Butte High was finally beaten at the state finals in 1993, losing to Billings Skyview. The Bulldogs were second that year and dropped down to fifth place the next year. It appeared the Bulldogs' dynasty was over and that they were once again just another team competing at the state tournament.

The true mark of a champion is how they handle defeat. Instead of going further down the ladder, in 1995, Jim and his wrestlers came roaring back to win another state championship. It was Street's 14th state wrestling championship. Following the tournament, Street was named the Class AA Wrestling Coach of the Year for the 14th time in his career.

After finishing second in 1996, Street's team was back on top again in 1997. They placed second in 1998. During the 18-year run, Street's teams won the state title 15 times and only once, in 1994, did his team not bring home a state trophy. He produced 41 individual state champions during his coaching career at Butte High School.

It is a remarkable accomplishment by a man who turned a doormat program into the state's best, marking him as one of the best coaches to every grace the sidelines in Montana high school sports.

The final period ended for Jim Street on May 1, 1998. He turned in his resignation as the head coach of the Butte High Bulldogs wrestling program. His records will likely not to be matched by any coach in any sport ever again in Montana.

If appearance means anything, then the first look at Uncle Dick Sutton revealed a homeless bum with no where to go. Uncle Dick Sutton always wore a raggy, old suit with no tie, baggy pants and without fail had an unlit cigar hanging from his mouth.

Appearance is one thing, but underneath the surface Uncle Dick Sutton was a major player in the Butte entertainment business. The Louisville, Kentucky, native first came to Butte in 1892 as part of the Uncle Tom's Cabin troupe. After the show was finished, Sutton decided to stay. In a short time, he acquired the rights to lease the Grand Opera House from John McGuire, the dean of theater in the community.

Sutton operated the Grand Opera House and then built the Family, the Lulu and Sutton theaters. The Sutton was later named the Broadway in 1915 when Sutton sold it to the Ansonia Amusement Company.

Sutton became a giant in the entertainment world. He helped organize the Northwest Theatrical Association which booked New York shows throughout the region. During the late 1890s and early 1900s, Sutton had almost every major stage talent and show of that time perform at one of his many Butte theaters. The largest of his empire, the Sutton, featured most of the major plays. The top flight shows, musical concerts and vaudeville acts filled his theaters all the time.

In addition to running his own string of theaters, Uncle Dick had his own troupe with at least two shows on the road all the time.

Sutton was revered as "Uncle Dick" to most in the entertainment business because of his generosity. Sutton was known for giving actors down on their luck money to pay for meals until they got back on their feet.

Sutton's Broadway Theater showed the first motion pictures in Butte, a film on the 1897 heavyweight championship fight between Bob Fitzsimmons and James Corbitt which Fitzsimmons won with a 14th round knockout. The event was a success, but Sutton never thought the motion picture would become such a big deal. He called it a fad, a "crackpot experiment" that would not last.

Unfortunately for Sutton, he was wrong. Theater performances and companies became a second line form of entertainment, a development that made Uncle Dick Sutton call it quits. He sold his theaters and died in California on October 2, 1924. His remains were brought back to Butte where the final curtain call, his burial, took place at a local cemetery.

Meaderville was noted for its restaurants and night clubs. The most famous place in the small neighborhood was the Rocky Mountain Cafe operated by Teddy Traparish.

Ted Traparish was like many immigrants who came to this country looking for an opportunity. Traparish was a bit different because he knew the value of money and was astute enough to figure out how to put more coins in his pocket.

His example of taking care of his money came after getting off the boat and arriving in this country. Ted was asked if he had anything of value with him. Traparish told the attendant all he had of value was his vest. The immigration authorities took his vest and ripped it open discovering that Ted had sewn coins inside the vest for safe keeping. He had a different way of protecting his money a habit he carried with him the rest of his life.

After arriving in Butte, Traparish got a job stacking boxes at the Butte Brewery for a dollar a day. It took awhile, but Traparish saved and soon had enough money to buy a bar in the business district.

Traparish was successful at the bar and tried to expand his operations by purchasing the Rocky Mountain Cafe in Meaderville with two partners, Louie Bugni and Pete Antonioli. Bugni dropped out of the partnership after the night club was destroyed by fire. Traparish and Antonioli moved their business down the street and took over the Golden Fan Club. They renamed the place the Rocky Mountain Cafe. Pete Antonioli also moved on to other things so Ted Traparish had the night club to himself.

The Rocky Mountain soon became the primary night spot in Meaderville and Ted Traparish played the part of Butte's best known nighttime host.

"Ted Traparish really was a great host," said Bill Antonioli. "He knew everyone in the place and went around making sure everything was okay. The people knew when they came to the Rocky Mountain Cafe that they'd get a great meal and have a friendly chat with Teddy."

Ed Bartoletti said, "A big reason for Teddy's success was his commitment to The Anaconda Company. Ted had over $1 million in stock invested in Anaconda at one time. When it came time for entertaining guests, Company officials always went to the Rocky Mountain Cafe. Ted took care of The Company's guests and in turn Anaconda took good care of him."

Traparish made lots of money running his restaurant and made sure he showed off his wealth to local residents. Every year, Ted purchased a new Cadiallac. He also paid his restaurant workers well and provided money to local kids who were looking for a few coins to go to the movie house.

"Ted Traparish was a very respected man in Butte," said Antonioli. "He was very generous with the money he made at the restaurant. Teddy provided meals to many people during the hard times of the Great Depression. He was constantly giving kids money who never had a nickel to their name."

Emily Sherman recalled, "Teddy was really a great guy. When we went to the business district, we had to wait an hour to catch a street car back to Meaderville. If Teddy spotted you, he'd pick you up and take you to Meaderville. I don't think he ever knew my name, but he remembered my face and knew I was from Meaderville. That's all that mattered to Teddy. He was always trying to help kids in our neighborhood."

Stella Ossello said, "Teddy helped more than just kids. There was this one fellow we all called Danny 'the bum.' He lived at the Leonard Mine and spent his day bumming things from people around Meaderville. I know Teddy gave Danny meals and sometimes money to keep him going."

Bartoletti remembered, "Teddy was a real high roller. He told me one time that during the 1929 stock market crash he lost over $1 million. Ted said he had to borrow $300,000 to just pay off his debts, but he was quick to point out that he was able to pay the note off in a few short years."

Traparish never did marry. He lived at the Finlen Hotel with his brother, George, who was a cook at the Moxom Cafe in the business district.

The good days of a great meal along with a friendly chat with Butte's nighttime host, Ted Traparish, eventually came to an end. The Berkeley Pit expanded into Meaderville putting an end to the neighborhood and Teddy Traparish's Rocky Mountain Cafe. It was the end for a generous man, a great restaurant, a way of life, Meaderville's wide-open night time gambling restaurants and bars.

Since the early days, Butte folks loved a parade and no one enjoyed all the fun more than Tony "the Trader" Canonica. Tony called himself, "A Living Legend" and "A World Ambassador of Goodwill." He entered any parade available making appearances in high school and college homecoming parades, the St. Patrick's Day festivities, Dillon's Labor Day parade, Helena's Last Chance Stampede and many other events. Butte's Fourth of July parade was where Tony the Trader made his real mark. He appeared in the annual event 57 straight years from 1935 through 1992. Tony was honored for his longevity by being selected as the 1982 Fourth of July parade grand marshall.

Canonica dressed in various costumes for the march down the street many times with young kids from the East Side tagging along in costumes which Tony provided. He appeared as everything from Buffalo Bill to Uncle Sam. Tony never lost his enthusiasm for a parade or for self- promotion. He always told people how much he loved Butte and how much he loved being the center of attention in a parade. Anyone who attended even one Fourth of July parade in Butte remembered Tony the Trader.

Tony was born in Butte on March 28, 1915. His father, Antone, was a well-known tinner owning a shop on South Arizona Street. In addition to his duties as a tinner; Tony said his father also operated a still and did some bootlegging on the side.

Tony became a self-made business person at a young age. He went around his neighborhood collecting junk in his little red wagon. Once the junk was in his wagon, it took some bartering and money for a person to get it out of his possession. He also made money peddling newspapers in the red light district and working at various duties in numerous Uptown theaters. But, it was buying and selling junk that Tony loved and he started his own business with a loan from his father. Tony, even as an old man remembered the vote of confidence from his dad.

Tony's first Trading Post was at 201 South Arizona. The location changed a number of times through the years, but one thing never changed: Tony's ability as a smart businessman. He built up his collection of junk by purchasing everything inside vacated hotels like the State, Jeffrey and Arizona. Tony bought everything from wall to wall. This included everything from beds, mats, light fixtures, sinks, toilets and pipes. If it had value, it was now Tony the Trader's. Through these massive buyouts, Tony had more junk than anyone could imagine. Many things which were "junk" became antiques, and the prices jumped accordingly.

Tony said everything had a price tag on it and sooner or later someone would buy it. Many people came into his store to look. Sometimes when a person asked how much he'd sell a particular item for Tony would say, "It's not for sale today." It was one way Tony could determine just how much a person was willing to pay for an item.

Through the years Tony made a handsome sum of money from his crafty business dealings. This led to purchasing various apartments and buildings in the Uptown area. It also led to numerous donations to various charities.

Tony also helped in some civic projects. One was keeping Montana Tech a four- year institution. In 1987, the Montana Legislature was looking at reducing the Butte college to a two-year school. Students organized a bus trip to Helena to rally lawmakers to kill the measure. Tony went along for the bus ride to Helena, his first trip ever to the State Capitol. Once inside the dome, Tony was all business. He asked security people where the Governor's office was located. The security personnel pointed down the hall, but also added that Governor Ted Schwinden was probably very busy and could not see him. Tony never paid any attention to the security people. Down the hall he went to the Governor's office. Once inside he told the secretary, "I'm Tony the Trader, Butte's Ambassador of Goodwill and I'm here to talk to the Governor about this here measure to close Montana Tech". The secretary immediately told the Governor who dropped everything to come out and greet Tony the Trader.

Tony spent a few minutes with the Governor and, of course seizing the moment, made sure he got his picture taken with the highest state official in Montana. He then left the Governor's office, went outside and participated in the student rally, which soon turned into a parade led by, you guessed it, Tony the Trader.

Tony died on April 20, 1993 in his modest, sparsely furnished home on the East Side. An auction of his goods some months after his death lasted three days and had to be moved to the Civic Center because Tony had so much junk.

Butte has been described by many as a "macho" town. A town where man is king. But, make no mistake about it, the women of the community played a critical role in the development of the richest hill on earth. The strength and accomplishments made by the women are evident in one of the most powerful unions ever created, the Women's Protective Union.

The roots for the Butte women's union were planted on June 5, 1890. The initial group had 34 members and was led by president, Delia Moore. It was not the first women's union developed in the country, that distinction belongs to the International Workingmen's Association which formed a separate female chapter in San Francisco on May 25, 1886.

Even though the Butte's Women's Protective Union was not the first, it quickly became the most powerful in the nation.

The idea behind a women's union was to provide a equal voice for female employees with their male counterparts in the industrial conditions and wages at the work place. When the union was created in 1890, women were still 30 years away from winning the right to vote. In addition, women were denied an opportunity to make a living in many fields. They did not have a strong voice in government, business, education and many other facets of every day life. The Women's Protective Union provided a voice through numbers.

It is not surprising that an organization like the Women's Protective Union developed in a union strong-hold mining camp like Butte. The rate of mine accidents and deaths in Butte were the highest in the world. Many women became widows overnight when their husbands were killed in the mines. The women became the main bread-earner in the family with a number of kids to feed.

The mine widows, in most cases, were not well-educated or well-trained in a particular craft and thus became a prime target for exploitation by cunning business people. These ladies were forced to take minimal paying jobs washing clothes, running elevators, waiting tables, cleaning hotel rooms, making dresses, cooking at boarding houses, serving as nursing maids, ushering at theaters, making candy, serving as bucket girls at boarding houses, clerking in local stores and, in a last desperate act, being prostitutes in the red light district to make a living. The women needed protection and the formation of the union in 1890 was the answer.

The Women's Protective Union was unique because it did not require a member to perform a certain occupation to be included in the group. A second stipulation for membership was that a woman had to work outside of her home.

The first union members saw their group as an agent for social change and social justice. A couple of years after forming, the WPU had already created a library, developed a housing assistance program for their members, tried to obtain medical and child care for members and provide legal-aid assistance. A job training program was established in 1895 to help women acquire the necessary skills to be effective in the work place.

The Women's Protective Union took steps in 1896 to campaign for civil and political equal rights for its members. A few years later in 1898, they were demanding a national health insurance plan, unemployment insurance and a retirement plan which was 40 years prior to the development of such programs by President Franklin Roosevelt.

The prospects of changing national policy by the Women's Protective Union did not produce as much success as its ability to solve problems right in its own backyard of Butte.

In 1903, the WPU demanded and received a reduced work schedule, specifically a 10-hour work day, one of the first such agreements ever reached in the country. The 10-hour work day established in Butte occurred before such arrangements were achieved in other western cities like Denver, San Francisco and Seattle.

A major victory for the organization occurred in 1904 when the Women's Protective Union forced all non-union hiring halls to cease their operations in Butte. This forced women workers to come through its union to acquire a job. This arrangement stayed secure into the 1950s.

In the early years, the union affiliated itself with a number of organizations. At one time, they were associated with the Industrial Workers of the World, better known as the Wobblies, the American Labor Union and Butte's Miners' Union. The Women's Protective Union found its niche in 1907 when it joined up with the Hotel Employees and Restaurant Employees International Local # 457. Even with the new association, the group maintained the name of the Women's Protective Union and was still a female-only organization.

The Women's Protective Union won a major victory in 1920 earning its members a wage of at least seventeen dollars a week. This wage was three dollars higher than the national average at the time.

The strength of the union could be reflected in higher wages and also in the number of women joining their group. The original 34 members in 1890 had grown to 229 by 1918. A decade later in 1929, that number had doubled to 508. The Women's Protective Union peaked at 1,149 members in 1955.

The political clout of the union was used as a tool by other groups. In 1926, the Butte Miners' Union leaders asked members of the Women's Protective Union to urge non-union members to join their ranks.

The power of the union could still be felt 80 years after it was first formed. In 1970, a local restaurant tried to force female employees to wear short-skirt bunny outfits. The Women's Protective Union felt the uniforms were demeaning to women and successfully argued against such outfits.

The battle over short skirts was one of the last achievements realized by the Women's Protective Union. Legal proceedings forced the union to accept male waiters and cooks into its association in August 1973. The name of the group was changed from the Women's Protective Union to Culinary and Miscellaneous Employees Union Local # 457.

The long history of the Women's Protective Union was over. Yet, its achievements for the rights of working women were every bit as important as the concessions achieved by the miners in their battles with The Anaconda Company.

Being a city which attracted so many immigrants coupled with the independence treasured by Westerners, Butte has produced many interesting people. Only a few have been mentioned here, but this captures some of the variety of people, both living and now gone, who have made the city a special place.

Another unique thing about Butte is nicknames, a phenomenon which probably came from the miners, particularly immigrants, who picked up a "handle" which was sometimes easier to say than their real Old Country names. The practice grew so that sometimes a Butte person's real name was not known until the newspaper printed their obituary. Thanks to years of research by local native, Alex Koprivica, the following provides some of Butte's more colorful nicknames.

A - Art Kearney, Awful Kanofle,

B - Babe Brady, Bag Ears Lohtinen, Bagga Klune, Baggers Sullivan, Baldy Quilici, Banger Harris, Banjo Kangas, Batty Richards, Beanie Dallas, Beano McCormick, Beans Collins, Bear Meat Robinson, Beatle Bartoletti, Bed Bug Boyle, Beefy Kearney, Beer Cronin, Bengo Sullivan, Biddy Cavanaugh, Big Lip Burns, Bimbo Chintoni, Bingo Crnich, Binty O'Brien, Bio Mattix, Black Jim Lynch, Birdie Aho, Blackie Keane, Blackie Webster, Blonde Patrick, Bloody Bill Bato, Bluebird Lubick, Bo Grmoljez, Boise Mudro, Bolo Sullivan, Bone Nouack, Bones Pettibone, Bones Thatcher, Booba Powers, Boogs Choinard, Boots Strah, Boozer Boyle, Breezy Lane, Brick Dennehy, Broncho Pete, Bruno Hagl, Buba Aguette, Bubba Maloney, Bucky Carden, Bud Fleming, Buffalo Head Gardner, Bulgy Eyes, Bull Flynn, Bull Serdan, Bullets Kasun, Bum Webster, Bumbo Madden, Butch Starin, Butch Snow, Butter Driscoll, Butter O'Leary, Buzz Ferriter, Buzzy Winston

C - Callahan the Bum, Canary Legs Carrots Damond, Car Slugs Merrifield, Chick Nylund, Chicken Liz, Chile Kearney, Chink Seymour, Chis Harrington, Chow Hanley, Chow McGarry, Chucksie Holland, Chucksie Kasun, Chunky Thatcher, Coke Dennehy, Coke Jones, Cokie Joe Keefe, Cold Cash Warren, Con the Horse, Cookie O'Gara, Country Ueland, Cosy Koprivica, Cousie Rowe, Creamery Mikovich, Crete Boyle, Crow Kane, Crying George Rooney, Cub Potter, Curly Darraugh, Curly Harrington, Curly Kramer, Cutsy Nichols

D - Dago Shea, Damie Kelly, Dandy Jim, Darko Young, Dead Dog Harrington, Dealo Shea, Dee Horn Daniels, Deke DeCorey, Denny the Buck Harrington, Diego Red, DieMite Duff Duffy, Digger Shea, Dike Helehan, Divie Owens, Dixie LaHood, Doc Harrington, Dodger Adams, Dog Eye Gleason, Doggy Fagan, Dooley Mehrens, Dome Driscoll, Droopy Drawers, Dry Bones Leary, Dubby Kiely, Dubler Dan, Ducky Kelly, Dud Malkovich, Duke Schroeder, Dumbo Jones, Dummy Janhunen, Dusty Walsh, Dutch McCrea, Dutch Michalsky,

E - Ears Holland, Eat'em Up Jake, Ego Gustafson, Evel Knievel

F - Fat Hugo, Fat Jack Jones, Fatty the Gambler Gardner, Finny Shea, Flat Murphy, Frenchie St. Pierre, Frog Cheff, Frostie Winters,

G - Gaga Ranovich, Ganty O'Leary, Gas Bags Kassalainen, Geek McMahon, Gelo Jackelini, Gitch Combo, Gooby Vaughn, Gooch Robinson, Googs Boyle, Goona-Goona Riley, Greasy Tomich, Greek Orlich, Granny Grannolm, Gubba Shea

H - Haiki Foley, Hamer Duran, Hammerhead Hogan, Happy Kraft, Harp Cote, Harp Sheehan, Harry the Bandit Harrington, Harvey Downey, Heinie Johnson, Hick Olsen, Hindi Groo, Hobo McCarthy, Holligan Moran, Honest John Corcoran, Honie Kiely, Hook Leahy, Hoot Gibson, Horse Shea, Huck Driscoll, Hula Kalafatich, Hula Sullivan, Humpy Thomas, Hunk Asanovich, Hymie Dennehy

I - Indigo Shaffer

J - Jakie Legs Luumi, Jazz Adler, Jebbie Rask, Jeff Sullivan, Jew Mose, Jiggs Dahlberg, Jiggs Kriskovich, Jinx Janhunen, Johnny Moxom Papich, Juice Evankovich, Jumbo Panion, Jumping Johnny, Juniper Koprivica, Juno Bruno

K- Kike Maloney, King Maloney, Koochy Kochevar, Kurtsy Jozovich

L - Lanky Spainy, Leggs Orlich, Liver Eating Johnson, Liz Bato, Long John Finnegan, Looper Mazzola, Lug Mulcahy, Lunk Lowney,

M- Maggie McGuire, Mags the Rag, Manny Lisac, Marbs Maloney, Mai Popovich, Mickey the Bird Sullivan, Mickey the Greek, Midnight Foley, Mink Fredrickson, Mitzi Koppo, Moldy Drawers, Moon Rogers, Moose Holland, Moose Pavlovich, Moose Petritz, Mope Dolan, Mope

Grant, Motor Mouth Gardner, Mouse Johnson, Moxy Tickson, Mucker Riley, Mudd Mudro, Mudro Kelly, Mugs Walsh, Munk Semansky, Mutt Cunningham, Muzz Faroni,

N- Nasty McNabb, Nickel Annie, Nig McGrath, Nob Hale, Nosey Ford, Notso Salo, Nubba Rowe

O- Oakie O'Connor, Obie Ashford, Obie Kopp, Obs Onkalo, Oike Hice, Ole Kearney, One-Eyed Dwyer, Onzie Powers, Oogie Popovich, Ookie Cook, Overcoat Willie Porter

P- Packey Bradley, Packy Buckley, Paddy Sixtoes Sullivan, , Paddy the Bum, Paddy the Pig Heikkenen, Parko Panion, Pat the Nig, Peewad Dennehy, Peewee Nevin, Pinky Duggen, Peachy Petritz, Peanuts Sullivan, Peeps Fortune, Peewee Nevin, Pegger Lee, Peg-leg Paddy Leggatt, Pepper Calcaterra, Peppy Stokina, Pesty Spear, Pickles McMeekin, Pin Pool George, Plug Dwyer, Pinky Duggen, Pitts Nevin, Pooch Lamuth, Poodles Fearon, Poo Doo Farren, Poop Ozanne, Popcorn Weller, Porky Powers, Porky Ruoho, Potts Prothero, Powder Puff Duggan, Pug Boyle, Pugnosed Gattiney, Punky Morris

R- Rabbit Cheff, Race Horse Gallent, Rags Shea, Rah Rah O'Brien, Ram Benich, Re-Re Driscoll, Red Gilligan, Red Wagon Jim, Reno Peterson, Rest Holland, Rivers Powers, Rocko Robbins, Rosie Owens

S- Sailor Pomroy, Salmon Bones Rowling, Sap Elakovich, Sarge O'Neill, Satch Kearney, Satchel Mazzola, Scar Face Charley, Scrap Iron Kavran, Seese Lisac, Seven Up Pete, Shadow Thompson, Shag Miller, Shagger Lyons, Shanghi Lill, Shanty Crowley, Sheet Iron Wier, Sherry Sullivan, Shiek Marcille, Shimmy Crnich, Shine O'Neil, Shoes O'Connor, Shoestring Annie, Shook Glogoski, Shorty Foley, Shrimp Mihelich, Skeet McCarthy, Skimmie Sullivan, Skinny Reardon, Skuck Stafford, Slats Sullivan, Slim Sever, Sly Jim Sulivan, Slug Sullivan, Smiles Norris, Smoke Martinich, Snitch Marsenich, Snowball Adams, Socks Traynor, Sonny Hicks, Sparky Andrews, Specks McGarvey, Speed Granger, Spider McCollum, Spokane John, Spooks Lane, Spud Buckley, Squeaky Wallace, Squirt Nurmi, Stack Spearman, Starey Eyes, Stick Bennets, Stiff Shirted Jerry Mullins, Stinky Garrett, Straight Back Dan Shea, Stormy Weathers, Stretch Brown, String Bean, Stubby Lane, Sunny Nool, Swede Dahlberg, Swede Larsen

T- Tabie Daly, Tatic Harrington, Teak Kehoe, Ten Yard Murray, Termite Rossland, Terrible Terry Barry, Testy McCaughey, Three Fingers Brown, Three Fingers Jack, Tib O'Neill, Tiddy Mulcahy, Timer Kingston, Tiny Sefton, Tiny Sullivan, Tigue Jiles, Toady McGuiness, Tony the Trader Canonica, Took Storey, Toots Skedd, Two Bits Teppo, Tubba Schroeder, Tubie Johnson, Tucker McGree, Tudsy Cragwick, Tug

 Haltunen, Turk Oaas, Turkey Jones Nichols, Turtle Johnson, Tweed Morrison

W- Waffle Odgers, Wah Manovich, Weasel Serich, Weege O'Leary, Whistling Sam Alexander, Whitey Chor, Wing Russell, Winkie Erickson, Woody Wold,

Y- Yellow Bray, Yellowstone Kelly

Z-Ziggo Zigich, Zog Koprivica, Zogo Venuse, Zowie Grmolijez, Zupe Zumpano

REFERENCES USED IN CHAPTER FIVE

Copper Camp written by William Burkepublished in 1943
Anaconda written by Isacc Marcosson published in 1957
St. Patrick's Parish 100 years written by Chris Daly published in 1981
1987 interview Tony Canonica
1989 interview Chuck Davis
1989 interview Bill Hawke
1989 interview Sam Jankovich
Butte's Big Game written by Pat Kearneypublished in 1989
The Montana Standard newspaper
Elmer Miller interview *The Montana Standard*
Notes from Alex Koprivica
1994 interview Carl Rowan
1996 interview Ed Bartoletti
1996 interview Bob Koprivica
1997 interview Dallas Doyle
1997 interview Tony Jurenic
1998 interview Bill Antonioli
1998 interview LaVerne Combo
1998 interview Janet Cornish
1998 interview Paul Cote
1998 interview Jack Ferriter
1998 interview Carol Gilmore
1998 interview Mike Judd
1998 interview Bob Kearney
1998 interview Bob Leipheimer
1998 interview Judy Martz
1998 interview Bob McCarthy
1998 interview Dave Micheletti
1998 interview Mary Mollish
1998 interview John Orizotti
1998 interview Guy Ossello Jr.

1998 interview Stella Ossello
1998 interview Don Peoples
1998 interview Chuck Richards
1998 interview Ernie Richards
1998 interview Bruce Shepperd Jr.
1998 interview Emily Sherman
1998 interview Doug Smith
1998 interview Oliver Steele
1998 interview Jim Street

Looking for a chance in America at Meaderville Drug Store
photo courtesy Jerry Bugni, World Museum of Mining

LaVerne and Gitch Combo
photo courtesy Pat Kearney

Don Peoples
courtesy Cathy Peoples

Judy Martz
courtesy Judy Martz

Bruce Shepperd and son Bruce
at their candy store
courtesy *The Montana Standard*

Steve Faulkner - photo courtesy Pat Kearney

Harry "Swede" Dahlberg
photo courtesy
1956 Butte High annual

Manus Duggan
photo courtesy
World Museum of
Mining

Granite Mountain Memorial dedication ceremony June 8, 1996
photo courtesy Pat Kearney

George Steele
photo courtesy Dan Steele

Carl Rowan
photo courtesy
The Montana Standard

Monsignor Michael English
photo courtesy
<u>St. Patrick's Parish 100 years</u>

Fat Jack Jones
photo courtesy
World Museum of Mining

Janet Cornish
photo courtesy Pat Kearney

Charlie Judd
photo courtesy Esther Judd

Dallas Doyle
photo courtesy Pat Kearney

Bob Koprivica
photo courtesy
Bob Koprivica

Evel Knievel
photo courtesy Jack Ferriter

Luigi - photo courtesy World Museum of Mining

John Orizotti
photo courtesy John Orizotti

Guy Ossello Sr.
photo courtesy Guy Ossello Jr.

Jim Street
photo courtesy Barbara Street

Mary Mollish
photo courtesy Frank Mollish

Teddy Traparish
photo courtesy Jerry Bugni

Uncle Dick Sutton
photo courtesy World Museum of Mining

Lydia Micheletti
photo courtesy Dave Micheletti

Con Kelley
photo courtesy
The Anaconda Company

Tony "The Trader" Canonica - photo courtesy Wes Harr

Pork Chop John's - photo courtesy Pat Kearney

Gamer's Cafe - photo courtesy Pat Kearney

CHAPTER SIX

Games

The various ethnic groups that came to Butte brought with them many of their favorite activities from their home countries, including Gaelic football, Irish hurling, Cornish coursing, Italian bocce, Scotch curling, soccer, rugby, skating and "shinny," which later developed into ice hockey, a favorite of the French-Canadians and Scots.

The new immigrants also tried their luck participating in many American games. One of the miners' favorites was the rough-and-tumble sport of football. Miners could display their manhood above the ground rather than a couple of thousand feet below it. Football was played without any type of protection and was mainly confined to a contest of running the football at one another until one of the two teams scored.

The first squad in Butte was formed in 1893 by a group of men fresh from college. They set up a game with students from the Montana College at Deer Lodge, a school that was only open for a brief time. The Butte team won easily, 34-6. The next seven years, the Butte club traveled throughout the western region of the United States taking on other local teams. The club played 36 games and won 23.

The interest developed from this team carried over into the high school ranks. Butte High School grabbed the spotlight with excellent teams. Butte High beat Fort Shaw to win the first-ever Montana high school championship game played in 1900. Butte dominated the early years of high school football in the state. In 1907, the "Purples," as they were referred to back then, beat a team from Spokane High School, 5-4, to win the Northwest Pacific Region Championship in a contest played at the Columbia Gardens field.

The next year the Butte High team, coached by George Downer, battled Englewood High School of Chicago in the national championship game played at the Columbia Gardens. The Chicago club won the contest 11-4.

Butte Independent Football League

What made football unique in Butte was not the local high school, but the formation of a semipro independent football league. The teams in the league represented various athletic clubs formed in the numerous neighborhoods around town. It was a well-structured league that fluctuated from four to six teams. The league was set up and in full operation long before a meeting in the Midwest which led to the creation of the National Football League in 1920.

"Some old-timers told me the advent of professional football began in Butte, Montana," said Dublin Gulch player Tony Stosich. "It was the idea which began here that others cashed in on when they formed the National Football League."

The Butte Independent Football League was like the NFL in that games were generally played on Sunday afternoons. Prior to 1921, the games were at Hebgen Park or the Columbia Gardens field; then at Clark Park from 1921 to 1937, and finally at Butte High Stadium, later called Naranche Stadium, from 1938 to 1941.

Vince Downing said with a laugh, "I remember spending a lot of time in the pigpen watching those Independent League games. Only a handful of kids had enough money in those days to go to games. So the way to get in was to go to the pigpen at the end of one side of Clark Park and watch the game for free behind this wired fence. The pigpen was always filled with kids when the Independent League teams played at Clark Park."

John Shea observed, "Another way to get in free was to carry the headgear for some of the players. You walked right on the field with them and served as a manager for the day."

Stosich noted "Clark Park was an excellent field. It was fast and always solid. The only thing it lacked was grass, but, heck, we didn't care."

Crowds at the Independent League games ranged from a couple of hundred to two- or three-thousand depending on who was playing and what was at stake. In similar fashion to the NFL, players competing in the Butte Independent League received money for their services. Winners took home 60 percent of the gate receipts which were split among the 22-team members. The losers' share was 40 percent.

Stosich said, "The most I ever made was $62 for the whole season. Of course, the money was not really the reason you played the game."

The battles on the gridiron all came down to a matter of pride. The players were former high school and college stars plus miners who never went to high school; they simply wanted to prove their toughness on the gridiron.

"That was damn tough football," said Torger Oaas, the son of long-time Englewood manager Turk Oaas. "They beat the hell out of each other and it was even worse when the Anaconda Anodes came to town to play one of the Butte teams. They absolutely hated each other and would do whatever it took to win the game."

Stosich recalled, "The games against Anaconda were just like a street fight. We got into fights with the Anodes all the time and they were a tough team. Mickey Kane, their running back, was one of the hardest guys in the league to bring down. He was always good for five or six yards. Moose Rouse and I mixed it up on the field and then one time we got into a fight on Park Street. It was a war every time we played Anaconda."

John Shea agreed. "Any time a Butte team battled the Anodes it was always murder. There was plenty of blood spilled on the field when that match took place."

Former Hub Addition player Rich Navarro added, "It was very tough, physical football. You always came out of those games with all sorts of bumps and bruises."

Rudy Tomazich, who played for Centerville, characterized the contests as "60 minutes of pure hell. There were very few player changes during the game. You played both ways and you had to be tough as hell to play in the league."

Manhood was everything in these battles. A typical game matched the Anaconda Anodes and Dublin Gulch in 1933. The Anaconda players bragged about how they were going to kick the hell out of Dublin Gulch come Sunday afternoon. Coach Birdie Aho of Dublin Gulch responded as quoted in *The Montana Standard:* "Let them come because we're as tough as they are!" Dublin Gulch prevailed 1-0 after winning a California playoff by a 26-yard advantage. The California playoff system had just been installed before the 1933 season to prevent ties. When a game ended in a tie the ball was placed on the 50-yard line. Each team alternated with an offensive play until both sides had five plays. The team with the most yardage after five plays by both teams was declared the winner.

The roots for the Independent League began shortly after the turn of the century when football teams were formed by the Centerville Athletic Club and the Englewood Athletic Club. They challenged each other to a game or tried to line up a contest with local high school or college teams. It really didn't matter who they played just so long as they got a chance to play.

More squads were formed around 1910: the Butte Ramblers from Centerville, a team from Anaconda, and the Stevens Addition of Butte. The first full year of league action was held in 1914 with five teams participating: Centerville, Deer Lodge Valley, Reynolds McDowell, South Butte and Englewood. Centerville took league honors with a perfect 4-0 record.

The Centerville team wore red, crimson, or maroon uniforms. Local newspaper reporters used them all as the team's color at one time or another. In fact, the Centerville team let the local high school, Butte Central, wear its uniforms in a 1916 game against Butte High because Central's uniforms had not arrived. When Central's team came out on the field the Butte High players called them "Maroons" because of the color of the uniform. The color stuck and so did the nickname for Butte Central.

Centerville did more than just donate its uniforms. It dominated the league winning the championship a record 10 straight times from 1913 to 1923. The "Reno Reds," "Hilltoppers," "Highlanders" or "Redskins," as Centerville was sometimes called, had complete command of the league. Centerville dominated to the point that it wasn't seriously challenged until 1919 in a 0-0 tie with Englewood. A second game was played on December 7, 1919, in snowy conditions with temperatures around zero at the Columbia Gardens field. Centerville's Tommy Fitzpatrick booted a 35-yard field goal with a minute to go in the game to give the Reno Reds a dramatic 3-0 victory.

The Hilltoppers were managed by Otis Lee and later by "Cash and Carry" Ted Warren, with George Bourquin serving as the coach. Managers were key components of each team because their primary duty was to find jobs for the players. A majority of the players who came to town got employment in the mines. Most of those jobs were above the ground and were day shift so players could practice at night.

Centerville team members changed into their practice uniforms at the Buffalo Mine, then walked a few blocks up Main Street to their practice location at Mullen Field. The field had street lights nearby, enabling the club to practice at night.

Centerville was led by quarterback "Hook" Leahy. A key member of the backfield was running back Tom "Sheet Iron" Wier, who got the name "Sheet Iron," as legend has it, because he took pieces of sheet iron and put them inside his pants in the upper thigh area for protection. Among players during Centerville's ten-year championship run were Frank and Bob Darragh, "Spottie" Williams, "Dolly" Sullivan, "Goula" Mulcahy, "Bittah" Rodgers, "Willow" Sullivan, "Kack" O'Connell, "Flossie" Sullivan, "Bunny" Shea, Ray Bray, "Chick" Shea, "Senator" Pat Holland, Tom Walsh and Tom Grady.

Centerville finally lost a league game on October 30, 1921, when "Swede" Lindstrum scored the lone touchdown in a 7-0 Englewood victory. Yet, the Reno Reds avenged that loss with a 13-0 win over Englewood in the title game played on December 18, 1921.

The Hilltoppers had a scare in the 1922 championship contest against the Hub Addition. Centerville won 10-3 on one of the strangest plays in league history. Hub Addition punted the ball to Centerville with Tommy Wier making a fair catch at his own 49-yard line. Wier called for an onside kick which was legal during that season. The kick forced both teams to move back 10 yards while Wier booted the ball back to the Hub Addition. The ball went into the end zone. Hub Addition players thought the ball in the end zone meant that the play was dead and the ball would come out to the 20-yard line where they would go on offense. The Centerville players saw the ball in the end zone and the Reds' "Flossie" Sullivan fell on it scoring a touchdown. Hub Addition players vehemently protested, insisting the ball was dead. The referee ruled in favor of Centerville, giving them a touchdown and ultimately the league title. The onside kick was outlawed the following season, too late as far as the Hub Addition was concerned.

Other rules for the rough-and-tumble game also were changed through the years. One was the dead ball rule which was discarded prior to the 1933 season. Previously, a player did not have to be tackled to the ground to have the whistle blown ending action. Under the new rule, a ball carrier had to be on the ground before the play was stopped. A second change allowed players to throw the football anywhere behind the line of scrimmage. Prior to the season, a player had to be five yards behind the line before tossing the ball.

The greatest change for the 1933 season involved breaking tie games through a California playoff. The previous season, the Hub Addition and Dublin Gulch played to a 0-0 tie in the championship game. Because no playoff system was in force, both teams were declared champions. League officials always wanted to have a winner regardless if it was a title game or just a league contest. So they installed the California playoff system of breaking a tie through yardage gained on five offensive plays for each side.

This system worked well, but it also produced some strange results. The most bizarre took place in the 1940 championship game between the Anaconda Anodes and the Hub Addition. The Anaconda club was clearly the best team in the league in 1940 winning five of six games heading into the title match. The Hub Addition lost three of its first four games, but won three of its next four contests. The Anodes completely dominated the championship game, moving up and down the field, but failed to score. When the final gun went off the game was tied 0-0. In the California playoff, the Hub Addition came out victorious by one-yard. Three feet became the difference between winning and losing a title.

Another rule opened the door for the Hub Addition's surprising win over Anaconda in 1940. During the season, league officials had the fourth and fifth place teams meet in a playoff game with the Hub Addition beating Dublin Gulch 20-0. League rules allowed the team that won the playoff game, to pick up the best players from the club that got beat. So, the

Hub Addition which lost three of its first four games, now had reinforcements— Dublin Gulch's best players—to continue through the playoff wars.

"When we picked up those Dublin Gulch players like Tony Stosich it made all the difference in the world," recalled Rich Navarro. "We needed all the reinforcements we could get against the Anodes because they were very tough to beat that year."

Rule changes helped open up the game. So did the persistence of league president Bob Corette during the 1930s. Corette said the league would fold after the 1936 season unless teams put more gate receipt money into uniforms and protective gear rather than keeping the cash in their own pockets. He was also concerned about sagging attendance which he blamed on too many running plays. Corette urged teams to open up the game with more passing for the fans. He also insisted on a championship game at the end of every season. Prior to 1936, a title game was played only if the top two teams had identical records or had not played each other during the season.

Even with better rules and equipment, the games were not without their share of trouble. A controversial call by an official could lead to total chaos. The game between Anaconda and Englewood on October 23, 1932, ended in controversy when an official's interference call decided the outcome in favor of Anaconda 6-0. An Englewood player punched the referee after the final gun which led to a free-for-all involving players from both sides and hundreds of fans who poured onto the Clark Park field.

The Independent Football League was indeed a very serious form of football and meant everything to the players, coaches, managers and fans from the various neighborhoods. It also had some special features for players to add to their fun. A "secret weapon" was adding booze in the water bucket.

"I was sitting on the Centerville bench one game serving as manager," said John Shea. "I went to take a drink from the water bucket and I could hear my dad screaming at me to come over and see him. He pulled some coins out of his pocket and gave me enough money to go buy a soda. He told me not to drink out of the water bucket. Later on, I found out why."

Meaderville, Walkerville, the Hub Addition, Dublin Gulch and the Anaconda Anodes were other teams besides Centerville and Englewood that played in the league.

Centerville obviously was a key club in the circuit because of its early dominance. They finally lost the league title to Dublin Gulch 10-7 in the championship contest played on November 7, 1924. Dublin Gulch was led by Emil "Shimmy" Crnich who booted a field goal and tossed a touchdown pass in the game.

Once it lost the league title, Centerville never again could boast about being champion. They lost the championship to the Hub Addition in 1925 and the Anaconda Anodes in 1928. Following the 1928 title loss, the Reno Reds never again supported a team with a winning record and dropped out of the circuit on August 27, 1941, shortly before the kickoff to a new season.

The Centerville woes happened despite the fact it had one of the league's best players in "Huck" Driscoll, who started in the Reno Reds' backfield from 1929 to 1939. Other colorful characters on the Centerville teams included Gene Harvey, "Red" Snyder, "Sheets" McCarthy, Tim Dennehy, Willie Inkret, "Stowie" Maxwell, Johnny Dixon, Rudy Tomazich, Edo Shea, and Mike O'Hara. Centerville coaches besides George Bourquin included "Biddha" Rodgers, Harold Eaton, Frank "Pop" Bender, Vivian Burr, Tim Dennehy, Jack Leary, Jim Freebourn, and "Ears" Holland.

Rudy Tomazich said what hurt Centerville the most was "a lack of consistency in the head coaching position. We seemed to have a new coach every year and it would mean a new system to learn with new plays. The other clubs had a consistent coaching order through the years while Centerville was always getting a new face which really hurt us."

Meaderville had a squad from 1917 through the 1921 season, but never had a winning record. Even though Meaderville did not win many games, it supplied one of the league's best players in Emil "Shimmy" Crnich, the quarterback. He and his favorite receiver Russ Penhale were a deadly duo that every team had to contend with when they battled Meaderville. Another key player was "Beans" Randono. The team was led by coaches Metlin and Bertoglio.

Walkerville played a couple of games in 1919 and 1920 before joining the league full time in 1921. Walkerville, called the "Stars," had tough luck in league competition. During its five years in the league, from 1921 to 1925, it won only one game and, oddly enough, it was the last game Walkerville ever played beating Englewood 3-0 on November 15, 1925.

Key players on the Walkerville Stars were "Pep" Downey, "Brick" Mueller, "Straight" Downey, "Zoolie" Reynolds, "Chink" Downey, "Bull" Harley, Martin Fox and Bill Jenkins who played halfback despite having only one arm. Coaches included "Slug'em" Sullivan, "Lefty" Ryan, Jim Combo and "Fat" Maloney.

The Hub Addition was a major force once it joined the league in

1917. The Hubs, known as the "Kelly Green" because of their uniform color, was consistent, winning league titles in 1925, 1927, 1929, 1932, 1936 and 1940. They practiced at the Hubs playground area near the Anselmo Mine yard. The players changed into their gear at the fire station on the corner of Excelsior and Caledonia Streets, then walked about six blocks to their practice field.

The Hubs were noted for having the best line in the circuit, but seemed to lack quality backfield players, although one back in the 1920s who was consistently good was "Reeka" Nugent. Other key players were "Stub" McGrath, "Soapy" Schaeffer, "Dome" Driscoll, "Wee" Brennan, "Lip" Crowley, John Meglen, "Chink" Sullivan, "Zoolie" Reynolds, "Feets" Lewis, Bart Riley, "Moose" Arndt, "Buzzy" Winston, Johnny Inkret, Mike O'Leary, Jim Bertoglio, "Ole" Reardon, Joe Riley, Jim Freebourn, "Binty" O'Brien, "Snake Hips" Sullivan, John and Joe Hazen, Roy Babich, Bill Flynn, Bob Cosgrove, Dan McCarthy, Rich Navarro, Jack McCarthy, "Monk" Semansky and Frank Little.

The longtime coach of the Hub Addition was Joe McGlone. Other skippers of the Kelly Green were "Skimmett" Dee, Chester Pittser, Bill Spears, John Hazen, Joe Riley, "Reeka" Nugent, and Dan McCarthy. Andy Peoples was club manager for many years.

Dublin Gulch began playing games in 1920 and joined the league full time in 1921. Dublin Gulch was a mainstay in the circuit, winning numerous championships. The first title won by the men wearing orange and black uniforms came in 1924 when they knocked off 10-time league champion Centerville.

The most bitter rivalry in the league was the annual showdown between Dublin Gulch and Centerville. It was like a civil war every time these two teams from the hill battled on the flats at Clark Park. The rivalry was based on the location of the two communities being close to each other on the hill and on the fact that Dublin Gulch ended Centerville's 10-year league title streak.

"The kids from Centerville would come down on the trolley car to go to the game," recalled Eddy Crnich from Dublin Gulch. "The Centerville kids loaded up with rocks before they left and when the trolley stopped in Dublin Gulch they would fire off their rocks at the Dublin Gulch kids trying to get on the car. Once everyone was aboard, the kids from both sides would be fighting all the way to the ball field."

John Shea of Centerville said, " I remember the Dublin Gulch kids tossing rocks and anything they could find at us as we came down the hill. When the game was over if we won they would toss rocks at us again as we rode the trolley through their neighborhood. If they won, the Dublin

Gulch kids would simply laugh at us. It was a very bitter rivalry."

Crnich laughed when he remembered that "it was such a rivalry that even the women got involved in it. My father told me that Centerville women used to beat on him with their purses as he was trying to leave the field after the game. He said the women hurt him worse than any Centerville player had on the field."

Rudy Tomazich said, "The women from Dublin Gulch were just as bad. Once I saw a Dublin Gulch lady take her shoe off and start beating Centerville players after Andy Groo and Johnny Hinch had gotten into a fight after the game."

Dublin Gulch was nicknamed "Comanches," "Gaels," or "the team from Hungry Hill." A dominant characteristic about Dublin Gulch was they always had someone who could throw the ball. They were blessed with outstanding quarterbacks like Emil "Shimmy" Crnich, Ralph Olsen, Birdie Aho and Al Zupan.

"Dublin Gulch was a tough team to play because they threw the ball so well," remembered Eddy Crnich. "My father, 'Shimmy' Crnich, had such an accurate arm that the opponent just tried to contain him. The other teams could always find a way to stop the run, but the Gulch's passing game made them hard to play."

Tomazich said he thinks "Al Zupan was the best player in that league when I played. The other teams hated to play against him because he could beat you in so many ways. When he ran with the football his knees got so high he would hurt people."

Other notable team members included "Bishop" Leary, Willard Thrasher, "Duke" Tevlin, "Coke" Dennehy, "Dago" Shea, "Tatie" Harrington, "Bones" O'Rourke, "Rags" Shea, Andy Groo, "Petsy" Spear, Dick Leary, Tony Stosich, "Fish" Lyons and "Kike" Maloney. A number of men led the Comanches on the war path as the head coach, including "Fat" Maloney, "Butter" Driscoll, "Birdie" Aho, "Petsy" Spear, "Fish" Lyons, and Myles "Kike" Maloney.

The Anaconda Anodes, sporting purple and copper as their colors, joined the league in 1926 and always seemed to be in contention for the championship. They won the league title six times in 1928, 1930, 1931, 1935, 1937 and 1939.

The most popular Anaconda player was "Street Car" Stergar. Other star athletes for the Anodes included Jim Emmons, Pat Sugrue, "Doc" Beal, Rube Shagina, Jim Rouse, "Wild Horse" Jenkins, "Bubs" Long, Moose Rouse, Oren Eccelston, "Old Krony" Domitrovich, Ted Bubash, Tim Calnan, Mickey Kane, and Joe Calnan.

Tomazich said, "The guy from Anaconda I remember the most was

Moose Rouse. He had to be the dirtiest player I ever competed against in my life. You would get tackled in a pile and Rouse would be going after your nose or mouth to try and inflect some more damage. He was just a mean son-of-a-gun."

The heart and soul of Anodes football was Jim Emmons. He served as both a player and coach for many years. Other coaches for Anaconda included Ray McCarren, "Doc" Beal, Gene Burris, Frank Mueller and Pat "Tubba" Connors.

The Englewood team started about the same time as Centerville during the first decade of the 1900s. They were called the "South Side" and represented the tough luck team of the league. They lost hard-fought title games to Centerville in 1919 and 1921. Englewood, also called the "Lowlanders," dropped the 1930 championship game to Anaconda before finally winning the crown in 1934 with a 19-0 victory over Dublin Gulch. The team wore gray and crimson uniforms through the 1926 season. They tried to change their luck by going to a blue and white color in 1927.

If there was a dominant theme to the club it was the number of former Butte High players who donned on the "Blues" as some liked to call Englewood. The best player to battle for Englewood was former Butte High star Ralph Olsen who both played and coached. Other star players were Tom Wier, Jim O'Keefe, Tim Harrington, "Lip" Crowley, "Tac" Barry, Tom Penaluna, Joe Meglen, Oscar Dahlberg, "Dummy" Janhunen, Jerry Sullivan, "Spike" Sullivan, Bob Keane, Johnny Dixon, Vic Leary, Jerry Murphy, Frank Meglen, Nig McGrath, Bill Pederson and Pete Vuich. Coaches besides Olsen included Allan McDougal, Leonard Daems, "Duke" Schroeder, "Lip" Crowley, "Kack" O'Connell, Ray "Feet" Lewis, Ray Erickson, Vic O'Leary and "Dummy" Janhunen.

When Centerville dropped out of the circuit in 1941, Englewood became the longest tenured club in the league making it appropriate that it won the last championship game, beating Anaconda 6-0 in the final contest ever played in the league on November 30, 1941. Seven days after that victory the Japanese bombed Pearl Harbor and triggered the start of World War II. The Butte/Anaconda Independent League, as it was known since the Anodes joined the circuit in 1926, was disbanded to never return.

Butte/Anaconda Independent Football League

Year	Champion and Title Game Score (When It Was Played)		
1913	Centerville		
1914	Centerville		
1915	Centerville		
1916	Centerville		
1917	Centerville		
1918	NO SEASON - FLU EPIDEMIC		
1919	Centerville 3	Englewood 0	
1920	Centerville		
1921	Centerville 13	Englewood 0	
1922	Centerville 10	Hub Addition 3	
1923	Centerville 13	Dublin Gulch 3	
1924	Dublin Gulch		
1925	Hub Addition 7	Centerville 3	
1926	Dublin Gulch 10	Hub Addition 3	
1927	Hub Addition		
1928	Anaconda 6	Centerville 0	
1929	Hub Addition		
1930	Anaconda 32	Englewood 0	
1931	Anaconda		
1932	Hub Addition 0	Dublin Gulch 0	# declared co-champions
1933	Dublin Gulch		
1934	Englewood 19	Dublin Gulch 0	
1935	Anaconda		
1936	Hub Addition 34	Anaconda 6	
1937	Anaconda 6	Hub Addition 0	
1938	Dublin Gulch 3	Anaconda 0	
1939	Anaconda 13	Englewood 7	
1940	Hub Addition 2	Anaconda 0	*California playoff
1941	Englewood 6	Anaconda 0	

Following World War II, there was an effort to bring independent semipro football back to Butte. Local tavern owner, Charlie Judd, formed the Butte "Buzzies" independent team in 1949. The first action for the Buzzies, under the direction of Coach Bob Sparks, came on October 16, 1949, when they took on the Anaconda Anodes at Naranche Stadium. The local club in its red and white uniforms won 22-0. The two squads met two more times during the month with both games ending in a tie.

The Buzzies played the University of Montana Cubs, losing 6-0. They also split a pair of games with a Billings Independent team to close out their 1949 season.

The next year was a highlight season for the Buzzies. The squad polished off the Billings team twice. They whipped a club from Lowry Air Base in Denver, 14-6. The next opponent to come to town was the Seattle Ramblers. The Buzzies won 6-0 before a crowd of over 5,500 people at Naranche Stadium.

The fan interest was certainly evident, but the lack of opponents, plus the high cost of equipment hurt the efforts to rekindle independent football in Butte. During the next few years, under Coach Larry Connors, the Buzzies played games in the Seattle area and met local schools like Carroll College and the Montana School of Mines. By 1952, the efforts of redevelopment of independent football had fallen short of the goal line and the team was disbanded.

The Buzzies were led by quarterback Alex Chavez. They also featured strong running efforts from Bill McKechnie, Matt Cassick and Jack Coyne. Other players included Jim Bennett, Jim Biggens, Bill Boston, Claire Boulet, Bill Brock, Don Cohn, Al Cutler, Art Day, Jack Doble, Frank Donovan, Bob Edwards, Joe Ferko, Kevin Foster, Jim Garrett, Chuck Goggin, Bob Griffith, Mark Hampton, George Huddleston, Bill James, Gus Janhunen, John Kello, George Krempasky, Jack Leary, John Masonovich, Joe Matkovic, Dean Mattix, Mort Mayo, Bill Mirich, Jim Morrissey, Eulijio Navarro, Bob Neubauer, Jerry O'Neill, Don Puich, Harold Reed, Bill Renouard, Ed Rosich, Rod Salo, Bob Sandlin, Dave Satterthwaithe, Bob Schulte, Jim Scown, Monk Semansky, Charles Shontell, Sid Smythe, Lauren Southers, John Stajcar, Bo Stanich, Charles Twardus, George Vucurovich and Bud Weldon.

Independent football was gone, but the promotion of the game was carried on by the Butte High Silver B's. The football letter-winner club was formed in September 1940, by five former Butte High players Wreck Donnelly, John Curtis, John "Butter" Driscoll, Stanley "Midge" Griffith and Duke Schroeder to promote Butte High athletes.

" I am amazed at how long the Silver B's has been functioning," said longtime member Bill Hawke. "When the group was started they wanted to do so many different things, but were not sure where to begin. I thought it all might become just a fly-by-the-night organization, but it survived and continues to get stronger every year."

One of the first projects undertaken by the Silver B's was the Soldiers Memorial Shrine next to Butte High School. It was completed and dedicated to Butte High veterans of World War II on May 26, 1947. Through the years the organization has helped numerous times supplying equipment and other things to help the Bulldogs' football team.

"I think longevity is what makes this organization so unique," said Silver B's member Dan Peters. "There is a loyalty factor that has built up through the years for football players at Butte High School. Its really hard to explain, but every person who has played for Butte High and later became a Silver B can experience that special feeling."

Former Silver B's secretary/treasurer Glenn Welch said, "I have received calls from people all over the country. They ask me all kinds of questions about how our organization got started and how it's able to continue through the years. Some want to know how they can start a similar organization in their town and keep it going. I think one of the big reasons for our success has been the pride that Silver B members have for the school and the game of football."

The first induction ceremony took place on October 11, 1940, prior to an important Big Six League match between Butte High and Anaconda. Fifty-seven letter-winners from 1893 to 1916 attended that Silver B's dinner. The list included six men who earned a letter for Butte High's first-ever football team in 1893: Fay Curtis, C. H. Gallagher, Lee Hawley, George Heimback, James Person and John Wulf. In all, 16 Silver B's at the first banquet had earned their letter prior to 1900.

After the first induction dinner, Butte High battled Anaconda in football action. The Bulldogs easily won the game 26-0 before over 9,000 fans at Butte High Stadium. The victory came a week after the Bulldogs had suffered a heartbreaking 8-6 overtime loss to Great Falls. The Silver B's win over Anaconda propelled the Bulldogs on a five-game winning streak that would climax with a 19-0 victory over Billings in the state title game.

Each year since 1940 an induction ceremony for former Bulldog football letter-winners from 25 and 50 years ago has taken place prior to the Bulldogs second to last home game of the season. The inductees become members of either the Silver or Golden B's club. Only actual letter-winners may attend the banquet. Family members are not allowed at the function. Prior to the game, Silver and Golden B members visit with the Butte High football team; then, they are introduced to the crowd and proudly march across the field.

"When I was a player it was like a cardinal sin to lose on Silver B's night," said former Bulldog player Gus Janhunen. "The Silver B members came into the locker room prior to the game to talk to everyone. It got you fired up and then they marched across the field which really got you going. It was very tough beating Butte High School on Silver B's night."

Peters said, "When I was head coach it was always an honor to bring a Silver B member in before the game to talk to the kids. I had former coach, Sam Jankovich, give a talk once and it really got the team ready for their game that night. Every team in the state hated to come to Butte to play the Bulldogs on Silver B's night. It was just a special night for the players and the entire Silver B organization."

The standard rule instituted by longtime coach Swede Dahlberg was that a player had to compete in 12 quarters during a season in order to earn a football letter. The rule is still used over 50 years later.

"It was darn tough to letter at Butte High especially under Swede Dahlberg," said Peters. "The small group of individuals who got a letter every year certainly earned it. Swede had a rule of playing 12 quarters and if you were even one quarter short you did not letter. It was that simple and every player knew it. Thankfully, that standard of 12 quarters was carried on by the coaches after Swede retired."

After each season, the Silver B's host a dinner for the most recent Butte High football team regardless of its record. The head football coach awards letters to the players who qualify.

"I remember going to my first dinner where I received a letter," said Silver B's member George Paul. "I felt it was quite an honor because the Silver B's was such a special organization. I couldn't wait until the day I could join.

"I recall sitting with Silver B's member, Al Ducich. During the course of the night, I told him it would be such a great honor to sit next to him 25 years down the road when I would be inducted and you know that's exactly what happened. You cannot put a price tag on a moment like that and the bond that has developed between the members of the Silver B's."

The Butte High Silver B's is one of the most unique organizations in the entire country. Bulldog players of the past are not forgotten at Butte High. They become a symbol of the game they love through the Silver B's.

Butte Copper League

The new immigrants arriving in Butte loved the national pastime of baseball. The rough-and-tumble sport of football may have been closer to the heart of miners, but baseball was just as great a passion for many Butte citizens. Baseball emerged as a local crowd pleaser in 1902 when William Clark had a large grandstand and ballfield built at the Columbia Gardens. The grandstand could hold 1,600 fans and, with additional open bleachers down the left field line, some games boasted attendance figures up to 3,000.

The new Columbia Gardens park allowed Butte to field a team in the Pacific Northwest League in 1902. The club drew large crowds to the

Gardens facility. The Butte team, under the direction of manager "Honest John" McCloskey, won the league title in its first year of competition. Butte had a record of 72 wins and 47 losses. Seattle was second, two-and-half games behind. Other squads in the circuit were Helena, Portland, Tacoma and Spokane.

The next summer, Butte's professional baseball team again won the title, this time in the renamed Pacific National League. The name change resulted after the California League expanded north to include teams from Portland and Seattle in their renamed Pacific Coast League.

The expanded Pacific Coast League created a war for players and teams. The Pacific Northwest League countered the expanded California League by renaming its circuit the Pacific National League on March 6, 1903. It placed teams in Los Angeles, San Francisco, Portland and Seattle to compete directly with the Pacific Coast League. Other teams in the Pacific National League were Tacoma, Helena, Spokane and Butte.

The Pacific National League had its share of problems in 1903. Near the season's midway point, the Portland team moved to Salt Lake City and started the year over with a brand new record. At the time of the transfer, Butte was leading the league by one game over Los Angeles. The problems in Portland spread across the league over the next month. Los Angeles, San Francisco, Tacoma and Helena all dropped their teams before the end of the year.

By the end of the summer of 1903, only four teams were left in the Pacific National League: Butte, Seattle, Spokane and Salt Lake City. Butte won the title with an 85-62 record. Spokane was second, followed by Seattle and Salt Lake City. The dismantling of the Pacific National League illustrated that professional baseball was on shaky grounds. Butte fielded a team in 1904, competing in a league with Salt Lake City, Boise, Idaho and Spokane. The next summer, Butte "struck out." The Mining City had no pro baseball team. Butte was back in professional baseball from 1906 to 1908, competing in the Northwestern League.

That was followed by a three-year absence before professional baseball returned. As part of the Union Association League, Butte competed from 1911 through 1914 with teams from Salt Lake City, Great Falls, Boise, Helena and Missoula. Poor attendance plagued the Butte club which played at a new field called McCloskey Field in the Warehouse District. The field later was renamed Hebgen Field, and then Bob Koprivica Park.

Butte was without a professional baseball team in 1915. The team returned to action in 1916 and 1917, competing in the Northwestern League along with Great Falls, Vancouver, Spokane, Portland and Seattle. The start of World War I put an end to the league following the 1917 season.

When the war ended a new type of league was developed within the city. It was called the Butte Mines League. The league was supported by the various mining properties in the community. Baseball players came to Butte with hopes of being spotted by a major league scout. The players were given "soft" surface jobs at the mines in return for their services on the diamond.

The league consisted of four to six teams. The ACM club sponsored by The Anaconda Copper Mining Company was the only squad to compete in all eight seasons of the league. Black Rock, North Butte and Timber Butte all participated only in the 1920 season. Colo-Pitts played from 1920 to 1924. Black Spec was a league member from 1921 to 1923. Black-Pitts played one year in 1924 and took league honors. The Montana Power Company and the Anaconda Anodes each joined the circuit in 1922. The Anodes took the league title in 1922 and 1926.

The team with the most success was the Clarks. They competed from 1921 to 1927, winning the league three times in 1923, 1925 and 1927.

Some of the players went on to compete at the big league level. The most notable were Frank Crosetti, who played and coached for years with the New York Yankees, and Earl Averill, who later became a member of the Cleveland Indians. Averill competed for the Anaconda Anodes in 1925. He went on to play 12 years in the big leagues from 1929 to 1941. He led the American League with 232 hits during the 1936 season. He was inducted into the Baseball Hall of Fame at Cooperstown, New York in 1975.

The games were played at Clark Park which was constructed and put into use in 1921. The league attracted large crowds. The biggest attendance was recorded on September 7, 1923, when the Clarks beat the Anodes 13-4 in a league playoff game before a crowd of 9,812 fans. It was the second straight win for the Clarks as they won the best-of-three series. The playoff series was the second in Butte Mines League history as the top two teams finished with the same record. In 1922, the Anodes had won a two game playoff sweep against ACM

The Butte Mines League lasted through the 1927 season.

<u>Butte Mines League</u>

League champion

1920	ACM	
1921	ACM	
1922	Anodes	beat ACM 2-0 in best of three

1923	Clarks	beat Anodes 2-0 in best of three
1924	Black Pits	
1925	Clarks	
1926	Anodes	
1927	Clarks	

After the Mines League fired its last pitch, Butte joined the State Amateur League and also developed a loosely-formed city league which continued through 1943.

Before the summer of 1944, a new league, the Butte Copper League, was formed by a group of Butte men. The Copper League provided a home run in terms of action for Butte baseball fans for the next 16 years, proving to be the most fruitful local circuit in the city's history. William McGonigle was elected as the league's first president. McGonigle served as a key figure for the league until his death in 1949.

"Bill McGonigle was a really big reason why the Copper League was able to develop," Rudy Tomazich said. "He ran a tight ship and kept everything in order."

Gus Janhunen remembered: "Everything had to be in order when Bill McGonigle ran the show. My father was an umpire in the league. Prior to each game, McGonigle made sure the umpires' entire uniforms were in perfect order, right down to the shine in their shoes, before he'd let them go out onto the field."

McGonigle was followed as league president by John Good from 1949 to 1956. Bill Cullen took over in 1957 and ran the league through 1959. Jim Kello was in charge in 1960. Other principal founders included Nick Hubber who served as the circuit's secretary/treasurer, statistician Jean Jordan, plus board members Bill Cullen, Ed Gerry and Lou Spears.

The four teams in the new league in 1944 were the Navy-12 Engineers from the Montana School of Mines, Miners Union, McQueen and Silver Bow Parks. Each team played 27 games against their three opponents with the School of Mines easily winning the title. The squad, coached by Bill Cullen, also was declared state champions after whipping a Great Falls team in a doubleheader played at Clark Park.

The roots for growth in the Butte Copper League were evident the next summer. During league play, more than 25,000 fans walked through the turnstiles at Clark Park. A playoff series followed the regular season. McQueen won the title, beating Silver Bow Parks 8-7 in a dramatic fifth and deciding game in the best-of-five series. McQueen's Sid Hoar hit a three-run homer in the bottom of the last inning to help his club win the title before a record crowd of 1,386 fans at Clark Park.

The next summer, with World War II now over, league attendance almost doubled over the previous year. Figures show 47,911 fans took in the action. A major attraction besides the solid play was the price of admission. It cost an adult 25 cents to go to attend. Kids 12 to 18-years-old paid 5 cents and kids under 12 got in free.

"The Copper League gave something for the people to do," said Jim Hanley, a former player. "It was real cheap entertainment for many people who never had a lot of money during that time. You simply lived for the summer to either play or watch Copper League games."

Tomazich said, "Why, people would come home from work, grab a sandwich and head out to the ballpark. It was a big deal to come out to Clark Park and watch the Copper League during the summer months.."

Former McQueen manager Jim Kello recalled, "Only a few people had cars in those days. Everyone filled up the city buses and headed out to the ballpark during the summer."

Rich Navarro said, "During the playoff series, you had to be at the park at least an hour early just to get a decent seat. They packed the grandstands for the finals and it was good, quality baseball."

Glenn Welch , who played for McQueen, recalled, "We felt it was a good, solid league and we sure had plenty of fun playing in the Copper League. You could make some pretty decent money playing in the Copper League for a summer. They would divide the gate revenue up between the teams at the end of the year. It came to a pretty good chunk of money by season's end."

"Sly" Jim Sullivan, a former player for South Side, said, "I think a good example of how talented the league was revolved around all-star games. The House of David and some of the Pioneer League pro baseball teams came to Butte to play a collection of all-star players from the Copper League. The all-star squad from the Copper League won most of those games. It was just an indication of how talented the league was against solid outside competition."

The 1946 season marked the first appearance of the North Side team which replaced the Montana School of Mines in the four-team league lineup. The North Side made it to the championship finals before getting beat in four games by regular season king Silver Bow Parks.

The expanding league added a fifth team in 1947, the South Side.

The North Side club dominated play during the 1947 regular season In fact, it won the regular season title for a record four straight years between 1947 to 1950; however, only once during that span did it take the playoff series championship.

The lone title for the North Side came in 1947 when it won three straight against Silver Bow Parks after dropping the first two games o the best-of-five series. The North Side won the final game before a new league record crowd of 5,331. During their five-game series with the Silver Bow Parks, more than 20,000 fans flocked inside Clark Park to see the action.

Tomazich , who managed the North Side team said, "That series really was the beginning of a bitter rivalry which developed between Silver Bow Parks and the North Side. After Silver Bow Parks won the first two games of the series, their fans had put together a big championship buffet dinner. They were going to host the players after they took the third game to win the series. Well, my players found out about it and they were as mad as hell. We won the third game and came back to win three straight and take the title. My players never let the Silver Bow Parks guys nor their fans forget about that buffet dinner."

Remembering the rivalry made Gus Janhunen laugh. "The thing I remember most about that rivalry was how much the fans from both sides got on the players. First, they would take out their frustrations on the players from the other side and then once in awhile they started hollering at each other up in the grandstands."

Joe Zderick of Silver Bow Parks remembered, "It really got to be something in the stands for both sides. The main cheerleaders for the North Side were 'Ears' Holland and his wife, Lena. On the other side for Silver Bow Parks you had Hank and Rose Desjardins. Boy, could those two couples get the fireworks going during a game."

The strong four-year run for the North Side featured some of the league's best players. The list was headed by the double play combination of second basemen Wilbur Johnson and shortstop Jim McCaughey. Johnson went on to play professional baseball making it to the Class AAA level in the Philadelphia Phillies organization. He later became a major league scout. The North Side featured John Podgorski, Lefty Rundle, George Cavan, Len Connors, Maury Mulcahy, George Vucurovich, Rich Navarro, Mike Perkovich, Mun Doran, Jim Lukas, John Little, Bill Leybold, Skippy Veale, Joe Hill and Bill Kambich plus some of the league's best hurlers in Jim Sweeney and Tom Mulcahy. Rudy Tomazich was the manager.

"Rudy Tomazich was the best baseball man I ever met," Hanley said. "He taught the theory of baseball. He instructed you on percentages and what happens when you did this or what are your chances if you tried that. He was an excellent teacher and its reflected in the success Rudy had as a manager in the Copper League."

Janhunen supported that opinion. "Rudy really knew the game," he recalled. "He would try just about anything to win a baseball game. I had a tremendous amount of respect for him."

Tomazich played in the Copper League during the 1946 season after returning to Butte from his World War II duty. During the year, he hurt his shoulder, which ended his career and forced him into managing to stay in the game he loved. During an eight-year stretch, from 1947 to 1954, Tomazich led his team to either the regular season or playoff title seven times.

The 1948 championship series saw Silver Bow Parks whip the North Side 5-3 in the decisive fifth game. Silver Bow Parks always seemed to have players who could hit the ball. They were led by Al Hockaday who won the league batting title in 1945 and 1947. Silver Bow Parks players won the league batting title five times, the most by one club. Other Silver Bow Parks players to take the title were Don Olson, Bob McLaughlin and Jim "Gus" Janhunen. The first batting title for Janhunen was 1954. He came back to capture the crown in 1958 and join Hockaday as the only two players to ever win the championship more than once. Other key performers for the Silver Bow Parks included Jack Pomroy, Jim Wedin, Rod Salo, Matt Spremic, "Beans" Collins, Bob Phillips, Ray McLaughlin, Gene Carlson and Tom Logan. The key pitchers were Lefty Mehrens and Joe Zderick. The club was managed by Jim Freebourn.

The crowds during the 1948 championship series were the best ever. The final contest of the five-game series was played before a league record 5,338 fans. The 1948 season was the high-water mark for attendance in the league. During the summer, 136,019 fans paid their way into Clark Park. The crowds the next summer were good, but not like 1948. The top attendance during the playoffs hit only 2,990.

The South Side led by their manager, Sonny Hicks, took the league playoff series in both 1949 and 1950. South Side always played the role of an underdog in the playoffs. During their two-year run as playoff champions, they never supported a winning record in the regular season.

What the South Side had was Herb Plews, perhaps the best player in league history. He hit a league record .508 during the 1949 season to capture the batting title. Plews went on to play at the major league level for the Washington Senators.

"Herbie Plews was an excellent baseball player," said Janhunen. "Plews was perhaps the best the league ever produced." Other key players for the South Side included Owen Bush, Jess Hodges, Jack McMahon, Van Vilet, Stan Syskowski and Babe Kovich. The South Side had a great money pitcher in "Sly" Jim Sullivan who won the final game in their 1950 playoff championship series victory over McQueen.

In 1951, competition came from the newly formed Butte Softball

League. The new activity had an impact on the Butte Copper League.

Hanley believed that "what softball did was cut into the player rosters in the Intermediate League. Kids could play in the Intermediate League until they were 19 or made the American Legion team. The Intermediate League was the main feeder program for the Copper League. When softball got started, a lot of those Intermediate League players switched over to softball. The Copper League started to lose its main base for growth and started to see the quality of their younger players decline. It did not take long to see the talent level at the Copper League start to slip."

Tomazich disagreed. "I am not sure the loss of the Intermediate League had that much to do with the reduction in the quality of players in the Copper League. In the early years we got kids in here from all over the country to play in the Copper League. These college players would learn about the league through competing with guys who had already played in the Copper League. Boy, we got some top-notch kids in here playing and the fans realized the talent that was in town. The college kids from around the country simply just stopped coming to Butte to play and that hurt the quality of the league and attendance.

"I also think more people purchasing cars led to other activities for folks besides just coming out to the ballpark every night."

Glenn Welch remembered: "There were some players from out-of-state who came here to play. I think one of the keys to success in the early years was not so much the out-of-state guys as it was the number of players who came to Butte from around the area. I recall playing with Charlie Moore from Deer Lodge. He was just one of many players from Anaconda, Deer Lodge, Helena, Dillon and other places around the region who came into town just to participate in the Copper League."

Rich Navarro believes "bringing players into town really hurt the league. The local kids would get a chance to play until some of the college kids from outside of town finished school and came to Butte to play in the Copper League. A number of local kids were put on the bench and that did not sit well with many local fans."

Television may have helped end local baseball, according to "Sly" Jim Sullivan who believes that TV was what hurt the Copper League games. "I remember getting our first TV in 1951. They had big league games on and people now had a choice to sit in front of the TV and watch the big leaguers play or come out and watch us. Unfortunately, we soon became the second choice for many fans."

Another impact was identified by Joe Zderick. "One of the big factors that really hurt the Copper League was Little League. Prior to the formation of Little League, the kids played a lot of games during the day.

It was a lot of fun and the kids really learned the fundamentals of the game. When Little League started their games were at night and many parents elected to go watch their kids play rather than go out to Clark Park. The parents took over and really took a lot of the sheer fun of playing out of the game for the kids."

World events also hurt the league in the summer of 1951. The North Side, after competing for only five years in the league, folded due to their club's roster being raided by the US Army. A number of North Side players enlisted and fought their battles not on the diamond at Clark Park, but in the mountains of Korea.

The North Side's loss was the Miners Union club's gain. The squad acquired Rudy Tomazich as a manager. They also got one of the North Side's best players in Jim Sweeney, who won the league batting title in 1951 with a .424 average. But it was on the mound rather than at the plate that Sweeney could best dominate a game because he was one of the league's best hurlers. Sweeney won the league's ERA title with a 2.00 mark in 1953. He pitched two shutouts during the 1954 championship series against Silver Bow Parks as the Miners Union won the playoff title in five games. The Miners Union team dominated the championship playoffs during a four-year stretch, winning the league title in 1951, 1953 and 1954.

The Miners Union club also featured players John Kennedy, George Mudro, Jim Hanley, Tom Pomroy, Don Williamson, Dick Roche, Bill Lepetic and "Crying" Jim Gregory.

The lone playoff series loss by the Miners Union during that four-year stretch came in 1952 against McQueen. The key to success for McQueen was pitcher Tom Mulcahy, who had a perfect 9-0 record during the season. The club also had the league's best hitter in Don "Lefty" Orlich who smacked the ball around for a .413 average. McQueen also featured players Rusty Smyth, Glenn Welch, Steve Kasun and Rod Salo

The Butte Copper League headed in a new direction in 1952. The circuit was expanded to five teams as the East Helena Smelterites joined the league. It was the first time a team from outside of Butte competed in the Copper League.

A player on the East Helena roster was Charlie Pride, who later achieved national fame as a country music singer.

"I remember Charlie Pride really started his music career right here in Montana while playing in the Copper League," said Sly Jim Sullivan. "After we got through playing a game in East Helena, everyone would head to the bar. Charlie would take off his baseball shirt, pull out his guitar and the next thing you knew he was up singing and entertaining the crowd.

"A few years later, there was Charlie Pride in the headlines as one of the biggest country singers in the country."

The trend of expansion continued in 1955 when a squad from Helena and Anaconda joined the fun. The Copper League was now up to seven teams. The Anaconda Anodes won both the 1955 regular season and playoff titles. They whipped the Helena Wranglers three games to two in the championship series, winning the decisive game 4-3 behind winning hurler Lefty Mehrens.

The expansion of the league outside of Butte hurt the local teams. The Helena, East Helena and Anaconda clubs could consolidate all the talent in their respective towns into one team. Prior to expansion, many of those players had been traveling to Butte to compete on one of its local teams. Even though it had lost a valuable talent source, Butte still fielded four teams. But, although it was a bigger community, Butte did not have enough quality players to fill out four solid teams. And so, it became clear early in the league expansion that the Butte clubs had to do things differently in order to compete.

The first experiment was to consolidate team rosters like the South Side and Miners Union did in 1956. The South Side also tried a combined club with Silver Bow Parks in 1957. The Miners Union and McQueen squads joined forces in 1959. But, the various combinations simply did not work. During a four-year span, from 1955 to 1959, only one Butte club, the 1957 McQueen team coached by Jim Kello, was able to capture the playoff series title, beating Miners Union

"The 1957 championship series was really special," recalled Kello. "It was the first time in a few years that two Butte teams played for the title. I was in my glory when McQueen won because I beat Rudy Tomazich, who was managing the Miners Union. Rudy was such a good baseball man and to beat him in a championship series was a great thrill."

The lack of competitive Butte teams hurt attendance. So did the fact that the Copper League's home, Clark Park, was destroyed by fire on May 1, 1957. The inferno that destroyed the grandstands at Clark Park forced league officials to scramble quickly to be ready for the 1957 season. A new baseball complex built at Grand Avenue and Garfield Street was called Duggan Memorial Field after Jack Duggan, who donated the land to the city for the ball diamond. A thousand temporary seats were installed along with a 12-foot high wooden fence surrounding the field. But, the cozy confines of Clark Park were gone and so were most of the fans.

"Duggan Memorial Field never had the same feel as Clark Park," Hanley said. "It lacked the atmosphere of being at the ballpark like Clark

Park had with its big grandstands. Clark Park was also kept in immaculate shape. You never got a bad hop at Clark Park. The care given Duggan Memorial Field was simply not there like Clark Park."

Zderick said, "At Clark Park they always announced scores from major league games and things like that. That all went away when Clark Park went up in flames like a cardboard box."

Kello remembered that "Clark Park smelled like baseball the moment you walked inside. It was everything that Duggan Field lacked in terms of atmosphere. Duggan Field had no real grandstands. The temporary seats were put in from the Civic Center. There were no permanent toilet facilities. The whole complex was not friendly for the fans."

Tomazich remembered some of the problems with Duggan Field. "We built this big fence all the way around the complex. The first year a big wind storm came through town and wiped out part of the fence. It was a tough place to maintain."

Copper League organizers decided to try a new approach in 1960 by eliminating teams from outside Butte. League officials hoped the move would turn around the sagging attendance for games at Duggan Memorial Field. Four teams —the South Side, McQueen, Miners Union and a new North Side team — competed during the summer. The South Side dominated, winning 21 of 22 games to capture the league championship.

The outstanding South Side team, managed by Jim Patrick, featured the league's best hitter in Dan "Dusty" Sullivan who clubbed a .458 batting average. The South Side polished off Miners Union 13-8 on August 27, 1960, to sweep the championship series in three games. That marked the final game in Butte Copper League history. A lack of fan interest during the 1960 season forced officials to fold the league after the season.

"The Copper League produced some quality baseball especially for a bunch of working folks," said Janhunen. "Sure, they brought some players in from the outside to compete, but overall it was mainly just working folks having a good time. If you look at the number of players who went on to compete at the pro level then you can understand that the Copper League was indeed solid baseball."

Hanley said, "It's criminal that the Copper League folded. It was great for kids giving them something to do in the summer. It was great for fans because they got quality entertainment without paying a lot of money. It was simply a lot of fun!"

Butte Copper League

League champions	Regular season champs
1944 Montana School of Mines Navy V-12	School of Mines
1945 McQueen beat Silver Bow Parks 3-2 in best of five	McQueen
1946 Silver Bow Parks beat North Side 3-1 in best of five	Silver Bow Parks
1947 North Side beat Silver Bow Parks 3-2 in best of five	North Side
1948 Silver Bow Parks beat North Side 3-2 in best of five	North Side
1949 South Side beat Silver Bow Parks 3-0 in best of five	North Side
1950 South Side beat McQueen 3-1 in best of five	North Side
1951 Miners Union beat Silver Bow 3-1 in best of five	Silver Bow Parks
1952 McQueen beat Miners Union 3-1 in best of five	Silver Bow Parks
1953 Miners Union beat Silver Bow Parks 3-2 in best of five	McQueen
1954 Miners Union beat Silver Bow Parks 3-2 in best of five	Silver Bow Parks
1955 Anaconda beat Helena 3-2 in best of five	Anaconda
1956 East Helena beat Anaconda 3-0 in best of five	East Helena
1957 McQueen beat Miners Union 3-1 in best of five	McQueen
1958 Helena beat McQueen 3-1 in best of five	Helena
1959 East Helena beat Helena 3-2 in best of five	Helena
1960 South Side beat Miners Union 3-0 in best of five	South Side

Butte Copper League Batting Champions

1944	"Fish" Papnich	McQueen	.385
	Stan Mayra	School of Mines	.385
1945	Al Hockaday	Silver Bow Parks	.491
1946	John Podgorski	North Side	.388
1947	Al Hockaday	Silver Bow Parks	.444
1948	Bill Kambich	North Side	.457
1949	Herb Plews	South Side	.508
1950	Don Olson	Silver Bow Parks	.415
1951	Jim Sweeney	Miners Union	.424
1952	Don Orlich	McQueen	.413
1953	Bud Sautter	South Side	.397
1954	Jim Janhunen	Silver Bow Parks	.500
1955	Bob McLaughlin	Silver Bow Parks	.448
1956	Dwayne Annala	McQueen	.438
1957	George Vucurovich	Miners Union	.448
1958	Jim Janhunen	McQueen	.436
1959	Earl Fred	Helena	.404
1960	Dan "Dusty" Sullivan	South Side	.458

Another attempt at the development of a new city baseball league was made when the Industrial League was formed in 1967, with four teams — Montana Power, the Anaconda Company, Stauffer Chemical, and the Miners Union. The league had a difficult time drawing people at the new baseball complex called Alumni Coliseum on the campus of Montana Tech, formerly the School of Mines. A good crowd for the league was a couple of hundred fans. The league threw its last pitch in the summer of 1970. That was the final strike out for adult baseball in town as players went back to the dugout looking for something else to do during the summer.

"The big thing that hurt the Industrial League was the lack of quality players competing in the circuit," Tomazich said. "The interest in baseball had dropped off in the town and there simply were not enough good, quality kids playing the game."

Baseball was down, but not out in Butte. The Pioneer League expanded its pro rookie circuit awarding Butte a franchise called the Copper Kings on February 6, 1978. The team joined clubs from Great Falls, Billings, Idaho Falls, Lethbridge, Medicine Hat, Calgary and Helena. The club was owned by Charlie Greathouse and Fred Nichols of New Haven, Connecticut. The first general manager was Bruce Manno.

The Butte Copper Kings had its first-ever game on June 23, 1978, losing to Idaho Falls, 15-11.

During their first year in the league, Butte played as a co-op club receiving players from various major league teams. In its second year, the club reached an agreement to compete as a farm team for the Milwaukee Brewers. During the next 20 years, the Copper Kings became a farm team for a variety of big league clubs including the Kansas City Royals, Seattle Mariners, Texas Rangers, Tampa Bay Devil Rays, and Anaheim Angels. The Copper Kings provided the first steps out of the batter's box for future major league players like Cecil Fielder, Julio Franco, Jeff Frye, Rey Sanchez, Ernest Riles, Robb Nen and many others.

Pennant fever hit a high mark in 1981 when the Copper Kings captured their only league championship beating Calgary in the playoffs.

Boxing

Team sports were popular in Butte, but so were individual activities. The most popular recreational sport since miners first set foot in the valley was boxing. If a fight was not taking place in a bar or alley, then a ring was set up to do things in a more civilized way.

The interest in the sport was keen and, with prize fights banned in many states, Butte was a top-ranked boxing center in the United States at the turn of the 20th century. A number of heavyweight champions including John L. Sullivan, Jim Jeffries, and Bob Fitzsimmons all had exhibition bouts in Butte.

In a 1902 exhibition, heavyweight champion Jim Jeffries got a scare when local miner Jack Munroe stayed with him through four bloody rounds to earn $500 at the Broadway Theater. Jeffries offered Munroe $1,000 to go another four rounds, but the Butte man refused. Munroe, a Canadian who came to Butte to work in the mines, knocked Jeffries down for a count of nine. Referee Dunc McDonald gave Munroe the decision. Munroe was offered a chance to take Jeffries' crown in a 1904 bout in San Francisco. Jeffries won the rematch with a second-round knock out.

Heavyweights dominated the fight game, but in Butte the smaller contestants proved to be the crowd favorites. One was Stanley Ketchel, who came to Butte from Grand Rapids, Michigan, and honed his skills as a bouncer in local gambling joints. Ketchel's first professional fight was a one-round knockout of Kid Tracy on May 2, 1903. Ketchel fought many times in Butte and eventually, after moving away from the city, won the world middleweight championship with a second-round knockout of Jack Sullivan on February 22, 1907, in San Francisco. Ketchel followed up that win by beating light-heavyweight champion Jack O'Brien.

Ketchel continued to move up the boxing ladder taking on Jack Johnson for the heavyweight title on October 16,1909. He knocked the champion down before getting knocked out in the 12th-round of their title bout.

Ketchel was just one of many good fighters developed in Butte. A crowd favorite during the 1920s was Joe Simonich, called "the Butte Assassin." Simonich was considered the toughest, roughest welterweight of his day. He beat champion Pete Latzo in Chicago on March 10, 1927. Latzo forced Simonich to come in overweight so the bout could not be sanctioned as a title contest. Simonich later went on to floor former champion Mickey Walker, the only time Walker was ever knocked down in a prize fight. Simonich fought 106 times winning 76 bouts with many of his fights ending in no decision.

Another major attraction in the 1920s was "the Pride of Sacred Heart School," Namen "Dixie" LaHood, who began his career in 1923. A highlight for LaHood was in 1925 when he whipped Abe Goldstein shortly after Goldstein had lost his world bantamweight crown. LaHood also beat Vic King, the Australian bantamweight champion, in Seattle in 1925. LaHood declared himself the uncrowned bantamweight champion of the world. LaHood's career was cut short by hand injuries and he retired in 1933.

When gladiators like Ketchel, Simonich or LaHood fought, they packed the uptown theaters. At prize fights held at the race track facility south of town, thousands of fans would cram into the complex to watch.

"Butte was a very good fight town especially in the 1920s and '30s," former boxer Jimmy Shea said. "It was the best boxing town west of the Mississippi River except for maybe San Francisco. We saw boxers from places like Pennsylvania come out to Butte just to train. They got jobs working as bouncers in bars like the Board of Trade. So they were doing some training while working as well. It was a tough town and if you were looking for a fight you always could find one."

Former boxer George Thomas said, "It seemed like every parish had a boxing team in Butte. The CYO (Catholic Youth Organization) championships were a big event. You had to be a good boxer and a tough guy to win in that tournament. There were simply a lot of good boxers here in every section of this community."

CYO events were eventually replaced by numerous local boxing teams, coached by Wes Dowling, Bill Barry, Doc Jordan and others. During the 1950s, the Butte Boxing Club was the best in Montana.

The tradition established in the early days was carried on throughout the 20th century by numerous professional and amateur boxers in Butte. The list of prominent fighters includes Jack Cloward, Joe Antonietti, Eli Thomas, George Thomas, Sonny O'Day, Daniel McCarthy, John Masonovich, Leroy Romero, Mick O'Brien, Norman Ygnatowiz and Vince Dunfee.

Handball

The strong influence of the Irish led to another favorite pastime in Butte, handball. The game has roots in Ireland that go back many years. In 1884, the Gaelic Athletic Association in Ireland identified handball along with Gaelic football and hurling as three purely Irish games.

Handball found a place in Butte shortly after a flood of Irish immigrants came to the mining camp in the 1880s. When the Ancient Order of Hibernians built a hall on Main Street in Centerville in 1900, the facility included a two-wall handball court. The nearby Mountain Con Mine had handball courts built next to the miners' dressing rooms.

Handball is a difficult sport to learn. It fit in just right with the Irish in their tough times trying to make a living underground in the Butte mines. Only dedication to the sport and the perfection of the off-hand will lead to success on the handball court.

"Handball is such a tough game because you have to use every bone in your body," said Bill Lee. "Its the one sport I know where you always have to be injury-free to be competitive. You can not have a bad knee, twisted ankle or anything wrong with you and be able to compete. It's you against your opponent inside four walls with no teammates to help out. If you're not ready both mentally and physically you're going to get whipped.

"I've seen some great athletes in various sports who really struggled in handball. Its just such a difficult game to master."

The sport started to grow enormously after the Irish Christian Brothers opened a new high school for boys in 1924. The school included handball courts where the Christian Brothers could display their skills playing handball and providing discipline to students who got into trouble.

The courts at Boys' Central, an outdoor three-wall court behind the Immaculate Conception School Gymnasium and the Elks Court helped produce some of Montana's best handball players. The early pioneers included Ray Gallant, Joe McCarthy, Jack Cavanaugh, Jack Whelan and Bob Brady, who won the 1953 United States Handball Association Championship.

The sport continued to grow in the 1970s, 1980s and 1990s as stars emerged like Bill Peoples, Steve Stanisich, Mike McLaughlin, Tom Zderick, Butch Starin, Rick McLaughlin, Bill Lee, Justin Balkenbush and Tom Pomroy.

Peoples started to dominate play in the state when he captured the 1970 Montana Open Singles title, a championship he won 14 times. In addition, he won the 1973 and 1975 NCAA singles title. Bill also was a member along with his brother, Bob, and Butte teammate Tom Zderick on the 1973 University of Montana squad which captured the NCAA Championship.

As a way to encourage more youngsters to get involved in the sport. Butch Starin led an effort to build new three-wall outdoor courts near East Middle School. "We needed to do something about getting kids interested in the sport," Starin said. "My wife, Mary Kay, and I put $1,000 in a separate bank account and called it 'Courts for Kids.' It was the seed money we needed to get going. From there it was a matter of going out and raising the necessary capital to get the project done. It took us about four years to raise $17,000 to take care of all the materials needed for the courts.

"The key to getting the project done was all the volunteer support we got from various people and organizations. We were able to have the Anaconda Job Corps do all the masonry work for the court. Jim Blankenship and his construction company donated time and a lot of material to blacktop all around the courts. Tom Pomroy Sr. and his son, Tom, did all the carpenter work to construct the footings.

"Tom Morris, Jim Michelotti and so many others were also very helpful in getting things accomplished. Somehow all the work paid off and we got the courts finished."

The project was completed in 1995. The next generation of Butte handball players began refining their skills to carry on the city's tradition of producing great handball players.

"One thing I know the three-wall courts did was expose every kid attending East Middle School to handball," Starin said. "They know what the game is and through PE teacher Tom Pomroy they are starting to pick up the finer points of the game. Tom holds tournaments and the kids seem to enjoy the competition. We need that so handball can remain a Butte tradition for the future."

Veterans Day Race

One of Butte's most unique sporting events takes place every year on Veterans Day, November 11. Few people pause today when November 11 arrives. The time has little meaning to many who fail to remember the significance of the moment. The year was 1918 and the eleventh hour on the eleventh day of the eleventh month of that year marked the end of "the war to end all wars," when the armistice was signed bringing World War I to an end. Veterans Day was created to remember the war's end and honor all the men and women who served and died for their country.

Butte, like thousands of communities around the country, holds special memorial services every year on Veterans Day, but the city also commemorates the day with some hardy competition. On that eleventh hour on the eleventh day in the eleventh month, a cannon can be heard throughout the community, signaling the start of the annual Butte Veterans Day Race, easily the oldest race in Montana and ranking as one of the 25 longest-held races in the United States.

The foot race was started in 1934 by former World War I veterans C. Owen Smithers and Charlie MacAuliffe. Smithers operated a photography company in town while MacAuliffe served as the athletic director and coach at the Montana School of Mines. That first three-mile distance through the streets of uptown Butte drew 22 competitors with Butte High School student John Dougherty crossing the finish line first. Since that 1934 race, the event has been held annually every year except during World War II from 1942 to 1945.

The distance of the race has varied through the years from two miles up to five. For various reasons, the course and location have also changed nine different times through the years.

One thing that has never changed is the challenge of the race in the high mountain air of Butte, located 5,500 feet above sea level. Besides the high altitude, the weather is also a major factor in the race held in early November. The temperature has been as warm as 60 degrees above zero and as cold as well-below zero with snow and ice on the streets. Regardless of weather conditions, the race is held every November 11.

The 1985 men's winner Matt Rothermel, a competitor in the 1992 United States Olympic trials, called Butte's Veterans' Day Race, "the toughest race" he ever participated in during his running career. Rothermel won the event in temperatures hovering around zero with snow on the ground and slippery, icy streets to negotiate.

During the first few years, the race was open to all-comers. Following World War II, the event became a race only for high school runners, attracting hundreds of spectators to the start/finish line area at City Hall on Broadway Street.

Butte High runner Lester Sodja was the first athlete to win the race more than once taking top honors in 1947, 1948 and 1949. Other multiple high school boys winners included the 1951 and 1952 champion Chuck Smith of Butte Central, the 1957 and 1958 king Geoffrey Chance of Butte High, the 1959 and 1960 champion Stewart Stadler of Butte High, the 1963 and 1964 first place finisher Bob Davis of Butte High, the 1971, 1972 and 1973 champion Dave McDougal of Butte Central, and the 1974 and 1975 king Mike Houlihan of Butte High.

Bob Davis, the 1963 and 1964 winner, did not get to compete his senior year in 1965 because his family moved to Minnesota. Davis said, "The hardest thing about leaving Montana was missing that race my senior year. It was absolutely a fabulous event and the crowds at the finish line were just incredible."

The event started to change with the advent of the running boom of the 1970s. First, high school girls got a chance to participate in their own race. The first girls' winner was Rose McCormick of Butte Central in 1972. The next year a race was set up for junior high students with Tim Curry of West Junior High and Liza Merrifield of East Junior High winning the boys and girls competition.

The increasing interest in running during the 1970s eventually forced race officials to open the race to everyone. The first open Veterans Day race took place in 1976 with Bill Kearney, a Butte Central student, taking the men's trophy while Mary Whelan, another Butte Central athlete, captured the women's title.

Since the race was first opened to all competitors in 1976, some of the best men's and women's runners from Montana have come to Butte on Veterans' Day. The list of notable male runners who have competed and won include Jim Hatcher of Helena, Matt Rothermel of Bozeman, Stan Zezotarski of Helena, Bob Stingley of Great Falls, Patrick Judge of Helena, Tony Banovich of Billings, Tom Raunig of Missoula, and Ray Matteson of Butte. Some top female runners who have participated and won the race include Debbie Raunig of Missoula, Ann Danzer of Helena, Nicole Murray Hunt of Bozeman, plus Mary Dean and Susan Kaluza both of Butte.

The event took on international flavor in 1989 when the race had its first foreign winner, Ted Calchpole of Australia.

The most important development of opening the race to everyone has been the participation by families. It has become common to see numerous family members competing in the event. This has led to some families producing multiple winners. Debbie Raunig of Missoula won the women's race in 1985 and 1986 while her brother, Tom of Missoula, took top honors in 1987. The Stingley family of Great Falls had multiple winners with Jacque taking the gold in the 1987 race while her husband, Bob, won the men's competition in 1988. First cousins, Mary Whelan and Liza Merrifield, both of Butte, each won the women's open race more than once. Mary did it twice, while Liza took top honors four times.

The one family with the greatest tradition in the race is the Kearneys of Butte. The ties for this family go all the way back to the second annual event in 1935. James Kearney was edged at the finish line by Jack Pachico of Butte High. Two years later, in 1937, James Kearney won the race with his brother, Martin, placing third. Martin took top honors in the 1940 race. After participating in the 1941 and 1946 race, Martin Kearney became race co-coordinator with C. Owen Smithers, a position Martin held until his death in 1970. The Kearney tradition continued through Martin's six sons, Marty, Pat, Bob, Tim, Bill and Mike plus lone daughter, Linda who all competed in the race. Bill Kearney won the event twice in 1976 and 1980 while Linda won the kids 14-and under competition in 1978.

The next generation of Kearney winners began in the 1996 race when Bill's daughter, Natasha, won the 14-and under age group for girls in the 2 1/2 mile event.

At least one member of the Kearney family has either been an active participant or race coordinator for the annual event in 57 of the 60 Butte Veterans Day races missing only the 1934, 1936 and 1977 races.

The Butte Veterans' Day race has a special flavor for families and other participants. The Butte's Veterans Day race has provided a unique experience with a colorful history and tradition.

Butte Veterans Day Race

Men's Division

Year	Winner	School/town
1934	John Dougherty	Butte High
1935	Jack Pacheco	Butte High
1936	Andy Slatt	Montana Tech
	Henry Tyrand	Butte High
1937	Jim Kearney	Butte
1938	Richard Parent	Butte High
1939	Walter Taylor	Butte High
1940	Marty Kearney	Butte
1941	Joe Lynchehan	Butte Central
1942	No race due to World War II	
1943	No race due to World War II	
1944	No race due to World War II	
1945	No race due to World War II	
1946	Claire Renouard	Butte Central
1947	Charles Twardus	Butte High
1948	Lester Sodja	Butte High
1949	Lester Sodja	Butte High
1950	Lester Sodja	Butte High
1951	Chuck Smith	Butte Central
1952	Chuck Smith	Butte Central
1953	Ted Molthen	Butte High
1954	Wendell Glenn	Butte High
1955	Tom Monaghan	Butte Central
1956	Robert Morgan	Butte High
1957	Geoffrey Chance	Butte High
1958	Geoffrey Chance	Butte High
1959	Stewart Stadler	Butte High
1960	Stewart Stadler	Butte High
1961	Fred Martin	Anaconda High
1962	Don Brunell	Butte High
1963	Bob Davis	Butte High
1964	Bob Davis	Butte High
1965	Terry Eamon	Butte High
1966	Gary Keltz	Butte High
1967	Howard Johnson	Anaconda High
1968	Tim Finley	Butte Central
1969	Dave O'Brien	Anaconda High

1970	Dick Hofacker	Butte High	
	Men's Division		**Women's Winner**
1971	Dave McDougal	Butte Central	
1972	Dave McDougal	Butte Central	Rose McCormick Butte Central
1973	Dave McDougal	Butte Central	Rose McCormick Butte Central
1974	Mike Houlihan	Butte High	Mary Whelan Butte Central
1975	Mike Houlihan	Butte High	Liza Merrifield Butte High
1976	Bill Kearney	Butte Central	Mary Whelan Butte Central
1977	Ed Foley	Butte	Rose McCormick Butte
1978	Mike Houlihan	Butte	Laura Callahan Butte High
1979	Mike Houlihan	Butte	Deirdre Caughlan Butte
1980	Bill Kearney	Butte	Liza Merrifield Butte
1981	Stan Zezotarski	Helena	Charlene Clark Dillon
1982	Jim Hatcher	Helena	Ann Danzer Helena
1983	Tony Banovich	Butte	Debra Raunig Missoula
1984	Jim Hatcher	Butte	Ann Danzer Helena
1985	Matt Rothermel	Bozeman	Debra Raunig Missoula
1986	Jim Hatcher	Helena	Debra Raunig Missoula
1987	Tom Raunig	Bozeman	Jacque Stingley Great Falls
1988	Bob Stingley	Great Falls	Susan Kalusa Butte
1989	Ted Calchpole	Australia	Susan Kalusa Butte
1990	Ray Matteson	Butte	Mary Dean Butte
1991	Jim Hatcher	Helena	Susan Kalusa Butte

	Men's Division		Women's Winner
1992	Ray Matteson	Butte	Susan Kalusa Butte
1993	Ton Banovich	Billings	Susan Kalusa Butte
1994	Jim Hatcher	Helena	Susan Kalusa Butte
1995	Patrick Judge	Helena	Katie Green Butte High
1996	Patrick Judge	Helena	Nicole Murray Butte
1997	Jason Hamma	Missoula	Susan Kalusa Butte

	14 and under Boys' Winner		Girls' Winner
1973	Tim Curry	Butte	Liza Merrifield Butte
1974	Andy Kautzman	Butte	Liza Merrifield Butte
1975	Bud Williams	Butte	Jenny Pascoe Butte
1976	Chuck Richards	Butte	Laura Callahan Butte
1977	Scott Fitzpatrick	Butte	Tina Diebold Butte
1978	Dave Wulf	Butte	Linda Kearney Butte
1979	Bob Whelan	Butte	Kelly Peck Butte
1980	Bill Sage	Butte	Rhonda Ferkovich Butte
1981	Bill Sage	Butte	Rhonda Ferkovich Butte
1982	Jim O'Neill	Butte	Rhonda Ferkovich Butte
1983	Eric Allen	Butte	Shelly LeMere Butte
1984	Mark Comba	Butte	Heather LaFontaine Deer Lodge
1985	Don Foley	Butte	Heather LaFontaine Deer Lodge
1986	Mike Clark	Butte	Heather LaFontaine Deer Lodge

	14 and under Boys' Winner		Girls' Winner
1987	John Castner	Butte	Wendy Lutgen Helena
1988	Russ Erickson	Butte	Cassie Floras Great Falls
1989	Jeremy Hamma	Butte	Jennifer O'Connell Bozeman
1990	Bob Miller	Butte	Shyloh Steffan Hardin
1991	Jim Miller	Butte	Katrina Lovshin Butte
1992	Jim Miller	Butte	Trish Burby Butte
1993	Mitch Cunningham	Butte	no girl runners
1994	Mitch Cunningham	Butte	no girl runners
1995	Mitch Cunningham	Butte	no girl runners
1996	John Lovshin	Butte	Natasha Kearney Helena
1997	Jake Sorich	Butte	Mariah Heaney Anaconda

The City of Champions

The trait to work hard to compete for a goal developed by early day miners has carried over to athletics especially at the high school level. The two Butte schools, Butte High and Butte Central, have been very successful. The story can be told by the number of state championships the two schools have won. Butte has taken more state titles in football, boys' basketball and wrestling than any other community in Montana. In the 1980s, Butte was referred to as "The City of Champions" due its tremendous success on the athletic field in both boys and girls athletics.

The lessons of hard work have made athletics more than just a form of entertainment in the community. It is a reflection of the pride and determination established by the first immigrants. That reflection can be found in the epic battles on the gridiron during the Butte/Anaconda Independent Football League, the fast-paced action of the Butte Copper League, the tough wars inside a boxing ring and a handball court, the challenge of competing in the annual Butte Veterans Day Race and the many fire truck rides enjoyed by Butte high school teams after taking the state championship.

The Butte sports scene has its own unique colorful history just like mining, ethnic groups and neighborhoods.

REFERENCES USED IN CHAPTER SIX

The Butte Daily Post newspaper
The Montana Standard newspaper
The Montana Standard newspaper interview Birdie Aho 1933
1985 interview Matt Rothermel
BUTTE'S BIG GAME by Pat Kearney in 1989
The Butte Daily Post newspaper
The Montana Standard newspaper
Article by Janice Downey for the University of Montana published in 1991
BUTTE'S PRIDE - THE COLUMBIA GARDENS by Pat Kearney in 1994
1997 interview Bob Davis
1997 interview Jimmy Shea
1998 interview Ed Crnich
1998 interview Vince Downing
1998 interview Jim Hanley
1998 interview Bill Hawke
1998 interview Gus Janhunen
1998 interview Jim Kello
1998 interview Bill Lee
1998 interview Rich Navarro
1998 interview Torger Oaas
1998 interview George Paul
1998 interview Dan Peters
1998 interview John Shea
1998 interview Butch Starin
1998 interview Tony Stosich
1998 interview Jim Sullivan
1998 interview George Thomas
1998 interview Rudy Tomazich
1998 interview Glenn Welch
1998 interview Joe Zderick

Early day Butte
boxing match
photo courtesy
World Museum
of Mining

Three-wall
handball court
East Middle School
photo courtesy
Mike Kearney

Start of 1994 Veterans Day Race
photo courtesy Lou Kearney

Baseball at Columbia Gardens
photo courtesy Jerry Bugni, World Museum of Mining

Chapter Seven

Heritage

Butte is the town that put Montana on the map. Less than seven years after copper was extensively mined here, the territory of Montana became a part of the United States. The town's colorful history is unique. In recent times people have realized the precious jewel of Butte and have taken steps to capture its heritage, tradition and history.

World Museum of Mining

The early 1960s was a tough time for Butte citizens. The Berkeley Pit was totally changing the landscape of the community. Neighborhoods like the East Side, Parrot Flat, Meaderville, McQueen and East Butte were being destroyed for the betterment of mining.

During this time, the Butte Exchange Club began to discuss how to capture the history of mining in the community. They began actively developing the idea of a mining museum. In 1964, the organization crafted a set of by-laws for a group called the World Museum of Mining. The new group was chartered as a non-profit educational corporation.

By the spring of 1965, the Butte Exchange Club had worked out an agreement with The Anaconda Company to lease the 33-acre Orphan Girl Mine property west of the Montana Tech campus for $13 a year. The goal was the development of a World Museum of Mining.

Club member Rayworth Howe was the club member that was the push behind the project. In April 1965, he called for a work party on a Saturday afternoon to clean up the Orphan Girl starting the process for the World Museum of Mining. One of the first volunteers to arrive for the clean up party was Dave Johns. It ignited Johns into a life-long commitment to the Mining Museum.

"Ray Howe was really the leader in the early days of the project," said Johns. "He really got the ball rolling on the project. When we started, I don't think anyone knew exactly what we were going to do. We did draw up some plans, but none of the things from the initial concepts ever went into the World Museum of Mining. In fact, some early members of the board of directors wanted to develop a Disneyland theme, but that never made it past the talking stage."

Dick Skates said, "I think one of the things that made the World Museum of Mining a success was we always maintained that it would emphasize mining only. When tourists come through the gates, they see a bit of what mining was like back in the old days. Its something they don't see in many places."

The World Museum of Mining opened its gates to tourists for the first time on July 19, 1965. Since then thousands of visitors from around the world have toured the museum.

Work crews started to create an old mining camp with various offices and other buildings in a place they named "Hell Roarin Gulch."

"When we first got started, there were no funds in the bank," recalled Johns. "We tried to get mining companies to donate money, but with no success at all. Financially we really struggled in the beginning. Thanks to the little merchandise store we started in the old Orphan Girl hoist house and other funding sources we slowly started to get our feet on the ground.

"The only major company who gave us a hand at all in the beginning was the Montana Power Company. I had a connection as an operations head at the company which helped secure large equipment for the Mining Museum. When someone wanted to give us a donation, we were able to eventually move it to Butte through the help of MPC. Company workers hauled a donated item back to Butte after taking some MPC material to the site where the donated item was located. Rather than take an empty truck back to Butte, the donated item for the Mining Museum was placed aboard the MPC vehicle and hauled back to town.

"We got things like a switch locomotive from The Anaconda Company's Great Falls Smelter. It was amazing the amount of donated materials we received from around the state and country. This was done before antiques became popular. Thanks to the Montana Power it made the development of the Mining Museum a reality in a few short years."

There were other firms besides the Montana Power Company that helped haul things to the site. Roberts' Rocky Mountain Equipment through the help of its owner, Joe Roberts, did transport some old buildings to the Mining Museum.

Roger Pierce, a graduate student from Montana Tech, paid for the transportation of the St. Helena's Catholic Church from Meaderville to the Mining Museum. Another church from Brown's Gulch also found a new home at the tourist site. The Anaconda Company donated homes from neighborhoods sections cleared out for its Berkeley Pit. The houses were hauled to the site and made into new artifacts for tourist viewing.

"Besides St. Helena's Church, we also got some things left behind in the Meaderville homes," said Ed Bartoletti, an early president of the World Museum of Mining. "There were a number of items people simply could not haul when they left Meaderville that had some value at the Mining Museum.

"The boarding houses in Finn Town were also filled with some valuable stuff left behind by tenants. We hauled a lot of truck loads of antiques up to the Mining Museum from Finn Town.

"Probably the most interesting place to go through was at the vacated Hibernia Hall in Centerville. There were old flags, guns, books, uniforms, statues and other things left behind by the Hibernians. We got a beautiful statue of the Irish writer, Robert Emmett. There was also a very interesting letter from Ireland left behind addressed to Montana Senator Thomas Walsh asking for assistance to help free the people in Ireland from the English."

John Shea said, "Its nice that they saved some of the things in the Hibernia Hall. Unfortunately, one of the most valuable aspects at both the Hibernia and Sons of St. George's Halls were the bricks. Both buildings had turn of the century bricks that were cleaned and shipped to Georgia for use in building new homes."

Other key early contributors to the Mining Museum were Clay and Tellie Moore of Helena. They had collected lots of old mining relics. The couple donated more than 25 truck loads of material to the World Museum of Mining.

Even with all the donated material and buildings it took long hours with a volunteer labor of love to make the World Museum of Mining a place to remember Butte's past.

"When we started building things, there was no money," recalled Johns. " I remember straightening out nails during the week nights so I could take them on Saturday up to the Mining Museum to construct something.

"We never did things without having a plan first. I built a scale-model at home of every building we constructed. I always got the approval of the board of directors before starting a project. Every plan had the board's blessing before we ever put a hammer in our hands."

Skates remembered, "We had to recycle more stuff than you can image. We stripped wood one time out of the old Hennessy's Building so we could use it up at the Mining Museum. Going out and scrounging was the only way we could construct things at the Mining Museum because we had very little money."

Through the years there were buildings constructed like a caretakers house, blacksmith shop, drug store, assay office, school, general store, optometrist's office, saloon, barber shop, post office, Hibernia Lodge, Chinese laundry, herb shop, tobacco shop, brothel house, photographer's shop, Knights of Pythais Hall, union hall, bank and so many other structures in the newly created town of Hell Roaring Gulch.

"I really liked the type of work we did up at the Mining Museum," said Skates. "You had to do a little bit of everything from being a carpenter to some electrical work. It was really satisfying once you completed a new project."

Besides all the buildings, a group of volunteers was formed to recapture and preserve old photographs of Butte.

"When we started, there were pictures scattered all over the place," said Al Hooper. "We had them laying on the floor, on top of cabinets, on tables and chairs. It was a real mess. Some were city photos while others were from the county. There was nothing in order and in many cases little information about individual photos. I thought it would take maybe six months to straighten out. Well, it actually took years because the number of photos we put in order only got larger as we went along."

Hooper's group cataloged over 7,000 Butte photographs. The photos were put in albums. The subject producing the most interest was the Columbia Gardens which filled up six albums of photos.

The general public saw the fruits of the labor put in by Hooper's group. They developed a slide show on various subjects which has been presented to numerous groups.

"You must have an interest in preservation to do the work the volunteers accomplished at the World Museum of Mining," Hooper said. "Its long, volunteer hours with your only pay check coming in the form of simply doing a good job."

Johns reflected, "The development of the World Museum of Mining is one of the most satisfying things I ever did. I have many tourists come up to me and comment on how the World Museum of Mining is so much superior to Virginia and Nevada City. Its an emotional satisfaction I receive through a comment like that one which keeps my enthusiasm up for continuing to make the World Museum of Mining a special place."

Skates recalled, "I remember one time a guy was watching us build some project at the mining museum. He told us we should get a job at Disneyland or the Lagoon because they were always looking for creative workers like we had at the mining museum."

One drawback to the success of the World Museum of Mining it is the lack of local people who visit the site. Figures indicate only 30 percent of the annual 40,000 visitors to Hell Roarin Gulch come from the community.

"Its really a shame that more Butte people have not visited the museum," said Skates. "It gives you a sense of what the old mining town was like. It is a treasure that more Butte people need to be aware of in the future."

Johns said, "I am very proud of everything we have done at the World

Museum of Mining. We have tried to recapture an era of the past that may not be Butte, but at least it gives you a feeling of what it might have been like. I believe its important especially for kids to know where the roots of their city are located in the glorious history of mining."

As the years pass the World Museum of Mining has become more of a treasure. Financially the Mining Museum has gone from no money to a healthy bank account and a full-time manager which is good news. It means the World Museum of Mining will continue to have a long, bright future displaying a piece of Butte's heritage, mining.

Butte Archives

The World Museum of Mining was started as a way to preserve mining heritage. A similar effort came years later to save important documents and records through the creation of the Butte Archives.

The birth of the Archives began with the death of the city government in 1977. When the city and county governments consolidated into one all the city officials moved from City Hall on Broadway Street to the County Courthouse on Granite Street.

All the city records were left in the vacated City Hall, including all birth dates stretching back to 1906 and death certificates back to 1901. A number of people went inside the old City Hall and took records without permission. A local group spearheaded by Bill Walker was formed to try to preserve all the paper work before it was taken away by residents or worse hauled out to the dump.

During the same time as consolidation, the new government was constructing a new public safety building for the police and fire departments on Montana Street. When the job was completed and both departments moved, Walker's local group asked local leaders for the now vacated fire station building on Quartz Street as a new home for the Archives.

Bill Walker was able to convince Butte Silver Bow Chief Executive Don Peoples that it was worth a try to establish Montana's first city archives. Peoples agreed to allow the local group to establish the Butte Archives. He also budgeted $5,000 a year for the project.

The Butte Archives opened its doors to the public for the first time in September 1979. Walker served as the first director. Since then, the center has seen a number of people hold the title including Mary Murphy, Chris Daly, John Hughes, Cathy O'Connor, Sara McClernan and Ellen Crain.

"The Butte Archives really became a focal point for people to save records," said John Hughes. "When people cleaned out an attic after grandma died, they always seemed to find old records and other things of interest. The establishment of the Butte Archives gave them to a place to send the documents knowing that they'd be preserved.

"I think the key group who got behind the Archives were the unions. They provided records and more importantly money to help the Archives grow as a center. The unions were able to help start the Butte Labor History Project which has been critical in helping preserve some of the key historical union sites and activities in the Uptown area."

In addition to the unions, the Butte Archives has been able to grow by acquiring key documents from around the world. An example is acquiring copies of the *Butte Independent* newspaper that was being stored at a Dublin, Ireland, library. The paper was published by James Mulcahy for the Butte Irish community from 1910 to 1931. Mulcahy shut down the press and went back to his native Ireland in 1931. He took with him copies of his newspaper.

Since its humble beginnings in 1979, the Butte Archives has continued to grow. The visitor counts topped 4,000 for the first time in 1996. Local studies indicate that 52 per cent of the people who visit the Archives are from out-of-state. Of this group, 25 per cent indicate their primary stop in their Montana stay was the Butte Archives, They wanted to find out more about their family genealogy or more about the history of Butte which later could be used in a research paper or the publication of a book.

"Each year we average helping out 16 different publication projects," said Ellen Crain, Butte Archives director. "We help provide information for magazine articles, films and books. The Butte Archives is such a tremendous resource for acquiring solid information. Since opening back in 1979, we have assisted people from all over the world with their various projects on Butte."

The World Museum of Mining and the Butte Archives have assured future generations that the colorful history of Butte will be available.

REFERENCES USED IN CHAPTER SEVEN

Hell Roarin Gulch Gazette published Summer 1996
The Montana Standard newspaper
1996 interview Ed Bartoletti
1997 interview John Hughes
1998 interview Ellen Crain
1998 interview Al Hooper
1998 interview Dave Johns
1998 interview John Shea
1998 interview Dick Skates

World Museum of Mining aerial view
photo courtesy World Museum of Mining

World Museum of Mining
photo courtesy Pat Kearney

World Museum of Mining
photo courtesy Pat Kearney

Looking for information at the Butte Archives
photo courtesy Pat Kearney

CHAPTER EIGHT

The City of Can Do

Butte, Montana is a town with a different spirit. The spirit can be traced back to the early mining days where one mistake could be fatal. It could mean the loss of your husband, son or brother. The Butte people always lived on the edge of disaster.

Despite the threat of danger, the people have always had a belief that anything could be overcome if enough hard work and determination were put to productive use. Such was the case late in the 20th century when Butte was beset by problem after problem. Rather than give up, or leave town, the people blended into one. The result was something few people thought could be achieved, a "Can Do" attitude leading to national recognition.

Industrial Park

Since the first settlers came to Butte in the 1860s mining was the principal form of employment. Anaconda Company officials told residents numerous times that its mining operations at the Berkeley Pit could not go on forever. In the 1960s, city fathers realized Butte needed to diversify its economy in order to survive. It was one reason why the Industrial Park was created south of town on Basin Creek Road.

The Industrial Park was the seed for other development activities. Through the help of the federally subsidized Model Cities' program, Butte was able to acquire seed money to purchase the 250-acre Industrial Park site.

The first major industry to call the Industrial Park its home was the Port of Butte. In 1983, it took the name the Port of Montana. The facility was constructed for $750,000 and put into operation in 1972.

The 55,000-square foot warehouse was built at the urging of officials from the Port of Seattle. They were having trouble with a lack of space and labor unions in the early 1970s. Despite the fact that Butte was over 00 miles inland from the Pacific Ocean, some felt the concept could work for two reasons.

The first key point was Butte's location at the intersection of two interstate highway systems, I-15 going north and south plus I-90 traveling east and west. The two highways connected at Silver Bow just a few miles northwest of Butte.

The second factor was the Union Pacific rail lines. The UP system came north to Silver Bow. Union Pacific provided an alternative for rail shipping in Montana.

Large containers taken off ships in Seattle could be put on trucks and hauled immediately to Butte for storage. Materials also could be shipped by rail to Butte and then taken either west to Seattle or south to California for shipping overseas.

The Port of Montana, the first inland port of its kind in the United States, provided Butte with an opportunity to develop international trade from its own backyard. Through the years, the Port of Montana became a temporary home for Japanese Kawasaki motorcycles, Indonesian rubber, Japanese wire, lumber, plywood, and medical supplies.

The development of the Port of Montana led to a second transportation project in 1985. The Scoular Grain Company of Omaha, Nebraska, built a $2.6 million grain terminal at the end of the Union Pacific rail lines at Silver Bow. A major chunk of the construction money, $1.8 million came through federal money.

The Scoular Grain Company was able to utilize the UP lines. It gave Montana grain producers an alternative to shipping their product through the monopoly Burlington Northern had on rail transportation in Montana. In 1980, Burlington Northern gained a major advantage in the state when the Milwaukee Railroad discontinued their operations. It forced grain operators with only one choice to haul their commodity by rail, Burlington Northern.

The Scoular Grain Terminal proved popular with many state grain producers. During its first year of operation, the new Scoular facility handled over three-million bushels of wheat far more than terminal officials had estimated they'd handle.

The grain terminal was followed up by a $900,000 Lumber Transit Loading Center built within a half-mile of the Scoular Grain Plant. The transportation hub allowed companies a new option to ship timber by rail on the Union Pacific rail system.

The success of the Port of Montana, Scoular Grain and the Lumber Transit Center did exactly what Industrial Park officials had hoped for when they formed their board of directors which was creating jobs outside of the mining industry.

Another successful project at the Industrial Park followed the Port of Montana. In 1974, two years after the Port went into business, the federal government invested over $50 million in a component development integration test plant. It was called the MHD test facility which stands for magnetohydrodynamics. The plant was used for a number of years as a test site for the development of a cleaner way to burn coal.

In 1996, the site was turned over by the Department of Energy to a private corporation, Mountain States Energy. The plant was converted to serve other purposes. MSE developed a number of clean up programs like the first National Mine Water Pilot Program. Its research mode turned from cleaner coal to a cleaner environment through experimental programs geared to clean up the mine waste in Butte.

The MHD plant led to other types of employment like NCAT, the National Center for Appropriate Technology in 1976. NCAT, under the direction of the Department of Energy, was designed to protect natural resources, assist inventors and help low income people with technical information to meet or beat rising energy costs. Between 1978 to 1981, NCAT printed 13 different consumer-oriented publications on how to do things for energy efficiency. Later, NCAT expanded its role into agriculture, providing technical assistant for rural areas of the country.

The economic developments of the Port of Montana, MHD Test Plant, NCAT, and other things came when Butte was suffering through some very difficult times. The main component of Butte that was crumbling was the Uptown business district.

Uptown Nightmare and Rebirth

The 1970s was a decade that everyone would like to forget when it comes to Uptown Butte. The Butte Plaza Mall had just been opened prior to the start of the decade. A number of the Uptown district's customers were now heading south for their shopping needs.

The Anaconda Company announced plans in 1972 to mine in the Uptown business district. They said it would invest $18.5 million in the mining plan while laying off 643 workers in their force.

If that was not enough bad news another enemy reared its ugly head during the decade which the district had no control over, fire.

There had been numerous blazes in the Uptown district ever since the first structures were created in the 1870s. The Symons' Store was damaged by fire on September 24, 1905 with 60 businesses lost and over $1 million in damage. The O'Rourke Block on Main Street went up in smoke on July 30, 1912, with 16 businesses being impacted by the inferno. A couple of months later, on September 1, 1912, the Thomas Block on Park Street was destroyed with 14 business establishments being affected. The Butte Hotel went up in smoke on August 9, 1954, with an estimated damage listed at $1 million. The inferno left 125 people homeless.

A hundred years after the first flames appeared in Uptown the ten-year period of the 1970s did more to shape the district than the previous 90 years combined. During the decade, a number of fires gutted the business district of much of its charm and turned some elegant architecture into a series of vacant parking lots.

The destruction actually began shortly before the start of the 1970s. On June 24, 1969, a blaze took out the Heidelberg Inn and Al's Photo Shop on the corner of Broadway and Main Streets.

A year later, on November 8, 1970, the Moxom Cafe on Broadway Street went up in smoke. A year later, the Currie Tire plant at 121 South Montana Street was destroyed by flames. Three months later, on February 9, 1972, the vacant Lennox Hotel across from the Butte Silver Bow Courthouse was engulfed in flames. Less than three weeks later, on February 28, 1972, the JC Penney's store was destroyed by an arson fire started with an explosion inside the store. It was the largest fire the Uptown had experienced. The estimated damage of the JC Penney's blaze was put at $2.9 million.

The JC Penney's fire destroyed not only the store, but half a block of city buildings on either side of the store's location at the corner of Park and Dakota Streets. When the smoke had cleared, 12 businesses were impacted by the inferno.

Firefighters were plagued by extremely cold temperatures during their efforts to control the blaze. Two different grand juries were established to investigate the arson blaze, but no indictments were ever returned.

"I firmly believe the JC Penney fire was set," said George Thomas, the owner of Thomas' Family Apparel located across the street from JC Penney's. "There was a large explosion inside the store before the flames. All the evidence points to arson.

"JC Penney's was simply an awful fire. I spent the entire night across the street at my store just trying to protect it from the flames. All the windows on my store front cracked because of the heat. I had to seal the windows to try and keep the smoke out."

Less than a year and a half after the JC Penney's fire, another blaze less than two blocks away destroyed another large portion of the district. On July 28, 1973, a fire ripped through the Medical Arts Building on the corner of Park and Main Streets. Better than 10,000 spectators watched the inferno completely destroy the building causing over $2.5 million worth of damage. There were 35 different businesses and stores inside the building that were displaced by the flames.

"The heat generated from the Medical Arts Fire was so intense I thought it would jump across the street and wipe out our store," said Chuck Richards, owner of Richards & Rochele's Mens' Store. "The windows in our store front cracked because of the heat. We had to gather some things and rush out the back entrance to get away from the blaze."

The JC Penney's and Medical Arts fires left two large vacant holes in the central core of the Butte business district. Except for a new office building on the corner of Park and Dakota Streets the two large holes remain vacant parking lots.

Less than 18 months after the Medical Arts blaze, another fire erupted on October 14, 1974. This time the blaze was across the street sandwiched between the JC Penney's and Medical Arts locations. Destroyed were four Butte businesses the Diana Shop, Gamers' Shoes, Gene's Furs and Copper City Chevrolet.

Less than a year later, juveniles started a fire in the Pennsylvania Building at 44 West Park Street. The blaze on August 20, 1975, left more people without a business to run and left Butte with another gapping hole in the center of the business district. The hole was replaced by Mural Park and a new office building constructed by the New York Life Insurance Company.

Historical architectural lovers felt a loss on October 21, 1978, when the Silver Bow Block and the Inter Mountain Building on Granite Street, across from *The Montana Standard* newspaper building, were destroyed by fire.

The blaze was triggered by an electrical malfunction in the new Mother Lode restaurant.

Richards recalled, "It seemed like every time you turned around their was another fire. It was an awful time for the area."

By the end of the 1970s, the Uptown district had been brought to its knees by the mercy of flames. There were 16 different major fires during the short ten-year period.

The Uptown was crippled and could no longer consider itself the economic hub of the city.

The decade closed on an even further sad note when officials from the Hennessy's Store announced in July 1979 that they were closing its Uptown store in February 1980. It meant the loss of 100 jobs, a $1 million dollar annual payroll and the elimination of the Uptown's last large department store.

The uptown was struggling for survival; however, long before the spirit of "Can Do" arrived and long before the flames of the 1970s fires, officials had taken steps to preserve the area. In 1962, the United States Secretary of Interior designated Butte as a national historic landmark above Front Street, east to the Berkeley Pit, north to Walkerville and west to Montana Tech.

The area of the historic district is larger than similar designations in American cities like Boston, Philadelphia and New York City. The historical region is rivaled only in land-mass by Lowell, Massachusetts, a preserved prototype of 1800 Northeast industrial center.

Following a decade of fires, the Butte Silver Bow government created the Urban Revitalization Board in 1979.

The mission of the group was to promote, renovate and rescue historic buildings in the area through a tax increment fund. When improvements were made in the area to a building, the extra taxes paid on the improvements went back into the district to help renovate other sections of the area.

In 1981, the Butte Historical Society started a five-year study to inventory each building inside the historical landmark district. It led to the creation of a Butte Silver Bow Historic Preservation Officer in 1984. This allowed one person to gather information and photograph each building.

By 1983, the URA had developed enough of a backing that it could give business owners who restored their buildings a 50 percent matching grant. The extra funds allowed building owners the push they needed to refurbish their dwellings.

In a few short years, the facades for the Curtis Music Hall, M & M Cigar Store, Exer-dance Building, Christie's Furniture, Decorating Etc., Butte Booksellers and the Thomas Block were all completely redone. A majority of the work was done through Fred Quivik of Renewable Technologies and the architectural firm of Walter and Steve Hinick.

"The URA provided the shot in the arm that the Uptown district needed," said Chuck Richards, a store owner. "It provided the district with hope when it looked like all hope was lost for the future of the area."

One of the first new companies calling Uptown Butte home was the Butte Business Development Center. It was housed in the old Boys' Central High School building. The Butte Business Development Center was the home of Montana's first municipally operated incubators. The idea behind an incubator was to help small businesses grow while proving common services like secretarial help and management expertise.

In 1986, the Butte Business Development Center was opened. In its first two years, the center helped eleven new businesses get off the ground creating 55 new jobs. The incubator was creating new opportunities as the city started to turn the corner on economic development.

Our Lady of the Rockies

Bob O'Bill was a worker for Atlantic Richfield in its massive Berkeley Pit. Like the Uptown business district the 1970s had not been overly kind to O'Bill. His wife, Joyce, had a serious health problem. She was rushed to St. James Community Hospital in Butte shortly after Christmas in December 1979.

Once at the hospital, O'Bill was told by doctors that his wife needed surgery in the morning. When O'Bill returned home, he began praying that his wife would be okay. He thought about what a fellow worker, Danny Ramierez, had told him about Our Lady of Guadeloupe, the patron saint of Mexico. O'Bill prayed to Our Lady of Guadeloupe and promised her if his wife could be spared in tomorrow's operation that he'd build a statue devoted to her in the mountains overlooking Butte.

Joyce O'Bill made it through the operation. Once home, Bob O'Bill told his wife about the promise he made to build a statue to Our Lady of Guadeloupe. Joyce thought the idea was far-fetched so did some of the workers that O'Bill approached at work. Despite their concerns, some of the men agreed to give O'Bill a hand to work on his promise.

In the spring of 1980, O'Bill began his quest to build a statue in the mountains. First, a site had to be selected. O'Bill wanted to put the statue on top of the East Ridge of the Rocky Mountains just east of Butte on the Continental Divide at a place called Saddle Rock. The site looked straight down on the city.

It took O'Bill over a year to gain access to the land and receive the necessary permission from federal agencies and local land owners to go ahead with his project.

In the spring of 1981, O'Bill went to the manager of ARCO's Berkeley Pit operations, Frank Gardner, and asked to borrow some equipment to construct a road to the statue location. Gardner agreed to give O'Bill and his small crew of workers some gear to start the process of building a road up the side of a mountain.

Next O'Bill went to Butte businessman, Joe Roberts. Roberts had operated a successful equipment shop near O'Bill's home for years. O'Bill got Roberts to agree to help supply more equipment and manpower for the road project.

Roberts called a group of business people together on the night of April 19, 1981, at his office. Roberts and fellow Butte businessman, Bob Koprivica, both agreed to give the project $1,000 each to start the work.

During the next four months, O'Bill and his crew of Mike Cerise, Bob O'Connor, Al Beavis and Bill Fisher began the long process of constructing a road. Beavis was the trigger man with years of experience in the use of dynamite. He had worked with explosives inside the Berkeley Pit. O'Connor and Cerise had a background in operating a bulldozer to help plow the road. O'Bill and Fisher did the labor chores for building the road.

In August 1981, the road to the site was completed. Roberts and O'Bill had a press tour of the site. The immediate reaction to the project was not overwhelming with Roberts and O'Bill being heavily criticized for months in the local *The Montana Standard* newspaper for a project now called "Our Lady of the Rockies."

O'Bill tried to stay away from the controversy and stuck to construction work. Joe Roberts had to deal with the critics and also try to raise money. Roberts had a local metal sculptor, John Mazzola, design a potential sample statue. This did help raise some money. Roberts wanted some changes made for the larger statue on top of the mountain. Roberts and Mazzola could never agree on a final design so Roberts turned his attention elsewhere for a statue concept.

He eventually went to one of his employees, Leroy Lee, and asked him if he could build a statue. At first Lee balked at the idea because their were no plans or designs for the statue. Bob O'Bill left a small nine-inch statue with Lee in his shop. After examining the statue for a few weeks, Leroy Lee felt he might be able to build a statue out of the small model.

Lee began molding the statue out of iron steel that Roberts had picked up at various mine sites. Along with the help primarily of Ron Hughes and Vic Duran he began to construct a hand for the statue.

Once Lee completed the hand, he became convinced that a statue could be built. By December 1983, Lee and his co-workers had constructed a large face. By the next spring, a complete head and shoulders were done.

As the statue started to take shape more and more financial support arrived at the door of Joe Roberts. One gentlemen who stopped at the shop to congratulate Roberts and his crew was Warren Nelson of Nevada. Nelson had close ties with Nevada's Senator Paul Laxalt. This relationship proved to be a critical component for the completion of Our Lady of the Rockies.

While Joe Roberts raised money and support, workers continued to develop a statue site on top of the East Ridge. The road was just the beginning of the hard work facing the men on the summit. A flat platform area needed to be developed on top of the mountain ridge which was covered with solid granite rock. It took workers three years to blast away the rock.

Through the help of a local retired engineer from The Anaconda Company, Laurin Riehl, a platform design was built and completed on the mountaintop in September 1985. Riehl developed a circular platform for the statue which ensured stability once the steel structure was put into place.

One of the few things the entire work force had little control over was the transportation of the statue to the site. Through the help of local

Butte native, Joe Monahan, who was working in Washington DC, the process of obtaining a helicopter to transport the various pieces of the statue from the Roberts' Rocky Mountain Equipment Yard to the East Ridge had begun.

Monahan went through various folks at the Department of Defense trying to obtain a helicopter. Meanwhile, Warren Nelson from Nevada talked to Senator Paul Laxalt about the project. He wanted Laxalt to visit his close friend, President Ronald Reagan, about participating in the statue lift. The President was for the project as were some key members of both the Senate and House. Lawmakers who pushed for the airlift included Arizona Senator Barry Goldwater, Montana Senator John Melcher, Nevada Senator Paul Laxalt, and Montana Congressmen Pat Williams. Through their pressure on the Department of Defense, a Sikorsky Skycrane helicopter and crew from the Nevada Air National Guard were made available to the statue coordinators.

On December 17, 1985, the airlift of Our Lady of the Rockies statue began from the yard at Roberts' Rocky Mountain Equipment. The crew from the Nevada Air National Guard was assigned to transport the various pieces to the top of the mountain. The crew consisted of Captain Marc Comstock the pilot, Chief Warrant Officer Bruce Britton the co-pilot, Staff Sergeant Tim Bortner the flight engineer and hoist operator, Chief Warrant Officer Robert Colemen a ground coordinator, Staff Sergeant Steve Petersen a ground coordinator and Staff Sergeant Hank St. Clair a ground coordinator.

The airlift began at 11 on the morning of December 17, 1985. The airlift was broadcast live on local radio station KBOW-AM by News Director, Connie Kenney. When Kenney reported that the airlift was about to take place, many Butte citizens rushed from their homes, office buildings and school classrooms to watch. Hundreds of people lined up outside the gates of the equipment yard next to the Montana street exit of the interstate highway looking at the Sikorsky Skycrane helicopter in action.

The first day of the airlift saw the skirting and the base piece for the statue being hauled to the mountaintop. The lone hold up during the day was the weather. A dense fog on the mountain kept the crew grounded most of the day. They waited for the area to clear so the base section of the statue could be brought to the mountainside.

The second day of the airlift found the winds howling up the side of the mountain at better than 35 knots. It made the process of putting the second piece of the statue at its new home extremely difficult. The helicopter crew had to lower the second section down on the mountaintop platform. From there workers used a crane to put the second piece into place.

The third section weighed over 19,000 pounds. It was the largest piece of weight that Comstock and his crew had ever tried to lift. They got the piece off the ground and to the mountaintop platform without any trouble at all.

When the third day of the airlift arrived everything started out peacefully with the winds calm on the mountaintop. The ironworkers on the summit rejoiced because they felt a lack of wind helped make their job much easier. No wind on the mountain actually made putting the next section into place even more difficult.

When the helicopter crew arrived with the fourth section there was little or no wind on top of the mountain. The Sikorsky Skycrane crew needed the lift provided by the wind to help stabilize the craft so the ironworkers could grab hold of the tag lines to put the section into place. The lack of wind forced the statue piece to spin as the helicopter had to use even more power to stay afloat. The Sikorsky Skycrane chopper eventually lost power as it hovered right above the ironworkers. The iron section came down and hit on the inside of the statue as the ironworkers scattered trying to avoid being clipped by the steel structure. Through a miracle, no one inside the statue was injured.

The momentum of the chopper forced the fourth section to come out from inside the statue as the Sikorsky Skycrane crew battled the helicopter down the mountainside with no power. The crew regained control of their aircraft and took it down near the airport where the steel piece was rested on a sandpile.

Later in the afternoon, when the winds picked up the helicopter crew decided to try again to move the fourth section. This time the air transport went smoothly with the section being put into place with little trouble.

The next day was Friday, December 20, 1985. It was day four of the airlift. After a mechanical problem developed on the aircraft during the transport of the fifth section of the statue, a delay took place while the helicopter was repaired. Once finished, the fifth section was easily put into place.

Later in the day, the Sikorsky Skycrane helicopter and its crew took the final piece, the head section of the statue, to its new home on top of the East Ridge. The final piece went in easily shortly after 4 P.M. on December 20, 1985. The hook was released and Our Lady of the Rockies statue was in place.

The promise Bob O'Bill made six years before had come true. The miracle of building a 90-foot, 60-ton statue had been finished. It was a project that united the entire town and created a "Can Do" attitude in Butte.

"The magnitude of completing the Lady of the Rockies had a tremendous impact not only on Butte, but on everyone who even heard about the project," said Don Peoples. "I was attending a Montana League of Cities and Towns meeting in Billings the day the statue was finished. I kept calling home to see if the airlift was completed. When I finally got news it was finished, I announced it at the meeting. Every person in the room got up and starting clapping.

"After the meeting, I caught a plane ride to Helena where my son, Donny, was attending college. We drove back to Butte together and I never will forget coming down that mountain and seeing Our Lady of the Rockies for the first time. It was one of the best feelings I ever had as a person. It gave the town a degree of hope that we could survive the mining closure and go on to new and better things."

No single project had ever captivated Butte like Our Lady of the Rockies. A community befuddled by problems like high unemployment at 15 percent, a lack of construction, a mangled Uptown business district and an uncertain future now seemed to have a renewed hope. It was a monumental turning point for a community that seemed to have so very little going for it.

A New Home

A few months before the airlift of Our Lady of the Rockies Butte native Fritz Daily and his son, Fritz, took a ride on their motor bikes south of town near the Beef Trail Ski Area. It was here that the proposed Columbia Gardens II project had been launched. The project ran into financial trouble in the late 1970s and never was completed.

Columbia Gardens II was the result of the Columbia Gardens amusement park east of Butte being shut down by The Anaconda Company in 1973. The Company wanted to use the land for a proposed mine which was in operation for less than two years.

The Columbia Gardens had been a mainstay for Butte families for the 74 years of its existence. It was a wonderful place for kids who could take an adventure on the amusement rides like the roller coaster, the carousel and the bi-planes or participate in the playground area with some of the most unique playground equipment in the country. All that was gone in September 1973.

The Anaconda Company had donated some money toward the Columbia Gardens II plan, but it was not enough to finish the project. The playground equipment and some of the other landmarks were moved to the proposed new park. The gear was put into place, but when the money ran out for construction the equipment was left to rust away.

This was the site that Fritz Daily and his son encountered in May 1985. The two entered the park area and saw rusty equipment in terrible shape. The elderly Daily could not believe how bad a shape the equipment was as he tried to explain to his son how elegant this gear once was when located east of Butte.

At the insistence of his son Fritz Daily wrote an article to the Reader's Speak section of *The Montana Standard* newspaper which was published on May 15, 1985.

Recently my son and I took a motorcycle ride south of Butte. We rode to the top of the hill that overlooked some of the old Colum bia Gardens' equipment. I reminisced with my son about some of the old equipment and some of the great times that my family and friends had at theGardens. He suggested that we ride down and look at theequipment. As we rode around, I was amazed to find thata lot of the equipment was still in good condition. I wasalso astonished and sick to see that a lot of the equipment was disinte grating by weather. It broke my heart to see at least 50 of the old park benches and three roller coaster cars simply destroyed due to weather. As we talked Fritzie said to me, " Dad, why don't we do something about this?" He said, " You know I love Butte and want to live here just like you."I said, " I think the best thing to do is let the people of Butte know the equipment is there and what is happening to it." Well people, the equipment is there and we need to do something about it before everything is destroyed. I have heard that Anaconda donated $750,000 to save the equipment. I have heard the equipment is owned by several different groups of people. That's all history. Its time for whoever owns the equip ment to make it available to the children of Butte. In my opinion, the equipment should be moved to Stodden Park or some other parks in Butte. Anyone who has any say about this equipment should step forward and show Butte your generosity. To leave this equipment to deteriorate any further without the children us ing it is one of the greatest tragedies in the history of Butte-Silver Bow.

Fritz Daily
1057 West Steel

Following his article, Daily went to see Butte Silver Bow Chief Executive Don Peoples. He was told by Peoples that a number of attempts had been made by his office to move the equipment into town. Peoples indicated that the Butte Junior League had just begun working with the Butte Ski Club, owners of the equipment, to try and find a more productive use for the gear.

Peoples felt the best way to handle the situation was to form a task force. The task force committee included Fritz Daily as chairmen, Madeline Daniel and Robbie Taylor of the Butte Junior League, Don Peoples, Rick Griffith and Jim McCarthy from Butte Silver Bow, Roger Baker and Paul McHugh from the Butte Ski Club, Butte legislator Joe Quilici, Butte Silver Bow Council of Commissioner Dale Dart, plus private citizens Ray Reynolds, Oakie O'Connor, John Mazzola, Pete Oren and Georgia Bryne.

At first the Butte Ski Club balked at any attempt to move the Columbia Gardens playground equipment out of its backyard at the Beef Trail. The Butte Ski Club had spent a number of years trying to maintain the gear with no funds coming from any entity except its own Club. It had cost the Ski Club plenty of money to maintain the equipment.

When the task force finally sat down with the entire Butte Ski Club membership on August 2, 1985, some Club members had prepared a statement which related their feelings toward the gear and their role in its upkeep.

> "*In 1973, The Anaconda Company stated that they planned* to destroy the Columbia Gardens. The citizens of Butte formed a committee called, 'Save the Gardens'. The Anaconda Company made a settlement payment of about $550,000 in bonds to the committee. Through an agreement with The Anaconda Com pany the Gardens ran for one more year. The cost of $125,000 for the 1973 operation came out of the settlement made by The Anaconda Company. At that point, The Anaconda Company and the Save the Gardens committee entered into a contract in which the Butte Ski Club donated 70 acres of their land at the Beef Trail Ski Area to the Gardens' project with the stipulation that if it did not materialize, or was not running in three years, the land and equipment would become the property of the Butte Ski Club."Allen McKenzie kept all accounting records for the Columbia Gardens Foundation. Also, as The Anaconda Company representative on the Foundation, McKenzie decided on the time and the place of the equipment placement. Although the actual amounts spent can

> only be given by McKenzie, other members of the board have given a rough estimate of the dollars spent and have balanced the books approximately. When the committee was disbanded, the remainder of the money went to the Butte Junior League. They spent the funds on an ice machine for the Butte Skating Club. No money was given to the Butte Ski Club. Nor was there ever any work done to the Butte Ski Club buildings. Nor was there any benefit to the Butte Ski Club members. "The Butte Ski Club has been the target of attack because of its original desire to give the youth of Butte and the city of Butte 70 acres of land for the future Columbia Gardens. In the ensuing time, the Club has been criticized because it held the equipment together in one place. We have had vandalism and have had to obtain a caretaker. Our taxes have increased, and we have lost income for years be cause of the equipment. "We have been open to any realistic plan to run the equipment for the youth of Butte. The plan must have provisions for supervising during its use."

The Butte Ski Club members were very angry the issue had gone to the press with no chance for them to respond. They felt the negative publicity had hurt the reputation of the club.

"It was a delicate situation, trying to deal with the Butte Ski Club," said Madeline Daniel. "The group was very apprehensive about turning over the playground gear. They certainly felt they had acquired a sense of ownership to the equipment."

Fritz Apostel, a Butte Ski Club member said, "We had clearly established ownership of the gear. In the contract reached with The Anaconda Company, the Butte Ski Club agreed to donate part of our land for a park. If the park was not operational within three years the land and all the equipment reverted back to the Butte Ski Club. In our opinion that was our equipment".

Rick Griffith recalled, "They were very protective of the gear and I can see why. The Butte Ski Club had spent a lot of years nursing the Columbia Gardens equipment. If it was going to be moved, someone had to prove to them that the gear would be protected and maintained."

Through some delicate negotiations the Butte Ski Club allowed the task force to come up with some alternative ideas about putting the playground equipment back into the hands of Butte kids. The task force came up with four possible solutions.

The first plan was moving the equipment to Stodden Park. It was the city's largest park, but with plenty of modern playground gear already in place task force members felt the Columbia Gardens equipment it did not fit in well and might create over use of Stodden Park. The cost of moving the equipment was calculated at $44,000.

The second option was moving the gear to Clark Park. The task force felt this was a possible proposal. The park was large enough to hold the gear. It also fit the theme of the Columbia Gardens because Clark Park was named after the founder of the Columbia Gardens, William Clark. The cost to transport and put the gear in place at Clark Park was put at $206,000.

The third solution was upgrading the proposed Columbia Gardens II site at the Beef Trail. The cost was put at $241,000. An additional $30,000 annually was needed to maintain the park. This was much higher than the other two ideas because its location was four miles south of the city limits.

The fourth plan was to split up the gear into two city parks, Chester Steele and Father Sheehan. The cost was put at $204,000, but task force committee members did not like the idea of splitting up the gear.

Following a series of public hearings, the options for the Columbia Gardens playground equipment were narrowed down to two choices: move the gear to Clark Park or upgrade the Beef Trail site. A bond issue was put before Butte voters to see if they wanted to spend the money to fix up the equipment.

On June 3, 1986, Butte voters went to the polls to decide the issue. The ballot for moving the gear to Clark Park was 3,593 for the proposal and 2,029 against the idea. The voters rejected keeping the gear at the Beef Trail by a count of 3,254 to 1,401.

Shortly after the results were official, Don Peoples ordered his city workers to start moving the Columbia Gardens' gear out of the Beef Trail Ski Area. During the winter of 1987, all the equipment was restored in local Butte Silver Bow shops by city workers. By June 1987, the Columbia Gardens playground was put into place at Clark Park. The Butte children once again had the gear to play on and reminisce with their parents about the fabled Columbia Gardens.

"For me it was one of the most satisfying things I ever worked on," said Daily. "When it was finally in place, people could once again share a piece of tradition that is so unique to the town through the Columbia Gardens playground equipment."

Peoples remembered, "I was pleased the transfer to Clark Park went so smoothly. It was really a last ditch effort to try to save the playground equipment. It was near an end if something was not done soon with the gear."

The "Can Do" attitude is evident in another project which got off the ground in the 1980s, the United States High Altitude Sports Center.

A month before the Our Lady of the Rockies statue was transported to the East Ridge a large banquet was held at the Copper King Inn to kick off the process for a new $6.5 million high altitude world-class speedskating facility in Butte. The banquet attracted over 1,000 people who came to hear five-time Olympic gold medalist, Eric Heiden, speak on behalf of gaining financial support for the rink.

The enthusiasm for speedskating in Butte can be traced back almost to the roots of the city. The cold winters and high altitude made for ideal skating conditions. During the turn of the century, speedskating events were held at Lake Avoca, south of town. There were also races at the Holland Rink located just south of Montana and Front Streets.

The man-made Lake Avoca was drained in 1939 to pave the way for an 18-hole golf course. The Holland Rink was a mainstay for speedskating until after World War II. In 1946, a section of the large wooden fence surrounding the rink collapsed. Rather than repair the fence, officials decided to tear down the entire wooden structure and eliminate the rink.

The loss of the Holland Rink forced local officials to concentrate their efforts on speedskating at the Clark Park facility. It was here that many of the grade school winter carnivals took place. It allowed spectators a chance to sit in the grandstands and watch the events. All that changed on May 1, 1957, when the grandstands for the Clark Park were destroyed by fire.

A temporary rink was installed through the help of Butte mayor, Hanna Griffith, and Butte Recreation Director, Bob Sparks. The rink was helpful in providing practice for local skaters Judy Morstein and Sylvia White who went on to make the 1964 United States Olympic team. Another Butte skater, Martin White, just missed qualifying for the Olympic squad.

Despite inadequate training facilities, Butte produced a host of skaters who competed well in state, regional and national competition. The showing of Butte athletes impressed the heads of national speedskating organization. They elected to hold the 1980 National Indoor Speedskating Championships at the Butte Civic Center.

The meet was a success, further vaulting the interest in speedskating in the community. One person who realized the potential of speedskating was Martin White, the young man who just failed to make the Olympic team. White felt if funding sources were developed, Butte could build a world-class speedskating oval. It could serve as a training center for the United States national team.

White unveiled his plans for the United States High Altitude Sports Center at the Copper King Inn banquet on the night of November 12, 1985. The speedskating oval would be only the third 400-meter refrigerated rink ever built in the United States. The other two facilities were in Lake Placid, New York, and West Allies, Wisconsin. The big difference between those two rinks and the Butte oval was altitude. Butte, a mile above sea level, allowed ice to laid down earlier in the fall and maintained longer than either the Lake Placid or the West Allies' facilities.

Prior to the completion of the Butte rink, members from the American team had to travel to Europe in the fall to get in early ice training. Once the Butte rink was completed, the Americans could stay in their own country to prepare for the speedskating season.

A bigger factor than even ice was the altitude of Butte. The new facility allowed for high altitude training which allowed skaters to be better prepared for major meets. White predicted that once the facility was completed skaters from around the world would come to Butte to train and compete.

On August 1, 1986, ground breaking ceremonies were held at the United States High Altitude site located east of the Bert Mooney Airport and south of the Butte Country Club. The event attracted attention from around the globe with United Nations' ambassadors from Australia, Ausria and Yugoslavia attending the festivities.

Through lots of hard work, enough of the complex was complete so Butte could host a men's and women's World Cup event at the new United States High Altitude Sports Center in November 1987. It was the first world championship speedskating event ever held in Montana.

Despite the fact that only 1,800 temporary seats were available, the wo-day event attracted 3,000 spectators each day. Fans came from all corners of Montana to watch some of the world's best compete. The fans who did not get seats elected to bring lawn chairs and blankets and sit on the north side of the rink.

The World Cup attracted 120 athletes from 16 different countries. The nations represented included Austria, Canada, East Germany, Finland, France, West Germany, Italy, Japan, Netherlands, New Zealand, Norway, Portugal, Sweden, Switzerland, Australia and the United States. The only major speedskating country not present at the meet was the Soviet Union.

In addition to the athletes, fans from around the world came to Butte s did numerous press reporters. Butte was back in the world news again his time not for copper, but its newest jewel, a first-class, 400-meter speedskating oval.

The meet featured the fastest skaters in 10 of 11 events. The field included Olympic gold medal winners Karin Kania and Christina Rotenburger of East Germany, Gaetan Boucher of Canada, plus Tomas Gustafson of Sweden.

The American team was well-represented by future five-time Olympic gold medalist, Bonnie Blair, and future Olympic men's gold medalist, Dan Jansen. During the two day meet, both won their 500-meter races. Yet, the big hero of the weekend was Butte native, Dave Silk, who was skating on the USA team. He skated well before the home folks, taking fourth place in the 1500-meter event.

The high altitude and fast ice produced some outstanding times for the early season meet. No new world records were set, but a number of the top skaters had their personal best times ever. Some skaters felt the ice was outstanding and claimed that the Butte complex was already one of the five fastest rinks in the world.

The thing that impressed the athletes and the world visitors the most was not the ice, altitude or cold temperatures. It was the warm hearts of the Butte citizens.

A number of people from the community brought hot soup, sandwiches, cookies and other hot dishes to the Sports Center so athletes could snack during the two-day meet. It was the type of hospitality that surprised and delighted the global crowd and the athletes.

The two-day event was declared a rousing success. Butte officials announced at the end of the weekend that the facility was scheduled to host another World Cup meet the next winter. It began the process of the United States High Altitude Sports Center attracting more state, regional national and international meets.

Just like Our Lady of the Rockies and the transplanting of the Columbia Gardens' playground equipment the spirit of "Can Do" paid off for Martin White and the volunteers of the United States High Altitude Sports Center. Butte now had a first-class speedskating oval.

Veterans' Memorial

The spirit of "Can Do" also had a strong impact on another project that actually was started a few months before the Our Lady of the Rockies statue was finished.

On April 30, 1975, the United States pulled out of Vietnam permanently. The war to contain Communism in Southeast Asia was over. The Vietnam War had deeply divided our country with many people holding protest demonstrations to end the conflict. Lost in all the controversy was the young American soldiers who went to battle in the war.

Ten years to the day that America left Vietnam on April 30, 1985, a "homecoming" ceremony took place at the top of the Big Butte for Vietnam Veterans. Some veterans from Butte and the surrounding area held a candle light vigil on top of the mountain to honor their brave, young friends who did not come home.

The ceremony touched the hearts of many within the community. Butte Celebrations, a non-profit organization in charge of many local events, elected to make the Vietnam Veterans the grand marshalls of Butte's annual Fourth of July parade.

Vietnam Veterans from around Montana came to Butte and marched down Harrison Avenue leading the 1985 Fourth of July parade. It was Butte and Montana's opportunity to finally welcome home the Vietnam Veterans.

The gesture by the community did not go unnoticed by the local Vietnam Veterans' group called, "Tripwire." Shortly after the Fourth of July, they began discussions on what they could do as a thank you to the community. During the next few months, Tripwire members began talking about developing a Veterans' Memorial at the entrance of Stodden Park.

"We really received so much support during the parade that we simply felt there had to be a way to pay back the people of Butte," said Andy Kankelborg. "We never wanted something like a statue that people could ook at. We wanted something functional that people could use and compliment all the other memorials built around town."

The city already had a number of memorials. There was the bronze World War II soldier statue near Butte High School at Soldiers' Memorial Park honoring fallen comrades from that war. The statue had been built in 1943 by John Weaver, an artist from Anaconda. The statue displayed an American soldier standing on the beach of Guadalcanal Island. The statue and park were officially dedicated on May 25, 1947. The driving force behind the park was the Butte High Silver B's. It was a group of former Butte High football letter-winners. The park listed all former Butte High tudents who fought in World War II and placed in bronze squares the names of the 125 Butte High students killed in the conflict.

Near that memorial was a World War I granite bust that honored oldiers from that conflict. Across town, Butte Central High School also had a memorial dedicated to all their former students killed in World War and II.

Tripwire members wanted a centralized Veterans' Memorial. The unctional item dedicated to Vietnam Veterans would be an amphitheater.

Kankelborg recalled, "We felt an amphitheater could be used all year y the entire community. During the summer, its a great spot for an outdoor concert plus it can be used for special ceremonies like Veterans' Day and Memorial Day."

In the spring of 1986, Tripwire members began pouring concrete for the foundation of the amphitheater. To help gain more exposure and money for their project they organized a foot race sponsored by Jim Thompson and Thompson's Distributing. It was called the "Coors American Challenge Road Race." The event was a success with money and attention starting to filter into their organization.

The next step by Tripwire was to move and refurbish the World War II soldier statue at Butte High School. It was put directly in front of the amphitheater. The statue had been badly damaged by weather, neglect and students. Through the help of local artist, John Mazzola, the statue was restored.

The statue was made of reinforced concrete which made it extremely difficult to restore. Mazzola had to carefully refurbish the statue with a diamond-tip chisel. It allowed him to clean out battered sections of the statue. Next he replaced the fractured sections with lag bolts and opened up pores in the cement with nitric acid. All this was needed so the newly placed cement adhered to the concrete already on the statue. Mazzola called it one of his most difficult challenges ever. He finished the project by the end of the spring in 1986.

The statue continued to have problems related to the weather. A decade after Mazzola finished his touch up work another renovation was needed. This time the statue's sculptor, John Weaver, and his son Henry came to Butte to refurbish the Soldier's Statue.

Despite the troubles with the Soldiers' Statue, Tripwire members achieved a monumental point in their quest for an amphitheater on July 22, 1986. The wooden beams for the complex were put into place. By the end of the summer of 1986, most of the amphitheater was finished.

Tripwire members constructed some flower beds around the amphitheater and built handicap ramps leading up to the stage.

In addition to the amphitheater and Soldiers' Statue, Tripwire members hauled the cross monument from old Boys' Central down to Stodden Park. It was set in concrete near the Soldiers' Statue.

The only plan they could not complete was moving the massive World War I bust from near Butte High School to the new Veterans' Memorial. Tripwire members did try to move the bust, but the monument was so large it tipped over equipment. The only other option for moving it was to cut it into sections and then move it to Stodden Park. Rather than attempt such a major project, they elected to leave the monument in place.

In less than 18 months after being honored as grand marshall of Butte'

Fourth of July parade, Tripwire members had developed and constructed the most complete Veterans' War Memorial in Montana. The cost of the project was over $30,000.

"It was a great effort by everyone," said Kankelborg. "We have about 40 Tripwire members. A majority of them came to do the job and they left the minute any type of press people came around the project. They did not do the memorial for any type of publicity. It as a personal thing and their way of saying thank you.

"We could've not done it without the tremendous support we received from the community. There were folks like Jim Thompson who got behind the project and made it a reality."

The actions of Tripwire rubbed off on former Korean War veterans. Tripwire members encouraged the Korean Vets to try to come up with a monument to their comrades.

"We looked at a lot of different designs before coming up with an idea off a belt-buckle," Neil Neary said with a laugh. "The buckle had the type of wording and map about Korea that we liked so we went with it as the theme for the Korean War Memorial.

"We wanted to make the monument a state-wide deal for all Korean War Veterans because there was no Montana memorial to honor the Korean War Veteran."

The Butte Korean War group asked each of the 56 counties in the state to submit a stone for the memorial. Each county could develop any type of stone they desired. Some counties were able to do it while others simply did not have the financial resources to complete the project. Neary's group stepped in to help the financially-strapped counties by picking up their construction bill. In order to pay the bills, the veterans held a number of dances, auctions and other events. It took eight years, but the veterans raised in excess of $25,000 and got another $25,000 donated in materials.

The word KOREA was spelled out on a plain cement wall using plaques from each of the 56 counties in Montana. The Korean War Memorial was finally dedicated on June 22, 1996, some 10 years after the first concrete footings were poured by Tripwire members creating Butte's Veterans' Memorial.

The memorial is made of dyed-concrete, standing 23 feet high and 24 feet long. A 6-foot by 3-foot square map of Korea made in starlight granite adorns the center of the memorial. The map depicts the 38th parallel, some major Korean cities and locations of some of the wars major battles.

Neary reflected, "It was very satisfying to finish the Korean Memorial. You must give a lot of credit to the Tripwire members because it was through them that we even got started.

"The neat thing about the Veterans Memorial at Stodden Park is we have something from ever conflict the United States fought in during this century except the Persian Gulf War. Heck, we've got plenty of room there for those veterans to built their own memorial and I hope some day they do it. It has something for every veteran who ever defended this country in a time of battle. Its something everyone can be proud of in Butte, Montana."

The action of "Can Do" by making the Vietnam Veterans the grand marshalls of the Fourth of July parade mushroomed into Montana's most complete war memorial.

Butte Sports Hall of Fame

The spirit of "Can Do" carried over to another unique project called the Butte Sports Hall of Fame.

Shortly after Our Lady of the Rockies statue was finished, a Christmas party was held for some Butte-Silver Bow workers in the conference room at the Butte Civic Center. During the course of the evening, a conversation developed about what could be done to add to the newly completed conference room on the second floor of the arena. Butte Silver Bow Chief Executive Don Peoples felt one of the ways to enhance the room was to create a Civic Center Hall of Fame filled with pictures. The photos could show various events of Montana's first multi-purpose sports arena which was completed in 1952.

A few weeks after the conversation Peoples decided to take action on the proposal. He wrote a letter to the Board of Directors of the Butte Civic Center on January 3, 1986.

> Since the renovation of the Butte Civic Center board room in the summer of 1985, it appears that something is missing and an added attraction is needed to liven up its appearance. A Civic Center Hall of Fame would be appropriate in capturing the history of the Civic Center from its very beginning to the present date. The Hall of Fame could feature photos, presentations of the many historical athletic events and non-athletic events of the past. It could also feature its key performers of these past events. To execute this task of gathering the informational dates and precise photos, I feel it is necessary to appoint a committee of individuals who have knowledge and the interest in getting this project off the ground and completed. With the Civic Center Board's ap proval, I would like to ask Ron Kenison, Jim Kello, Mick O'Brien,

Rob Harrington, Jack Ferriter and a representative from the Civic Center Board to serve on this committee. It is the feeling of many Butte sports enthusiasts that this added attraction in the new board room, a Hall of Fame and the record number of events puts the Butte Civic Center a step above other athletic events and multi-purpose buildings in the State of Montana.

Mr. Don Peoples
Chief Executive
Butte-Silver Bow

The initial committee never did get the project off the ground, but that changed in November 1986. The group was reorganized, enlarged and now called the Butte Sports Hall of Fame. The reorganized committee had 16 people, Don Peoples, Civic Center manager, Ric LeCoure, committee chairman, Pat Kearney, served as ex-officio members, Civic Center ticket manager, Ellen Nugent, worked as secretary with 12 voting members: Mick O'Brien, Ron Kenison, Gus Janhunen, Betty Merrifield, Jim Kello, Jack Ferriter, Oakie O'Connor, Jim Kambich, Dan Sullivan, Mick Delaney, Fraser MacDonald and Shirley Shea.

The committee had to begin the process from ground zero. There were no city-wide sports hall of fame in Montana, and very few around the United States. How do you develop by-laws? How do you select nominees? How do you honor inductees? How do you pay for it all? Those were just some of the hurdles the committee had to overcome.

In keeping with the "Can Do" spirit, within two weeks of their first meeting the group had developed a series of by-laws for the Butte Sports Hall of Fame. They also created a theme that the Butte Sports Hall of Fame would honor outstanding athletes, coaches, individuals and teams who made a significant contribution to Butte athletics.

In less than two months, the committee had compiled a list of 47 nominees and 14 teams for consideration into the Butte Sports Hall of Fame. Perhaps the most amazing feat of the creation, development and first election of the Butte Sports Hall of Fame was that it was all done in secret. The committee wanted to make sure when the first announcement was released its impact would be positive.

The creation of the Butte Sports Hall of Fame was made public on February 2, 1987, in the board room at the Civic Center. Some of the elected inductees were asked to come to the Civic Center for a press conference about the arena.

One of the 13 individuals elected into the first class of inductees, Bill Cullen, said, "I walked into one of the biggest surprises of my life!"

The 13 initial members were inducted into the Butte Sports Hall of Fame at a banquet held on May 9, 1987 at the Copper King Inn. The list of individuals included Butte High coach Harry "Swede" Dahlberg, Olympic speedskater Sylvia White Blaine, baseball coach Bill Cullen, Butte Central football player Danny Hanley, Butte High track star Bob O'Malley, Butte Central basketball player Joe Kelly, Olympic speedskater Judy Morstein Martz, Butte Central all-around athlete Jim McCaughey, Butte High all-around athlete Bob O'Billovich, Butte High track star Bob Hawke, Butte High football great Milt Popovich, Montana Tech professor Walter T. Scott, and former Butte Central football coach Jim Sweeney. In addition, three teams were inducted into the Butte Sports Hall of Fame, the 1908 Butte High football team, the 1927 Butte High football team and the 1950 Butte Central basketball team.

Each individual received a Montana-shaped wooden plaque. A second identical copy was placed in the conference room at the Butte Civic Center. A plaque for each team inducted was also placed on the wall in the newly created Butte Sports Hall of Fame.

Since that initial effort, the Butte Sports Hall of Fame committee took a number of key steps to ensure that the shrine became a lasting tribute to athletic accomplishments in Butte. Perhaps the most important decision was to hold the election and induction every two years. The committee felt this added renewed enthusiasm to the project.

Another key development was the rotation of committee members after each election. A committee person could serve for three elections and then was taken off the board to be replaced by a new member. This enabled the committee to consistently rotate new members onto the board prior to every new election.

The committee developed a Hall of Fame shrine in the lobby area of the Butte Civic Center. In 1991, the plaques on the wall in the conference room were transferred downstairs to the lobby. The committee also began working on plans for a Hall of Fame area to be build at the west end of the Civic Center lobby.

In 1993, the committee created a time formula for the induction of high school state championship teams and squads which made a significant contribution. This ensured that all state championship teams one day will have a place of honor in the Butte Sports Hall of Fame.

"Butte prides itself on being called the city of champions," said Jim Kello. "The Butte Sports Hall of Fame has become such a tremendous way of bringing these great champions back together to celebrate a remarkable accomplishment.

"I know as the manager of the 1953 Butte American Legion baseball team that won a state title it was an incredible honor to be inducted into the Butte Sports Hall of Fame. The bond developed by my team was special and to be able to come back together again to celebrate was neat."

Judy Martz said, "To be inducted into the Butte Sports Hall of Fame was one of the highest honors of my life. When your peers elect and then honor you is such a fulfilling accomplishment that is hard to describe what a great experience it is to receive such a compliment."

Don Peoples reflected, "If ever there was a fun project to work on the Butte Sports Hall of Fame was it. I grew up with idols like Jim Sweeney and Swede Dahlberg. To take these individuals who have meant so much to Butte and put them in a city hall of fame is a special thing. The Butte Sports Hall of Fame will always be one of my fondest memories as the Chief Executive of the local government."

The Butte Sports Hall of Fame becomes more special with each new induction ceremony. It is a place of honor and also a place to remember. It was a lot of work that was sparked by a mere conversation at a Christmas party. Less than two years after that spark, Butte had Montana's first city-wide sports hall of fame and another accomplishment in its spirit of "Can Do".

New Life

The spirit of "Can Do" impacted the community. In 1985, there was over $26 million in construction projects in Butte. The figure was as much as the previous five years combined. A majority of the construction was taking place on Harrison Avenue with fast-food chain restaurants like McDonald's and Arby's being built.

In 1988, local officials felt so good about the improvements they sent in an application to become an All-America City. Butte's application focused on three major developments, the creation of the mining company, Montana Resources, the development of the United States High Altitude Sports Center and the creation of the Butte Business Development Center.

There were 850 cities from the around the country that turned in applications to the National Civic League. Butte made the first cut down to 25 towns. It allowed the city to make a formal presentation.

After a long process, Butte was declared one of the few All-America Cities in the country. The announcement came just five years after Atlantic Richfield had suspended mining sending 700 workers to the unemployment line and raising questions about the survival of the community. It was a remarkable turn around for a town some thought might soon be a ghost town.

Don Peoples said, "I think there are two reasons why Butte became an All-America City. The first is the enormous community spirit that had been created by things like Our Lady of the Rockies and the High Altitude Sports Center. The second reason was the community was willing to take some chances. The local government took a chance giving Montana Resources a tax break to get the shovels rolling again. We took a chance on the Business Incubator and the High Altitude Sports Center. All those projects were real gambles and the city took plenty of chances that worked."

Butte the "Can Do" City, the city of Our Lady, the city of the United States High Altitude Sports Center, the city which saved the Columbia Gardens playground gear, the city of a new Veterans' Memorial, the city of a Sports Hall of Fame, the city of a revitalized Uptown district, the city of a new business incubator was now an "All-America City".

Butte, Montana, the richest hill on earth, had come back to life in a big way.

REFERENCES USED IN CHAPTER EIGHT

The Montana Standard newspaper
Miracle on the East Ridge by Pat Kearney published in 1990
The Smithsonian magazine November 1992 article by Dan Baum and Margaret Knox
Butte's Pride- The Columbia Gardens by Pat Kearney published 1994
notes from Butte Sports Hall of Fame meetings
notes from NCAT publication
Butte Archives
1985 Fritz Daily Reader's Speak article for *The Montana Standard*
1985 Butte Ski Club letter
1986 Don Peoples letter to Butte Civic Center board
1987 interview Bill Cullen by *The Montana Standard*
1994 interview Fritz Apostel
1994 interview Fritz Daily
1994 interview Madeline Daniel
1994 interview Rick Griffith
1998 interview Andy Kankelborg
1998 interview Jim Kello
1998 interview Judy Martz

1998 interview Neil Neary
1998 interview Don Peoples
1998 interview Chuck Richards
1998 interview George Thomas

1987 World Cup action
photo courtesy Karen Sullivan

Bob O'Bill

Joe Roberts

Skycrane helicopter gets ready
to life the second section
photo courtesy Joe Lee

Head section moves toward the
East Ridge
photo courtesy Joe Lee

Our Lady of
the Rockies
photo
courtesy
Pat
Kearney

Vietnam Veterans Amphitheater
photo courtesy Mike Kearney

Korean War Memorial dedication June 22, 1996
photo courtesy Pat Kearney

Korean War Memorial dedication June 22, 1996
photo courtesy Pat Kearney

1991 Butte Sports Hall of Fame banquet
photo courtesy Lou Kearney

Renovated facade at
Curtis Music Hall
photo courtesy
Pat Kearney

Crossing the monkey bars at Clark Park
photo courtesy Pat Kearney

Sliding at Clark Park
photo courtesy Pat Kearney

Columbia Gardens cowboy swings at Clark Park
photo courtesy Pat Kearney